I Dada, Gyda
Oddiwrth El

xxxx.

Nadolig 1990.

ATONEMENT AND JUSTIFICATION

Atonement and Justification

*English Evangelical Theology 1640–1790
An Evaluation*

Alan C. Clifford

CLARENDON PRESS · OXFORD
1990

Oxford University Press, Walton Street, Oxford OX2 6DP
Oxford New York Toronto
Delhi Bombay Calcutta Madras Karachi
Petaling Jaya Singapore Hong Kong Tokyo
Nairobi Dar es Salaam Cape Town
Melbourne Auckland
and associated companies in
Berlin Ibadan

Oxford is a trade mark of Oxford University Press

Published in the United States
by Oxford University Press, New York

© A. C. Clifford 1990

All rights reserved. No part of this publication may be reproduced,
stored in a retrieval system, or transmitted, in any form or by any means,
electronic, mechanical, photocopying, recording, or otherwise, without
the prior permission of Oxford University Press

British Library Cataloguing in Publication Data
Clifford, Alan C.
Atonement and justification: English evangelical
theology 1640–1790.
1. Christian doctrine. Atonement. Theories, history
I. Title
232'.3'09
ISBN 0-19-826195-0

Library of Congress Cataloging in Publication Data
Atonement and justification: English Evangelical theology,
1640–1790: an evaluation / Alan C. Clifford.
Includes bibliographical references.
1. Atonement—History of doctrines. 2. Justification—History of
doctrines. 3. Owen, John, 1616–1683. 4. Wesley, John, 1703–1791.
5. Calvinism—England—History of doctrines. 6. Arminianism—England—History of
doctrines. 7. Grace (Theology)—History of doctrines. I. Title.
BT263.C55   1990   234'.7'094209032—dc20   89-28186
ISBN 0-19-826195-0

Phototypeset by Cotswold Typesetting Ltd., Gloucester
Printed in Great Britain by
Bookcraft Ltd., Midsomer Norton, Avon

To
MARIAN
John, Katie, Hywel
and David
and
the Memory of
the 'Authentic'
JOHN CALVIN

SOLI DEO GLORIA

Preface

THE origins of this book may be traced back to my pastorate (1969–72) in Northampton, an East Midlands town made famous by the ministry of Dr Philip Doddridge from 1729 to 1751. Interest in Doddridge the preacher and hymn-writer led to an interest in his theology. I soon realized that his 'moderate' Calvinism was rather different from the 'five-point' orthodoxy I had embraced a decade before, chiefly through the writings of George Whitefield and J. I. Packer. My interest was heightened when I discovered Doddridge's references to John Calvin's views on the extent of the atonement, in his Academy lectures. This interest did not subside with my move to a new pastorate in Gateshead, so I undertook a course of part-time, external, M.Litt. research in Doddridge's theology at the University of Newcastle upon Tyne (1972–7). I became convinced that there were historical, philosophical, theological, and exegetical grounds on which to question certain dogmatic details of the neo-Calvinist revival. My conclusions were confirmed by the appearance in 1979 of R. T. Kendall's book *Calvin and English Calvinism to 1649*.

However, Dr Kendall was unable to pursue his research as far as John Owen, whose classic treatise on the atonement, *The Death of Death*, was appealed to by every 'Calvinist' as the last word on the subject. Thus any attempt to settle this question would involve an in-depth investigation of John Owen's treatise. Having been encouraged by my Newcastle tutor, the Revd Professor B. M. G. Reardon, to continue my studies, I undertook a course of doctoral research in the School of Theology at the University College of North Wales, Bangor (1979–84), under the tuition of the Revd Professor R. Tudur Jones.

I soon realized that the subject of justification was as much involved as the doctrine of the atonement in the historic Calvinist –Arminian controversy. Indeed, these closely related subjects have a perennial interest for theologians and church historians, if only because of the numerous controversies thay have occasioned. No serious study of the New Testament can ignore subjects which bear so directly on those two questions, 'What is Christianity?' and 'Who is a Christian?' It is unlikely that interest in the underlying issues will subside as long as serious answers to these questions are sought. This book, based on my thesis, is intended as a contribution to a debate of more than passing historical interest, although its matter is confined to a particular period in church history. While some of the doctrinal distinctives of Arminianism are also criticized, the book is chiefly intended as a reply to John Owen. My conclusions surprised no one more than myself; others must judge for themselves whether they are valid.

With regard to matter, attention is focused on the writings of John Owen (1616–83) and John Wesley (1703–91), men whose eminence and importance are unquestioned, and who may be regarded as the leading English representatives of the Calvinistic and Arminian traditions within British evangelicalism. The period in question covers the 150 years between 1640 and 1790, encompassing the careers of our two main theologians. To provide a 'middle ground' in the debate, the contributions of Richard Baxter (1615–91), Owen's erstwhile Nonconformist colleague and occasional opponent, and John Tillotson (1630–94), who became Archbishop of Canterbury, figure prominently in the discussion.

With regard to method, this book is both comparative and evaluative. It is not merely an excursion into the field of historical theology. As well as surveying the contrasting ideas of the two main theologians within their historical context, I attempt to reach a verdict. Biblical criteria and exegesis are employed to compare convictions and test their validity. To supplement the main comparison between Owen and Wesley, the claims of Baxter and Tillotson to provide a tenable alternative to the views of the main disputants are also tested. The entire discussion takes place against the wider background of Reformation theology, where a comparison with the teaching of John Calvin in particular provides, in certain instances, some illuminating insights in the course of the debate.

Such a treatment of the issues before us is made possible because the four theologians shared a common commitment to the Protestant rule of faith. Like Calvin and the other reformers, they all regarded Holy Scripture as normative and authoritative; the axiom of *sola scriptura* allowed of no discussion. The particular fascination and importance of the debate arises from the fact that the four representative theologians reached very different and far-reaching conclusions in the course of expounding not the obscure, but the seemingly perspicuous, areas of New Testament teaching. The analysis is concerned to explain differences where they occur, and the evaluation attempts to provide an alternative solution where possible.

That Owen, Baxter, Tillotson, and Wesley represent four major ecclesiastical traditions within British Protestantism is largely incidental to this book. Congregationalism, Presbyterianism, Anglicanism, and Methodism are not, as such, under review, although it is recognized that each leader played a significant role in the shaping of a denominational ethos. It is a fact that they all had common religious roots—that is, they were all ordained in the Church of England. It is also true that their particular doctrinal emphases explain in great measure how their ecclesiastical differences emerged. However, the main preoccupation of the analysis is with their soteriological opinions. The fact that Wesley was not a contemporary of the others in no way affects the investigation, which is concerned primarily with their convictions rather than their careers. However, preparatory to the main debate, brief biographical sketches introduce the quartet of divines in chronological order. These do not claim to be exhaustive; they merely attempt to place our theologians in the context of their times, providing a glimpse of the spiritual and intellectual motives which produced those writings most relevant to the main themes of this book.

And now to acknowledge my debts. Believing that I had the best tutor available in 'Dr Tudur' (as his students affectionately address him), I will always be grateful to him for his knowledge, wisdom, and kindness. He was always just and generous in assessing my work. Since I was in pastoral charge of a Norfolk village church—I was a part-time, external student—Dr Tudur's prompt and encouraging postal responses to my efforts were all the more important.

I am also grateful to the Revd Professor R. Buick Knox, formerly of Westminster College, Cambridge, who kindly welcomed me on my first visit to the college library. As my external examiner, he made my viva a most stimulating hour. Thanks are also due to the Revd Dr Geoffrey F. Nuttall, whose kind encouragement dates from my Northampton ministry. He wisely questioned the high orthodox criteria by which I initially assessed Doddridge and Baxter. Once 'liberated', I discovered unexpected gold. The Revd Dr R. T. Kendall's interest in my book was perhaps predictable. However, I am grateful for his useful criticisms as well as his encouragement and support. I am also grateful for the kind and efficient assistance received from the Revd Dr A. Skevington Wood during the later stages of preparing this book.

Thanks are also due to several brethren in the Christian ministry, whose constant encouragement and interest in my book has been invaluable. I refrain from naming them lest I incriminate them! Suffice it to say that we embrace the theological and pastoral implications of this book. To be able to preach from John 3: 16 without any high orthodox inhibitions is a privilege. It is my hope that others may yet join us.

My research presented no great problems regarding material. I had possessed for many years the complete *works* of John Owen (an original twenty-four-volume set). A retired Methodist minister in Cornwall was willing to sell me his complete set of Wesley's *works*, later beautifully re-bound by a friend. Quite providentially one day in Norwich, I obtained the three folio volumes of Tillotson's *works* at a bargain price. For access to the numerous and rare tomes of Richard Baxter, and also the secondary sources, I am exceedingly grateful to the staff of the University Library and the Westminster College Library in Cambridge. I also wish to thank the staff of Tyndale House Library in Cambridge. The efficient postal services of Dr Williams's Library and the Evangelical Library, London, have been greatly appreciated.

I should also like to express my gratitude to the Oxford University Press. I will always regard it as an immense privilege that this book was published by them. Their interest stretches over a long period, and I shall always remember their courteous and patient encouragement. Special thanks are due to my church. Without their willingness to grant me a two-month sabbatical, it is doubtful that this book would ever have reached publication.

Lastly, my wife and four children deserve gratitude words cannot express. Although 'daddy's book' consumed more time than he would have wished, they were utterly unselfish in their demands.

My middle son, Hywel, deserves warm commendation for initiating his father in the mysteries of word-processing. There were times when encouragement was much needed, but a patient, understanding, and enthusiastic wife never failed to supply it.

A. C. C.

Great Ellingham,
1989

Contents

List of Illustrations   xiv
List of Abbreviations   xv

I. THE THEOLOGIANS

1. John Owen (1616–83)   3
2. Richard Baxter (1615–91)   17
3. John Tillotson (1630–94)   33
4. John Wesley (1703–91)   51

II. THE THEOLOGY: ATONEMENT AND GRACE

5. Authentic Calvinism   69
6. The Legacy of Aristotle   95
7. Doctrinal Dilemmas   111
8. The Meaning of the Cross   125
9. The Verdict of Scripture   142

III. THE THEOLOGY: FAITH AND JUSTIFICATION

10. The Reformation Heritage   169
11. Christ's Righteousness and Ours   186
12. The Obedience of Faith   202
13. Paul and James   221

Conclusion   240
Bibliography   245
Index of Biblical Citations   259
General Index   262

List of Illustrations

1. John Owen — 2
2. Richard Baxter — 18
3. John Tillotson — 32
4. John Wesley — 50
5. John Calvin — 68

List of Abbreviations

Further details of works in this list, other than periodicals, may be found in the Bibliography.

Appeal I, II	Wesley, 'An Earnest Appeal to Men of Reason and Religion'; 'A Farther Appeal', *Works*, viii. 1–239
ATR	*Anglican Theological Review*
BOT	*The Banner of Truth*
BQ	*Baptist Quarterly*
BSB	*Bulletin of the Strict Baptist Historical Society*
CM	*Churchman*
Comm.	Calvin's *Commentaries*
CT	Baxter, *Richard Baxter's Catholick Theologie*
DA I, II	Wesley, 'Dialogues' (I, II) 'between an Antinomian and his friend', *Works*, x. 257–274
DAB	*Dictionary of American Biography*
DD	Owen, 'Salus Electorum, Sanguis Jesu; or The Death of Death in the Death of Christ', *Works*, x. 139–428
Dis. A.	Owen, 'A Display of Arminianism', *Works*, x. 1–137
DNB	*Dictionary of National Biography*
DP	Wesley, 'A dialogue between an Predestinarian and his friend', *Works*, x. 250–7
EC	Baxter, *An End of Doctrinal Controversies*
EQ	*The Evangelical Quarterly*
Homilies	*Sermons or Homilies, Appointed to be Read in Churches*
Inst.	Calvin *The Institutes of the Christian Religion*
JF	Owen, The Doctrine of Justification by Faith', *Works*, v. 1–500
JTS	*Journal of Theological Studies* (new series)
MHB	*The Methodist Hymn Book*
Notes	Wesley, *Explanatory Notes upon the New Testament*
Paraphrase	Baxter, *A Paraphrase on the New Testament*
PCC	Wesley, 'Predestination Calmly Considered', *Works*, x. 197–249

PHSE	*Journal of the Presbyterian Historical Society of England* (1913–71)
PJ	Wesley, 'Preface to a Treatise on Justification', *Works*, x. 304–33
PRSC	Puritan and Reformed Studies Conference
RB	Baxter, *Reliquiae Baxterianae, or Mr Richard Baxter's Narrative of the Most Memorable Passages of his Life and Times*
SJT	*Scottish Journal of Theology*
TW	*The Works of the Most Reverend Dr John Tillotson*
UR	Baxter, *Universal Redemption of Mankind*
URC	*The Journal of the United Reformed Church Historical Society* (1972–)
WHS	*Proceedings of the Wesley Historical Society* (1893–)
WTJ	*The Westminster Theological Journal*

Since the Authorized Version of the Bible (1611) was the English version generally quoted by the main theologians in this book, all Scripture quotations are taken from it. When other versions are quoted, this is indicated as follows: RV = Revised Version (1881–4); RSV = Revised Standard Version (1946–52); NIV = New International Version (1970–8); NKJV = New King James Version (1979–82).

PART I
The Theologians

I. JOHN OWEN

I
John Owen (1616–83)

HIS SIGNIFICANCE

Dr John Owen is assured of an honoured place in the annals of the Christian church. His eminence is soon apparent to students of the religious and political tumults of seventeenth-century England. His accomplishments were not merely confined to religious affairs; the interaction between religion and politics during the Puritan revolution involved him in both arenas, and his activities earned him just renown. Yet three centuries were to pass before an adequately researched biography would appear.[1] Even then, material is wanting adequately to portray Owen the man, compared with the personal information available about his contemporary Richard Baxter. However, Peter Toon concludes his fine study by saying, 'Owen shines through the available material as a truly great man, whose one basic concern in word and deed, book and action, was the proclamation of Jesus Christ and His gospel.'[2]

Friends and foes alike have been generous in their praise of Owen. He was 'the Calvin of England' to a fellow Congregationalist from Newcastle,[3] whereas Anthony Wood, the bitter Anglican critic, conceded that Owen was an 'Atlas and Patriarch of Independency.'[4] Despite numerous instances of theological disagreement, Baxter was not slow to describe Owen as an 'excellent man' of 'rare parts and worth'.[5] In the next century Philip Doddridge—whose views reflected Baxter's theology—could still speak warmly of 'the great and excellent Dr Owen'.[6] Even John Wesley, whose antagonism towards Owen's theology is too conspicuous to miss, could applaud him as 'an unexceptional judge of men and manners'.[7] The nineteenth-century saw no abatement of praise for Owen. In the 1850 edition of Owen's complete works W. H. Goold wrote, 'It would be presumption to enter upon any commendation of John Owen as an author and divine. His works will continue to gather around them the respect and admiration of the Church of Christ, so long as reverence is cherished for the Christian faith.'[8] When the first volume of the Goold edition of Owen's works was republished by the Banner of Truth Trust in 1965 (sixteen of the original twenty-four being reprinted), the jacket proclaimed the author as 'The greatest British theologian of all time.'

Understandably, Congregational scholars honour Owen's name. Dr Erik Routley said he was 'the greatest of the Puritan scholastics',[9] while Dr Geoffrey Nuttall emphasizes the 'centrality' of Owen in pre-Restoration Congregationalism, a position which became yet more striking after 1660.[10] Dr R. Tudur Jones writes that Owen possessed an 'uncanny ability to keep in touch with people of all kinds both within and without the circle of Congregational Churches and his quiet and dignified influence upon those in authority made him the nerve-centre of the Congregational resistance to the penal code'.[11]

HIS LIFE

John Owen was born at Stadhampton, Oxfordshire, in 1616, the son of a Puritan clergyman. One brief reference to his childhood is all we possess: 'I was bred up from my infancy under the care of my father, who was a nonconformist all his days, and a painful labourer in the vineyard of the Lord.'[12] So, just four years old when the Pilgrim Fathers sailed for America, John was nurtured in principles which were to direct his life. After attending a small grammar school in Oxford, he entered Queen's College in 1628, graduating BA in 1632 and MA in 1635. Soon after this he was ordained deacon by John Bancroft, bishop of Oxford, and in 1637 he became a private tutor in the family of Sir Robert Dormer at Great Milton, not far from Oxford.

In 1642, the year in which the civil war began, Owen moved to London. For some five years his spiritual pilgrimage had been plagued by doubt and melancholy, a common feature of Puritan piety. Hearing an unknown preacher instead of the renowned Edmund Calamy at St Mary's Church, Aldermanbury, Owen experienced assurance of salvation. Around this time he was also engaged on his first book *A Display of Arminianism* (1643),[13] which he dedicated to the parliamentary Committee of Religion. Thus, with head and heart convinced, he became a recognized champion of the Calvinism then in vogue. A consequence of this public attention was his presentation to the living of Fordham in Essex.

Late in 1643 Owen married Mary Rooke, the daughter of a clothier from nearby Coggeshall. Following the battle of Naseby (1645) and the end of the first civil war, he was invited to preach before Parliament, and in the published sermon, 'A vision of unchangeable mercy',[14] he describes the recent providential successes of Puritanism as 'England's visitation.' His move to Coggeshall in 1646 coincided with a reappraisal of the prevailing Presbyterian theory of church order. He thus became a Congregationalist, his views being published in *Eschol; or Rules of Direction for the Walking of the Saints* (1647).[15] Soon after this he published the results of several years' hard study in a work which proved to be his most famous and controversial treatise: *Salus Electorum, Sanguis Jesu; or The Death of Death in the Death of Christ* (1647).[16] This expounds the doctrine that the atonement of Christ is limited exclusively to the elect, and remains the classic high Calvinist statement on this subject to this day.

In 1648 Owen was chaplain to the parliamentary forces under General Fairfax at the siege of Colchester. While preaching again before Parliament in 1649 the tall, imposing Owen greatly impressed Oliver Cromwell, who invited him to accompany him to Ireland. At about this time, Owen's periodic controversies with Richard Baxter began. In his *Aphorismes of Justification* (1649) Baxter took issue with Owen's *Death of Death*, the debate focusing on the precise nature of the atonement. Owen's rejoinder was entitled *Of the Death of Christ, The Price He Paid* (1650).[17] In March 1650 Owen's reputation was further enhanced by his appointment as preacher to the Council of State, and in the same year he was again Cromwell's chaplain on the expedition to Scotland.

It was inevitable that Owen's scholarly prowess should be recognized. In 1651 he was appointed dean of Christ Church, and in the following year vice-chancellor of the University of Oxford. Then in 1653, contrary to his wishes, he was created DD. In 1654 he was chosen as a 'trier' or member of the Committee for the Aprobation of Publique Preachers, set up to oversee Cromwell's new religious settlement. Far from being a mere academic, Owen helped organize the defence of Oxford against the threatened uprising of 1655.

During his period as vice-chancellor Owen published several works against Arminianism and Socinianism. Of special importance are his *Doctrine of the Saints' Perseverance* (1654)[18] and *Vindiciae Evangelicae* (1655).[19] However, he did not confine his polemics to strictly doctrinal issues. He was equally concerned to elucidate the character of true Christian experience and this he did in his treatise *Of Communion with God the Father, Son and Holy Ghost* (1657),[20] a work which was to involve him in considerable controversy.

Owen ceased to be vice-chancellor in 1657. His attempt to reconcile a traditional scholastic policy with a more radical religious outlook had not been entirely successful. Shortly after the Protector's death in September 1658, he was involved in more congenial activities, taking a prominent part at the Savoy Assembly in preparing the Declaration of Faith and Order[21] of the Independent or Congregational Churches. The following year saw him accused of involvement in the plot to remove Richard Cromwell from power, but he denied the charge. However, he was actively engaged in securing the support of General Monck and the army for the Independents. As sympathy for the Restoration increased, Owen was ejected from his deanship at Christ Church, being replaced by the Presbyterian Dr Edward Reynolds (later bishop of Norwich). From this time, he rapidly disappeared from public life, retiring to his estate at Stadhampton in 1660.

Quietness did not mean idleness, even if his activity was now to be largely pastoral and literary. His duties as pastor of a church consisting largely of former friends and associates of Oliver Cromwell did not prevent him from publishing his monumental Latin treatise *Theologoumena pantodapa*[22] on the history of religion and theology (1661). The following year saw the publication of *Animadversions on a Treatise Entitled Fiat Lux*,[23] a work which so pleased Lord Clarendon for its refutation of Roman Catholicism that Owen was offered preferment in the restored Anglican church. However, the former Lord Protector's chaplain declined the offer. Indeed, with the passing of the Act of Uniformity in 1662, he gave expression to his Nonconformist principles in *A Discourse concerning Liturgies and their Imposition*.[24] He also championed the cause of religious liberty in a number of anonymous tracts. While his family moved to the home of the prominent Nonconformist Sir John Hartopp at Stoke Newington, he himself was preaching a good deal in London and Oxford, and in 1665 he was prosecuted under the Conventicle Act for holding meetings in his home at Stadhampton.

In 1667 Owen was actively engaged with others in persuading Parliament to introduce a Toleration Act. However, such pleas made little impression at this time. He was also involved in discussions with Richard Baxter about Nonconformist unity, but these proved abortive; the two divines held to differing conceptions of the church. Despite their various differences, Owen's letter to Baxter reveals the magnanimity for which he was famous. He regrets that a severe cold prevents him from enjoying Baxter's company, and he judges Baxter's proposals 'worthy of great consideration'. The conclusion of the letter reflects the spiritual bond between the two men: 'Sir, I shall pray that the Lord would guide and prosper you in all studies and endeavours, for the service of Christ in the world, especially in this your desire and study for the introducing of the peace and love promised among them that believe, and do beg your prayers.'[25]

An easing of restrictions on the Nonconformists came in 1672 with the Declaration of Indulgence, for which Owen personally thanked the king. In 1673, the year of the Test Act, Owen's church united with the congregation of the deceased Joseph Caryl at Leadenhall Street in London. In the following year he was again embroiled in controversy, when William Sherlock published criticisms of Owen's earlier work *Communion* (1657). In particular, Sherlock attacked his theory of the imputation of Christ's righteousness to the believer. Owen's reply provided some groundwork for his major treatise on the subject, *The Doctrine of Justification by Faith*,[27] published in 1677. In the midst of all this literary activity Owen knew domestic sadness, for his first wife, to whom he was deeply attached, died in 1675. He married again, however, in the following year.

In his remaining years, a number of works flowed from Owen's pen, covering various doctrinal, controversial, and practical subjects. His breadth of learning and range of concern are fully evident in his *Discourse Concerning the Holy Spirit* (1674)[28] and the masterly *Exposition of the Epistle to the Hebrews* (1674).[29] His *Inquiry into the Original Nature . . . . . and Communion of Evangelical Churches*

(1681)[30] was occasioned by Dean Stillingfleet's attack on the Nonconformists. This proved to be his final controversy.

As Owen's life drew to its end, his literary pursuits reflected a growing preoccupation with more personal and eternal issues. *The Grace and Duty of Being Spiritually Minded* (1681)[31] is an example of this, as are the posthumously published *Meditations and Discourses on the Glory of Christ* (1684).[32] Owen's final letter—written to Charles Fleetwood two days before he died—reveals the depth of his piety: 'I am going to him whom my soul hath loved, or rather who hath loved me with an everlasting love; which is the ground of all my consolation .... I am leaving the ship of the church in a storm, but whilst the great Pilot is in it the loss of a poor under-rower will be inconsiderable .... '[33] The printing and proof-reading of the *Glory of Christ* was being supervised by William Payne, a minister from Saffron Walden in Essex, who visited Owen at Ealing on the day he died, 24 August 1683. On seeing his friend, Owen exclaimed, 'O, brother Payne, the long-wished-for day is come at last, in which I shall see the glory in another manner that I have ever done or was capable of doing in this world.'[34]

Five years later the Glorious Revolution brought to an end the absolutist pretensions of the Stuarts and the sufferings of Nonconformists. The religious liberty which Owen had laboured so long to achieve was finally granted in the Toleration Act of 1689.

HIS CONTRIBUTION

Owen's *Display of Arminianism* (1643) was an instance of the author's astuteness. With the Puritans in the ascendancy, the treatise met a public need. The subject was 'artfully chosen'[35] and Owen was anxious for recognition. A tangible consequence of the book's success was his presentation to the living at Fordham. Toon admits that the treatise 'was no masterpiece',[36] and J. I. Packer describes it as a 'competent piece of prentice-work, rather in the nature of a research thesis'.[37] None the less, Thompson was right to say that 'it is rich in matter which must have staggered the courtly theologians of the age .... it is hung all round with massive Calvinistic armour'.[38] The *Display* defends 'the central core of orthodox Calvinism',[39] with Owen's Aristotelian methodology much in evidence. Goold regrets the acerbity of Owen's style, suggesting also that the assessment of Arminianism lacks discrimination; Arminius' views are not sufficiently distinguished from those of his followers, and too often Arminianism is confounded with Pelagianism. These criticisms notwithstanding, the book continued to attract attention; even John Wesley could not ignore it in his controversy with the Calvinist Rowland Hill in 1772.[40]

Of far greater importance was Owen's second major work, and his first masterpiece, *Salus Electorum, Sanguis Jesu; or The Death of Death in the Death of Christ* (1647). It was the result of 'more than seven years' serious enquiry'.[41] Owen believed that the heart of the debate with Arminianism concerned the nature and extent of the atonement, and his work fully reflects that belief. Packer's only reservation about Owen's performance is his style; despite the 'lumbering literary gait',[42] Packer considers that the Puritan spoke the last word on this subject. 'He was sure in his own mind that a certain finality attached to what he had written', and in Packer's opinion 'time has justified his optimism'.[43]

Thompson kindly describes Owen's style as that of 'the elephant's grave and solid step', but he also agrees that 'The characteristic excellencies of Owen's mind shine out in this work with great lustre ... comprehension and elevation of view ... intellectual strength ... [and] ... the presence of a heavenly spirit.'[44] Despite such applause, Thompson questions whether Owen has established 'the whole truth' on the subject of the atonement. Without doubting the particular efficacy of the atonement in the ultimate salvation of the elect, he wonders whether Owen does justice to those biblical expressions which imply a universal dimension to the atonement. Of course, as Thompson points out, Owen believed in the infinite sufficiency of the atonement, but he questions whether Owen's exposition at this point is entirely satisfactory.

William Orme, writing a generation before Thompson, is even more specific. While granting that the *Death of Death* is distinguished 'by all that comprehension of thought, closeness of reasoning, and minuteness of illustration, which mark the future productions of the author', yet he is not entirely satisfied: 'There is too much reasoning on the debtor and creditor hypothesis.'[45] In other words, Owen's doctrine of limited atonement relies too heavily on the commercial analogies employed in the biblical description of sin. In short, sin is not a quantitative but a qualitative concept. Like Thompson, Orme concedes that Owen believed in the infinite sufficiency of the atonement as the basis for evangelistic enterprise, but he thinks Owen's exposition of the subject is not always in harmony with this consideration.[46]

Goold is seemingly as unhappy as Thompson and Orme. He even attempts to excuse Owen by suggesting that the basis of evangelism 'was never formally before the mind of our author'.[47] This is not in fact true, and Owen makes himself perfectly clear on this point, how satisfactorily is yet to be determined. It must be said in passing that Orme rejects Owen's commercialism in favour of the governmental theory of the atonement, a view vigorously opposed by Owen himself; this is one of the issues discussed in the present book.

Richard Baxter's contribution demands partial consideration at this point, since he took issue with Owen in his *Aphorismes of Justification* (1649). At the heart of the commercial theory of the atonement is the idea that Christ, by his death, paid the debts of the elect on their behalf. For this reason, no provision is made for the non-elect. Accordingly, Owen urged that Christ made the 'exact payment' demanded by the law of God for the sins of the elect—the *solutio ejusdem*.[48] In an appendix to his *Aphorismes* Baxter argued that for a number of reasons Owen's view was incoherent and that, by virtue of the nature of his mediation, Christ 'paid' not the exact, but an equivalent payment—the *solutio tantidem*.[49]

Baxter's basic point is that since human sin is threatened with eternal punishment, whereas Christ's sufferings were terminated by his resurrection, it makes no sense to say that he paid the exact payment demanded by the law. Realizing that Baxter had touched on a matter of crucial importance for his entire argument, Owen responded with *Of the Death of Christ, the Price He Paid* (1650).[50] After confessing that he 'meddled too forwardly with Dr Owen',[51] Baxter resumed the argument in his *Confession of Faith* (1655). There he argues that the *solutio ejusdem* theory was 'at the bottom of antinomianism'. If Christ has satisfied the law's demands in exact, quantitative terms then believers may disregard the law with impugnity. This brought forth a further rejoinder from Owen in an appendix to his *Vindiciae Evangelicae* (1655), entitled 'Of the death of Christ and of justification'.[52]

Thompson clearly questions the propriety of such 'scholastic phrases',[53] and William Cunningham fails to perceive the importance of the controversy.[54] The matter is thoroughly discussed in this book. The terminology is easily rescued from obscurity, and its importance will become evident in due course; indeed, the case for the doctrine of limited atonement hangs on this issue.

In commenting on Owen's 'orthodox Calvinism', Toon is not assuming an exact correspondence between Owen's teaching and the theology of John Calvin.[55] The precise relationship between the views of the Puritan and those of the Reformer will be investigated in this book as an issue of considerable interest and importance. There can be no doubt that Owen believed he was advocating the same position as that adopted by Calvin and the other reformers of the sixteenth-century.[56] However, R. T. Kendall and others have questioned whether Calvin's 'Calvinism' and the theology of the Westminster Assembly (1643-9) can be regarded as quite the same thing.[57] Other authors have presented evidence from the formularies and literature of the Anglican Reformation which make J. I. Packer's support for Owen appear somewhat anomalous.[58]

Owen's thesis in the *Death of Death* is not only opposed to Arminianism; it is directed equally against the hypothetical universalism of the French Reformed Academy at Saumur—commonly known as 'Amyraldianism'[59] after Moise Amyraut (Amyraldus), its leading exponent. Owen accepts the popular view that Amyraldianism was simply another heterodox deviation from Reformed orthodoxy, but fails to consider Amyraut's claim, in his *Defence de la doctrine de Calvin* (1644), that it was the seventeenth-century high orthodox theologians, rather than himself, that had significantly departed from Calvin's original theology. It is important, therefore, to ask which of the contending theological positions is the true heir of Calvin's theology. When Packer says that 'Calvinistic thinking is the Christian being himself on the intellectual level',[60] he begs the question, 'What is true Calvinism?' Owen's assumption is thus shared by Packer, who fails to make more than a passing reference to the Amyraldian view.[61] He rightly links Baxter with this movement since his activities in this country parallel the debate on the Continent.[62] The claim that Calvin's theology and its 'high orthodox' derivative are to be distinguished will be considered in particular relation to John Owen as well, as part of the general background to this book.

Turning to Owen's treatise *The Doctrine of Justification by Faith* (1677), we find that it has something of a prehistory. It arose from the controversy with William Sherlock, rector of St George's Botolph Lane, who, seventeen years after its publication, wrote against Owen's work *Communion* (1657). Owen had argued that the imputation of Christ's active, as well as his passive, obedience was the basis of the believer's justification before God. Sherlock argued that such a theory made personal obedience and holiness quite redundant. Owen then published his *Vindication*, asserting a position he was to defend three years later in his main treatise on justification.

In 1658, a year after the treatise *Communion* appeared, Owen was involved in the preparation of the Savoy Declaration of Faith and Order. Chapter XI, 'Of justification', shows a highly significant modification of the corresponding chapter of the Westminster Confession, on which it was largely modelled. Whereas the Presbyterian document could be defended against Sherlock's type of objection, the Congregational one states the very position which Sherlock had criticized. Where Westminster speaks of an imputation of 'the obedience and satisfaction of Christ', Savoy states that the believer's 'whole and sole righteousness' consists of 'Christ's active obedience unto the whole Law' as well as his 'passive obedience in his death'.[63] The significance of all this, and the degree to which Owen was able to refute the charge of an incipient antinomianism, are matters requiring careful investigation.

It is interesting to note that, according to Baxter himself, the acceptance of the Savoy alterations at the 1658 Assembly was not a true reflection of opinion. Some who had been silent at the time, and who sympathized with Baxter's sentiments, declared that 'it was chiefly Dr Owen's doing'.[64] Regarding the theology of Savoy on the subject of justification, it is significant that whereas neither Baxter nor Wesley took exception to the Westminster version, they did have reasons for objecting to the Savoy statement. The reasons for this are discussed in considerable depth in this book.

This background to Owen's treatise on justification shares an important parallel with his views on the atonement. Just as significant differences are claimed between the Puritans and the Reformers on the latter, so the same may be said of the former. Toon states that the 'orthodox' view of justification—comprising forgiveness of sin plus a further imputation of Christ's active righteousness—is to be attributed to Calvin's successor Theodore Beza rather than to Calvin himself, who equated the imputation of righteousness with forgiveness.[65] Toon does not document this at any length, though the matter will receive careful examination in this book. The view of several modern scholars that Beza was also responsible for the high orthodox modification of the Reformation doctrine of the atonement[66] confirms the suggestion that Beza's influence on Reformed thought was fundamental and far-reaching.

Returning to Owen's treatise itself, we find that Toon questions Perry Miller's widely accepted thesis that Puritan federal theology was a device to remove the harshness of predestinarianism. In Owen's overall argument the divine purpose of predestination figures prominently.[67] Indeed, he is concerned with the justification of the elect according to the covenant of grace. Not surprisingly, Packer views Owen's treatise as a 'classic work',[68] reinforcing Goold's comment (in 1851) that 'it is still the most complete discussion in our language' of the subject of justification.[69]

For all their obvious sympathy with Owen, both Orme and Thompson were somewhat critical of his treatise. 'The great extent of this work is one of the strongest objections to it', wrote Orme. 'It is unfavourable to that simplicity with which the Bible states all its doctrines . . . . It gives divine truth too much the appearance of artificial or systematic arrangement, and by the very terms which it employs, exposes it to opposition, and oppresses it with explanations that impede rather than forward its progress.'[70] Thompson agrees with Orme that Owen's treatment of the nature of justifying faith tends to 'perplex' an enquirer, although he is quick to point out that such a censure is not to be confined to Owen. In his view, on the subject of faith 'The Puritan divines, with their scholastic distinctions, were far inferior to the theologians of the Reformation.'[71]

This book is concerned to examine the evidence on which these criticisms are based, and to consider their serious and far-reaching implications. This will provide a perspective on Owen's place in British theology, and afford a basis for an informed comparison with the views of John Wesley and the 'middle way' theologians Richard Baxter and John Tillotson.

By way of conclusion, we may observe that none of Owen's critics has ever presumed to doubt his intellectual brilliance or his theological greatness. It is fascinating to discover that the physicians ascribed the lingering character of his death 'to the strength of his brain'.[72] This will come as no surprise to students of his works, overawed as they are by the sheer cerebral power of his scholarship. But we should not forget his essential humility. It is best illustrated by the great respect he had for the preaching of John Bunyan. Once, asked by the King why he listened to the uneducated tinker, Owen—much less of a preacher than a theological author—replied, 'Could I possess the tinker's abilities for preaching, please your majesty, I would gladly relinquish all my learning.'[73]

NOTES

1. P. Toon, *God's Statesman: The Life and Work of John Owen* (Exeter, 1971). Earlier biographies: J. Asty, 'Memoirs of the life of John Owen', in *A Complete Collection of the Sermons of John Owen* (London, 1721); E. Williams, 'Life of Owen', In Owen's *Exposition of the Epistle to the Hebrews* (London, 1790); W. Orme, 'Memoirs of Dr Owen', in *The Works of John Owen, DD*, i, ed. T. Russell (London, 1826); A Thompson, 'Life of Dr Owen', in *The Works of John Owen, DD*, i, ed. W. H. Goold (London, 1850); J. Moffat, 'Introductory sketch: life of Owen', in *The Golden Book of John Owen* (London, 1904); *The Correspondence of John Owen (1616–1683): With an Account of His Life and Work*, ed. P. Toon (Cambridge, 1970); S. B. Ferguson, 'John Owen and his Christian life', in *John Owen on the Christian Life* (Edinburgh, 1987). See also *DNB*; *Biographia Britannica*, v. (London, 1760), 3291.
2. Toon, *God's Statesman*, p. 178.
3. *Memoirs of Ambrose Barnes*, ed. W. H. D. Longstaffe (London, 1867), 16.
4. *History of the University of Oxford*, ed. J. Gutch (Oxford, 1791), ii. 650.
5. Quoted in Orme, 'Memoirs', at p. 359.
6. *The Works of the Revd P. Doddridge, DD*, ed. E. Williams and E. Parsons (Leeds, 1802–5), ii. 223.
7. *The Works of the Revd John Wesley, AM*, ed. T. Jackson (London, 1840), vi. 311.
8. *Works of John Owen*, i, p. vii.
9. *English Religious Dissent* (London, 1960), 10.
10. *Visible Saints: The Congregational Way, 1640–1660* (Oxford, 1957), 39–40.
11. *Congregationalism in England, 1662–1962* (London, 1962), 71.
12. Toon, *God's Statesman*, p. 3; Owen, *Works*, xiii. 224.
13. *Works*, x. 1 ff.
14. *Works*, viii. 1 ff.

15. *Works*, xiii. 51 ff.
16. *Works*, x. 139 ff.
17. *Ibid.* 429 ff.
18. *Works*, xi. 1 ff.
19. *Works*, xii. 1 ff.
20. *Works*, ii. 1 ff. For an analysis and exposition of Owen's pastoral theology see Ferguson, *John Owen*.
21. *The Savoy Declaration of Faith and Order*, ed. A. G. Matthews (London, 1959).
22. *Works*, xvii. 1 ff.
23. *Works*, xiv. 1 ff.
24. *Works*, xv. 1 ff.
25. *Correspondence of John Owen*, pp. 136–8.
26. *Works*, ii. 275 ff. For Sherlock (1641–1707) see *DNB*.
27. *Works*, v. 1 ff.
28. *Works*, iii. 1 ff.
29. *Works*, xviii. 1–xxiv. 485.
30. *Works*, xv. 187 ff.
31. *Works*, vii. 261 ff.
32. *Works*, i. 273 ff.
33. *Correspondence of John Owen*, p. 174.
34. Toon, *God's Statesman*, p. 171.
35. *Biographia Britannica*, v. 3291.
36. Toon, *God's Statesman*, p. 15.
37. Introductory Essay to Owen's *Death of Death* (London, 1959), at p. 23.
38. 'Life of Dr Owen'. p. xxxii.
39. Toon, *God's Statesman*, p. 15.
40. Wesley, *Works*, x. 363.
41. Owen, *Works*, x. 149.
42. Introductory Essay, 25. Subjective impressions in this respect vary interestingly. Goold says Owen's style is 'deficient in grace and vivacity; his mode of discussing a subject is often tedious and prolix' (Owen, *Works*, x, p. vii). Wood, O.'s contemporary, thought he had 'a great command of his English pen' (*Biographia Britannica*, v. 3295). Doddridge considered O.'s style 'very obscure', yet he also said that 'it resembles St Paul's' (*Works*, v. 430).
43. Introductory Essay, p. 23.
44. Owen, *Works*, i, p. xxxviii.
45. 'Memoirs', p. 59.
46. *Ibid.* 61.
47. Owen, *Works*, x. 141.
48. *Ibid.* 267.
49. *Aphorismes of Justification* (London, 1649), Appendix, 137 ff.

50. *Works*, x. 429 ff.
51. *RB* i. 107.
52. *Works*, xii. 591 ff.
53. Owen, *Works*, i, p. xxxix n. 4.
54. *Historical Theology* (London, 1960 edn.), ii. 307.
55. *God's Statesman*, p. 15.
56. *Dis. A.* 6; *Works*, vii. 74; iii. 229.
57. R. T. Kendall, *Calvin and English Calvinism to 1649* (Oxford, 1979), 2.
58. N. F. Douty, *The Death of Christ* (Swengel, Pa., 1972), 114 ff.
59. B. G. Armstrong, *Calvinism and the Amyraut Heresy: Protestant Scholasticism and Humanism in Seventeenth-century France* (Madison, Wisc., 1969). For useful surveys see R. Nicole, 'Amyraldianism', in *The Encyclopedia of Christianity*, ed. E. H. Palmer (Wilmington, 1964), i. 184–93; T. M. Lindsay, 'Amyraldism', in *Encyclopaedia of Religion and Ethics*, ed. J. Hastings (Edinburgh, 1908), i. 404–6.
60. Introductory Essay, p. 10.
61. Ibid. 23.
62. Baxter says that he declined to pursue his 'small tract of *Universal Redemption*' in view of Amyraut's reply to Spanheim which 'opened my very heart, almost in my own words' (*Aphorismes*, Appendix, p. 164). Although he eventually completed the MS, he refrained from publishing it for the sake of peace. The work was published posthumously in 1694.
63. A. G. Matthews, *Savoy Declaration*, p. 90. Criticism of the Savoy Declaration was far from muted; see Owen's reply to Pierre Du Moulin (*Correspondence of John Owen*, p. 165). For Du Moulin see *DNB*.
64. Baxter, *Catholick Communion Defended* (1684), ii. 8. See also *EC* 266.
65. Toon, The Emergence of Hyper-Calvinism in English Nonconformity, 1689–1765 (London, 1967), 15–16.
66. Armstrong, *Calvinism*, pp. 37 ff.; Kendall, *Calvin*, p. 29. For a survey of the literature see Nicole, 'John Calvin's view of the extent of the atonement', *WTJ* 47 (1985), 197–225.
67. Toon, *God's Statesman*, p. 170; A. P. F. Sell, *The Great Debate* (Worthing, 1982), 40.
68. 'The Doctine of justification in development and decline among the Puritans', in *By Schisms Rent Asunder* (PRSC, London, 1969), at p. 19.
69. Owen, *Works*, v. 3. Goold's claim is to a degree made obsolete by J. Buchanan, *The Doctrine of Justification* (1867; fac, London, 1961).
70. 'Memoirs', pp. 308–9.
71. Thompson 'Life of Dr Owen' p. xcvi.
72. S. B. Ferguson, 'John Owen on Christian piety', *BOT* 191–2 (1979), at p. 47.
73. Toon, *God's Statesman*, p. 162.

2
Richard Baxter (1615-91)

HIS SIGNIFICANCE

If John Owen was 'the leading figure among Congregational divines',[1] Richard Baxter was 'the outstanding figure among ejected ministers'.[2] He is justly famous for his energetic pastoral ministry at Kidderminster from 1641 to 1660. He was equally noted for his distinctive theological and ecclasiastical position, in which he advocated the 'middle way' between the extremes of the day. A prophet of ecumenical comprehension, he was less successful in ending the Protestant fragmentation of his day than in his evangelistic and pastoral activities. However, his 'pacific vision' has earned him just renown, even if his methods were deficient in realism and common sense.

Baxter's autobiography, the *Reliquiae Baxterianae*,[3] provides an abundance of detailed information about his life and times. Together with his numerous theological treatises and practical writings, the *Reliquiae* reflect a character of great complexity. The seemingly inconsistent nature of Baxter's accomplishments have led to highly conflicting judgements about him. To Packer, he was 'the most outstanding pastor, evangelist and writer on practical and devotional themes that Puritanism produced',[4] yet, 'as a theologian, he was, though brilliant, something of a disaster'.[5] Writing from a similar theological perspective, W. N. Kerr notes that 'Baxter, without intention, demonstrated Arminian tendencies',[6] a view which in the minds of some has disqualified Baxter forever. Such verdicts as these clearly reflect the current revival of interest in the type of theology espoused by John Owen.

Older assessments were more generous. To Lord Morley, Baxter was 'the profoundest theologian of them all',[7] and the historian S. R. Gardiner thought him 'the most learned and moderate of the Dissenters'.[8] C. E. Surman reflects current ecumenical aspirations when he describes Baxter as 'an outstanding theologian and

2. RICHARD BAXTER

ecclesiastical leader' and 'would-be apostle of Christian peace'.[9] These varied judgements confirm the impression that the versatile Baxter cannot be neatly categorized. As N. H. Keeble points out, Baxter has proved an elusive figure. 'Modern scholars claim him as both Puritan and Anglican; as representative of the central moderate Puritan and as its "stormy petrel"; as a rationalist and a mystic; as a Calvinist and an Arminian; as a fully integrated personality and as an "utterly self-divided man"'.[10] G. F. Nuttall sees him as an 'individual figure', as 'one who agreed with most men about some things but could never agree with any of them about everything'.[11] In his own lifetime Baxter exasperated those who insisted on rigid theological categories. In the years following his death, his distinctive outlook was identified as 'Baxterianism'[12] and a definite 'middle way' tradition was to emerge by this name.

This book investigates the charge that Baxter's *via media* was a theological disaster. It attempts to evaluate his claim that his theological outlook represents a coherent alternative to the theological positions personified by John Owen and John Wesley. Although Baxter's doctrinal contribution is the primary concern of this book, the impact of his practical and devotional works cannot be ignored. Indeed, his writings have had a truly 'catholic' appeal. Matthew Henry,[13] Philip Doddridge,[14] John Wesley,[15] George Whitefield,[16] C. H. Spurgeon,[17] Archbishop Trench,[18] and J. I. Packer[19] have all commended his practical writings. In a sense, Dr Johnson expressed a universal verdict when he urged Boswell to 'read any of them; they are all good'.[20] Judging by a recent reissue of a selection from *Practical Works*,[21] it would seem that the author of *The Saints' Everlasting Rest*, *A Call to the Unconverted*, and *The Reformed Pastor* is still able to command the attention of his readers 300 years on.

HIS LIFE

Richard Baxter was born at Rowton, Shropshire, in 1615, of modest yet godly beginnings. His upbringing was not marked by the advantages enjoyed by the younger Owen; his education at Wroxeter and Ludlow was largely informal and he was denied the opportunity of attending university. None the less, Puritan piety found a ready response in the precocious Baxter, whose religious concerns were awakened around 1630 through popular Puritan authors. He mentions 'a poor day-labourer' who 'had an old torn book which he lent to my father, which was called *Bunny's Resolution* . . . . And in the reading of this book (when I was about fifteen years of age) it pleased God to awaken my soul . . . '[22] The reading of the 'heavenly Dr' Sibbes's *Bruised Reed* furthered his spiritual progress.

After studying logic under Francis Garbet of Wroxeter and engaging in further private theological study, Baxter was ordained by the bishop of Worcester in 1638 and licensed to teach at Richard Foley's school in Dudley. Although his attachment to the Church of England was attended with some scruples, Baxter became a curate at Bridgnorth in 1639. Despite his zeal, his ministry there seemed fruitless, for 'the people proved a very ignorant, dead-hearted people'.[23] At about this time, Baxter's sympathy for Nonconformity was aroused by the 'et caetera oath'.[24] He now entertained serious doubts about diocesan episcopacy, which were reinforced by the romanizing measures of Archbishop Laud.

Baxter accepted an invitation to a living at Kidderminster, where he was to exercise an extraordinary ministry for nearly twenty years. 'And thus I was brought, by the gracious providence of God, to that place which had the chiefest of my labours and yielded me the greatest fruits of comfort.'[25] His description of the impact of his ministry is famous: 'In a word, when I came thither first there was about one family in a street that worshipped God and called on his name, and when I came away there were some streets where there was not passed one family in the side of a street that did not so.'[26]

With the advent of the civil war, Baxter's support for he parliamentary cause incensed the royalists of Worcestershire. So, his life being threatened, he became an army chaplain at Coventry from 1642 to 1645. After the battle of Naseby he served as a chaplain in Colonel Whalley's regiment for about two years. His five-year acquaintance with religious life in the army found him opposed to its rampant sectarianism and especially to its emphasis upon the orthodox doctrine of 'free grace' at the expense of godliness of character. This close encounter with antinomianism profoundly influenced his conception of the Christian life.

Baxter left the army in 1647. The rigours of a military chaplaincy contributed to his ill health, and he spent some time convalescing at the home of Sir Thomas Rouse. Though indisposed, he conceived his first two books at this period; and in 1649, he returned to Kidderminster, when they were published. In the *Aphorismes of Justification*—a work which clearly reflects his army experiences—he made the first of his many forays against antinomianism; in an appendix, he criticized John Owen's *Death of Death*. The other work was the celebrated *Saints' Everlasting Rest*, which became instantly popular. Numerous other practical and polemical works were published during the Kidderminster years, including the famous *Gildas Salvianus: The Reformed Pastor* (1656) and *A Call to the Unconverted* (1658). Of the *Call* he declared, 'I published this little book, which God hath blessed with unexpected success beyond all the rest that I have written (except *The Saints' Rest*).'[27]

In 1660 Baxter left Kidderminster for London. He was involved in plans to restore Charles II to the throne, and he preached before Parliament at St Margaret's, Westminster. After the Restoration he became a chaplain to the king and was offered the bishopric of Hereford, which he refused. He took a prominent part in the Savoy Conference of 1661, where he stood shoulder to shoulder with moderate Episcopalians and Presbyterians. Still uncomfortable with several features of the Book of Common Prayer, he contributed to the liturgical discussion by producing his *Reformed Liturgy*, written in the space of fourteen days.

Baxter attempted to return to Kidderminster, but was prevented. With the restoration of king and church in full flood, the Puritans found few sympathizers. So, three months before the Act of Uniformity came into force (24 August 1662), Baxter bade farewell to the Church of England in a sermon at Blackfriars. Of 'this fatal day' he wrote: 'When Bartholomew Day came, about one thousand eight hundred or two thousand ministers were silenced and cast out .... And now came in the great inundation of calamities .... Hundreds of able ministers, with their wives and children, had neither house nor bread...'[28] In September of this eventful year, Baxter married Margaret Charlton. Twenty-one years her husband's junior, she was a convert of his Kidderminster ministry. After living for a while at Moorfields, they retired to Acton in Middlesex. They lived happily together for nineteen years, until a grief-stricken Baxter laid his wife to rest in 1681, ten years before his own death.

Despite constant ill-health and uncongenial living conditions, Baxter continued his ministry when and wherever possible. His *Reliquiae* provide a noble, moving, and highly informative account of the ravages of the plague and the great fire of London. Flanking these calamities were two of his important publications, *The Divine Life* (1664) and *Reasons for the Christian Religion* (1667). Dr Johnson considered the latter work 'the best collection of the evidences of the Christian system'.[29] Ever concerned to promote Christian unity, Baxter was involved in discussions with John Owen in 1669. These talks proved fruitless, for differing conceptions about the nature of the church and doctrinal subscription made progress impossible.[30]

There can be no doubt that disunity was a constant source of grief to Baxter. Living at a time when creeds proved constantly divisive, he was ready to declare, 'I can as willingly be a martyr for love as for any article of the Creed.'[31] Not surprisingly, he was a reluctant Nonconformist. He was always interested in schemes for comprehending the Nonconformists within the established church. In 1674 he drafted a bill for comprehension with John Tillotson, hoping to unite moderate opinion of both sides.[32] Such schemes were kept alive until 1689, but the convocation of that year showed a greater sympathy with 'high church' sentiments than with the 'liberal' views of Tillotson, Baxter, and the Presbyterians.[33]

The last twenty years of Baxter's life saw no abatement of his phenomenal literary industry. His publications reflect a continuing concern for church unity and theological consensus. His *Cure of Church Divisions* (1670) and *Richard Baxter's Catholick Theologie* (1675) are typical of this period. The latter work, a heavy folio, contains the sum of his solutions to the theological controversies of the day. It reveals an eclectic *via media* between the high Calvinism of theologians like John Owen and the Arminianism later to be embraced by John Wesley.

Baxter shared the sufferings of the Nonconformists, being imprisoned for a week at Clerkenwell in 1669 and for twenty-one months at Southwark in 1684–6. The second imprisonment is associated with his trial at the hands of the notorious Judge Jeffreys, in which he was accused of libelling the Chuch of England in his *Paraphrase on the New Testament* (1685). Notwithstanding his moderate criticism of episcopacy, Jeffreys accused him of being a thoroughgoing Presbyterian. When he tried to defend himself, the Judge's scurrility knew no bounds:

Richard, Richard, dost thou think we'll hear thee poison the court? Richard, thou art an old fellow, an old knave; thou hast written books enough to load a cart, every one as full of sedition, I might say treason, as an egg is full of meat. Hadst thou been whipped out of thy writing trade forty years ago, it had been happy.[34]

In the closing years of his life Baxter was engaged in further disputes over antinomianism, occasioned by the republication of Tobias Crisp's sermons in 1690. This led him to publish *The Scripture Gospel Defended*. His final theological compendium was *An End of Doctrinal Controversies*, published in 1691, the year of his death. Important posthumous publications included *Universal Redemption of Mankind* (1694), a treatise on the atonement written more than forty years earlier, and the *Reliquiae* (1696), edited by Matthew Sylvester.

Baxter had indeed written enough books to load a cart. Keeble lists a total of 141 publications, many of them large folios, not to speak of collections of his sermons and prefaces to works by other authors.[35] It has been estimated that he wrote more than twice as much as Owen. Probably his last work, *The Certainty of the World of Spirits* (1691), expresses the 'other-worldliness' of one who lived and laboured that he and others might enjoy everlasting rest. At the end, his expectation was sure. The day before he died, he declared to Dr William Bates, 'I have pain, there is no arguing against sense, but I have peace, I have peace.'[36]

HIS CONTRIBUTION

Unlike Owen, whose views on the subjects under review tend to be confined to a few separate treatises, Baxter expressed his thoughts copiously and repeatedly in numerous publications. He even admitted that 'fewer well studied and polished had been better' than the plethora of his hasty output. 'I wrote them', he says, 'in the crowd of all my other employments, which could allow me no great leisure for polishing and exactness, or any ornament; so that I scarce ever wrote one sheet twice over, nor stayed to make any blots or interlinings, but was fain to let it go as it was first conceived'.[37]

When Baxter's tedious analytical method is added to his self-confessed indiscipline, he is clearly open to the charge he frequently levelled at others, that of 'overdoing'. Powicke, who lists this as a fault which impaired Baxter's influence, admits that he simply shared 'the common Puritan abuse of the inherited scholastic way', but asserts that in Baxter's case 'it was carried to a singular length'.[38] Keeble disagrees on the grounds that Baxter refused 'to pass over difficulties or to spare the reader, eschewing all over-simple solutions, neglecting nothing'.[39] As Baxter urged so frequently himself, the truth is probably 'half-way'. He certainly aimed in his polemical writings at a 'thorough simplicity' of verdict, since, as he wrote in 1670, 'It is SIMPLE CATHOLICK CHRISTIANITY which I plead for . . .'[40] However, the thoroughness tended to dominate the simplicity, often resulting in something less than perspicuity.

As with so much in Baxter's career and contribution, paradox is never far away. In his controversial pieces his aim was peace, but his style and method promoted antagonism. It is true that he sought 'the churches' peace',[41] but he was charged with causing 'many contentions'.[42] Yet he was totally unrepentant as to method, even if he did lament his tendency to use provocative language. In the preface to *Catholick Theologie* he presents this self-justification: 'If you say, physician heal thyself: Who hath wrote more of controversies? I answer, peruse what I have written, and you will see, it is of controversies, but *against controversies*, tending to end and reconcile . . . . I have meddled much with controversies in this book, but it is to end them.' Even if he was rather naïve in thinking that rational analysis could remove all disagreements, his objective is borne out by the title of his final polemical piece, *An End of Doctrinal Controversies*, which is something of a compendium of his theological views.

It is difficult not to imagine, despite his protestations to the contrary, that Baxter enjoyed theological debate. With regard to John Owen, G. P. Fisher says of him, 'Undoubtedly he was fond of breaking a lance with the great Independent.'[43] Indeed, Baxter was aware of his natural genius and was hardly reluctant to use it. He had 'an astounding capacity for instant analysis', says Packer, and 'could run rings round anyone in debate'.[44] However, it is being less than fair to Baxter not to acknowledge that he engaged in controversy for practical and pastoral ends. He believed that truth supported his conclusions, but mere victory in debate was never his object. His one concern was to clarify those theological issues which, when misunderstood, led to practical errors and difficulties.

If any one issue persuaded him to adopt a polemical stance, it was antinomianism. As Keeble writes:

For the man who declared 'Practical divinity . . . my soul doth live on, and is the happiest part of my learning', there was one controversy which could not be ignored. The antinomian challenge, which Baxter detected not merely in libertine extremism, but in any version of Calvinism which regarded man's moral effort and obedience as incidental to salvation, posed such a threat to the nature of true Christianity as to demand attention.[45]

This one issue gave Baxter no rest. His first book, *Aphorismes of Justification* was his opening shot in a number of engagements and in the last year of his life *The Scripture Gospel Defended* proved to be his parting one.

Little sympathy has been shown towards Baxter's views on justification. From the beginning, although his *Aphorismes* were directed at antinomians, many who had nothing but contempt for libertine ideas of grace thought he had swung too far in the direction of legalism. He sought to discredit his opponents by insisting that Christians were not lawless when saved by grace. At the heart of his scheme is the idea that faith is the Christian's justifying righteousness according to the gospel, God's 'law of grace'. Faith by its very nature embraces trust and obedience, for Christ is both Saviour and Lord. To orthodox minds, the mere suggestion that the believer's obedience had a bearing on his justification appeared to sail dangerously close to the Roman Catholic conception of salvation, thus threatening the theology of the Reformation.

More recent criticisms of Baxter's views have concurred with the general response to his *Aphorismes* when they first appeared.[46] Such was the hostility shown that he retracted the book.[47] Although he lamented many of the book's expressions, statements in his later works reveal that his position underwent no fundamental change. Orme was correct to say that he 'adhered to the substance of its sentiments to the last'.[48]

One of the purposes of this book is to examine Baxter's contribution to the debate about justification *vis-à-vis* the conflicting opinions of John Owen and John Wesley. The suggestion will be examined that Baxter's critics have tended to minimize the exegetical foundations of his theological case, relying upon assumptions which are themselves questionable. This is not to say that Baxter may be entirely vindicated, but to propose that an important mistake in his theology arises from a neglected quarter. Once this is made plain, a solution to the Puritan debates about the doctrine of justification begins to emerge which is thoroughly consistent with a correct interpretation of the Reformation principles of *sola fide, sola gratia,* and *sola scriptura.*

Baxter's involvement with John Owen over the atonement has already been referred to. It should also be remembered that Baxter's posthumous treatise *Universal Redemption* (1694) was withheld from publication in the 1650's 'partly because many narrow minded brethren would have been offended with it' and partly because it would have needlessly duplicated the work of Bishop Davenant, Moise Amyraut, and Jean Daille.[49] Even then, his views are sufficiently evident in the *Aphorismes* and the *Confession of His Faith* (1655), a fact which occasioned an attack on his position by Louis Du Moulin, Camden Professor of History at Oxford.[50] Baxter was singled out as Amyraut's 'only proselyte in England', an error he was not slow to correct. Quite apart from the fact that he was convinced of his views long before he had heard of Amyraut, many others had taught the same things before him. Baxter cites the English delegates at the Synod of Dort, including Bishops Hall and Davenant. Among others, Archbishop Ussher, Dr William Twisse (first prolocutor of the Westminster Assembly), and the Puritan court chaplain Dr John Preston are appealed to. In claiming their support, he hastens to add that his view of the atonement is to be carefully distinguished from the Arminian view, namely universal redemption in a middle sense—'That Christ died for all men, so far as to purchase them pardon and salvation on condition they would repent and believe; and for the elect, so far further as to procure them faith and repentance itself.'[51]

Baxter also contests Du Moulin's assertion that all the members of the Westminster Assembly were opposed to the Amyraldian view. He personally knew several who 'profest themselves for the middle way of universal redemption'.[52] Indeed, one may cite Edmund Calamy, Dr John Arrowsmith, Richard Vines, Dr Lazarus Seaman, and others in this connection.[53] It is a fact that Robert Baillie, one of the Scottish commissioners at the Assembly, actually complained of the influence of Amyraldianism: 'Unhappily Amyraut's questions are brought in on our Assembly. Many more love their fancies here than I did expect . . .'[54]

With reference to the Westminster Confession itself (especially ch. VIII), Baxter emphatically denies that it opposes 'Amyraldus' method'. On the contrary, he asserts it was deliberately framed so as not to exclude the Amyraldian view. He was assured by 'an eminent divine, yet living, that was of the Assembly', that 'they purposely avoided determining that controversy'.[55] While it would appear from the detailed statements of the Confession (ch. III. vi; VIII. v, viii) that Baxter's 'middle way' was rejected, at least by implication, he himself understood matters otherwise. His unqualified commendation of the Assembly is famous: 'The divines there congregate were men of eminent godliness and learning . . . . the Christian world . . . had never a Synod of more excellent divines (taking one thing with another) than this Synod and the Synod of Dort were.'[56]

Baxter's reference to the Synod of Dort appears to be an even more surprising concession. Owen's editor, W. H. Goold, found it difficult to reconcile Baxter's rejection of Owen's view of the atonement with his admiration for the divines of Dort.[57] Indeed, Baxter's words are truly remarkable when he declares: 'In the article of the extent of redemption, wherein I am most suspected and accused, I do subscribe to the Synod of Dort, without any exception, limitation, or exposition, of any word, as doubtful and obscure.'[58] The solution to Goold's perplexity is not difficult to find, for unlike the Westminster Confession, and contrary to their popular image, the Canons of Dort contain a clear statement about the universal sufficiency of the atonement.[59] It is from the very same perspective that Amyraut himself was able to rebut the charge of heterodoxy. In short, while neither Baxter nor Amyraut questioned the 'effectual application' of the atonement in the salvation of the elect, they were able to affirm, on the authority of the Synod of Dort, that there was a universal dimension to the atonement.

With the advantage of hindsight, one may observe that had the Westminster Confession followed the Canons of Dort more closely, debate over the atonement might have been reduced considerably. It will be said that Owen also affirmed the infinite sufficiency of the atonement, and that no seventeenth-century divine seriously questioned the idea. However, it will be demonstrated that his view of the nature of the atonement militates almost as much against Dort as against Baxter. This is to suggest that Baxter is closer to Dort than Owen is, in the sense that high Calvinists of the Owen school pursued an ultra-orthodox course in their debate with the Arminians. It is therefore a mistake to assume a concurrence of sentiment where Owen and the divines of Dort are concerned, if Baxter can endorse the Canons as he does. It is interesting to note Owen's impatience with those who questioned the views of the English bishops at the Synod on the subject of regeneration,[60] when he himself summarily rejected Davenant's 'middle way' *Dissertatio de morte Christi* (1650) as being 'repugnant unto truth itself'.[61] Indeed, Owen was not quite consistent.

Even though Baxter thought that no significant theological gap existed between Dort and Westminster, Owen would not have tolerated the thought that Baxter could claim such credal support. This might suggest that Owen had refined the ultra-orthodox tendencies of the Westminster Confession even further in his *Death of Death*. Baxter evidently thought so, for he linked Owen with Francis Cheynell, describing them as 'the over-orthodox Doctors'.[62] If, therefore, Owen's high orthodoxy is not quite the same thing as Dort Calvinism, it becomes interesting and legitimate to ask where Baxter is to be placed on the theological spectrum, and according to what credal norms. Was he a Calvinist or not? This question has become more meaningful since R. T. Kendall raised questions about the character of Calvin's 'Calvinism.'[63]

As has been noted, Baxter defies any neat categorization, and earlier attempts to place him have revealed considerable disagreement.[64] However, in his *Catholick Theologie* he is careful to claim Calvin's support for his view of the atonement.[65] As Amyraut himself eulogized Calvin, enlisting his support against his ultra-orthodox critics, so Baxter expressed his admiration for the Genevan reformer in a way Owen never did. 'I know no man, since the Apostles' days, whom I value and honour more than Calvin, and whose judgement in all things, one with another, I more esteem and come nearer to.'[66] This book will reassess Baxter's theological position by evaluating the conflicting evangelicalisms of Owen and Wesley.

NOTES

1. A. G. Matthews, ed. *Calamy Revised* (Oxford, 1934), p. 376.
2. Ibid. 39.
3. Edited by Matthew Sylvester (London, 1696), this was 'a confused and shapeless hulk' according to J. M. Lloyd-Thomas, whose abridgement appeared in 1931. The *Reliquiae* are usefully discussed in O. C. Watkins, *The Puritan Experience* (London, 1972), 121–43. In addition to W. Orme's 'A life of the author', in *The Life and Writings of Richard Baxter*, i, (London, 1830), and J. C. Ryle's valuable essay in *Light from Old Times* (London, 1890), there are 20th-cent. studies: A. R. Ladell, *Richard Baxter: Puritan and Mystic* (London, 1925); F. J. Powicke, *A*

Life of the Revd Richard Baxter 1615–1691 (London, 1924); id., *The Revd Richard Baxter: Under the Cross 1662–1691* (London, 1927); G. F. Nuttall, *Richard Baxter* (London, 1965); N. H. Keeble, *Richard Baxter: Puritan Man of Letters* (London, 1982).

4. Introduction to *The Reformed Pastor*, ed. W. Brown (London, 1829; fac. Edinburgh, 1974), at p. 9.
5. 'The doctrine of justification in development and decline among the Puritans', in *By Schisms Rent Asunder* (PRSC, London, 1969), at p. 27.
6. In *The Encyclopedia of Christianity*, ed. E. H. Palmer (Wilmington, Del., 1964), i. 605.
7. *The Autobiography of Richard Baxter*, ed. J. M. Lloyd-Thomas (London, 1931), p. vii.
8. Ibid.
9. *Richard Baxter* (London, 1961), 11; 19.
10. *Richard Baxter*, p. 22.
11. *Richard Baxter and Philip Doddridge: A Study in a Tradition* (London, 1951), pp. 1–2.
12. T. Edwards, *The Paraselene Dismantled of her Cloud, or Baxterianism Barefac'd* (London, 1699).
13. J. B. Williams wrote of Henry, 'The practical works of Mr Baxter, especially, occupied a very exalted place in his esteem; they are more frequently cited in his manuscripts than the productions of any other author' (*Memoirs of the Life, Character and Writing of the Revd Matthew Henry* (London, 1828; fac. Edinburgh, 1974), p. 221).
14. The young Doddridge wrote of 'Mr Baxter's incomparable writings', declaring that 'Baxter is my particular favourite' (*The Correspondence and Diary of Philip Doddridge, DD*, i, ed. J. D. Humphreys (London, 1829), 368; 460). In his maturity Doddridge stated of Baxter, 'He is inaccurate, because he had no regular education', but thought he might be regarded as 'The English Demosthenes ... Few were ever instrumental of awakening more souls' (*Works*, v. 431).
15. Wesley wrote of 'honest Richard Baxter', calling him a 'loving, serious Christian' (*Works*, ii. 312). He published abridgements of Baxter's *Aphorismes* and *Saints' Rest*, remarking of his *Reformed Pastor* that it was 'worth a careful perusal' (*Works*, viii. 290).
16. Whitefield's early reading included Baxter's *Call to the Unconverted*, which 'much benefited me' (*George Whitefield's Journals*, ed. I. Murray (London, 1960), 62). During a visit to Kidderminster in 1743 he wrote to a friend, 'I was greatly refreshed to find what a sweet savour of good Mr Baxter's doctrine, works and discipline remained to this day' (*Works*, ed. J. Gillies (London, 1771), ii. 47).
17. Spurgeon sought refreshment after preaching by asking his wife to read the *Reformed Pastor* to him; 'perhaps that will quicken my sluggish heart' (*The Early Years* (London, 1962), 417).

18. The archbishop considered that *The Saints' Rest* possessed 'a robust and masculine eloquence' (cited in H. Martin, *Puritanism and Richard Baxter* (London, 1954), 127–8).
19. Packer still considers that 'Baxter was a great and saintly man; as a pastor, evangelist, and devotional writer, no praise for him can be too high' ('The doctrine of justification', p. 27).
20. James Boswell, *Life of Johnson* (London, 1960), ii. 472.
21. *The Practical Works of Richard Baxter: Select Treatises* (Grand Rapids, Mich., 1981).
22. *Autobiography*, p. 7.
23. Ibid. 18.
24. This was one of the measures adopted to stem the tide of Puritanism; see W. H. Hutton, *A History of the English Church From the Accession of Charles I to the Death of Queen Anne, 1625–1714* (London, 1903), 82–4.
25. *Autobiography*, p. 25.
26. Ibid. 79.
27. Ibid. 96.
28. Ibid. 175.
29. Ibid., p. xxiii.
30. *The Correspondence of John Owen*, ed. P. Toon (Cambridge, 1970), 136–45.
31. *Autobiography*, p. ix.
32. *RB* iii. 110; 157.
33. F. Proctor and W. H. Frere, *A New History of the Book of Common Prayer* (London, 1929), 206.
34. *Autobiography*, p. 262.
35. Keeble, *Richard Baxter*, pp. 156 f; also A. G. Matthews, *The Works of Richard Baxter* (London, 1932).
36. *Autobiography*, p. 266.
37. *RB* i. 124.
38. *Baxter: Under the Cross*, p. 253.
39. *Richard Baxter*, p. 67.
40. Ibid. 24.
41. Nuttall, *Richard Baxter*, p. 65.
42. Powicke, *Baxter: Under the Cross*, p. 234.
43. 'The writings of Richard Baxter', *Bibliotheca sacra*, 9 (1851), at p. 309.
44. Introduction to *The Reformed Pastor*, p. 9.
45. *Baxter: Under the Cross*, p. 69.
46. Orme, 'A life of the author', p. 448; Powicke, *Life of Baxter*, p. 241; Martin, *Puritanism*, p. 135; C. F. Allison, *The Rise of Moralism* (London, 1966), 162; Packer, 'The doctrine of justification', p. 26; Kerr, in *Encyclopedia of Christianity*, i. 604.

47. See *Rich. Baxter's Confession of His Faith* (London, 1655; not paginated), p. [xxxv].
48. 'A life of the author', p. 448. In the Preface to his *Catholick Theologie* (1675), Baxter reflected on his *Aphorismes* (1649) thus: 'And being young, and unexercised in writing, and my thoughts yet undigested, I put into it many incautelous [sic] words (as young writers use to do) though I think the main doctrine of it sound'.
49. *RB* i. 123.
50. For Du Moulin (1606–80) see *DNB*.
51. *Aphorismes*, Appendix, p. 164; Preface to *Certain Disputations of Right to Sacraments* (London, 1658); not paginated).
52. Preface to *Certain Disputations*.
53. See *Minutes of the Sessions of the Westminster Assembly of Divines*, ed. A. F. Mitchell and J. Struthers (London, 1874), pp. lv, 152–9 (hereinafter cited as *Minutes*).
54. Ibid., p. xxvi.
55. Ibid., pp. liv ff.; Preface to *Certain Disputations*.
56. *RB* i. 73.
57. Owen, *Works*, x. 430.
58. Cited by Orme, *Works*, i. 456.
59. Article 3 of the second canon states that 'The death of the Son of God is the only and most perfect sacrifice and satisfaction for sin; and is of infinite worth and value, abundantly sufficient to expiate the sins of the whole world.' See *The Creeds of the Evangelical Protestant Churches*, ed. H. B. Smith and P. Schaff (London, 1877), 586 (hereinafter cited as *Creeds*).
60. Owen, *Works*, iii. 229.
61. *Works*, x. 432.
62. *RB* ii. 199.
63. *Calvin*, pp. 2, 13.
64. Orme wrote that none should 'question the Calvinism of Richard Baxter' ('A life of the author', p. 436), whereas Fisher declares that 'he can hardly be styled a Calvinist' p. 307. Martin calls Baxter a 'liberal Calvinist' (*Puritanism*, p. 134), while Kerr shows more perception, affirming with Dowden that B. was 'too Arminian for the high Calvinists and too Calvinistic for the Arminians' (*Encyclopedia of Christianity*, p. 603–4.
65. *CT* II. 51.
66. Cited by P. Schaff, *The History of the Christian Church* (Edinburgh, 1883), viii. 136. Keeble's assessment is therefore wholly inaccurate: 'Though we may wonder that Baxter could say "I am no Arminian", it is no surprise to find him denying whole-hearted allegiance to Calvin' (*Richard Baxter*, p. 72).

3. JOHN TILLOTSON

3
John Tillotson (1630–94)

HIS SIGNIFICANCE

Like Baxter among the Puritans, Dr John Tillotson represents the policy of moderation within post-Restoration Anglicanism. He is probably the most famous example of that religious outlook known as latitudinarianism.[1] J. R. H. Moorman expresses much that was true of Tillotson and the 'men of latitude'[2] when he says,

> They were, on the whole broad-minded men, tired of controversy and the intensity of religious feeling in which they had grown up and anxious for a quiet life in the pursuit of goodness and righteousness. They believed intensely in reason, and had the utmost dislike and contempt for the various forms of ecstatic individualism which were then beginning to be known as 'Enthusiasm'.[3]

The mild-mannered, introverted Tillotson was an altogether different kind of man from the extrovert Baxter, yet their views on the nature and unity of the church were close. If his career was generally less dramatic than that of the Puritan, his place in the annals of English Christianity is assured. Though his primacy was short and uneventful, he was considered 'the wisest and best man that ever sat in the primatial chair of Canterbury'.[4] Dr Edward Carpenter believes that 'If character in itself qualified for office, no man could have had greater claims to Canterbury than John Tillotson. He was intelligent, liberal and warm-hearted.'[5]

The archbishop's most enduring claim to fame in his preaching; he was possibly the only primate who took front rank in his day as a preacher. One of the most attractive features of his pulpit performances was their remarkable lucidity,[6] even if their theological content proved unacceptable to those who demanded stronger opinions.[7] Baxter avoids the more extreme verdicts of others when he declares that Tillotson 'preached well',[8] being one of 'the best and ablest of the Conformists'.[9]

Horton Davies, however, finds it difficult to understand the popularity of Tillotson's preaching.[10] James Downey is of a similar mind, though he concedes that it is 'almost impossible to exaggerate the influence of Tillotson upon eighteenth-century theology and preaching.... The years 1720–40 are the period of greatest vogue for Tillotsonian theology and ethical preaching'.[11] As late as 1778 Dr Johnson was constrained to admit his fame;[12] and in the next century Lord Macaulay acknowledges that 'Tillotson still keeps his place as a legitimate English classic.'[13]

Attempts to explain Tillotson's success vary considerably. Cragg considers that his approach represented a sane alternative to the fanaticism of the Puritan sects.[14] R. Tudur Jones observes a correspondence between Tillotson's style and the 'demands of the new science for a precise and unambiguous medium of expression'.[15] Similarly, Moffat quotes approvingly Sir Leslie Stephen's view that 'for the time, reason and Christian theology were in spontaneous alliance',[16] and accordingly concludes that Tillotson's 'excellence lay in seeing that this involved moral requirements as well as mental'.[17] Not surprisingly, he was accused of rationalism and moralism, although the charges are probably excessive. However, allowing for the belief in the Protestant view of grace which is conspicuous in his sermons, Louis G. Locke concludes that his 'religion led unintentionally toward Deism'.[18] It is certain that the deists applauded his stress on the 'reasonableness' of Christianity.[19]

If there are clear parallels between Tillotson's view of Christianity and the 'supernatural rationalism' of John Locke, it is equally important to note the affinity between the archbishop and some of the Protestant Dissenters whose clear-cut evangelicalism cannot be questioned. Tillotson's Puritan origins, his early sympathy with Presbyterianism, and his lifelong desire to comprehend the more moderate Dissenters within the state church explain much of this. Davies acknowledges that, in addition to the rationalism of the Cambridge Platonists, Tillotson's outlook embraced 'the seriousness of the Puritans'.[20]

Baxter's commendation of Tillotson has already been noted. For some, this might confirm their suspicions about Baxter's own supposedly rationalistic tendencies.[21] However, none could question the fervent evangelicalism of men like Matthew Henry and Philip Doddridge, who regarded both Baxter and Tillotson highly. While studying law at Gray's Inn, young Henry heard many of the

London preachers. Of all the sermons he sampled, he remarked, 'There are not many desirable. Dr Tillotson's are best',[22] and in later life he could write of 'That great man Archbishop Tillotson'.[23] In 1721, three years before he acquired Baxter's works, Philip Doddridge declared to his brother-in-law, 'In practical divinity, Tillotson is my principal favourite.'[24] Even after Baxter became the dominant influence in Doddridge's life, he held Tillotson's sermons in high esteem.[25] When lecturing to his own students in later years, he alluded to more than the 'beautiful simplicity' of Tillotson's style; he also remarked 'He had some puritanical expressions.'[26]

Not all eighteenth-century evangelicals shared his admiration. Notwithstanding their warm regard for Doddridge,[27] George Whitefield and the Wesley brothers were thoroughly antagonistic towards Tillotson.[28] In their view, the latitudinarianism of Tillotson and his school had been largely responsible for the spritual lethargy of the Church of England. Remembering that David Hume's sceptical rejection of miracles had been influenced by the very type of reasoning Tillotson had employed against transubstantiation,[29] L. G. Locke is correct to conclude, 'If on one hand rationalism led eventually to scepticism, on the other, it certainly produced the reaction which we know as the great revival movement of the following century, of which Methodism is a large part.'[30]

HIS LIFE

John Tillotson was born at Sowerby near Halifax in 1630. His father was a prosperous clothier and a decided Calvinist. After receiving a grammar-school education, first at Colne in Lancashire and then at Halifax, John entered Clare Hall, Cambridge, in 1647. His tutor was the Presbyterian divine David Clarkson,[31] and he shared rooms with another Puritan, Francis Holcroft.[32] The master of Clare was Ralph Cudworth,[33] one of the 'Cambridge Platonists'. Initially Tillotson was much attracted to the Puritans, and their intellectual keenness impressed him. He was an avid reader of William Twisse[34] and a great admirer of Thomas Goodwin.[35] However, at some stage in his university career he began to entertain doubts about certain features of Puritan fundamentalism. His reflective and non-partisan disposition welcomed the cool, logical style of William Chillingworth's *Religion of Protestants* (1638).[36] Here was a book which challenged the aggressive dogmatism of Rome but also raised questions about bigotry of every kind.

Ill health interrupted his studies for a while, and he returned to Sowerby to convalesce. He eventually graduated BA in 1650 and MA in 1654, having been elected a fellow of his college in 1651 in succession to David Clarkson.

At this time, Tillotson's sympathies still aligned him with the Presbyterians, and he supported the protectorate of Oliver Cromwell. In 1656 he left Cambridge to become tutor to the son of Sir Edmund Prideaux, Cromwell's attorney-general. Tillotson was in London at the time of the Protector's death in September 1658. A week later he was present on a fast-day at Whitehall; there in the presence of the new Protector and his family were John Owen, Thomas Goodwin, Joseph Caryl, and Peter Sterry. According to Birch,

> The bold sallies of enthusiasm, which Mr Tillotson heard upon this occasion, were sufficient to disgust a man less disposed to it than he was both by temper and principles. God was in a manner reproached with the deceased Protector's services, and challenged for taking him away so soon. Dr Goodwin, who had pretended to assure him in a prayer, a very few minutes before he expired, that he was not to die, had now the assurance to say to God, 'Thou hast deceived us and we are deceived.' And Mr Sterry, praying for Richard, used these indecent words, next to blasphemy— 'Make him the brightness of the father's glory, and the express image of his person.'[37]

This incident, if true (its authenticity has been contested),[38] promoted Tillotson's growing disenchantment with Puritanism.

His personal attachments began to change, and during a visit to London in 1660 by the bishop of Galloway, Dr Thomas Sydserf, he was ordained. His episcopal orders notwithstanding, Tillotson was still a Presbyterian sympathizer, so he was ejected from his fellowship at Clare. He was also present as an auditor at the Savoy Conference of 1661 with the Presbyterian commissioners. In the same year he preached at St Giles, Cripplegate, in one of the 'morning exercises',[39] in the absence of Dr William Bates, another eminent Presbyterian. However, upon the passing of the Act of Uniformity in 1662 Tillotson conformed, thus severing his formal links with the Presbyterians.

Tillotson's unique style of preaching was beginning to attract attention. After a curacy at Cheshunt in Hertfordshire and a brief appointment as rector of Kedington in Suffolk, he was elected as preacher at Lincoln's Inn and also as Tuesday lecturer at St Lawrence Jewry in 1663. His famous sermon, 'The wisdom of being religious',[40] was preached and published in the following year. In this response to the growing secularism of the age, his communication skills were used to the full: 'when it shall be counted brave to defy God, and every dabbler in natural philosphy, or mathematics, or politics, shall set up for an atheist; sure then it is high time to resist this growing evil'.[41]

The obvious impact of Tillotson's preaching aroused jealousy, especially among churchmen who doubted his real commitment to the Church of England. However, there was no denying that his labours 'contributed so much to turn the greatest part of the city to a hearty love of the church, and a firm adherence to the communion of it'.[42] Thus he was destined for high places, and preferment came quite rapidly. In 1669 he became royal chaplain and prebendary of Canterbury, and in 1672 dean of Canterbury. Three years later he was appointed prebendary of St Paul's.

If Tillotson was no longer a Presbyterian, his Anglicanism remained conspicuously Protestant. Indeed, he was frequently engaged in controversy over Roman Catholicism. This commenced with *The Rule of Faith* (1666), the only formal treatise that he ever published, and for which he was created DD. A significant proportion of Tillotson's sermons were directed against the church of Rome, which did not endear him to the king. His sermon on 'The hazard of being saved in the church of Rome' (1672),[43] preached at Whitehall, resulted in the permanent absence of the duke of York from the Chapel Royal. The 'popish plot' of 1678 occasioned another of his anti-Roman discourses, this time before the House of Commons. Even then, while decrying the persecuting spirit of Rome, the magnanimous Tillotson refused to admit that like should meet with like: 'But I speak it to awaken your care thus far, that if their priests will always be putting these pernicious principles into the minds of the people, effectual provision may be made, that it may never be in their power again to put them in practice.'[44] Consistently with his generous nature, he gave warm support to the French Protestant refugees following the revocation of the Edict of Nantes in 1685.

Tillotson never totally lost his Puritan sympathies. He married a niece of Oliver Cromwell in 1664, and maintained close friendships with the leading Nonconformists. He tearfully admitted his error when John Howe, a former chaplain to the Protector, contested some aspersions he had cast up on the Reformers in a hastily prepared sermon preached before the king.[45] The idea of comprehending the Nonconformists within the state church always appealed to him. In 1674 he drafted a bill for comprehension jointly with Richard Baxter.[46] However, support from the king and the bishops was not forthcoming.

In 1678 Tillotson preached at the Yorkshire Feast—a gathering of expatriate Yorkshiremen—urging the Church of England to make concessions to the Nonconformists. For this he was severely criticized. He also took an interest in the efforts of the Nonconformist Thomas Gouge to promote education and evangelization in Wales.[47] Typical of his keen sense of justice was his willingness to apologize to the Quaker William Penn for having supported those who suspected he was a Jesuit. In 1687, after losing a daughter and suffering a mild stroke, Tillotson wrote to a friend who was dying of cancer. This moving letter reveals a warm personality combined with an essential Puritan piety and pastoral concern:

> I pray God to fit us both for that great change, which we must once undergo .... I commend you to the Father of all mercies, and the God of all consolation, beseeching him to increase your faith and patience, and to stand by you in your last and great conflict; that when you walk through the valley of the shadow of death, you may fear no evil; and, when your heart fails, and your strength fails, may you find him the strength of your heart, and your portion forever. Farewell, my good friend; and whilst we are here, let us pray for one another, that we may have a joyful meeting in another world.[48]

On the advent of the Glorious Revolution of 1688, Tillotson was invited to preach thanksgiving sermons before the Prince of Orange at St James and at Lincoln's Inn.[49] With the passing of the Toleration Act in 1689, he and his friends promoted another comprehension scheme, and a bill was laid before Parliament. Tillotson persuaded the king to summon Convocation, and a commission met to consider possible concessions to the Nonconformists. Extensive alterations to the Book of Common Prayer found favour with many. However, 'high' church opinion prevailed in Convocation and the reforming measures were rejected.[50]

Tillotson's sermon 'Of the eternity of hell torments',[51] preached before the queen at Whitehall in 1690, brought considerable odium upon him. He was unjustly accused of undermining the received doctrine by arguing that the divine threatenings are primarily conditional. His 'deterrent theory' was misunderstood and viewed with suspicion.[52] *The Life of Jesus Christ Considered as our Example*[53] and *The Precepts of Christianity not Grievous*[54] were seen as specimens of his eudaemonistic view of Christianity. He was thought to have departed from the theology of the Reformation in his sermons on faith and justification,[55] in which he follows the controversial views of Bishop Bull's Latin treatise *Harmonia Apostolica* of 1669.[56]

Tillotson had been appointed dean of St Paul's early in 1689. With much reluctance, he became archbishop of Canterbury in 1691. His sincere sense of unworthiness and the depth and reality of his piety are evident in the meditations and prayers he composed on the eve of his consecration.[57] Throughout his brief primacy he conscientiously sought to uphold the Toleration Act, although in some quarters his liberalism and magnanimity were misinterpreted.

Tillotson's 'reasonable' theology aroused suspicions of Socinianism. He consequently revised and published his four sermons 'Concerning the divinity and incarnation of our blessed saviour' in 1693,[58] but this failed to satisfy some of his critics. Unlike Baxter, the gentle Tillotson was no match for his persistent critics and his spirit was broken. Weary of controversy, he endeavoured to promote domestic piety in 'Steadfastness in religion' and other sermons.[59] His final sermon was on 'Sincerity towards God and man',[60] preached a few months before his death. After suffering a stroke during a service in Whitehall on 18 November 1694 he lingered for four days, during which 'He continued serene and calm, and in broken words said, that he thanked God he was quiet within, and had nothing to do, but to wait the will of heaven.'[61] When he died King William declared, 'I have lost the best friend that I ever had, and the best man that I ever knew.'[62]

HIS CONTRIBUTION

With the notable exception of *The Rule of Faith*—an apologia for the Protestant doctrine of Holy Scripture *vis-à-vis* the Roman

Catholic doctrine of tradition—the vast majority of Tillotson's published works are sermons. Thus his literary activities were significantly different from those of Owen and Baxter. This is not to imply that he avoided the theological issues of the day. What marks him out is a relatively uncomplicated and less scholastic way of expounding the Bible.

Tillotson's sermons on the atonement and justification do not begin to compare with the lengthy treatises of Owen and Baxter, but his style reveals a remarkable gift for brevity and lucidity. If this is to commend his virtues, we should remember that some questioned his orthodoxy. A cool, conciliatory manner was viewed with suspicion by those for whom orthodoxy and pugnacity were all of a piece. Yet he was unrepentant. He thought that 'the less men's consciences were entangled, and the less the communion of the church was clogged with disputable opinions or practices, the world would be happier, consciences freer, and the church quieter'.[63]

It is true that Tillotson lacked the thoroughness of Owen and the passionate directness of Baxter. Indeed, he tended to preach *about* the gospel rather than declare it. It is also true that the atmosphere of his sermons is often rational and moral, but this was not to the exclusion of all else. His deep suspicion of excessive emotion is plain; in this there is clear evidence of an over-reaction to Puritan extravagance. This being granted, it is incorrect to describe his sermons as 'frigid moral essays' without charm or interest.[64] Horton Davies has written, 'It was left to the Latitudinarians to conceive of a contradiction—Christianity without tears.'[65] This is a highly questionable generalization, at least where Tillotson is concerned. He could, at times, preach with a warmth not untypical of the most fervent evangelicalism:

In the blood of Christ we may see our own guilt, and in the dreadful sufferings of the Son of God, the just desert of our sins; *He hath born our griefs, and carried our sorrows,* . . . *He was wounded for our transgressions, and bruised for our iniquities*; therefore the commemoration of His sufferings should call our sins to remembrance, the representation of His body broken should melt our hearts; and so often as we remember that *His blood was shed for us*, our eyes should *run down with rivers of tears*; so often as we *look upon Him whom we have pierced*, we should *mourn over Him*. When the Son of God suffered, the *Rocks were rent in sunder*; and shall not the consideration of those sufferings be effectual to break the most stony and obdurate heart?[66]

Notwithstanding the emotional element in Christian experience, Tillotson believed that such an emphasis was only part of the New Testament conception of the Christian life. Piety must entail practice, and this, he believed, was a frequently neglected principle. That said, his sermons are far from being arid dissertations.

The extract quoted above serves to illustrate another important feature of the sermons. The sequence of biblical texts[67] woven into his prose is not incidental. Tillotson, no less than Baxter or Owen, was a meticulous expositor of Scripture; in this vital respect he remained a Puritan to the last. His critics have not always noticed that even when his views seem heterodox, he is carefully expounding a text of Scripture.

Tillotson often preached on texts and subjects neglected by others. In this he was seeking to redress the theological and pastoral imbalance. A case in point is the oft-criticized sermon 'The precepts of Christianity not grievous',[68] 'easily', says Downey, 'the most popular sermon in eighteenth-century England'.[69] While commending Tillotson and his colleagues for reasserting the need for morality in the decadence of post-Restoration society, Sykes accuses them of reducing it to the level of 'prudence' and 'worldly wisdom'.[70] He further argues that this outlook adapts 'the demands of Christianity to the infirmities of unregenerate human nature', promising 'the consolations of religion to the weakest of its professors;.[71] Davies is even more severe: Tillotson's style 'reduced Christianity to rationalism and moralism, the former diluting faith and the latter abandoning grace'.[72]

A careful study of the sermon in question—an exposition of the text 'And his commandments are not grievous' (1 John 5: 3)—exposes the superficiality of these criticisms. In drawing attention to the 'utilitarian' aspects of the gospel, Tillotson is not guilty of making Christianity attractive at the expense of its scriptural duties and requirements. In emphasizing the positive benefits of the godly life, he neither calls into question the pessimistic potential of human nature nor the necessity of divine grace to redeem it.[73] It is interesting to compare this sermon with John Calvin's comment on 1 John 5: 3,[74] for the similarity of exegesis is marked. As for Tillotson, he is far from 'diluting faith' and 'abandoning grace' when he argues:

'Tis true we have contracted a great deal of weakness and impotency by our wilful degeneracy from goodness, but that grace which the Gospel offers to us for our assistance is sufficient for us. And this seems to be the particular reason why the Apostle says here in the text that *his commandments are not grievous*, because he offers us an assistance proportionable to the difficulty of his commands and the necessity of our condition: for it follows immediately after the text, *For whosoever is born of God, overcometh the world*. Therefore, the commandments of God are not grievous, because every child of God, that is every Christian, is endued with a power whereby he is enabled to resist and conquer the temptations of the world.'[75]

In this statement, Tillotson is clearly steering a middle course between legalism and antinomianism.

Davies further fails to appreciate Tillotson's expository method in the three sermons on 'The life of Jesus Christ considered as our example.'[76] The preacher is accused of reducing Christianity to morality and of suppressing the truth of Christ's diety.[77] But Tillotson aimed to correct an imbalance; in his day it was common for Christ to be preached as 'saviour' but not as 'example'. It was predictable that those who highlighted the latter should be regarded as moralizers. However, his text could not be more explicit: '... leaving us an example, that ye should follow in his steps; (1 Pet. 2: 21).

What Davies repudiates as Tillotson's 'character reference'[78] for Jesus Christ is in fact a faithful exposition of our Lord's character according to the New Testament evidence. Since the context in 1 Peter 2 is concerned with Christian conduct, it is hardly surprising that Tillotson's exposition should reflect this emphasis. Even then, it is simply not true that he suppresses the orthodox doctrines of the incarnation and the atonement.[79] However, remembering the limited object he had in view in these sermons, one must seek his orthodoxy elsewhere. His sermons on 'The divinity and incarnation of our blessed saviour' and 'The sacrifice and satisfaction of Christ' were published to combat rumours that he favoured Socinianism. No candid mind can fail to detect the archbishop's decided convictions regarding the deity of Christ and his substitutionary atonement.

An advocate of broad theological consensus, Tillotson was suspected of Socinianism mainly because he stressed the rationality of Christianity. In refusing to concede that reason and revelation were mutually exclusive, what he regarded as a relationship to be fostered was construed by others as a flirtation with error. It was natural enough for the champions of 'orthodoxy' to suspect anyone who appealed to 'reason'. After all, the Socinians had argued that such doctrines as the incarnation and the trinity were both above and contrary to reason. Tillotson's 'rational supernaturalism' admitted the former but not the latter. However, he positively refused to give ground to the 'enthusiasts'. In his view it was dangerous as well as unnecessary to imply that religious belief was basically irrational.[80]

Cragg is correct to say that the latitudinarians were 'more ready to praise reason than to define it'.[81] Their conception seems to amount to nothing more than the use of rational processes in perceiving facts and evaluating arguments. They certainly shunned the secular rationalism of a later age, when unaided reason became the sole arbiter of all that was possible. Tillotson believed that 'religion is necessary to purify our minds'[82] and that the Christian's sanctified intelligence was an integral part of his experience. Again he is consistent with Scripture. Commenting on 1 Peter 3: 15, where the apostle urges Christians to 'answer everyman that asks you a reason for the hope that is in you', Tillotson says, 'If ye be questioned for being Christians, be ready to own your profession, and give a reason of it.'[83]

Tillotson and the latitudinarians were not alone in asserting the importance of reason. John Owen and Richard Baxter shared his emphasis.[84] Goold is incorrect when he says that Tillotson's 'greater rationalism' implied a sufficiency in reason apart from divine influences.[85] Tillotson, like Owen and Baxter, not only insists that sin has not suspended our rational faculties, but that the Holy Spirit is still necessary to 'illumine the mind' and 'remove the impediments which hinder our effectual assent to the gospel'.[86]

It is paradoxical that Tillotson, rather than Owen, has been viewed as the rationalist. Unlike Owen, he repudiated Aristotelian logic in favour of the a posteriori, inductive reasoning of the new empiricism. He was in many respects less doctrinaire than Owen, whose theology was significantly influenced by the older a priori, scholastic rationalism.

As has been noted, Tillotson's theology exhibits clear signs of over-reaction. In recoiling from the excesses of ultra-Calvinism in his youth, he went beyond the kind of moderate Calvinism embraced by Baxter towards Arminianism. Being a man of peace and 'moderate principles', he generally had little to say about the Calvinist-Arminian controversy. While his version of moderation placed him to the left of Baxter's position, Tillotson's part in the writing of Gilbert Burnet's *Exposition of the Thirty-nine Articles* (1699)[87] reveals a concern to tolerate Calvinism and Arminianism, to the exclusion of Pelagianism and antinomianism.

If much of Tillotson's theology may be rescued from undue approbrium, questions remain about his theology of justification. As has been noted, eighteenth-century evangelicals came to regard the late primate as an enemy of the Protestant Reformation. In a highly controversial comment attributed by him to John Wesley, George Whitefield was to declare that Tillotson 'knew no more about Christianity than Mahomet'.[88] This book is concerned to investigate these accusations, especially in view of the interesting similarity between Wesley's mature views on justification and those of the latitudinarian archbishop.

NOTES

1. G. R. Cragg, *From Puritanism to the Age of Reason* (Cambridge, 1966), 61 ff.
2. For Stillingfleet (1635–98), Wilkins (1614–72), Bull (1634–1710), Burnet (1643–1715), and other latitudinarians, see *DNB*.
3. *A History of the Church of England* (London, 1953), 255.
4. J. Hunt, *Religous Thought in England* (London, 1871), ii. 99.
5. *Cantuar: The Archbishops and Their Office* (London, 1971), 226. Biographical accounts of Tillotson have been generally few and slight. See G. Burnet, *A Sermon Preached at the Funeral of . . . John . . . Lord Archbishop of Canterbury* (London, 1695); F. Hutchinson, *The Life of the Most Reverend Father in God John Tillotson, Archbishop of Canterbuy* (London, 1717). For a fuller account see T. Birch, *The Works of Dr John Tillotson* (London, 1752; repr. London, 1820); this includes a memoir by T.'s pupil John Beardmore as an appendix. See also W. Nichol's account in the *Biographia Britannica*, vi (1763), as well as *DNB*; also the sketch by J. Moffat in *The Golden Book of Tillotson* (London, 1926). The most recent study is L. G. Locke, 'Tillotson: a study in seventeenth-century literature', *Anglistica*, 4 (Copenhagen, 1954), 1–165.
6. 'The attributes of Tillotson's oratory which most impressed hearers and readers were the lucidity of his language and the sinewy strength of his argument' (J. Downey, *The Eighteenth Century Pulpit* (Oxford, 1969), 26).
7. Cragg, *Puritanism to Age of Reason*, p. 67.

8. *RB* ii. 437.
9. Ibid. iii. 19.
10. D. H. M. Davies, *Worship and Theology in England from Andrewes to Baxter and Fox, 1603–1690* (Princeton, 1975), 182.
11. *Eighteenth Century Pulpit*, p. 24.
12. J. Boswell, *Life of Johnson* (London, 1960), ii. 179.
13. *History of England* (London, 1967), iii. 170–1.
14. *Puritanism to Age of Reason*, p. 64.
15. *Congregationalism in England, 1662–1962* (London, 1962), 130.
16. *English Thought in the Eighteenth Century* (London, 1876), i. 79.
17. *Golden Book of Tillotson*, p. 35.
18. 'Tillotson', p. 110.
19. Cragg, *Puritanism to Age of Reason*, p. 81.
20. *Worship and Theology 1603–1690*, p. 181.
21. See R. Thomas, 'Parties in Nonconformity', in C. G. Bolam et al., *The English Presbyterians: From Elizabethan Puritanism to Modern Unitarianism* (London, 1968), 103.
22. Quoted in J. B. Williams, *Memoirs of the Life, Character and Writings of the Revd Matthew Henry* (London, 1828; fac. Edinburgh, 1974), 25.
23. *An Exposition of the Old and New Testament* (London, 1886), vol. ii, p. v.
24. *The Correspondence and Diary of Philip Doddridge, DD,* ed. J. D. Humphreys (London, 1829–31), i. 44; *Calendar of the Correspondence of Philip Doddridge, DD,* (1702–51), ed. G. F. Nuttall (London, 1979), Letter 8, p. 2.
25. 'Doctor Tillotson has also prepared an admirable sermon, which he will quickly deliver in my chamber with his usual grace and sweetness' (*Correspondence and Diary*, ii. 139).
26. *Works*, v. 435.
27. A. C. Clifford, 'Philip Doddridge and the Oxford Methodists', *WHS* 42. 3 (1979), 75–80.
28. L. Tyerman, *The Life of the Revd George Whitefield* (London, 1876), i. 360; *The Works of the Revd John Wesley, AM,* ed. T. Jackson (London, 1840–2), vii. 433; *Charles Wesley's Earliest Evangelical Sermons*, ed. T. R. Albin and O. A. Beckerlegge (London, 1987), 67.
29. D. Hume, *Enquiries Concerning Human Understanding and Concerning the Principles of Morals*, ed. L. A. Selby-Bigge, 2nd edn. (Oxford, 1902), 109; *TW* iii. 314–15.
30. 'Tillotson' pp. 110–11.
31. See *DNB*. Clarkson preached Owen's funeral sermon in 1683 (P. Toon, *God's Statesman: The Life and Work of John Owen* (Exeter, 1971), 173.
32. G. F. Nuttall, 'Cambridge Nonconformity, 1660–1710: from Holcroft to Hussey', *URC* 1. 9 (1977), 241–58.

33. See *DNB*.
34. See *DNB*.
35. See *DNB*.
36. See *DNB*; W. Haller, *The Rise of Puritanism* (New York, 1957), 236 f.
37. T. Birch, 'Life of Tillotson' in *The Works of Dr John Tillotson*, vol. i, pp. xi–xii.
38. Toon shares Orme's suspicion that Burnet's account of these proceedings is prejudiced and unreliable (*God's Statesman*, p. 103). However, Burnet's information came from Tillotson, who was not known to indulge in misrepresentation.
39. *The Morning Exercise at Cripplegate, or Several Cases of Conscience Practically Resolved by Sundry Ministers* (London, 1661). The preachers' names were not printed until the 4th ed. (1677). The first sermon is by Dr Samuel Annesley (J. Wesley's grandfather), then minister of St Giles, the tenth by Tillotson. Although this was not published in the Barker ed. (1695), it was included by Birch (1752), whose ed. was republished in 1820.
40. *TW* iii. 1 ff.
41. Birch, 'Life of Tillotson', pp. xix–xx.
42. Ibid. xxi.
43. *TW* iii. 119.
44. Ibid. 209.
45. Birch, 'Life of Tillotson', p. xliv; Henry Rogers, *The Life and Character of John Howe, MA* (London, n.d.), 141 ff.
46. *RB* iii. 110; 157.
47. See Tillotson's funeral sermon for Gouge (1681), *TW* iii. 251 ff. Gouge was the son of the eminent Puritan William Gouge (d. 1653); see Haller, *Rise of Puritanism*, pp. 67 ff.
48. Birch, 'Life of Tillotson', pp. xci–xciii.
49. *TW* iii. 373 ff.
50. F. Proctor and W. H. Frere, *A New History of the Book of Common Prayer* (London, 1929), 206 f.
51. *TW* iii. 409 ff.
52. For a recent discussion of Tillotson's sermon see J. Carrick, 'Jonathan Edwards and the Deists', *BOT* 299–300 (1988), 22–34. Following Edwards's critique of Tillotson, Carrick misunderstands the sermon. Tillotson does not deny the doctrine of eternal punishment; he merely states that the primary purpose of God's threatenings is to deter sinners. If they fail to repent, God 'will execute these threatenings upon them, if they will obstinately stand it out with him . . . they who wilfully break his laws are in danger of eternal death'. (*TW* iii. 415.) Like Calvin (*Institutes* I. xvii. 14), Tillotson acknowledges a 'tacit condition' in the divine threatenings (*TW* i. 657), which is not to deny the certainty of punishment in the case of the unrepentant. Carrick also

accuses Tillotson of sympathizing with Origen's theory of a limited 1,000-year punishment for the wicked (pp. 28–9), but Tillotson twice refers to Origen only to refute him (pp. 413, 417). Furthermore, T.'s sermon is relevant to current interest in the doctrine of annihilation. J. R. W. Stott finds the concept of everlasting punishment 'intolerable' David L. Edwards with John Stott, (*Essentials: A Liberal–Evangelical Dialogue* (London, 1988), 314). Contrary to Tillotson's liberal reputation, he is surprisingly conservative on this issue: 'For if the *second death*, and to be *destroyed*, and to *perish*, signify nothing else but the *annihilation* of sinners and an utter extinction of their being ... then the fire of hell is quenched all at once, and is only a frightful metaphor without any meaning.' (p. 414). What is plain in Tillotson's theology is a concern to moderate an excessively severe conception of divine justice. However, he does not stress the benevolence of God to the exclusion of retributive justice altogether. See 'The justice of God in the distribution of rewards and punishments', *TW* i. 637 ff.

53. *TW* ii. 221 ff.
54. *TW* iii. 70 ff.
55. *TW* ii. 474 ff.
56. G. Bull, *Harmonia apostolica* (Oxford, 1842).
57. *TW* ii. 672 ff.
58. *TW* iii. 505 ff.
59. Ibid. 581 ff.
60. *TW* i. 1 ff.
61. Birch, 'Life of Tillotson', p. ccxxii.
62. Ibid. ccxxxviii.
63. Burnet, *Sermon Preached at Funeral of Tillotson*, p. 31.
64. See W. H. Hutton, *A History of the English Church from the Accession of Charles I to the Death of Queen Anne, 1625–1714* (London, 1903), 300; *Cambridge History of English Literature* (1912), viii. 303. For a discussion of Tillotson's style see W. F. Mitchell, *English Pulpit Oratory from Andrewes to Tillotson* (1932), 121 ff.; Davies, *Worship and Theology, 1603–1690*, 182; Downey, *Eighteenth Century Pulpit*, pp. 1–29; N. Sykes, *From Sheldon to Secker* (Cambridge, 1959), 150 ff.; id., *Church and State in England in the Eighteenth Century* (Cambridge, 1934), 256 ff.; L. G. Locke, 'Tillotson', pp. 112 ff.; A. Pollard, *English Sermons* (London, 1963), 26 ff.; Cragg, *Puritanism to Age of Reason*, 83–4.
65. D. H. M. Davies, *Worship and Theology in England from Watts and Wesley to Maurice, 1690–1850* (Princeton, 1961), 56. Davies thus endorses Hutton's assessment of Tillotson's preaching, but neither Moffat (*Golden Book of Tillotson*, p. 37) nor Pollard (*English Sermons*, p. 28) agree with him.
66. *TW* ii. 7.

48   The Theologians

67. Isa. 53: 4; Matt. 26: 28; Lam. 2: 18; Ps. 119: 136; Rev. 1: 7; Zech. 12: 10; Matt. 27: 51.
68. *TW* iii. 70 ff.
69. Ibid. 15.
70. *Sheldon to Secker*, p. 150.
71. *Church and State*, p. 262.
72. *Worship and Theology* 1603–1690, 184.
73. It is surely not mere prudence and worldly wisdom to argue from Christ's exhortations to 'love our neighbour as ourselves' (Matt. 22: 39) and 'to do to others as we would have them do to us' (Matt. 7: 12) as Tillotson does (*TW* iii. 71). It is hardly adapting Christianity to 'unregenerate nature' to state the necessity of repentance, the mortification of lusts and passions, humility, patience, contentedness, forgiveness and love of enemies, and self-denial for the cause of God and religion, all of which he does (ibid. 72–3).
74. Calvin believes that all difficulty in the Christian life stems not from 'the nature of the Law but from the vice of our flesh'. He also says that 'the sweetness and delight' suggested in the text applies only to those 'whom God begets again by His Spirit. . . . John confines these words, God's commandements are not grievous, to God's children, lest anyone should take them generally'. Again, like Tillotson, Calvin concludes that 'the Law is called easy in so far as we are endowed with heavenly power and overcome the lusts of the flesh' (*Comm.* 1 John 5: 3). This is the essential thrust of Tillotson's sermon.
75. *TW* iii. 73.
76. *TW* ii. 221 ff.
77. *Worship and Theology* 1690–1850 pp. 56–7.
78. 'No other age would surely have presumed to give Jesus Christ a testimonial of good character' (ibid. 56).
79. Tillotson could not be clearer: 'He that requires us to forgive our enemies, shed his own blood for the forgiveness of our sins; while we were enemies to him, laid down his life for us, making himself the example of that goodness, which he commands us to show to others' (*TW* ii. 242). The preacher's belief in the incarnation is as clear as his affirmation of the atonement when he asks—with obvious reference to Paul's christological statement in Phil. 2—'Can we be proud, when the Son of God *humbled himself and became of no reputation; emptied himself* of all his glory, and was contented to be despised and rejected of men?' (ibid. 242).
80. 'But if this be Socinianism, for a man to enquire into the grounds and reasons of the Christian religion, and to endeavour to give a satisfactory account of why he believes it, I know no way but that all considerate inquisitive men, that are above fancy and enthusiasm, must be either

Socinians or Athiests . . .' ('The efficacy, usefulness and reasonableness of divine faith', *TW* ii. 464).
81. *Puritanism to Age of Reason*, p. 65.
82. *TW* iii. 51.
83. *TW* ii. 376–7.
84. Baxter even places reason in the context of grace: 'Reason as reprieved in order to recovery, and reason as illuminated are certainly a sort of common grace' (*CT* ii. 160). Owen declared, 'Many things are above reason . . . which are not at all against it' ('The doctrine of the Holy Spirit explained and vindicated' (1668), *Works*, ii. 411).
85. Owen, *Works*, ii. 4.
86. 'Of the testimony of the spirit to the truth of the gospel', *TW* ii. 456.
87. Birch, 'Life of Tillotson', p. ccxxi; G. Burnet, *An Exposition of the Thirty-nine Articles of the Church of England*, ed. J. R. Page (London, 1841), p. 227.
88. L. Tyerman, *The Life of the Revd George Whitefield* (London, 1876), i. 360.

4. JOHN WESLEY

4
John Wesley (1703-91)

HIS SIGNIFICANCE

Unlike Owen, Baxter, and Tillotson, John Wesley needs little or no introduction. No other Christian denomination honours the name of its founder more than the Methodist Church honours him. When the denomination's new historical society was formed in 1893, it was called the Wesley Historical Society. Indeed, he has become something of a cult figure. J. C. Ryle wrote a century ago, 'If ever a good Protestant has been practically canonised, it has been John Wesley'.[1] Nearly two centuries after his death, there is no decline of interest in his life and his contribution to Christianity. His wide-ranging influence is reflected in the comments of public figures, secular historians, and Christian leaders of all denominations.[2] No study of the eighteenth-century can ignore him. His own conservatism notwithstanding, the rise of political radicalism cannot be explained without reference to him, and he occupies a place of unsurpassed eminence in the history of the Christian church. By any standard, he is unique.[3]

Like Richard Baxter, Wesley was a paradox. A devoted son of the Church of England, he fathered a breakaway church. An Oxford don, he became a preacher to the illiterate masses. An unbending Tory, he was a friend of the poor and enemy of slavery. Saintly and calm in a crisis, he could be irritable and dictatorial. Extravagant claims have been made for him, but, these apart, Stanley Ayling seems justified in regarding him as 'the single most influential Protestant leader of the English speaking world since the Reformation.'[4]

In a sense Wesley has become the property of the whole church. It is not difficult to find Anglicans, Presbyterians, Congregationalists, and Baptists expressing gratitude and admiration.[5] Bearing in mind the controversial themes being discussed in this book, the eminent Victorian preacher C. H. Spurgeon was surprisingly generous in his praise. His own Baptist and Calvinist convictions notwithstanding, he could declare that 'The character of John

Wesley stands beyond all imputation for self sacrifice, zeal, holiness and communion with God; he lived far above the level of common Christians, and was one of whom the world was not worthy.'[6] The same generosity was evident in Wesley's friend and colleague George Whitefield. As with Spurgeon, Whitefield's Calvinist convictions were not accompanied by personal disaffection for the Arminian evangelist. Despite their theological disagreements, he wanted Wesley to preach his funeral sermon.[7]

Calvinistic opinion has not generally been as magnanimous towards Wesley as it might have been.[8] After all, he was considered to have given fresh impetus to a deviant theology, despite his broad evangelical sympathies. Although the concerns of a growing secularized outlook have tended to relegate the Calvinist–Arminian controversy to the past, a renewed interest in Calvinism has had yet again to consider the implications of Wesley's influence. In recent decades, the Banner of Truth Trust—a neo-Calvinist publishing house—has endeavoured to exercise the same respectful charity towards Wesley as Whitefield and Spurgeon did. However, Arnold Dallimore's recent biography of Whitefield, published by the Trust, tends to project a favourable image of Whitefield at the expense of Wesley. The author's concern to compensate for the undue neglect of Whitefield's contribution makes him unnecessarily critical of Wesley.[9]

A more just assessment has been expressed by Maldwyn L. Edwards: 'The danger is that the towering figure of John Wesley may cause his biographers by lack of perspective to underrate the importance of Whitefield, and likewise that those who write about Whitefield may consciously attempt to restore the balance and, like Shakespeare's lady, "protest too much".'[10]

The Wesley literature is immense and ever growing.[11] This book makes an attempt to evaluate his theology from an entirely fresh perspective. Clarifying and redefining Calvinistic theology in terms of its sixteenth-century origins demands a reassessment of Wesley's own position, with consequences for our understanding of the controversy between him and Whitefield.

HIS LIFE

John Wesley was born at Epworth in Lincolnshire in 1703. He was the fifteenth child and second surviving son of the Revd Samuel

Wesley, an Anglican clergyman of the Tillotsonian type.[12] John had a distinguished Puritan ancestry, for both his grandfathers had been ejected for their nonconformity in 1662. Susannah Wesley's father was the patriarchal Dr Samuel Annesley, the Presbyterian rector of St Giles, Cripplegate. In later years Wesley was to reflect with pleasure that he came from a line of faithful ministers.[13]

John Wesley's mother was energetic, determined, and rigorous in the education of her children. She was the most dominant influence in the household, and John clearly inherited much of her strength of personality. Samuel was competent and zealous, but inclined to be irresponsible, not least in financial matters. However, he possessed considerable literary and poetic gifts, which John and more especially his younger brother Charles inherited.

John's remarkable escape from the Epworth rectory fire in 1709 impressed him with the conviction that God had preserved him for a special purpose. Entering Charterhouse in 1713, he came to acquire something of the fortitude which he displayed in manhood, not to speak of an ability to lead others. In 1720, Wesley entered Christ Church, Oxford, graduating BA in 1724. While all his academic promise was fulfilled, his religious life was no more than nominal. However, a change of attitude occurred in 1725: 'I began to alter the whole form of my conversation, and set in earnest upon a new life.'[14] This new seriousness brought a concern to study for the ministry. His father urged him to take holy orders, and he was ordained deacon by the bishop of Oxford in September 1725. He was then elected a fellow of Lincoln College in 1726, his impecunious father noting with pride, 'my Jack is Fellow of Lincoln.'[15] Wesley graduated MA in 1727, receiving priest's orders in the following year.

Wesley's early spiritual pilgrimage has been rightly described as legalistic and mystical. Encouraged by his parents, he became attracted to authors who inculcated 'the religion of the heart'. His intense pursuit of spiritual reality did not dispose him to scholastic theology, and his mother directed him away from the Calvinism of his forebears.[16] Hence he was influenced by the devotional works of Thomas à Kempis, Jeremy Taylor, and William Law.[17]

After spending some time as his father's curate at Wroote near Epworth, Wesley returned ot Oxford in 1729. He soon assumed leadership of the Holy Club, a small relgious society started by his brother Charles, then a student at Christ Church. They were known as 'methodists', but not by choice; the group's strict religious life earned this appellation from its critics, as Wesley, the conscientious Anglican, was always anxious to make clear.[18] Whatever the 'people called methodists' were to be in years to come, Wesley and his friends were 'high church' sacramentalists at this period. Strangers to the Reformation doctrine of justification, they sought to gain salvation by self-examination and prayer, frequent worship, and philanthropic endeavour. This piety permeated Wesley's famous university sermon 'The circumcision of the heart' (1733).[19]

In 1732, George Whitefield entered Pembroke College and was introduced to the Holy Club by Charles Wesley. Sharing the same intense religious aspirations, Whitefield was enlightened more by the writings of Henry Scougal and Joseph Hall than by the other mystical authors, and under such influences he experienced an assurance of salvation in May 1735. A full three years were to pass before the Wesleys could claim a similar experience. Shortly afterwards, the seeds of Whitefield's future Calvinism were sown by his reading of such Puritan authors as Richard Baxter, Joseph Alleine, and Matthew Henry.[20]

In 1735 John Wesley commenced his ill-fated career as a missionary to the new colony of Georgia. His ministry was plagued by personal uncertainty, persistent criticism, and a disastrous love affair, all of which contributed to a sense of frustration and failure. After his return to England in February 1738, he met the Moravian Peter Bohler, whose evangelical teachings he embraced after much discussion. Renouncing his legalistic ideas, he began to preach the doctrine of justification by faith alone. Then came his famous Aldersgate Street experience of 24 May, when his heart was 'strangely warmed': 'I felt I did trust in Christ, Christ alone, for salvation: and an assurance was given me, that he had taken away my sins, even mine, and saved me from the law of sin and death.'[21]

One of the most frequently quoted conversions in Christian history, the true significance of this experience has occasioned considerable discussion. If it was so decisive, why was he still troubled by subjective uncertainties, as his journal testifies?[22] In later years he even viewed it differently, implying that he had been a Christian before 24 May.[23] Indeed, it is difficult to deny this, for he was preaching justification by faith with deep conviction several weeks earlier. Taken in isolation, his experience would imply that assurance is of the essence of faith—the view of the Reformers—

John Wesley

and that without the element of 'feeling' no one can possess saving faith. It is surely significant that Wesley's subsequent pastoral experience led him to revise the Reformation view of saving faith,[24] for in the Methodist revival he sometimes encountered sincere Christians who lacked assurance.

None can doubt the impact of Wesley's 'baptism of assurance'. It established him as a militant evangelist. Together with his brother Charles, whose 'baptism' had taken place on 21 May,[25] Wesley joined forces with Whitefield, who actually pioneered the evangelistic movement. Methodism soon became a nationwide phenomenon as huge crowds gathered on village greens and at marketplaces, as well as other large open spaces, in London, Bristol, and Newcastle upon Tyne. The story of Wesley's ministry is best told by himself in his journal, which has been described as 'the most amazing record of human exertion ever penned by man'.[26] Wesley's account reveals a rich tapestry of events and experiences woven into the geography and social fabric of eighteenth-century Britain. J. C. Ryle's summary of Wesley's activity helps explain something of his uniqueness: 'For fifty-three years—from 1738 to 1791—he held on his course, always busy, and always busy about one thing—attacking sin and ignorance everywhere, preaching repentance toward God and faith toward our Lord Jesus Christ everywhere—awakening open sinners, leading on enquirers, building up saints—never wearied, never swerving from the path he had marked out, and never doubting of success.'[27]

The heralds of the Methodist revival had to suffer a good deal of antagonism before gaining widespread respect. Apart from incurring the disapproval of the religious establishment, the preachers were frequently attacked by the mob and bitterly abused in the press. The movement was also plagued by theological controversy. In spite of a common evangelicalism, the Arminian Wesley clashed with the Calvinist Whitefield. Notwithstanding Whitefield's obvious passion for evangelism, Wesley could not abide his theology. Their differences were made public in 1740 with the publication of Wesley's sermon 'Free grace,'[28] which brought forth a reply from Whitefield.[29] Wesley's long ministry was frequently punctuated by this controversy. In his view, Calvinism both hindered evangelism and promoted antinomianism. Thus he was often embroiled in debates over justification and sanctification.

Despite their theological differences, Wesley and Whitefield became personally reconciled in 1742. But Methodism was divided into two camps: the Arminian, or Wesleyan, Methodists and the Calvinistic Methodists. Welsh Methodism was virtually all Calvinistic,[30] and Whitefield presided at the first Calvinistic Methodist Conference in 1743. In England the countess of Huntingdon sided with Whitefield, and a separate body known as the Countess of Huntingdon's Connexion came into being. However, while their respective followers frequently aggravated the differences, the two great evangelists recognized that they were united by a central core of doctrine. Other Calvinists like Rowland Hill and Augustus Toplady were thoroughly hostile to Wesley, but a notable exception was the moderately Calvinist Charles Simeon of Cambridge, whom Wesley met in 1784.[31]

Unlike Whitefield, Wesley organized the groups of converts which were springing up all over the country. The first Methodist Conference met in 1744 and eventually, through a system of circuits and districts, the Methodist Connexion became a nationwide reality. Wesley's London base was the foundry at Moorfields, which remained the headquarters of Methodism until the City Road chapel was opened in 1778. Despite his organization, he refused to separate formally from the Church of England, even when many of the clergy opposed him. Though he welcomed the friendship and encouragement of such eminent Dissenters as Philip Doddridge,[32] he would never be drawn away from the established church. He insisted that the meetings of the Methodist societies were never to clash with services at the parish churches. There were a number of strains on his position as time went by. At his mother's suggestion, he welcomed the idea of lay preachers. When he ordained Thomas Coke for the American work in 1784, Charles accused his brother of becoming a Presbyterian.[33] All in all, it was inevitable that Methodism should find its own identity in the nineteenth-century.

John Wesley's single-mindedness made his unwise marriage to the widow Mary Vazeille less than happy; it demonstrated that itinerant preaching and home life do not mix. Whatever effect his wife's persistent jealousy had on him, nothing hindered his mission to the nation. In his tireless travels throughout the United Kingdom, it is estimated that he journeyed over a quarter of a million miles and preached 40 000 sermons. In eighteenth-century terms, given that roads were primitive and that he had to study on horseback, Wesley's achievement is phenomenal.

Although the main emphasis of Methodism was on personal salvation and holiness, it was not a pietist movement; indeed, its strong humanitarian concern raised the tone of the nation's domestic, moral, social, and even political life. Wesley believed in reaching the poor and underprivileged for Christ, often to the annoyance of the idle rich, with whom he rarely felt comfortable. However, the impact of Methodism was felt in high places. On one occasion King George III declared privately to Charles Wesley junior, 'It is my judgement, Mr Wesley, that your uncle and your father, and George Whitefield and Lady Huntingdon, have done more to promote true religion in the country than all the dignified clergy put together, who are so apt to despise their labours.[34]

The Wesley brothers enjoyed a unique relationship, in spite of periodic differences. Unlike his brother, Charles was somewhat temperamental. Though frequently masked by his brother's achievements, his own abilities were of no mean order. His immortal hymns are more than vehicles of praise; they also contain the theological distinctives of Wesleyan Methodism. Furthermore, as a preacher he was considered second only to Whitefield. Although ill health and domestic responsibilities eventually intervened, he was an active evangelist until 1756.[35] Confined mainly to London for the remainder of his life, Charles died there in March 1788.

While John Wesley disapproved of the American revolution of 1776, he was utterly opposed to slavery. After preaching his final open-air sermon at Leatherhead, Surrey on 23 February 1791, he wrote his final letter the next day to William Wilberforce,[36] encouraging him in the fight against slavery. After more than fifty years' labour as evangelist, author, and organizer and leader of the Methodist movement, he died on 2 March 1791. He summed up the abiding conviction of his life on his deathbed: 'The best of all is, God is with us!'[37]

HIS CONTRIBUTION

John Wesley is not known primarily for his writings.[38] He published no exhaustive commentary like Owen's *Hebrews*, and no devotional classic such as Baxter's *Saints' Rest*. It cannot be said that his sermons became models for later generations, as Tillotson's did.[39] However, while his journal is his permanent literary memorial, his sermons and other writings still possess an abiding theological worth.

Although Wesley is renowned as an evangelist, he also fulfilled the role of a pastor-theologian. In these capacities, he not only proclaimed the gospel; he insisted equally that those who believed it should live consistently with its precepts. As he understood his mission to be the preaching of 'scriptural holiness' in the prevailing conditions of his day, he saw Calvinism as the enemy to his evangelism, and antinomianism as a threat to its lasting success.

The *raison d-être* of Wesley's mission was the doctrine of universal redemption. His famous sermon on 'Free grace' (1740) reveals his dislike of Calvinism. As he saw it, the doctrines of election, reprobation, and limited atonement were a total negation of evangelistic enterprise. Aware of his views, Whitefield had discouraged Wesley from publishing the sermon in the interests of unity, but not long after Whitefield's departure for America Wesley did so. In his reply Whitefield argued that Wesley's theology was inconsistent with Article XVII of the Church of England, 'of predestination and election.' He then proceeded to insist, as Owen had done a century before that the atonement was limited to the elect: 'Our Lord knew for whom he died.'[40]

Whitefield's arguments had a profound if temporary influence over Wesley. Shortly after the 'Free grace' controversy, Wesley wrote a brief memorandum entitled 'Calvinistic controversy.'[41] Anxious to avoid 'needless dispute' with Whitefield, he declared his sentiments in a distinctly Calvinistic manner; but in affirming unconditional election, irresistible grace, and final perseverance, he significantly omitted limited atonement. Although he had been cautious about leaning 'too much towards Calvinism'[42] at the 1744 Methodist Conference, he was willing in his doctrine of grace to 'come to the very edge of Calvinism'[43] at the 1745 conference. It was probably the question of the extent of the atonement which turned the scales in favour of Arminianism. Wesley's 'moderately Calvinistic' phase was therefore temporary. In *Predestination Calmly Considered* (1752)[44] he gave permanent expression to those views for which he is famous.

If Whitefield's appeal to the Thirty-nine Articles was a source of embarrassment to Wesley, he was himself involved in an anomaly which Wesley was not slow to exploit. Just as surely as Article XVII acknowledges personal election, Article XXXI states that the atonement was 'for all the sins of the whole world, both original and actual'. Wesley appeals not only to the Articles, Homilies, and Catechism of the Church of England, but also to the writings of the Anglican Reformers, to vindicate his position.[45] (He later employed the same evidence against Rowland Hill in 1772.) His position therefore demands careful scrutiny, for it raises important questions about the precise nature of sixteenth-century Anglican theology. This assumes added importance in the light of recent discussions of Calvin's theology of the atonement.

Wesley's views on the doctrine of justification involved him in frequent controversy, and his writings reveal his constant preoccupation with the subject.[46] It is significant that his views altered through the years, despite his occasional denials.[47] The chief factor in these changes was the challenge of antinomianism, of both the Moravian and Calvinistic varieties.[48] The view of Count Zinzendorf and the Moravians that Christians never cease from being 'miserable sinners until death' alarmed Wesley, who believed that the saved sinner must be progressively different from his preconversion state. He considered Luther's apparent antipathy towards good works to be the source of antinomian libertinism. By 1741 he had come to regard Luther's *Galatians* as a 'dangerous treatise', confessing with shame that he had formerly esteemed the work highly.[49] Wesley therefore rejected 'solifidianism' as commonly understood. This marked a significant shift in his thought away from a strictly Lutheran view of justification, and the reasoning behind these and related changes requires investigation.

The views of Baxter clearly had an influence on Wesley. Baxter's *Aphorismes* were chosen as study material for the 1745 conference.[50] Wesley published an abridged edition of them in that year,[51] and the work went through four editions by 1797. It is noteworthy that Baxter's theory of a twofold justification is evident in Wesley's 1746 sermon 'justification by faith',[52] a fact which raises questions about his oft-repeated claim, frequently quoted by scholars, that he was loyal to the Reformation doctrine of justification.

Wesley's attitude to Tillotson is relevant at this point. In an unpreached sermon, 'True Christianity defended' he criticizes Tillotson's views on justification. Tillotson is charged with teaching that 'not faith alone, but good works also, are necessary for justification'.[53] Whitefield, who was severely reprimanded for attacking the late primate in 1740, cites Wesley as the source of the offending remark that 'the Archbishop knew no more of Christianity than Mahomet',[54] However, in 1755 Wesley abridged and published two of Tillotson's sermons in his *Christian Library*,[55] and in the preface the archbishop is described as a 'great man'. The suggestion is worth investigating that Wesley's change of opinion may be attributed to certain affinities between Tillotson's view and his own mature conception of salvation.[56] The plain fact is that his early, 'Lutheran' view of justification underwent a significant change in the face of the antinomian challenge. He thus came to appreciate some of the emphases made by Baxter and Tillotson, and his reputation suffered accordingly.

At the 1770 Conference the fear of antinomianism led to the view that good works, though not meritorious, were necessary conditions of salvation. To deal with the storm of opposition occasioned by the minutes, the 1771 Conference issued the statement that 'the Doctrine of Justification by Works' was 'a most perilous doctrine' and that 'in life, death, or the day of judgement' the Christian's confidence was in 'the alone merits of our Lord and Saviour Jesus Christ'. Works, though essential for salvation, had no meritorious value.[57]

Scholars explain the complexity of Wesley's theology of justification in different ways.[58] His frequent appeals to the formularies and writings of the Anglican Reformation are well known, but one wonders whether sufficient attention has been paid to John Calvin's influence on him. It is surely significant that on several occasions Wesley appealed to Calvin's views on justification.[59] In the light of his early rejection of Luther and the subsequent influence of Baxter (not to mention Tillotson), the Arminian Wesley's appeal to Calvin must surely raise questions about the true character of Calvin's theology of justification *vis-à-vis* its seventeenth-century derivatives. In seeking to make a comparative evaluation of the views of Owen and Wesley, the aim of this book is to supply answers to these questions.

NOTES

1. *Christian Leaders of the Last Century* (London, 1885, fac. Edinburgh, 1978), 64.
2. Macaulay considered that Wesley's 'eloquence and logical acuteness might have rendered him eminent in literature' and that his 'genius for

government was not inferior to that of Richelieu' (L. Tyerman, *The Life and Times of the Revd John Wesley* (1875), iii. 660). Gladstone wrote that Wesley's 'life and acts have taken their place in the religious history not only of England, but of Christendom' (quoted in A. Skevington Wood, *The Burning Heart: John Wesley, Evangelist* (London, 1967), 280–1). Lloyd George asserted that Wales 'owed more to the movement of which Wesley was the inspirer and prophet and leader, than to any other movement in the whole of its history' (J. W. Bready, *England: Before and After Wesley* (London, 1939), 181. Stanley Baldwin said that historians of the 18th Cent. 'who filled their pages with Napoleon and had nothing to say of John Wesley, now realise that they cannot explain nineteenth-century England until they can explain Wesley' (ibid.). The historian H. W. V. Temperley, after enumerating some of the greatest men of the 18th Cent., adds, 'But more important than any of these in universality of influence and range of achievement, were John Wesley and the religious revival to which he gave his name and life' (*Cambridge Modern History* (1909), vi. 77). Historians such as G. M. Trevelyan, Dorothy George, J. H. Plumb, and Christopher Hill have acknowledged the social and political impact of Methodism on English society. Thus secular historians have endorsed the conclusions of scholars like Bready (above) and B. Semmel (*The Methodist Revolution* (London, 1974)) that the well-known Halévy thesis is substantially true, namely that Methodism helped to improve and transform society in a non-revolutionary direction.

3. 'If the Damascus road explains Paul the Apostle; if the Milanese garden accounts for Augustine of Hippo, the doctor of the church; if the Black Tower of Wittenberg gave birth to Martin Luther as the pioneer Reformer; then Aldersgate Street, London, produced John Wesley the evangelist' (Skevington Wood, *Burning Heart*, p. 283). Tyerman concludes that 'Taking him altogether, Wesley is a man *sui generis*. He stand alone: he has had no successor' (*Life and Times*, iii. 660).

4. *John Wesley* (London, 1979), 318.

5. Dean Farrar, when canon of Westminster, wrote generously of one who had been ostracized by the church he loved, 'I say that even now I do not think we have done sufficient honour to the work Wesley did' (J. Telford, *The Life of John Wesley* (London, 1929), 377). Regretting the excessive adulation Wesley has received, J. C. Ryle wrote, 'Whether we like it or not, John Wesley was a mighty instrument in God's hand for good; and, next to George Whitefield, was the first and foremost evangelist of England a hundred years ago' (*Christian Leaders*, p. 105). The Presbyterian A. H. Drysdale was careful to point out Wesley's Presbyterian ancestry and his adoption of corresponding views of

ordination and church government (*The History of the Presbyterians in England* (London, 1889), 584, 589). For the Congregationalists, R. W. Dale was happy to acknowledge the debt which the older nonconformity owed to Methodism (see Telford, *Life of Wesley*, p. 377). For the Baptists, the aged John Clifford wrote in his diary for 9 Aug. 1922, 'Reading "Wesley's Journal" ... is one of my most refreshing occupations just now' (James Marchant, *Dr John Clifford, CH: Life, Letters and Reminiscences* (London, 1924), 265–6).

6. *The Early Years* (London, 1962), 173. See also id., 'John Wesley', *BOT* 68 (1969), 15–20; 69 (1969), 43–8; 70–1 (1969), 54–8.
7. Wesley, *Works*, vi. 158 ff.
8. A. M. Toplady, *The Works of Augustus M. Toplady*, *AB* (London, 1825), v. 318 ff. For Toplady (1740–78) see *DNB*; T. Wright, *The Life of Augustus Toplady* (London, 1911); G. Lawton, *Within the Rock of Ages: The Life and Work of Augustus Montague Toplady* (Cambridge, 1983). See also J. Gill, *A Collection of Sermons and Tracts* (1773), iii. 257 ff. (for Gill (1697–1771) see *DNB*).
9. A. A. Dallimore, *George Whitefield* (London, 1970–80), ii. 5 ff.
10. 'George Whitefield after two hundred years', *WHS* 37 (1970), 178–9.
11. After early biographies by Moore, Southey, and others, the first major work was Tyerman's (see n.1). See also J. H. Overton, *John Wesley* (London, 1891); J. Telford, *The Life of John Wesley* (London, 1899); C. E. Vulliamy, *John Wesley* (London, 1931); V. H. H. Green, *The Young Mr Wesley* (London, 1961); id., *John Wesley* (London, 1964); M. Schmidt, *John Wesley: A Theological Biography* (London, 1973); Skevington Wood, *Burning Heart*; Ayling, *John Wesley*; R. G. Tuttle, *John Wesley: His Life and Theology* (London, 1979). Special studies in Wesley's theology are: G. C. Cell, *The Rediscovery of John Wesley* (New York, 1935); W. R. Cannon, *The Theology of John Wesley: With Special Reference to the Doctrine of Justification* (New York, 1946); H. Lindström, *Wesley and Sanctification* (Stockholm, 1946); C. W. Williams, *John Wesley's Theology Today* (New York, 1960); J. Deschner, *Wesley's Christology* (Dallas, 1960); A. C. Outler, *John Wesley* (New York, 1964); R. C. Monk, *John Wesley: His Puritan Heritage* (London 1966); Semmel, *Methodist Revolution*. For further studies see E. P. Crow, 'John Wesley's conflict with antinomianism, Ph.D. thesis (Manchester, 1964); A. Lawson, 'John Wesley and some Anglican evangelicals of the eighteenth-century', Ph.D. thesis (Sheffield, 1974); A. Coppedge, 'John Wesley and the doctrine of predestination', Ph.D. thesis (Cambridge, 1976); J. B. Selleck, 'The Book of Common Prayer in the theology of John Wesley', Ph.D. thesis (Drew, 1983).
12. See Samuel Wesley's eulogy, *Poem on the Death of His Grace John, Late Lord Archbishop of Canterbury* (London 1695).

13. A. Skevington Wood, *Burning Heart*, pp. 19 ff.
14. Tyerman, *Life of Wesley*, i. 33.
15. Vulliamy, *Wesley*, p. 24.
16. Tyerman, *Life of Wesley*, i. 39–40.
17. Ibid. 35, 50.
18. See 'The character of a Methodist', *Works*, viii. 325–6.
19. *Works*, v. 190.
20. *George Whitefield's Journals*, ed. I. Murray (London, 1960), 62.
21. *The Journal of the Revd John Wesley, AM*, ed. N. Curnock (1909–16), i. 476.
22. Entries for 25, 26, 28, and 31 May; 3, 6, June (ibid. 476 ff.).
23. Tuttle, *Wesley*, p. 336; Wesley, *Works*, vii. 189–90; see also *Journal*, i. 423 n. l. For a recent discussion of Wesley's conversion date see P. E. G. Cook, 'Hearts strangely warmed: John and Charles Wesley, May 1738', in *Not by Might nor by Power* (London, 1988), 85–101.
24. Letter to Charles Wesley, in *The Letters of the Revd John Wesley, AM*, ed. J. Telford (London, 1931), ii. 108.
25. *The Journal of the Revd Charles Wesley, MA*, ed. T. Jackson (1849), i. 90 ff.
26. A. Birrell, KC, in Telford, *Life of Wesley*, p. xviii.
27. *Christian Leaders*, p. 78.
28. *Works*, vii. 356 ff.
29. Whitefield, *Journals*, pp. 563 ff.
30. J. Roberts, *The Calvinistic Methodism of Wales* (Caernarfon, 1934); E. Evans, *Daniel Rowland and the Great Evangelical Awakening in Wales* (Edinburgh, 1985).
31. For Simeon (1759–1836) see *DNB*. Wesley recorded the meeting on 20 Dec. (*Journal*, vii. 39), but Simeon gave a full account of the conversation in *Horae homileticae* (1832), i. xvii f. See also Tyerman, *Life of Wesley*, iii. 510–11; H. C. G. Moule, *Charles Simeon* (1892), 100–1; J. I. Packer, *Evangelism and the Sovereignty of God* (London, 1961), 13–14.
32. A. C. Clifford, 'Philip Doddridge and the Oxford Methodists', *WHS* 42. 3 (1979), 75–80.
33. F. Baker, *Charles Wesley as Revealed by His Letters* (London, 1948), 138.
34. F. C. Gill, *Charles Wesley: The First Methodist* (London, 1964), 188–9.
35. The final entry in his journal is for 5 Nov. 1756 (ii. 139).
36. *Letters*, viii. 265.
37. Tyerman, *Life of Wesley*, iii. 654.
38. J. H. Overton correctly states: 'The very last thing of which John Wesley was ambitious was literary fame' *Wesley* (1891), 169. Wesley's intentions are clear; what he said of his sermons applied to all his writings: 'Nothing here appears in an elaborate, elegant, or oratorical

dress. If it had been my desire or design to write thus, my leisure would not permit' (*Works*, v. 1).
39. This is not to deny that, with the *Explanatory Notes upon the New Testament* (London, 1755), the sermons constitute 'the standard doctrines of the Methodist Connexion', or to forget that they became recommended reading for all Methodists preachers.
40. Whitefield, *Journals*, p. 587.
41. *Works*, xiii. 478–9. Tyerman believes the document dates from 1743 (*Life of Wesley*, i. 349).
42. *Works*, viii. 267. Jackson cites the document as evidence of Wesley's tendencies at the time.
43. Ibid. 274.
44. *Works*, x. 197 ff.
45. *Works*, x. 255, 368. Whitefield was arguably influenced by the high Calvinism of Elisha Coles' *Practical Discourse on God's Sovereignty* (London 1673), rather than the 'Calvinism' of the Anglican reformers (see his *Journal*, p. 586).
46. 'Dialogues between an antinomian and his friend' (1745), *Works*, x. 257 ff.; 'A farther appeal to men of reason and religion' (1745), *Works*, viii. 45 ff.; 'Thoughts on the imputed righteousness of Christ' (1762), *Works*, x. 300 ff.; 'Thoughts on salvation by faith' (1779), *Works*, xi. 472 ff.
47. Tuttle attempts to divide Wesley's theological progress into three distinct periods: (1) salvation by grace through assurance (1738–47), (2) salvation by grace through faith (1748–62), and (3) salvation by grace through faith confirmed by works (1763–88). (*Wesley*, p. 331).
48. Semmel, *Methodist Revolution*, pp. 35 ff.
49. Ibid. 40; *Journal*, ii. 468.
50. *Works*, viii. 271.
51. See Wesley's Introduction (*Works*, xiv. 207).
52. *Works*, v. 48 ff. Wesley refers to justification 'at the sentence of the great day' as well as the sinner's justification by faith (pp. 52–3).
53. *Works*, vii. 433.
54. See Tyerman, *Life of Whitefield*, i. 360; Dallimore, *Whitefield*, i. 482–3; ii. 46–7.
55. The two sermons are 'Of the ordinary influence of the Holy Ghost on the minds of Christians' (*TW* ii. 298–310) and 'To speak evil of no man' (*TW* iii. 491–504). See Wesley's preface in *Works*, xiv. 222.
56. J. C. English, 'John Wesley and the Anglican moderates of the seventeenth-century', *ATR* 51. 3 (1969), 203–20; esp. p. 206, 'Wesley was dependent upon the moderates for a portion of his ideas.'
57. Tyerman, *Life of Wesley*, iii. 100.
58. Cannon, Williams, Schmidt, Outler, and Skevington Wood stress Wesley's dependence on Reformation theology, both continental and

English. However, his theory of a twofold justification is given little or no attention. Even Tuttle, who argues for a shift in Wesley's thought after 1763, refuses to admit that Wesley 'has changed his view of justification by faith' (*Wesley*, p. 336). For obvious reasons, other scholars have noted 'Anglo-Catholic' overtones, not only in Wesley's sacramental theology, but also in his theology of justification. M. Piette (*John Wesley and the Evolution of Protestantism* (London, 1937)) and U. Lee (*John Wesley and Modern Religion* (New York, 1936)) favour this view in the light of Wesley's stress on sanctification. Outler points out that although *sola fide* was a fundamental principle for him, faith came to be *prima* rather than *sola*; thus there was a parallelism between justification and sanctification both being by faith (*Wesley*, p. 251). However, he pleads too much for Wesley, to the neglect of Baxter's influence, when he says that 'this insistent correlation between the genesis of faith and its fullness marks off Wesley's most original contribution to Protestant theology' (ibid. 28). Likewise, Cell fails to do justice to Baxter's influence by simply arguing that W synthesized the Protestant ethic of grace and the Catholic ethic of holiness (*Rediscovery*, p. 361). Lindström, Deschner, and Monk take a more substantial look at Wesley's doctrine of final, as opposed to initial, justification without grasping the reasons for his modification of the *sola fide* principle. Deschner accuses him of missing the significance of 'Christ's imputed active obedience' (*Wesley's Christology*, p.183), without being impressed by his reasons for rejecting such a concept of imputation. Monk correctly highlights Baxter's attraction for Wesley, although he mistakenly describes Baxter as an Arminian. Following Deschner, he argues that Wesley 'breaks justification in two', even suggesting that Owen's dualistic alternative would have solved his basic difficulties (*Wesley*, p. 131).

59. In his preface to Goodwin's treatise on justification, Wesley insists that he employs the expression 'imputed righteousness' exactly as Calvin did (*Works*, x. 326). In his sermon 'The Lord our righteousness' (1765) he quotes from Calvin's *Institutes* (*Works*, v. 226). In the same year he insisted, 'I think on justification just as I have done any time these seven-and-twenty years [i.e. since 1738]; and just as Mr Calvin does. In this respect, I do not differ from him a hair's breadth' (*Journal*, v. 116). As late as 1770, the year in which the second Calvinistic controversy commenced, he argued in his tract 'What is an Arminian?' that Calvin never asserted justification by faith more strongly than the Arminians had done (*Works*, x. 345).

PART II
The Theology
Atonement and Grace

5. JOHN CALVIN (FROM A PORTRAIT BY HOLBEIN)

5
Authentic Calvinism

The theological viewpoints of Owen and Wesley represent the two main currents of evangelical thought in British church history. An acquaintance with their writings reveals not only their deep commitment to their respective convictions, but a lifelong antipathy to the other school of thought.[1] The Calvinist–Arminian controversy brought into conflict—albeit not personally and concurrently—two eminent contestants, both of whom regarded themselves as advocates of biblical Christianity. Despite a common Protestant heritage, their differing conceptions of the gospel were to prove a lasting cause of disunity.

Of all the divisive issues which have hindered theological consensus and unity amongst evangelicals, none has been more serious and far-reaching than the Calvinist–Arminian controversy.[2] Its seriousness is reflected in the fact that both schools have claimed the same starting-point. Each would identify with Luther's defiant stand at the Diet of Worms: 'My conscience is captive to the Word of God!' The controversy thus raised fundamental questions about Luther's belief in the perspicuity of Scripture and the possibility of a harmonious hermeneutic.[3] To an impartial observer, the Calvinist–Arminian debates of the seventeenth and eighteenth-centuries might suggest an inversion of Luther's axiom: the Word of God was captive to men's consciences. Was there anything inevitable about this seemingly perpetual, and still unresolved, source of discord?[4]

Scholars have shown that the rise of Dutch Arminianism in the early seventeenth-century was occasioned not so much by the balanced biblical theology of John Calvin as by the rigidly systematic form that this assumed in the hands of Theodore Beza (1519–1605), his successor in Geneva.[5] Jakob Hermanszoon, known to history by his latinized name Arminius (1560–1609), had studied under Beza in 1581–4. After becoming a pastor in the Reformed Church at Amsterdam in 1587, he began to feel uneasy about some of the emphases of Reformed orthodoxy. Whatever were the distinctives of Calvin's actual presentation of the gospel, Arminius' own sympathies began to change when he was asked to defend Beza's doctrine of predestination from a heterodox pamphlet circulating against it.[6]

After his appointment as professor of theology at Leiden in 1603, it was soon clear that Arminius had changed his mind on a number of sensitive theological issues. He eventually questioned the doctrines of unconditional election and efficacious grace. However, being summoned before the States of Holland in 1608 to answer charges of heterodoxy, he made statements which were cautious and moderate.[7] On being misrepresented by a document forged in his name, Arminius published this *Apology* in 1609, the year of his death. His views on the atonement were considered to be at variance with received opinion, for he affirmed that 'the price of the death of Christ was given for all and for every one'.[8]

Arminius clearly considered that there were serious discrepancies between certain plain statements in the Bible and the formulations of orthodox theology. He was thus giving expression to the view that Reformed theology, in the hands of Theodore Beza and others, had exceeded the bounds of the Protestant rule of faith in several respects. In short it was Beza, not Calvin, who had taught that Christ died only for the elect, a theological shift which had vital practical and pastoral implications, not least in the area of assurance of salvation.[9]

While it is clear that Arminius fell victim to over-reaction, it was very largely Beza's orthodoxy rather than Calvin's that he was objecting to. As has been shown, Calvin's theology was essentially Christological in its emphasis and inductive in its method of expounding Scripture. The doctrine of predestination has a relatively low profile in his thought; in the *Institutes* he expounds it towards the end of Book III, where it is seen as an *ex post facto* explanation of why some are not saved.[10] On the other hand, the decrees of predestination and providence constitute the motive of Beza's theology, its method being governed by the deductive principles of Aristotelian logic. Beza's method was to have serious implications for the evolution of Calvinistic thought, not least with respect to the extent of the atonement.[11] Scholastic rationalism was to replace Luther and Calvin's strictly exegetical approach to the Bible. Thus, in the wake of the Arminian revolt, Bezan tendencies were evident at the Synod of Dort (1618–19), where the Five

Articles of the Arminian Remonstrance of 1610 were condemned by the representatives of the Reformed churches in the famous five Canons.[12] The theology of Dort was further reinforced and developed by the Westminster Assembly (1643–9), in whose *Confession of Faith* high orthodoxy received full expression.[13]

Although the entire range of doctrines involved in the Calvinist–Arminian controversy possess great importance, the question of the extent of the atonement is at its heart. This was evidently how Owen saw the situation. After publishing a general critique of the Remonstrant's position in his first work, *A Display of Arminianism* (1643), he focused his attention on the subject of the atonement in *Salus Electorum, Sanguis Jesu; or the Death of Death in the Death of Christ* (1647). This treatise at once established itself as the definitive statement of the doctrine of limited atonement or particular redemption. In the opinion of J. I. Packer, Owen was so thorough in his work, so comprehensive in his treatment of the issues and arguments, that 'nobody has a right to dismiss the doctrine of the limitedness of atonement as a monstrosity of Calvinistic logic until he has refuted Owen's proof that it is a part of the uniform biblical presentation of redemption, clearly taught in plain text after plain text. And nobody has done that yet'.[14]

A century later, John Wesley also saw the extent of the atonement as the central issue in his controversy with Calvinism. His provocative sermon 'Free grace' (1740) launches the reader into the subject in its first sentence. As with Owen, Wesley had much to say on the other points at issue, yet the entire controversy hinged on the question of the extent of the atonement. That said, it might be thought that Wesley's sermon and all his published utterances on the subject are no possible match for Owen's treatise. How can one justify a comparison between the theologian and the preacher on such an important subject? There can be no question about Wesley's competence to produce an erudite response to Owen; his academic credentials have never been questioned. Even allowing for his busy schedule, he saw no need to argue his case against Calvinism in a specific treatise on the atonement.[15] As Arminius had noticed, there are no universalist texts dealing with election and regeneration, but there are several which assert a universal atonement. Thus, in his debates with the Calvinists, Wesley believed he had a prima-facie case in the bare word of God. Was he not on incontrovertible ground when he simply announced such texts as John 1: 29 and 3: 16, 2 Corinthians 5: 14 and 15, Hebrews 2: 9, and 1 John 2: 2, all of which suggest universality in the atonement?[16] It is for this reason that the Calvinists of Owen's and Wesley's generation felt especially vulnerable. Their conception of the gospel seemed threatened by a direct appeal to the Protestant rule of faith.

The recent resurgence of interest in Calvin's theology has an obvious bearing on the Calvinist–Arminian controversy. In evaluating the opposing viewpoints of Owen and Wesley, it is interesting to ask what their perception of Calvin was. This might be regarded as a foregone conclusion. After all, Owen was regarded as the 'Calvin of England' and Wesley was no friend of Calvinism. From this traditional perspective, it is assumed that Owen 'championed all the traditional Protestant tenets of Calvin and the Reformation'[17] while Wesley did not. However, the matter is not so simple. The fact remains that neither Owen nor Wesley ever referred to Calvin's precise views on the extent of the atonement, although we must assume they were not entirely ignorant of them.[18] As far as Wesley was concerned, one would imagine that he would have charged Whitefield, Toplady, and even Owen with going beyond their master's teaching, had he suspected that Calvin was a universalist. After all, in the debates over justification he was not slow to enlist Calvin's support.[19] Owen's silence with respect to Calvin may be accounted for in two ways: either he believed that no significant difference existed between Calvin's views and his own, or out of deference to the great Reformer he declined to criticize him. The former seems more likely, for Owen was not slow to criticize the Reformers in a general way regarding their idea that assurance was of the essence of faith.[20] Had he believed that Calvin taught universal atonement, he would have regarded him as an adversary of some note, especially when Arminians like John Goodwin appealed to Calvin's authority. In other words, although the Bible was the final court of appeal for both Owen and Wesley, it seems strange that Calvin was not specifically quoted by either of them in a controversy involving his name.

What, then, of the Calvinism of John Calvin? His theology of the atonement *vis-à-vis* the formulations of later 'Calvinists' has occasioned lively discussion, resulting in a sizeable corpus of scholarly literature.[21] Although opinion still seems divided, there is considerable evidence to suggest that, judged by seventeenth-century criteria, he did not subscribe to, nor believe in, the doctrine of limited atonement.[22] In short, Calvin was no Calvinist.

It remains true that in his presentation of the gospel Calvin did not share the inhibitions of his later disciples. Even if they always held him in high esteem, they were seemingly reluctant to use his universalist phraseology.[23] The advent of Arminianism clearly affected the linguistic liberty of orthodox theologians and preachers. They 'over-defined' their statements, placing themselves outside the explicit terminology of Scripture.[24] When preaching from texts like John 3: 16, they cautiously expounded 'world' to mean 'the world of the elect' in a manner Calvin would never have dreamed necessary. For him 'all' means all and 'world' means world, as in this typical statement: 'God commends to us the salvation of all men without exception, even as Christ suffered for the sins of the whole world.'[25]

It has, of course, been argued that had Calvin been faced with Arminianism, his formulation of the atonement would have reflected the precision of the Canons of Dort.[26] This is very debatable if the canons are interpreted in a high orthodox manner. Calvin would have spurned the Arminian denial of unconditional election, but he would not have penalized them for their statements about the extent of the atonement as such. It is true that Calvin affirmed the particular efficacy of the atonement in the light of election, but he was apparently never tempted to disregard the universalist language of Scripture to which the Arminians appealed. Faced by the decrees of the Council of Trent, he did not feel obliged to oppose the doctrine of limited atonement to the decree which said that Christ died for all men.[27]

Remembering Richard Baxter's surprising acquiescence in the Canons of Dort,[28] it is doubtful whether even Calvin would have considered them consistent with their popular image, that they teach a strict doctrine of limited atonement. Article 3 of the second canon states, 'The death of the Son of God . . . is . . . abundantly sufficient to expiate the sins of the whole world.'[29] Here is the suggestion that, notwithstanding the limited efficacy of the atonement, its universal sufficiency is as much part of its design. Allowing for some degree of ambiguity at this point, the second canon does not necessarily teach that the atonement's sufficiency is merely a consequence of its 'infinite worth and value'. Therefore, Dort really teaches a limited efficacious atonement, not a limited atonement as such. Such was the understanding of Baxter and Amyraut, and doubtless it would have been Calvin's too, judging by his comment on the repentant thief on the cross: 'Our Lord made effective for him His death and passion which he suffered and endured for all mankind . . .'[30]

Calvin was clearly at ease with the medieval formula adopted by Peter Lombard and Thomas Aquinas to describe the atonement: 'sufficient for all, efficient for the elect;.[31] An element of ambiguity in the term 'sufficient' permitted all schools to attach their own meaning to it. However, unlike later Calvinistic universalists, Calvin did not constantly resort to the words 'Christ's death is sufficient for all' when he meant 'Christ died for all'. He had no inhibitions about saying that Christ's sacrifice 'was ordained by the eternal decree of God, to expiate the sins of the world'.[32]

It is clear from Calvin's numerous utterances on the extent of the atonement that he sees a correlation between the 'free offer' of the gospel and a universal, all-sufficient provision of grace in the atonement. Calvin accepted a basic soteriological dualism, rooted in the supreme paradox of God's inscrutable purpose and revealed will.[33] Accordingly, from the perspective of God's revealed will, 'Christ died for all' means 'there is a sufficient provision of grace for all if only they believe'; from the perspective of his secret purpose, the efficacy of the provision is applied only to the elect. Calvin is prepared to formulate matters thus because he accepts the mysterious paradox of God's revealed and secret wills without attempting to grasp the inscrutable.[34]

Following Beza's interpretation of 'mere' or 'undesigned' sufficiency, Owen would not endorse Baxter's view of the Canons of Dort. As this book attempts to demonstrate, although Owen paid lip-service to the sufficiency–efficiency distinction, his commercial theory of the atonement led him to deprive the universal sufficiency of the atonement of all its value.[35] For Owen, the atonement is only sufficient for those for whom it is efficient. For Calvin, there really is something 'on offer', which all but the elect refuse.

Calvin's position received credal sanction in the French Confession of Faith (*Confessio fidei Gallicana*) of 1559 and the Heidelberg Catechism (1563).[36] In the former, a document Calvin personally helped to draw up, there is no trace of the doctrine of limited atonement. Notwithstanding a clear statement about divine election, the provision of the atonement is expressed in general, unrestricted

Authentic Calvinism

terms.[37] The answer to question 37 of the Heidelberg Catechism states that Christ 'sustained, in body and soul, the wrath of God against the sins of all mankind'. Modern attempts[38] to adapt the sense of this statement to a high orthodox view are invalidated by the views of David Pareus (1548–1622), pupil of the Catechism's co-author Dr Zacharias Ursinus (1534–83).[39] Reflecting his teacher's views, Pareus (who actually completed Ursinus' own commentary on the Catechism) affirms that as Christ 'died for all, in respect to the sufficiency of his ransom; and for the faithful alone in respect of the efficacy of the same, so also he willed to die for all in general, as touching the sufficiency of his merit.... But he willed to die for the elect alone as touching the efficacy of his death.'[40] It was Pareus, not Beza, who perpetuated the authentic view of Calvin after his death. Whereas the Dort canon is somewhat ambiguous, Pareus explicitly follows Calvin's view of a dual design in the atonement.

It is more than likely that Calvin would have rejected the Westminster Confession for its failure to include a reference to the universal sufficiency of the atonement.[41] In this respect the Westminster divines were the victims of an anti-Arminian over-reaction. In pursuing the particularist tendencies of the Synod of Dort one stage further, they formulated a doctrine of the atonement far removed from the sentiments of Calvin,[42] the *Confessio fidei Gallicana*, and the Heidelberg Catechism. As we have noted, some members of the Westminster Assembly sought to resist these trends. Edmund Calamy spoke with great insight when he declared:

> I am far from universal redemption in the Arminian sense; but that that I hold is in the sense of our divines [e.g. Bishop Davenant] in the Synod of Dort, that Christ did pay a price for all... that Jesus Christ did not only die sufficiently for all, but God did intend, in giving Christ, and Christ in giving himself, did intend to put all men in a state of salvation in case they do believe...[43]

Regrettably, Calamy's moderate position did not prevail. English Puritanism's answer to the sub-orthodox evangelicalism of the Arminians was thus an ultra-orthodox evangelicalism. Assisted by the contribution of John Owen, this over-reaction led to the more fatal extreme of hypercalvinism in the eighteenth-century via the Congregationalist and Particular Baptist Confessions of Faith (1658, 1689). Contrary to popular assumption,[44] a notable exception among the Particular Baptists was John Bunyan, whose views clearly endorse the Calvinism of Calvin, Ursinus, Pareus, and Calamy. Bunyan declares:

Christ died for all . . . for if those that perish in the days of the gospel, shall have, at least, their damnation heightened, because they have neglected and refused to receive the gospel, it must needs be that the gospel was with all faithfulness to be tendered unto them; the which it could not be, unless the death of Christ did extend itself unto them; John 3: 16. Heb. 2: 3. for the offer of the gospel cannot with God's allowance, be offered any further than the death of Jesus Christ doth go . . .[45]

Bunyan, however, was a rare exception. Amongst the Particular Baptists generally, exaggerated Calvinism gained ground. It is against this background that Wesleyan Methodism appeared as an almost justifiable corrective.

Baxter was clearly not alone in occupying the middle ground between high Calvinism and Arminianism. Like Amyraut in France, he attempted to moderate an over-orthodox mentality in favour of the original balanced theology of Calvin and his fellow reformers.[46] Contrary to the prevailing high orthodox trends of the day, it is easy to imagine how Amyraldianism, alias Baxterianism, was construed as heterodox deviation. yet Baxter was adamant; in his *Catholick Theologie* (1675) he cites extensively from Calvin and the other reformers, defending his position against high Calvinists and Arminians alike.

Baxter gave his name to an English free-church tradition of 'moderate' Calvinists, the most notable late seventeenth- and early eighteenth-century 'Baxterians' being the Presbyterians Daniel Williams (1644–1716)[47] and Edmund Calamy III (1671–1732)[48] and the Congregationalists Isaac Watts (1674–1748)[49] and Philip Doddridge (1702–51).[50] The Congregationalist Edward Williams (1750–1813)[51] and, to a degree, the Baptist Andrew Fuller (1754–1815)[52] perpetuated something of a Baxterian outlook. Nineteenth-century Scotland saw Ralph Wardlaw (1779–1853),[53] also a Congregationalist, arguing the moderate Calvinist case. The same must be said of Thomas Chalmers (1780–1847),[54] founder of the Free Church of Scotland, whose view of the atonement is hard to reconcile with Westminster Calvinism. On the denominational level the 'Calvinistic Methodist' or Presbyterian Church of Wales moderated its confessional position on the atonement in 1874,[55] while the Presbyterian Church of England revised its confessional standards in an Amyraldian manner in 1890.[56]

Across the Atlantic, the New England Congregational divine Joseph Bellamy (1719–90)[57] opposed both Arminianism and high Calvinism with the obvious approval and agreement of his mentor Jonathan Edwards (1703–58).[58] In the nineteenth-century, Baptists like A. H. Strong (1837–1921)[59] and J. P. Boyce (1827–80)[60] pursued an Amyraldian *via media*. For the Presbyterians, Albert Barnes (1798–1870)[61] also rejected the high Calvinist view of the atonement. It is equally clear that more conservative Presbyterian theologians like Charles Hodge (1797–1878),[62] Robert L. Dabney (1820–1898),[63] and William G. T. Shedd (1820–94),[64] while formally objecting to some of the speculative features of Amyraldianism, nevertheless embraced a clear moderate Calvinism. They certainly step beyond the Westminster Confession in their formulations of the atonement. In the present century noted Reformed theologians like R. B. Kuiper (1886–1966)[65] and John Murray (1898–1975)[66] cannot be seen to endorse every aspect of John Owen's theology of limited atonement.

Before continuing with our main theme, it is appropriate to take note of a contemporary debate in the Roman Catholic Church.[67] Indeed, in his *Catholick Theologie*, Baxter shows his awareness of the controversy between the Jesuits and the Dominians over grace, free will, and the atonement. In Spain the debate in 1582 between the Thomist theologian Domingo Báñez and the Jesuit Prudentius Montemayor paralleled the seventeenth-century debates between the Calvinists and the Arminians. Later, Báñez championed the efficacy of grace against Luis de Molina's treatise *Concordia* (1588), in which the author attempted to reconcile divine sovereignty with free will. The somewhat inconclusive peace imposed on the contending parties by Rome was overshadowed by the rise of Jansenism in France, occasioned by Cornelius Jansen's posthumously published treatise *Augustinus* (1640). Rejecting the Molinist conceptions of universal grace and free will, the Jansenists claimed the authority of Augustine for their views of efficacious grace and a limited atonement. This controversy made a Jansenist theologian of Blaise Pascal (1623–62), who brilliantly refuted the Jesuits in his *Lettres provinciales* (1657). There is clear evidence that Jansen misread Augustine in an 'ultra-Calvinist' sense, but that

Pascal himself, like Baxter, detected a broader understanding of redemption in Augustine's theology.[68]

Returning to Owen and Wesley, it is now possible to assess their respective theologies against the background of 'authentic Calvinism'. Remembering that they were ordained in the Church of England, it seems that both men were involved in serious anomalies arising out of their churchmanship. While it is commonly understood that Wesley's Arminianism was at variance with Reformed Anglican orthodoxy, Wesley refused to allow the Calvinists the luxury of condemning him on the technicality of subscription to the Thirty-nine Articles. In the controversy with Rowland Hill in 1772, he adroitly declared, 'I never preached against the Seventeenth Article, nor had the least intention of doing it. But did Mr Hill never preach against the Thirty-first Article, which explicitly asserts universal redemption?'[69]

Although Wesley's Arminian reading of Article XVII, 'On predestination and election', must be ruled out on historical–theological grounds, his reference to Article XXXI certainly suggests that the Anglican Church did not commit its ministers to the high Calvinism of Beza, Owen, Whitefield, and Toplady.[70] How, then, could Owen claim to be defending Anglican doctrine? In *The Display of Arminianism* (1643) he was largely correct to regard Arminianism as 'a doctrine so opposite to that truth our church hath quietly enjoyed ever since the first Reformation',[71] but the theological ground from which he viewed the encroaching error was itself questionable. It is somewhat ironic that the parliamentary committee to whose members Owen dedicated his work had been appointed to examine all innovations in doctrine and discipline illegally introduced into the Church of England since the reformation. Owen's high Calvinism was itself an innovation, for he was advancing a view of the atonement first expounded in the English church by William Perkins (1558–1602), who in turn had been influenced by Theodore Beza.[72]

When Owen described Davenant's 'Amryaldian' *Dissertatio de morte Christi* (1650) as 'repugnant unto truth itself',[73] he was dismissing the very teaching of the church in which he was ordained. Considerations of election apart, John Wesley could claim support for his views from 'the Church of England, both in her Catechism, Articles and Homilies',[74] and 'Bishops Ridley, Hooper, and Latimer, to name no more, were firm universalists'.[75]

Indeed, as may be surmised in Calvin's case, the English Reformers would not have quarrelled with the Arminian view of the extent of the atonement as such. The real issues at stake were fewer than Owen perceived them to be, being confined to the inscrutable way in which God sovereignly applied the benefits of redemption.

Owen thus overstated his case, judging by evidence which is both compelling and embarrassing. Article XXXI explicitly affirms that 'The offering of Christ once made is that perfect redemption, propitiation, and satisfaction, for all the sins of the whole world, both original and actual . . .' Consistent with this, the prayer of consecration from the service of holy communion states that Christ made 'a full, perfect and sufficient sacrifice, oblation, and satisfaction, for the sins of the whole world'. The catechism teaches the catechumen to believe that God the Son 'hath redeemed me, and all mankind', though it hastens to add, in Calvinist rather than Arminian fashion, that God the Holy Ghost 'sanctifieth me, and all the elect people of God'. The homily for Good Friday is equally clear: 'So pleasant was this sacrifice and oblation of His Son's death, which he so obediently and innocently suffered, that he would take it for the only and full amends for all the sins of the world.'[76]

The personal views of the Reformers are no less convincing. John Hooper (1495–1555) affirmed that Christ died 'for the love of us poor and miserable sinners, whose place he occupied upon the cross, as a pledge, or one that represented the person of all the sinners that ever were, be now, or shall be unto the world's end'.[77] Hugh Latimer (1485–1555) could preach that 'Christ shed as much blood for Judas, as he did for Peter: Peter believed it, and therefore he was saved; Judas would not believe, and therefore he was condemned'.[78] Thomas Cranmer (1489–1556) also says that Christ 'by His own oblation . . . satisfied His Father for all men's sins and reconciled mankind unto His grace and favour . . .'[79] John Bradford (1520–55) explains these universalist statements with reference to election when he asserts that 'Christ's death is sufficient for all, but effectual for the elect only'.[80]

The Elizabethan Anglicans were no different in their understanding. John Jewel (1552–71) wrote that on the cross Christ declared 'It is finished' to signify 'that the price and ransom was now full paid for the sin of all mankind'.[81] Elsewhere he proclaimed that 'The death of Christ is available for the redemption of all the world . . .'[82] Richard Hooker (1553–1600) states an identical view when he says that Christ's 'precious and propitiatory sacrifice' was 'offered for the sins of all the world . . .'[83] Against this theological background, John Davenant (1570–1641) argued that, notwithstanding God's secret decree of predestination, 'The death of Christ is the universal cause of the salvation of mankind, and Christ himself is acknowledged to have died for all men sufficiently . . . by reason of the Evangelical covenant confirmed with the whole human race through the merit of his death . . .'[84] This 'evangelical covenant', he adds is the basis on which 'Christ . . . sent his Apostles into all the world, (Mark 16: 15, 16) . . . On which words of promise, the learned Calvin has rightly remarked, *That this promise was added that it might allure the whole human race to the faith*'.[85]

The Caroline divines of the seventeenth-century, both before and after the Interregnum, generally adhered to an Arminian soteriology. Undeterred by scholastic Calvinism, they rejected double predestination, insisting that Article XVII could be harmonized with election based on faith foreseen. However, Arminianism could not be justly blamed for their view of the atonement, as Clement Barksdale made clear in 1653:

> You are mistaken when you think the doctrine of Universal Redemption Arminianisme. It was the doctrine of the Church of England before Arminius was borne. We learne it out of the old Church-Catechisme. I believe in Jesus Christ, who hath redeemed me and all mankind. And the Church hath learned it out of the plaine scripture, where Christ is the Lamb of God that taketh away the sinnes of the world.[86]

This was substantially John Wesley's defence against his high Calvinist critics. In his view the Arminians simply reaffirmed the teaching of the Reformation and the Bible.

It is surely significant that the eighteenth-century moderate Calvinists shared Wesley's view of the extent of the atonement, even if they distanced themselves from his understanding of Article XVII. In short, between the polarized positions of Wesley and Whitefield, the earlier 'Anglican Calvinist' tradition re-emerged in the wake of the Methodist revival. While shunning Arminianism, John Newton (1725–1807) still shared Wesley's aversion to high Calvinism:

> That there is an election of grace, we are plainly taught; yet it is not said, 'that Jesus Christ came into the world to save 'the elect', but that he came to save 'sinners', to 'seek and save them that are lost' . . . And therefore the

command to repent implies a warrant to believe in the name of Jesus, as taking away the sin of the world'.[87]

Charles Simeon of Cambridge (1759–1836) was even more emphatic:

> To say that he died for the elect only, is neither scriptural nor true. He died for all: according as it is elsewhere said: 'we thus judge, that if one died for all, then were all dead: And that he died for all . . .' (2 Corinthians 5: 14, 15) If all be not ultimately saved by his death, it is not owing to any want of sufficiency in his sacrifice to procure acceptance for them, but to their own impenitence and unbelief. . . . Here . . . we see the propriety of interesting ourselves with God in behalf of all, since for all without exception did Jesus die.[88]

Nineteenth-century Anglican evangelicalism perpetuated this tradition. The supreme example is J. C. Ryle (1816–1900), the first bishop of Liverpool. Having little sympathy for Arminianism, Ryle was equally aware of the threat posed by high Calvinism. After appealing to Davenant, Calvin, and other commentators, he concludes:

> Those who confine God's love exclusively to the elect appear to me to take a narrow and contracted view of God's character and attributes . . . . I have long come to the conclusion that men may be more systematic in their statements than the Bible, and may be led into grave error by idolatrous veneration of a system.[89]

W. H. Griffith Thomas (1861–1931)[90] represented the 'Anglican Calvinist' tradition in the early twentieth century, after which Anglican evangelicalism became polarized into the Arminian and high Calvinist schools in the persons of John R. W. Stott[91] and J. I. Packer.[92] The writings of both theologians fail to reflect accurately the full-blown soteriology of Reformation Anglicanism.

The evidence would seem to demand certain conclusions. If Wesley cannot really justify his Arminian conception of election within the context of Reformation Anglicanism, Owen certainly cannot do so with his concept of limited atonement. In short, Arminianism and high Calvinism are both deviations from 'authentic' Calvinism. Calvin and his fellow Reformers, both Continental[93] and English, were willing to accept paradox. They seemed able to balance the apparently conflicting elements of a doctrine of grace which was both general in provision yet special in application. They believed that faithful exegesis demanded their

The Theology: Atonement and Grace

conclusions. Unlike many seventeenth-century theologians, they successfully resisted the temptation to impose a logical strait-jacket on the Bible, thereby suppressing or modifying part of the textual data in the interest of certain theological emphases.

This book seeks to demonstrate that the main cause of the Calvinist–Arminian controversy was the re-emergence of Aristotelian scholasticism within Reformed theological thought. Once Beza's exaggerated orthodoxy gained ground, it was inevitable that the equally exaggerated Arminian reaction should set in. In the ensuing controversy John Owen became the undoubted champion of the Bezan school; he was inaccurately regarded as 'the Calvin of England'. Sufficient evidence has been adduced to indicate that the reformers would not recognize Owen's doctrine of the atonement as their own.

In many respects Richard Baxter emerges as the true advocate of Reformation Calvinism. Of course, judged by the criteria of high Calvinism, Baxterianism was bound to look like a compromise with Arminianism, just as the Arminians thought Baxter too Calvinistic. Baxter considered that, at their best, both high Calvinism and Arminianism were only emphasizing opposite sides of the same coin. They were both, in different though complementary senses, semi-Calvinist. He saw that as the Arminian was not all wrong, so the high Calvinist was not all right, and vice versa. For Baxter, as for Calvin, the supreme issue for the Reformed theologian was integrity of exegesis. His own words serve to highlight this priority: 'When God saith so expressly that Christ died for all, and tasted death for every man, and is the ransom for all, and the propitiation for the sins of the whole world, it beseems every Christian rather to explain in what sense Christ died for all, than flatly to deny it.'[94]

It is surely appropriate to end this chapter with full statements by John Calvin himself. His comments on John 3: 15–16 not only vindicate Richard Baxter; they also serve to provide unambiguous specimens of authentic Calvinism.

And indeed our Lord Jesus was offered to all the world. For it is not speaking of three of four when it says: 'God so loved the world, that he spared not His only Son'. But yet we must notice what the Evangelist adds in this passage: 'That whosoever believes in Him shall not perish but obtain eternal life.' Our Lord Jesus suffered for all and there is neither great nor small who is not inexcusable today, for we can obtain salvation in Him. Unbelievers who turn away from Him and who deprive themselves of Him by their malice are today doubly cuplably, for how will they excuse their ingratitude in not receiving the blessing in which they could share by faith?[95]

A statement like this surely refutes the popular assumption[96] that Calvin taught limited atonement. None the less, an all-sufficient, universal provision of grace is restricted in its efficacious application:

> It is incontestable that Christ came for the expiation of the sins of the whole world. But the solution lies close at hand, that whosoever believes in Him should not perish but should have eternal life (John 3: 15). For the present question is not how great the power of Christ is or what efficacy it has in itself, but to whom He gives Himself to be enjoyed. If possession lies in faith and faith emanates from the Spirit of adoption, it follows that only he is reckoned in the number of God's children who will be a partaker of Christ. The evangelist John sets forth the office of Christ as nothing else than by His death to gather the children of God into one (John 11: 52). Hence, we conclude that, though reconciliation is offered to all through Him, yet the benefit is peculiar to the elect, that they may be gathered into the society of life. However, while I say it is offered to all, I do not mean that this embassy, by which on Paul's testimony (2 Corinthians 5: 18) God reconciles the world to Himself, reaches to all, but that it is not sealed indiscriminately on the hearts of all to whom it comes so as to be effectual.[97]

NOTES

1. Only a year before he died, Owen viewed Arminianism as the 'ruin and poison of the souls of men' (*Works*, ix. 459). As late as 1789 Wesley was no less vehement: 'Calvinism . . . strikes at the root of salvation from sin' (*Works*, viii. 323).
2. Owen denies that the differences are 'of an inferior nature . . . One church cannot wrap in her communion Austin and Pelagius, Calvin and Arminius' (*Dis. A.* 7).
3. Luther did not deny that many passages were obscure to the uneducated, but he emphatically denied that anything is 'left obscure or ambiguous . . . all that is in the Scripture is through the Word brought forth into the clearest light and proclaimed to the whole world' (*The Bondage of the Will*, trans. J. I. Packer and O. R. Johnson (London, 1957), 74).
4. For an historical survey of the controversy see A. P. F. Sell, *The Great Debate* (Worthing, 1982).
5. See B. G. Armstrong, *Calvinism and the Amyraut Heresy* (Madison,

Wisc., 1969), 37 ff.; R. T. Kendall, *Calvin and English Calvinism to 1649* (Oxford, 1979), 29 ff.
6. Kendall, *Calvin*, pp. 141 ff. For studies of Arminius see A. W. Harrison, *Arminianism* (London, 1937); C. Bangs, *Arminius: A Study in the Dutch Reformation* (Nashville, Tenn., 1971).
7. Episcopius (1583–1643) and Limborch (1633–1712) went beyond their master, but on the subject of the perseverance of the saints Arminius says, 'Though I here openly and ingenuously affirm, I never taught that a true believer can either totally or finally fall away and perish; yet I will not conceal, that there are passages of Scripture which seem to me to wear this aspect' (*Declarations of the Sentiments of Arminius*, in *The Works of James Arminius, DD*, trans. J. Nichols (London, 1825), i. 603).
8. 'Let those ... consider how they can answer the following Scriptures [1 John 2: 2; John 1: 29, 6: 51; Rom. 14: 15; 2 Pet. 2: 1–3] ... He therefore who speaks thus, speaks with the Scriptures; while he who rejects such phraseology, is a daring man, one who sits in judgement on the Scriptures and is not an interpreter of them' (ibid. ii. 9–10).
9. 'In Puritan teaching, the doctrines of limited atonement and predestination often raised the question of personal assurance.' S. B. Ferguson, *John Owen on the Christian Life* (Edinburgh, 1987), 99.
10. Armstrong, *Calvinism*, p. 37.
11. A. E. McGrath, *The Intellectual Origins of the European Reformation* (Oxford, 1987), 194–5; B. Hall, 'Calvin against the Calvinists', in *John Calvin*, ed. G. Duffield (Abingdon, 1966), 27. For Beza see I. McPhee, 'Conserver or transformer of Calvin's theology? A study of the origins and development of Theodore Beza's thought (1550–1570)', Ph.D. thesis (Cambridge, 1979).
12. The Canons are popularly expressed by the mnemonic TULIP, where T = total depravity, U = unconditional election, L = limited atonement, I = irresistible grace, and P = perseverance of the saints. For the full texts of the articles of the Remonstrants and the Canons of Dort, see *Crisis in the Reformed Churches: Essays in the Commencement of the great Synod of Dort (1618–1619)*, ed. P. Y. De Yong (Grand Rapids, Mich., 1968), 207 ff.; H. B. Smith and P. Schaff, *The Creeds of the Evangelical Protestant Churches* (London, 1877), 581–97; J. Nichols, *Calvinism and Arminianism Compared* (London, 1824), 90–164.
13. H. Rolston, *John Calvin versus the Westminster Confession* (Richmond, Tenn., 1972); A. F. Mitchell and J. Struthers (eds.), *Minutes of the sessions of the Westminster Assembly of Divines*, (London, 1874), xi ff.
14. Introductory essay to his edn. of *The Death of Death* (London, 1959), 13.
15. Wesley's most substantial contribution to the debate was the brief treatise *Predestination Calmly Considered* (1752) (*Works*, x. 197–249).

16. Ibid. 206–8, 217.
17. P. Lewis, *The Genius of Puritanism* (Haywards Heath, 1979), 27.
18. The Arminian Puritan John Goodwin quotes Calvin's views on the extent of the atonement extensively in his *Redemption Redeemed* (London, 1651), 552–5. Owen's treatise *The Doctrine of the Saints' Perseverance* (1654) (*Works*, xi. 5 ff.) was a critique of the latter part of Goodwin's book. He clearly saw no need to duplicate his *Death of Death*, in which there is only one reference to Calvin (*DD* 275). In a letter to Walter Sellon in 1768, Wesley wrote, 'I am glad you have undertaken the "Redemption Redeemed." But you must in no wise forget Dr Owen's answer to it: otherwise you will leave a loop–hole for all the Calvinists to creep out. The Doctor's evasions you must needs cut in pieces . . .' (*Letters*, v. 96). W.'s intended successor John Fletcher was certainly aware of Calvin's views however; see *The Works of John Fletcher* (Salem, Ohio, 1974), ii. 71.
19. *Works*, v. 226; x. 326, 345.
20. *JF* 84.
21. See *EQ* 55. 2 (1983); also R. Nicole, 'John Calvin's views of the extent of the atonement', *WTJ* 47 (1985), 197–225.
22. See Appendix A, 'Did John Calvin teach limited atonement?', in C. Daniel, 'John Gill and Hypercalvinism', Ph.D. thesis (Edinburgh, 1983), 777–828.
23. Calvin generally employs the universal terms 'all' and 'world' in their natural sense of 'all without exception', although he believes this cannot be the case in 1 Tim. 2: 5–7. Kendall is not quite correct here (*Calvin*, p. 13 n. 2). P. Helm labours unconvincingly to prove that Calvin meant something other than what he wrote, even contradicting Calvin's explicit statements (*Calvin and the Calvinists* (Edinburgh, 1982), 46; cf. Calvin, *Comm*. Col. 1: 14).
24. John Murray, writing from the perspective of a later orthodoxy, virtually penalizes Calvin and his contemporaries for using the very generalities of scripture, as if 'fuller and more precise' definitions necessarily preclude error. See 'The importance and relevance of the Westminster Confession', *Collected Writings of John Murray* (Edinburgh, 1976), i. 317.
25. *Comm*. Gal. 5: 12. R. A. Peterson refuses to interpret Calvin's statements at face value (*Calvin's Doctrine of the Atonement* (Phillipsburg, NJ, 1983), 90). Calvin's comment on Gal. 5: 12 says more than Peterson claims. As in his comment on Rom. 5: 18, Calvin distinguishes between the atonement and the free offer, where one is seen to be dependent on the other.
26. J. I. Packer, 'Calvin the theologian', in *John Calvin*, ed. G. Duffield (Abingdon, 1966), at p. 151.
27. *Antidote to the Council of Trent* in J. Calvin, *Tracts and Treatises*

(Edinburgh, 1851), iii. 93. Calvin found nothing objectionable in the decree: 'The third and fourth heads I do not touch' (ibid. 109).
28. W. Orme, (ed.), *The Life and Writings of Richard Baxter* (London, 1830), i. 456.
29. Smith and Schaff, *Creeds*, p. 586. See W. R. Godfrey, 'Reformed thought on the extent of the atonement', *WTJ* 37 (1975), at p. 171.
30. *Sermons on the Saving Work of Christ*, trans. L. Nixon (Grand Rapids, Mich., 1980), 151.
31. Kendall misreads Calvin here (*Calvin*, p. 16). In his comment on 1 John 2: 2 C. says he accepts the formula; he only denies its relevance to the text. See also Calvin's *Sermons on Isaiah's Prophecy*, trans. T. H. L. Parker (London, 1956), 116.
32. *Comm.* Matt. 26: 24.
33. Roger Nicole produces a contradictory account of Calvin's position, failing to perceive the reformer's full-blown acceptance of the 'two-sidedness' of the atonement and claiming that 'most of the well-meant offers and invitations, human as well as divine, are not grounded in coextensive provision!' ('Calvin's view', p. 213). He then says, 'Calvin is also concerned to express the sufficiency of the work of Christ so that no one inclined to claim this work and to cast himself or herself on the mercy of God should feel discouraged by thinking that somehow the cross would not avail for him/her' (ibid. 217). Once it is seen that Calvin views the 'sufficiency' of the atonement in terms of 'coextensive provision' there is no need for such contradictory statements. Without such a provision there would be no basis for encouragement. Calvin is perfectly clear: 'Let us not fear to come to Him in great numbers, and each one of us bring his neighbours, seeing that He is sufficient to save us all' (*Sermons on Isaiah's Prophecy*, p. 144).
34. If Calvin's acceptance of God's 'hidden secret will' is unbiblical (but see his references to Deut. 29: 29 in *Inst*. iii. xxi. 3 and (*Comm*. Ezek. 18: 32), his theology is effectively Arminianized (M. C. Bell, *Calvin and Scottish Theology* (Edinburgh, 1985), 32).
35. '. . . it is denied that the blood of Christ was a sufficient price and ransom for all and everyone . . .' (*DD* 296).
36. Smith and Schaff, *Creeds*, pp. 356 ff.
37. A. C. Clifford, 'John Calvin and the Confessio Fidei Gallicana', *EQ* 58. 3 (1986), at p. 199.
38. Such as H. Hoeksema, *The Triple Knowledge: An Exposition of the Heidelberg Catechism* (Grand Rapids, Mich., 1976), i. 529–43, 641–2.
39. Godfrey, 'Reformed thought', p. 148. In failing to relate the sufficiency–efficiency distinction to Calvin's theology, Kendall mistakenly affirms that 'Ursinus espouses a limited atonement' (*Calvin*, p. 41).
40. Z. Ursinus, *The Commentary of Dr Zacharias Ursinus on the Heidelberg*

Catechism, trans. G. W. Williard (Columbus, Ohio, 1852; fac. Phillipsburg, NJ, 1985), 223; see also pp. 212–15.

41. R. L. Dabney believes that the Westminster Confession 'carefully avoids implying any limitation upon the infinite value and merit of Christ's sacrifice' (*The Westminster Confession and Creeds* (Dallas, 1983), 13). But since the Confession says nothing at all about the sufficiency of the atonement, unlike the Canons of Dort, Dabney has no grounds for his conclusion. Indeed, the language of the Confession (ch. VIII. viii) is restrictive by implication.

42. William Cunningham (1805–61) flies in the face of the evidence in denying that Calvin taught universal atonement (*The Reformers and the Theology of the Reformation* (London, 1862; fac. London, 1967), 397. Although he denies that it is conclusive, he cites Calvin's isolated reply to the Lutheran divine Heshusius as 'a very explicit denial of the universality of the atonement' (p. 396). Calvin says, 'As he adheres so doggedly to the words ['this is my body'], I should like to know how the wicked can eat the flesh of Christ which was not crucified for them, and how they can drink the blood which was not shed to expiate their sins?' For a discussion of this see Daniel, 'John Gill and Hypercalvinism', p. 818 ff. Alternatively, once it is seen that Calvin is opposing the theory of consubstantiation, an otherwise problematic statement makes sense beside his numerous universalist statements. He is virtually asking how unbelievers (or anyone for that matter) can feed on a crucified Christ simply be eating and drinking consecrated elements; for they themselves were not actually crucified as Christ was. Calvin is simply ridiculing the idea that unbelievers feed on Christ by feeding on mere symbols. See *Tracts and Treatises*, ii. 527.

43. Quoted in A. F. Mitchell and J. Struthers (eds.), *Minutes of the Sessions of the Westminster Assembly of Divines* (London, 1874), 152.

44. See T. J. Nettles, *By His Grace and for His Glory* (Grand Rapids, Mich., 1986), 57–72. Bunyan is aligned with Keach as a Particular Baptist.

45. 'Reprobation asserted', in *The Works of John Bunyan*, ed. G. Offor (London, 1855), at ii. 348. Although Nettles discusses this treatise, he omits any reference to the extract quoted here.

46. Alexander Gordon wrote that 'Baxter's Calvinism differed from that of the Westminster divines, simply by the purity of its adhesion to the original type, unaffected by the Arminian reaction. His Calvinism, like that of the framers of some of the Anglican formularies, admitted, nay insisted, that our Lord, by His death, had redeemed all mankind' (*PHSE* I. 2 (1915), 35).

47. See *DNB*; R. Thomas, *Daniel Williams: 'Presbyterian Bishop'* (Dr Williams's Library Lecture; London, 1964). Williams's Baxterianism is evident in his *Gospel-truth Stated* (London, 1692).

88   *The Theology: Atonement and Grace*

48. See *DNB*. Like Baxter and his grandfather, Calamy argues that 'the doctrine of particular election' is consistent with 'a general love of God to the world' (*Divine Mercy Exalted: or Free Grace in Its Glory* (London, 1703), p. iv.
49. See *DNB*; A. P. Davis, *Isaac Watts* (London, 1943), 107 ff. Watts expounds Baxterian Calvinism in his *Ruin and Recovery of Mankind* (1740); see *The Works of The Reverend and Learned Isaac Watts, DD*, ed. D. Jennings and P. Doddridge (London, 1753), vi. 287–8, for references to Calvin's universalism.
50. See *DNB*; G. F. Nuttall, *Richard Baxter and Philip Doddridge: A Study in a Tradition* (Dr Williams's Library Lecture; London, 1951). For a discussion of Doddridge's Calvinism see A. C. Clifford, 'The Christian mind of Philip Doddridge', *EQ* 56. 4 (1984), 227–42.
51. See *DNB*; Sell, *Great Debate*, 89 pp. ff.; R. Tudur Jones, *Congregationalism in England, 1662–1962* (London, 1962), 168–71. Also G. Thomas, 'Edward Williams and the rise of "modern Calvinism"', *BOT* 88 (1971), 43–8; 90 (1971), 29–35.
52. See *DNB*; A. H. Kirkby, 'The theology of Andrew Fuller and its relation to Calvinism', Ph.D. thesis (Edinburgh, 1956) *passim*. See also G. F. Nuttall, 'Northamptonshire and the *Modern Question*', *JTS* n.s. 16 (1965), at p. 119. Fuller, when accused of Baxterian sentiments, insisted that he was a 'strict Calvinist' rather than a 'moderate Calvinist' because he claimed to hold 'the system of Calvin' (*The Complete Works of Andrew Fuller*, ed. A. G. Fuller (London, 1831), i. pp. lxiv, cxv. He was obviously unaware of the close similarity between Calvin's actual views and those of Baxter. There is definite evidence that Fuller moved more in Baxter's direction; see the famous footnote in *The Gospel Its Own Witness* (1800) (ibid., i. 113–14).
53. See *DNB*; R. Wardlaw *Discourses on the Nature and Extent of the Atonement* (London, 1854); id., *Systematic Theology* (London, 1856), ii. 358 ff. He believed that high Calvinism provided too easy an excuse for the Arminians to reject true Calvinism (*Discourses*, p. lxxxvii).
54. See *DNB*. Chalmers says, 'If Christ died only for the elect, and not for all', ministers 'are puzzled to understand how they should proceed with the calls and invitations of the gospel . . . . Now for the specific end of conversion, the available scripture is not that Christ laid down His life for the sheep, but that Christ is set forth a propitiation for the sins of the world. It is not because I know myself to be one of the sheep, or one of the elect, but because I know myself to be one of the world, that I take to myself the calls and promises of the New Testament' (*Institutes of Theology* (1849), ii. 403, 406). Chalmers's views have more affinity with Edward Fisher's *The Marrow of Modern Divinity* (London, 1645) than with the Westminster Confession. The *Marrow* contains several statements which favour a Baxterian view of the atonement. See M. C.

Bell, *Calvin and Scottish Theology*, pp. 151 ff.; A. C. Clifford, 'Faith assurance and the Gospel offer', *The Monthly Record of the Free Church of Scotland* (Sept. 1988), at p. 204.

55. Calvinistic Methodism was more exclusive than Westminster Calvinism. Its Confession (1823) states, 'Trefnwyd i'w Berson ef gael ei osod yn lle y personau hyny (a hwy yn unig) a roddwyd iddo i'w prynu' *Cyffes Ffydd*: (Wrexham, *y corph o Fethodistiaid Calfinaidd, yn Nghymru* 1861), 52. ('It was ordained that [Christ's] Person should stand in the stead of those persons (and those only) who had been given him to redeem', *Confession of Faith of the Calvinistic Methodists or the Presbyterians of Wales* (English trans.; Caernarfon, 1900), 74). The 1874 amendment reads: 'That while we do not wish to make any alteration in what is stated in this article, we think it necessary to call attention to the opposite truth concerning the infinite sufficiency of the atonement, as it is set forth in the hymns of Williams of Pantycelyn, and in the writings of Charles of Bala, and Jones of Denbigh' (ibid. 129–30).

56. The Declaratory Statement of 1885 effectively restored the more moderate position of Calamy and others in the Westminster Assembly: 'That the Doctrine of Redemption set forth in the Westminster Confession, particularly in its reference to the election of some among mankind to eternal life, is held and taught in this Church together with other great truths which are vital to the Gospel, such as (1st) That the love of God to mankind moved Him to provide, by the gift of His Son to be a propitiation for the whole world, a way of salvation which in His Gospel is freely offered to all . . .' (*Digest of the Proceedings of the Synods of the Presbyterian Church of England 1876–1905*, ed. S. W. Carruthers (London, 1907), 16).

57. See *DAB*; J. Bellamy, *True Religion Delineated* (Edinburgh, 1788). He denies that 'Christ died merely for the elect', citing the views of Dr William Twisse, first prolocutor of the Westminster Assembly: 'I am ready to profess . . . that every one who hears the gospel, (without distinction between elect or reprobate) is bound to believe that Christ died for him, so far as to procure both the pardon of his sins and the salvation of his soul, in case he believes and repents' (ibid. 310).

58. Edwards wrote the preface to Bellamy's book, and his commendation of it is precise and deliberate: 'it will be found a discourse wherein the proper essence and distinguishing nature of saving religion is deduced from the first principles of the oracles of God, in a manner tending to a great increase of light'. There can be little doubt that the mature Edwards shared Bellamy's view of the atonement. Without questioning the efficacious redemption of the elect, Edwards grants that 'Christ in some sense may be said to *die for all*, and to redeem all visible Christians, yea, the whole world, by his death . . .' (*On The Freedom of the Will* (1754), in *The Works of Jonathan Edwards*, ed. E. Hickman

90   *The Theology: Atonement and Grace*

(London, 1834; fac. Edinburgh, 1974), i. 88). The very year in which Bellamy's book was published (1750) saw Edwards willing to subscribe 'to the substance of the Westminster Confession' (I. H. Murray, *Jonathan Edwards: A New Biography* (Edinburgh, 1987), 346). Edwards's words imply some reservation with respect to the details of the Confession. He clearly considered, like Baxter before him, that the 'substance' of the Confession was not inconsistent with a broader view of the atonement. For a discussion of Edwards's theological influence see A. C. Guelzo, 'Jonathan Edwards and the New Divinity', in *Pressing Toward the Mark: Essays Commemorating Fifty Years of the Orthodox Presbyterian Church*, ed. C. G. Dennison and R. C. Gamble (Philadephia, 1986), 147–67. Unlike Guelzo, Murray ignores both Bellamy's book and E's preface.

59. See *DAB*. Following the Amyraldian view, Strong rejected both the commercial and governmental theories of the atonement; see *Systematic Theology* (New York, 1890), 409 ff.
60. See *DAB*. As leading Southern Baptist theologian, Boyce viewed the atonement in a way that differs little from the Amyraldian view; see his *Abstract of Systematic Theology* (Philadelphia, 1887), 340.
61. See *DAB*. Barnes was a later advocate of 'new school' Calvinism, which derived its initial stimulus from Edwards and the New England theologians. Like Bellamy, he rejected the commercial theory of the atonement in favour of the governmental view; see *The Atonement* (New York, 1860), 230 ff.
62. See *DAB*. Hodge was the leading representative of 'Old School' Presbyterian Calvinism. He rejected the commercial view of the atonement as well as certain speculative features of Amyraldianism, but his view of the extent of the atonement is virtually Amyraldian. Reflecting Baxter's statement 'Christ therefore died for all, but not for all equally' (*CT* I. ii. 53), he writes that 'Augustinians do not deny that Christ died for all men. What they deny is that He died equally, and with the same design, for all men' (*Systematic Theology* (New York, 1873; fac. London, 1960), ii. 558).
63. See *DAB*. The Southern Presbyterian Dabney is very similar to Hodge. He even criticizes William Cunningham for taking a narrow view of the atonement's design (*Systematic Theology* (St Louis, 1878; Edinburgh, 1985), 529). He distances himself from John Owen's particularism: 'I have already stated one ground for rejecting that interpretation of John 3: 16, which makes 'the world' which God so loved, the elect world . . . Christ's mission to make expiation for sin is a manifestation of unspeakable benevolence to the whole world' (ibid. 535). See also 'God's indiscriminate proposals of mercy', in his *Discussions: Evangelical and Theological* (Richmond, Virg., 1890; fac. London, 1967), i. 282 ff.
64. See *DAB*. Shedd's discussion of the common/special grace distinction

is typically Amyraldian, as is his view that 'Atonement is unlimited, and redemption is limited. This statement includes all the Scripture texts: those which assert that Christ died for all men, and those which assert that he died for his people.... the sacrifice of Christ is unlimited in its value, sufficiency, and publication, but limited in its effectual application. (*Dogmatic Theology* (New York, 1894), ii. 470).
65. Kuiper plainly rejects the way some Calvinists assert the doctrine of particular redemption. Like Dabney, Hodge, and Shedd, he makes room for a broader design in the atonement than earlier Calvinists like Owen did; see *For Whom Did Christ Die?* (Grand Rapids, Mich., 1982), 6 and 78 ff.
66. Murray, while claiming to hold to a rigid redemptive particularism, is still ready to admit that there is a sense in which 'Christ died for non-elect persons' (*Collected Writings*, i. 68).
67. A. E. McGrath, *Iustitia Dei* (Cambridge, 1986), ii. 93–4.
68. Pascal wrote: 'Jesus Christ Redeemer of all. Yes, for He has made His offer as a man who has ransomed all who are willing to come to Him. If any die by the wayside, it is their misfortune; so far as He is concerned, He offered them redemption.... When you say that Jesus Christ did not die for all, you are taking advantage of weakness in men...' ('Notes for the "Writings on grace"', in *Pensées*, trans. J. Warrington, ed. Louis Lafuma (London, 1960), 215). Pascal notes that some receive grace by Christ's death who do not persevere in faith, but in the case of others 'Jesus Christ has desired their salvation absolutely, and brings them to it by certain and infallible means' ('Note on grace', in *The Provincial Letters*, trans. A. J. Krailsheimer (London, 1967), 28). Accordingly, Baxter wrote: 'As for *Augustine* and some *Protestants*, they oft deny that Christ redeemeth any but the faithful, because the word *redemption* is ambiguous, and sometimes taken for the price or ransome paid, and often for the *very liberation* of the captive sinner. And when Austin denieth common redemption, he taketh redemption in this *last* sense, for actual deliverance. But he asserteth it in the first sense, that Christ died for all. Yea, he thought his death is actually applied to the true justification and sanctification of some reprobates that fall away and perish, though the elect only are so redeemed and saved. Read yourself *Augustine*... and you will see this with your own eyes' (*CT* II. 57–8).
69. *Works*, x. 368.
70. In his 'Historic proof of the doctrinal Calvinism of the Church of England', *Works* (1825), i. 161 ff. Toplady fails to prove that limited atonement was taught before the late 16th cent. His reference to Andrew Willet's *Synopsis Papismi* (c.1600), in which the doctrine is asserted, only proves that the original Anglican position had been effectively amended through the influence of Beza and Perkins.
71. *Dis. A.* 6.

72. Kendall, *Calvin*, pp. 54 ff.
73. *Works*, x. 432.
74. *DP* 225.
75. *Works*, x. 409.
76. *Homilies*, p. 287.
77. *Later Writings of Bishop Hooper* (Cambridge, 1852), 31.
78. *Sermons by Hugh Latimer* (Cambridge, 1844), ii. 521.
79. *The Works of Thomas Cranmer* (Cambridge, 1844), i. 346.
80. *Sermons* (Cambridge, 1848), i. 320.
81. '*Apologia ecclesiae Anglicanae*', *The Works of John Jewel* (Cambridge, 1848), iii. 66.
82. *Homilies*, p. 310.
83. 'The laws of ecclesiastical polity', *The Works of that Learned and Judicious Divine Mr Richard Hooker*, ed. John Keble (Oxford, 1836), iii. 71.
84. 'A dissertation on the death of Christ', trans. J. Allport, in *A Commentary on the Epistle to the Colossians* (London, 1832), ii, at p. 401. For a similar view of the covenant of grace see N. Shepherd, 'The covenant context for Evangelism', in *The New Testament Student and Theology*, ed. J. H. Skilton (Phillipsburg, NJ, 1976), 54–65.
85. Ibid. 419.
86. Cited in J. W. Packer, *The Transformation of Anglicanism 1643–1660* (Manchester, 1969), 56.
87. *The Works of the Revd John Newton* (London, 1808), iv. 192–5.
88. *Horae homileticae* (London, 1833), xviii. 501–2.
89. *Expository Thoughts on the Gospels* (London, 1865), *St John*, i. 159.
90. Although Griffith Thomas warns against 'overpressing' the logic of predestination, he rejects the Arminian view of Article XVII: 'Election contingent on foresight is really not election at all, since the choice in such a case would be solely man's, and would leave no room for distinction due to Divine foreordination.' Yet with Luther, Calvin, and the best 'Anglican Calvinists', he declares that 'the Atonement means that God in the Person of His Eternal Son took upon Himself in vicarious death the sin of the whole world. The offer of mercy is made to everyone, since there is no sinner for whom Christ did not die, and every sin, past, present, and future, is regarded as laid on and borne by Him' (*The Principles of Theology* (4th edn., 1951), 247, 246, and 58–9).
91. As in Stott's early work *Basic Christianity* (London, 1958), the themes of election and the consequent efficacy of the atonement are conspicuously absent from his later book *The Cross of Christ* (London, 1986).
92. Reading Packer's *Evangelism and the Sovereignty of God* (London, 1961), 64–9, and his review of Stott's *Cross of Christ*, in *Christianity Today* (4 Sept. 1987), 35–6, no one can doubt Packer's high Calvinism.
93. Contrary to Kendall's claim, (*Calvin*, p. 13), Luther did not teach

limited atonement. In his comment on 1 John 2: 2 he states, 'It is certain that you are a part of the world. Do not let your heart deceive you by saying: "The Lord died for Peter and Paul; He rendered satisfaction for them, not for me." Therefore let every one who has sin be summoned here, for He has made the expiation for the sins of the whole world and bore the sins of the whole world.' ('The catholic epistles', in *Works* (St Louis, 1963), xxx. 237.) For Zwingli's 'Calvinistic' universalism see Daniel, 'Gill and Hypercalvinism', 516–17. Helm, whose defence of the traditional view of Calvin is as unconvincing as Cunningham's, suggests that since Karl Barth attributed the 'theological error' of limited atonement to Calvin, the traditional view is correct. This dubious argument might rather suggest that both critic and apologist are wrong. (P. Helm, 'Calvin and Calvinism', *Evangel* (Winter 1984), 7–10.) For a Barthian assessment of the issues see J. B. Torrance, 'The strength and weaknesses of Westminster theology', in *The Westminster Confession in the Church Today*, ed. A. I. C. Heron (Edinburgh 1982), 40–54; id., 'The incarnation and limited atonement', *EQ* 55. 2 (1983), 83–94.

94. UR 286.
95. *Sermons on Isaiah's Prophecy*, p. 141. Peterson writes of Calvin's views: 'There is too little evidence in the *Institutes* to reach a conclusion on the extent of the atonement. The lack of evidence in the *Inst.* should make us cautious when using the commentaries and sermons to determine whether Calvin taught limited or unlimited atonement. In his preface to the reader in the 1559 *Institutes* Calvin gave his own methodological statement that one should interpret his commentaries doctrinally on the basis of the *Institutes*' (*Calvin's Doctrine*, p. 90). This conclusion is clearly at variance with the facts. Even if Calvin's statements in the *Institutes* are not as full as those elsewhere, his teaching is no less clear: Christ became man 'to redeem the human race . . . We know well why Christ was at first promised—viz. that he might renew a fallen world, and succour lost man . . . . the salvation brought by Christ is common to the whole human race, inasmuch as Christ, the author of salvation, is descended from Adam, the common father of us all . . . . so long as we are without Christ and separated from him, nothing which he suffered and did for the salvation of the human race is of the least benefit to us' (*Inst.* II. xii. 4; II. xiii. ; III. i. 1).
96. The American Presbyterian R. C. Reed (1851–1925) reflects this in *The Gospel as Taught by Calvin* (London, 1979). Despite the title, Calvin's views on the atonement are nowhere quoted. The same assumption is shared by C. H. Spurgeon in his sermon 'Particular redemption' (1858). He appeals to the reformer thus: 'Calvin, after all, knew more about the gospel than almost any man who has ever lived, uninspired' (*The New Park Street Pulpit* (London, 1859), iv. 135).

However, Calvin is nowhere quoted. Furthermore, Spurgeon incorrectly appeals to 'the gospel of Calvin' when he says of the commercial theory, 'The mercantile idea of the atonement is the Biblical idea of the atonement' (*The Treasury of the Old Testament* (London, n.d.), i. 270-2). Despite his belief in limited atonement, Spurgeon was superior to his creed; in practice, he was closer to Baxter than to Owen and Gill.

97. *Concerning the Eternal Predestination of God*, trans. J. K. S. Reid (London, 1961), 148-9. Kendall is correct to say that the limited efficacy of an otherwise universal atonement is explained by Christ's intercession: 'While Christ *died* for all, "He does not pray for all"', Calvin claims' (*Calvin*, pp. 13-14). However, this only applies to the high-priestly intercession of John 17: 9. Calvin also admits that the prayer from the cross, 'Father forgive them . . .' (Luke 23: 34) shows Christ praying 'for all indiscriminately' (*Comm.* John 17: 9). He therefore seems to think that Christ prays in a special efficacious way for the elect, not that he prays only for them. This observation meets the objection made by Helm (*Calvin and the Calvinists*, pp. 36 ff.) and others that Calvin treats Christ's death and intercession inseparably. This is true, but does not prove that he taught limited atonement. It proves that, just as there are two aspects to the atonement in Calvin's mind—'sufficient for all/efficient for the elect'—so there are two aspects to his intercession, the two parts of his priestly work correlating in this 'dualistic' way. In the broadest sense, Calvin denies that Christ only prays for the elect, just as he denies that the atonement is only for the elect. Two years after his death, Calvin's biblical universalism was reflected in the *Second Helvetic Confession* (1566). See *Reformed Confessions of the Sixteenth Century*, ed. A. Cochrane (London, 1966), 220 ff., esp. at pp. 242, 246. The last of the great Reformation confessions, it was drawn up by Calvin's friend Heinrich Bullinger (1504-75), Zwingli's successor at Zurich. See M. Prestwich (ed.), *International Calvinism 1541-1715* (Oxford, 1985), at pp. 2-3. For Calvin and Bullinger, see *Letters of John Calvin* (Edinburgh, 1980).

6
The Legacy of Aristotle

The Protestant Reformers rejected the medieval scholastic theology in favour of a truly biblical one. In repudiating the speculations of the schoolmen they laid the foundations of a theology which, in both method and content, regarded the perspicuity of Scripture as axiomatic. In particular, the reformers shunned the kind of synthesis of divine revelation and human philosphy evident in the scholasticism of Thomas Aquinas. Aristotle was the villain of the piece; no longer were the opinions of 'the philosopher' to be placed beside the authoritative utterances of 'the apostle'.

Martin Luther's impatience with Aristotle is well known.[1] John Calvin also wrote of 'the great darkness of philosophers',[2] but his humanist training gave him greater discernment than Luther in the assessment of their medieval heritage. However, while Calvin did not entirely reject Aristotelian logic and terminology,[3] he spurned speculative metaphysics in his theology.[4] Without pretending that Calvin renounced reason as such, we may say that he was generally content to live with paradox and tension in his theology. His primary concern was to expound Christian teaching within the framework of revelation. Under no circumstances was 'theory' allowed to impose itself on the 'data', however unsatisfactory his conclusions might appear from a strictly logical standpoint.[5]

A number of scholarly studies indicate that beside Theodore Beza, Peter Martyr Vermigli (1500–62) and Girolamo Zanchi (1516–90) were responsible for reintroducing scholastic patterns of thought into Reformed theology.[6] Biblical theology thus assumed a significantly modified character by the late sixteenth-century. It was expounded deductively rather than inductively, and theory took precedence over the textual data, an approach totally alien to Luther and Calvin. Through the influence of William Perkins and others, Bezan scholasticism helped English Protestant theologians to outgrow their earlier antagonism to Aristotle.[7]

In his later works John Owen seems to lament the continuing

influence of Aristotle.[8] However, the *Death of Death*—an early work—reveals the scholastic influences then in vogue. The obtrusive complexity of Baxter's 'subtle metaphysics'[9] might not appear in Owen's general style, but it can be shown that when it suited his purpose, Owen could resort to scholastic methodology in a significant way. Indeed, the *Death of Death* is typically scholastic in its structure. Instead of providing an exegesis of the relevant scriptural data first, followed by various inferences and conclusions, the order is in fact reversed. Theological arguments are advanced and debated first (albeit with some reference to relevant texts) and the major exegetical discussion follows. There is evidence to suggest that Owen's arguments in the earlier parts of the treatise prejudice his biblical exegesis in the later sections. There is, in effect, an incipient rationalism at work.[10]

Owen's Aristotelian method is evident in the opening chapters of his treatise. His basic contention that the atonement is exclusively designed for the redemption of the elect is couched in the means–end terminology of Aristotle's metaphysics.[11] As far as he is concerned, there was one exclusive 'end' or purpose in the death of Christ. However, the set of concepts which he employs to establish his case 'end, means, moving cause, etc.) are derived not from the writers of the New Testament but from Aristotle. The philosopher's conception of teleology governs his understanding of the design of the atonement: 'The end of anything is that which the agent intendeth to accomplish in and by the operation which is proper unto its nature, and which applieth itself unto—that which any one aimeth at, and designeth in himself to attain, as a good thing and desirable unto him in the state and condition wherein he is.'[12] The concept of 'end' in this statement is fundamental to his thesis. It bears the same relationship to the subsequent exposition as Aristotle's similar statement does to the general argument of the *Nicomachean Ethics*,[13] a work Owen often refers to in his writings. A methodological parallel exists between Owen's *Death of Death* and Aristotle's *Ethics*. The philosopher's conception of teleology governs Owen's understanding of the atonement:

By the end of the death of Christ, we mean in general, both—first, that which his Father and himself intended in it; and secondly, that which was effectually fulfilled and accomplished by it . . . the end of Christ's obtaining grace and glory with his Father was, that they might be certainly bestowed upon all those for whom he died . . .[14]

The Legacy of Aristotle

Recent criticism of Aristotle's concept of a 'single end' is not without relevance to Owen. Indeed, it is doubtful whether the philosopher ever made coherent sense of the single, exclusive end. At times he argues that people govern their lives by reference to a single dominant end, while at others he argues for an inclusive end (other ends being embraced within the total plan of life).[15] In short, Aristotle's 'exclusive' theory cannot stand up before the data of human experience. This criticism of Aristotle has obvious application to Owen; it is questionable whether the New Testament account of the purpose of Christ's death is conceived in terms of a single, exclusive end.

Without denying that the chief purpose of the atonement is the salvation of the church, Owen cannot deny that the relevant New Testament passages use general rather than specific expressions. Even his textual citations prove this.[16] There is no text which exclusively limits the reference of God's love in Christ to the elect as such; indeed, it is proclaimed to the 'world' (John 3: 16, 2 Corinthians 5: 19, etc), even though texts like these are not immune from Owen's attempts to particularize them. Besides the ultimate end of the salvation of the elect, other, even 'thwarted', ends are accounted for in the total plan of God. In texts like John 1: 11, John 6: 32, and Luke 13: 34 (all of which Owen conveniently ignores), Christ is said to have come even for those who eventually rejected him. In short, his atoning death provided grace for a greater number than those who actually receive it. Governed as he was by Aristotle's notion of an exclusive end which must be realized, Owen was unable to grant this; he pleaded for the 'infallible efficacy'[17] of the atonement at the expense of significant textual data.

Owen's fear that the Arminian denial of God's sovereign choice might paralyse the atonement was understandable. The thought that the success of the gospel depended of human caprice was anathema to him. However, his response was needlessly excessive. After all, Calvin, Davenant, Amyraut, and Baxter never questioned the certain salvation of the elect when they affirmed a universal atonement. For the 'middle way' theologians, the atonement's design included general as well as special 'ends'. In other words, it was Aristotle rather than Paul who prevented Owen from saying, with Calvin, 'Although Christ suffered for the sins of the world, and is offered by the goodness of God without distinction to all men, yet not all receive him.'[18]

It seems, then, that Owen was governed more by Aristotelian than by Scriptural considerations. He actually imported alien philosophical criteria into his exposition of the gospel. His medieval-style references to Aristotle as 'the great philospher'[19] and 'the wise man'[20] are surprising. Indeed, when justifying the reality of devotion to Christ, why does he feel the need to quote 'the philosopher'?[21] For all his rhetoric, Baxter makes a valid criticism of 'great scholars in Aristotle's school': 'They that are so confident that Aristotle is in hell, should not too much take him for their guide in the way to heaven.'[22] Owen's early regard for Aristotle perhaps explains his inability to be thoroughly and exclusively scriptural. The words of Thomas Chalmers (1780–1847), written long after Aristotle had become *passé*, are certainly applicable to Owen and his generation:

> The middle age of science and civilisation is now terminated; but Christianity also had its middle age, and this, perhaps, is not yet fully terminated. There is still a remainder of the old spell, even the spell of human authority, and by which a certain cramp or confinement has been laid on the genius of Christianity.[23]

By Wesley's time the empiricist philosophers Locke, Berkeley, and Hume had all contributed to the dethronement of Aristotelian philosophy.[24] But as late as 1787 Wesley was prepared to admit that Aristotle possessed 'a universal genius'[25] and that his activities in the realm of natural history 'are to be commended'.[26] It was during the Middle Ages that 'Aristotle began to reign', and Wesley considered it 'the schoolmen's misfortune to neglect what was commendable in him, and to follow only what was blameworthy; so as to obscure and pollute all philosophy with abstract, idle, vain speculations'.[27] Needless to say, there is no trace of Aristotle's exclusive teleology in Wesley's sermon 'The end of Christ's coming.'[28] By appealing to such texts as John 1: 29 and Isaiah 53: 5, and also quoting from the Prayer Book, the Arminian Wesley simply announces 'biblically-revealed facts'.[29] In *Predestination Calmly Considered* he confidently affirms universal atonement in a manner Owen would have judged utterly simplistic: 'Now show me the scriptures wherein God declares in equally express terms, (1) 'Christ' did not die 'for all', but for some only. (2) Christ is not 'the propitiation for the sins of the whole world' . . . . Show me, I say, the scriptures that affirm these . . . things in equally express terms.

The Legacy of Aristotle

You know there are none'.[30] Wesley's method was therefore to utilize the perspicuity of Scripture. He believed he was safe in merely quoting the Bible, and he refused to theorize about self-evident truth: 'But the question is (the only question with me; I regard nothing else), What saith the Scripture? It says, "God was in Christ' reconciling the world unto himself . . ." '.[31]

In addition to the sermon and the tract, Wesley employed the medium of the popular hymn in his crusade against Calvinism.[32] The hymns of Methodism therefore constitute an important source for his thought. Although the vast majority of them were from the pen of Charles Wesley, Henry Bett is persuaded that the first of the *Hymns on God's Everlasting Love* (1741) is to be attributed to John.[33] The second verse of 'Father, whose everlasting love' is thoroughly explicit:

> Help us Thy mercy to extol,
>   Immense, unfathomed, unconfined;
> To praise the Lamb who died for all,
>   The general Saviour of mankind.[34]

Unlike other hymns of the period,[35] the hymns of the Wesleys were more than specimens of devotion. They were tools for doctrinal instruction, deliberately contrived to disseminate evangelical Arminianism. In so doing, John Wesley was not averse to stealing Calvinist terminology to make a very different point:

> Thy undistinguishing regard
>   Was cast on Adam's fallen race;
> For all Thou hast in Christ prepared
>   Sufficient, sovereign, saving grace.[36]

Although he did not entertain the thought that all would be saved, he basically contends that the immediate end of Christ's death is to make salvation possible to all. It is only efficacious to believers and, in true Arminian style, he insists that the divine decree preordains a general provision of grace without any predetermination of the number of the saved. In the final analysis the success of the gospel is rooted in the human response, for 'free grace' can never negate 'free will'.

Wesley's view of the freedom of the will has often been unjustly caricatured. However, his authentic teaching does contain paradoxical elements. On the one hand, he asserts that man in his natural sinful state 'is still in bondage and fear, by reason of sin . . . Such is the freedom of his will; free only to evil';[37] However, no man is any longer in his natural sinful state. As a result of common grace, Wesley insists, 'there is a measure of free-will supernaturally restored to every man.'[38] It is grace, therefore, which enables a person to respond to the gospel, not his mere unaided powers. Yet still the problem remains: does the efficacy of grace depend ultimately upon the God who is being gracious, or upon the individual's willing response to grace? In short, does God actually save men, or do men allow God to save them? Owen has no difficulty in assessing this type of argument: 'It is in our power to make the love of God and death of Christ effectual towards us or not.'[39]

Wesley is not afraid to admit the logic of his case, especially when he has the support of Scripture. Citing 2 Peter 3: 9 and John 5: 40, he declares that wilful rejection of Christ is the reason why some perish, not a reprobating will of God, 'If the oracles of God are true'.[40] However, Wesley does not seem to consider that the entire mission of grace might prove fruitless if left to the 'sovereign will of man'. Yet he confidently writes:

> A world He suffered to redeem;
>   For all He hath th'atonement made:
>   For those that will not come to Him,
>   The ransom of His life was paid.[41]

For Owen the consequences of the Arminian thesis are unthinkable; a hypothetical redemption is no redemption at all. The reason why all are not saved is that all are not redeemed. Christ's redemption is necessarily certain and assured. Therefore 'it cannot possibly be conceived to be universal unless all be saved'.[42] But if Wesley propounds a general atonement guaranteeing no acceptance, Owen argues for a limited atonement permitting no rejection; such is the logic of their respective positions. However, in reality Wesley knew many who embraced Christ, and Owen knew many who did not. Although Wesley's account appears to square with the textual evidence, he fails to allow for any effectual divine purpose which does not ultimately hinge upon the will of man. Alternatively, Owen's 'one end' conception of the atonement cannot make sense of the sin of unbelief. If unbelievers are guilty of rejecting Christ, whence their guilt, if Christ was not given for them? It is arguable, therefore, that Owen's Aristotelian theorizing and

Wesley's total reluctance to theorize lead alike to anomalous conclusions, neither of which are scriptural.

The position of Richard Baxter commends itself immediately as a view which attempts to synthesize the scriptural elements within high Calvinism and Arminianism. Against Owen, Baxter argued that there was more than one 'end' to the death of Christ; against Wesley, he would contend for an effectual purpose within God's dealings with mankind. Baxter considers that the biblical teaching demands an account which takes note of the universal and particular dimension of the atonement: 'The Father giveth up to Christ as Redeemer the whole lapsed cursed reparable world, (the several parts to several uses) and especially his chosen to be eventually and infallibly saved . . .'[43] In contrast with Owen's exclusive particularism, Baxter insists that the total character of the gospel demands a much broader scenario than Owen allows:

Christ's sacrifice for sin, and his perfect holiness, are so far satisfactory and meritorious for all men, as they render Christ a meet object for that faith in him which is commanded men, and no man shall be damned for want of a Saviour to die for him, and fulfil all righteousness, but only for the abusing or refusing of his mercy.[44]

Wesley would not quarrel with this statement as such. However, without granting every deterministic connotation of Owen's view, Baxter rejects the Arminian thesis that the ultimate success of the gospel is in human hands. Baxter refuses to theorize at the expense of paradox; in his view both Owen and Wesley 'explain away' the textual evidence in the interests of their respective theories. Against Owen's view, Baxter insists that the gospel is presented in the Bible as a 'conditional deed of gift to all the world';[45] against Wesley's view, he maintains that 'Christ . . . died for all, but not for all equally, or with the same intent, design or purpose'.[46] In short, divine predestination ensures that the elect embrace a salvation offered to all.

Needless to say, neither Owen nor Wesley would find Baxter's solution acceptable, albeit for very different reasons. However, notwithstanding the frustrations of submitting to the full range of textual data, Baxter believes that his account does justice to what is demonstrably Scriptural in the two opposing views. He rejects Owen's charge that 'Christ shed his blood in vain' if all are not saved. On the contrary, there are 'other ends' in the atonement beside the certain salvation of the elect; for instance, the universal blessings of providence are rooted in the atonement; that Christ is actually offered to all the world is another end fulfilled; lastly, Christ's provision of grace for all mankind is the basis on which ingratitude is judged. The position emerges clearly: Owen believes that grace is special to the elect alone; Wesley says it is common to all men. Baxter replies that, rightly understood, grace is both common and special. He insists that 'many sincere Christians' are mistaken to 'judge them inconsistent'.[47] Thus he sought to perpetuate the very kind of dualistic soteriology taught by Calvin and others in the sixteenth-century.

As for Owen's doctrine of grace, there is clearly a necessary connection between a limited atonement and a limited provision of grace. The exclusive 'end' of the death of Christ is to supply grace for the elect alone. This is the major thesis of the *Death of Death*, and it is stated repeatedly.[48] Grace, therefore, can only be special grace by definition; common grace finds no place, logically speaking, in Owen's system. It is all the more surprising, therefore, to discover that he does adopt a distinction between common and special grace, very much in the style of Baxter. Although there is little more than a hint of this in the *Death of Death*,[49] it is surprisingly conspicuous elsewhere. This very fact poses serious difficulties for the overall coherency of his theology of atonement and grace.

What is very uncharacteristic of the argument in the *Death of Death* is unexpectedly clear in *A Display of Arminianism*, published just five years earlier:

Concerning grace itself, it is either common or special. Common or general grace consisteth in the external revelation of the will of God by His word, with some illumination of the mind to perceive it, and correction of the affections not too much to condemn it, and this, in some degree or other, to some more, to some less, is common to all that are called. Special grace is the grace of regeneration, comprehending the former, adding more spiritual acts, but specially presupposing the purpose of God, on which its efficacy doth chiefly depend.[50]

It seems that the overwhelming logic of the *Death of Death* obscured Owen's doctrine of common grace only temporarily, for it reappears in later works. In *The Doctrine of the Saints' Perseverance* (1654) we read that 'There is an inferior, *common* work of the Holy

The Legacy of Aristotle

Ghost'.[51] In *A Discourse Concerning the Holy Spirit* (1674) we learn that 'even *common* illumination and conviction of sin have, in their own nature, a tendency unto sincere conversion'.[52] Both of these later statements reflect the 1643 view. If they express Owen's settled conviction, how can he possibly reconcile common grace with limited atonement? Furthermore, what is the origin of common grace and the basis of its provision? Owen himself answers these questions in his treatise on the Holy Spirit: 'All grace is orginally intrusted in and with Jesus Christ . . .'[53] Are we to understand that Christ has purchased common as well as special grace? The implication is clear: there is a procurement of grace which is broader than the thesis of the *Death of Death* will allow.

The anomaly is obvious. For Baxter, his doctrine of common grace correlates with his view of universal atonement. If Owen wishes to maintain such a view of grace, he cannot escape Baxter's view of the atonement; if the latter course is unthinkable, then he must discard his theory of common grace. Furthermore, if any criticism of the common–special grace distinction is to be levelled against Baxter, then it must also be applied to Owen. Indeed, the entire orthodox Puritan movement acquiesced in the distinction,[54] and there is evidence that Calvin employed it too.[55]

Calvinists are far from unanimous over the function and significance of common grace. It tends to be confined to the realm of providence rather than salvation.[56] However, Louis Berkhof, a twentieth-century Calvinist theologian, appears to make an important concession when he says that common grace 'does not effect the salvation of the sinner, *though . . . it may . . . have a soteriological aspect*'(emphases added).[57] Despite this observation, he is very anxious to distinguish such a view from that of the Arminians, who regarded common grace as a link in the *ordo salutis* and ascribe to it saving significance.

Returning to Owen and Baxter, it is clear that for both men common grace does possess redemptive, and not merely providential, connotations. Like Baxter, who argues that it helps men 'nearer to salvation',[58] Owen maintains that common grace has 'a tendency unto sincere conversion'.[59] In other words, common grace serves as an introduction to special grace. Like Baxter, Owen believes that when 'wilfulness and stubborness' prevent men from co-operating with the influences of common grace, only 'sovereign grace' (i.e. special grace designed for the elect alone) removes the innate resistance to the Holy Spirit.[60] In other words Owens' overall teaching involves him in a contradiction with serious consequences for his doctrine of a limited procurement of grace. In short, he is obliged either to adopt a view of the atonement hardly distinguishable from Baxter's, or to renounce his view of common grace.

If Owen wishes to retain his view of common grace, then it must affect his view of the atonement. His 'one-end' Aristotelian teleology is thus an embarrassment. More than the eventual salvation of the elect was comprehended in the death of Christ, as Baxter declares: 'Whatever good Christ giveth to any, that he from eternity decreed to give them. But we are agreed that he giveth not salvation to all men, and yet he doth give many and great mercies to all men.'[61]

If the atonement is not the meritorious source of common as well as special grace, then all those theologians from Calvin onwards who speak of common grace in soteriological terms cannot do so without adopting a broader view of the atonement than Owen allows. In this respect Calvin and Baxter are consistent. The absurd alternative is to say (in Baxter's words) that 'God giveth it to one part of men for Christ's death, and to the other part *not for his death*, but as *without it*'.[62] Unless one is to deny that providence is part of God's gracious activity, even confining common grace to providence demands a broader view of Christ's death than Owen grants.[63]

As has been noted, the other course open to Owen was to renounce his view of common grace altogether in favour of the narrow thesis of the *Death of Death*. It is surely significant that those who embraced Owen's particularism in later years did precisely this. In the transition from the 'high Calvinism' of Owen to the 'hyper' Calvinism[64] of Dr John Gill (1696–1771),[65] the eminent Particular Baptist theologian, the concept of common grace was rejected. Whereas Owen taught the distinction between 'common' and 'special' operations of the Holy Spirit, Gill denied the former, even with reference to those 'who enjoy the outward ministry of the word'. God 'does not vouchsafe his Spirit to convince of sin' those who are not chosen to salvation. If people are chosen, God 'calls them effectually by his grace'.[66] Given the exclusive thesis of Owen's *Death of Death*, Gill is arguably more consistent than Owen in rejecting a wider conception of grace than it logically allows. If Owen wishes to retain common grace, he must adopt Baxter's view;

The Legacy of Aristotle

if he wishes to maintain a limited atonement, he must agree with Gill.

As the true heir of Calvin's theology of the atonement, Baxter is able to identify with what is demonstrably scriptural in the otherwise opposing views of Owen and Wesley. He agrees with Owen's emphasis on divine election, and with Wesley's on universal atonement. However, faced with the paradoxical character of the biblical data, the 'dualistic' Baxter[67] had no sympathy either with the scholastic exaggerations of Owen or with the simplistic generalizations of Wesley. In the next chapter, attention is focused on some of the remaining doctrinal dilemmas confronting our theologians.

NOTES

1. Luther's lectures on the Psalms (1513–14) suggest that 'the discovery of Augustine was associated with a growing repugnance for Aristotle' (V. H. H. Green, *Luther and the Reformation* (London, 1964), 48). In his *Annotations on the New Testament* (1519) he complained that 'Aristotle is so in vogue that there is scarcely time in the churches to interpret the gospel' (cited in R. Bainton, *Here I Stand* (New York, 1950), 126; see also B. A. Gerrish, *Grace and Reason: A Study in the Theology of Luther* (Oxford, 1962), *passsim*).
2. *Inst.* I. xv. 8.
3. T. Lane, 'The quest for the historical Calvin', *EQ* 55. 2 (1983), at pp. 97 ff.
4. Although Calvin discusses the doctrine of the trinity using the traditional scholastic terms 'substance', 'hypostasis', etc., he is sensitive to the objection that such terms are foreign to the Scriptures. He wishes 'that such names were buried, provided all would concur in the belief that the Father, Son, and Spirit, are one God.... I am not so minutely precise as to fight furiously for mere words' (*Inst.* I. xiii. 5; I. McPhee, 'Conserver or transformer of Calvin's theology? A study in the origins and development of Theodore Beza's thought, 1550–1570, Ph.D. thesis (Cambridge, 1979), 354).
5. Lane, 'Quest', p. 98. Calvin warns against 'frigid speculations' in the early chapters of the *Institutes* (I. ii. 3). He argues that the textual data demands a two-sided perception of the will of God: secret and revealed. '... while in himself the will is one and undivided, to us it appears manifold, because, from the feebleness of our intellect, we cannot apprehend how, though after a different manner, he wills and

wills not the very same thing' (I. xviii. 3). Therefore 'Our true wisdom is to embrace with meek docility, and without reservation, whatever the Holy Scriptures have delivered' (I. xviii. 4).

6. B. G. Armstrong, *Calvinism and the Amyraut Heresy: Protestant Scholasticism and Humanism in Seventeenth-century France* (Madison, Wisc., 1969), 38 ff. and 127 ff.; McGrath, *The Intellectual Origins*, 191–6; McPhee, 'Conserver or transformer?', pp. 354 ff.

7. Latimer's changed attitude parallels Luther's rejection of Aristotle; he 'began to smell the Word of God and forsook the school-doctors and such fooleries' (R. Demaus, *Hugh Latimer* (London, 1903), 49, also 28–9). Thomas Hobbes (1588–1679) had his own reasons for spurning the 'vain and erroneous philosophy of the Greeks, especially of Aristotle' (*Leviathan* (London, 1965), 332); but the Puritan John Preston (1587–1628) regarded Aristotle as his 'tutelary saint' (R. T. Kendall, *Calvin and English Calvinism to 1649* (Oxford, 1979), 117). Another Puritan, John Flavel (1628–91), a near contemporary of Owen, actually accuses 'the schools of Epicurus, Aristotle and the Cartesians' of having 'troubled the world with a kind of philosophical enthusiasm'; yet he is prepared to admit that 'the helps philosophy affords in some parts of this discourse are too great to be despised .... The quality of the subject necessitates, in many places, the use of scholastic terms, which will be obscure to the vulgar reader ...' ('Pneumatologia: a treatise on the soul of man', *The Works of John Flavel* (London, 1820; fac. London, 1968), ii. 485–8). On the Continent a similar change of attitude was also evident; The philosopher G. W. Leibniz (1646–1716) sought to 'rehabilitate in some sort the ancient philosophy'. It is his view that 'our moderns do less than justice to St Thomas [i.e. Aquinas] and to other great men of that time and that their sentiments are much sounder than is imagined' (*Discourse on Metaphysics*, trans. P. G. Lucas and L. Grint (Manchester, 1953), 17. See also W. S. Howell, *Logic and Rhetoric in England 1500–1700* (Princeton, NJ, 1956), *passim*.

8. In 'Animadversions on a treatise entitled *Fiat Lux*' (1662) Owen complained that too many 'theological determinations ... are not delivered in the words that the Spirit of God teacheth, but in terms of art, and in answer to rules and notions' deriving from Aristotle (*Works*, xiv. 315). In 1677 he argued that the entire body of Roman Catholic theology was based on 'such terms, distinctions and expressions, as are so far from being in the Scripture', and that such would never have been introduced 'had they escaped Aristotle's mint, or that of the schools deriving from him' (*JF* 55–6).

9. Burnet wrote of Baxter, 'He had a very moving and pathetical way of writing, and was his whole life long a man of great zeal and much simplicity, but he was most unhappily subtle and metaphysical in

everything' (cited in G. P. Fisher, *The History of the Christian Church* (London, 1904), 433).
10. A simplified outline of Owen's treatise reveals the following: (1) Books I and II are concerned with the divinely appointed 'end' or purpose of the death of Christ; (2) Book III discusses the nature of the atonement in the light of this 'end'; the terms 'redemption', 'reconciliation', 'satisfaction', and 'propitiation' are expounded accordingly; (3) Book IV expounds the biblical texts relating to the extent of the atonement, to demonstrate that by design and nature the atonement is limited to the elect. The entire treatise assumes the validity of the following syllogism: (major premiss) the atonement provides an effectual salvation; (minor premiss) the elect are effectually saved; (conclusion) the atonement is designed for the elect alone.
11. Owen writes of end, means, and cause in traditional scholastic fashion; see Aristotle, *Metaphysics*, trans. J. Warrington (London, 1956), 4.
12. *DD* 160.
13. 'It is thought that every activity, artistic or scientific, in fact, every deliberate action or pursuit has for its object the attainment of some good. We may therefore assent to the view which has been expressed that "the good" is "that at which all things aim".' (*The Ethics of Aristotle*, trans. J. A. K. Thompson (London, 1953), 25).
14. *DD* 157; 203.
15. W. F. R. Hardie observes that 'Aristotle sometimes, when he speaks of the final end, seems to be fumbling for the idea of an inclusive end, or comprehensive plan' ('The final good in Aristotle's Ethics', in *Aristotle: A Collection of Critical Essays*, ed. J. M. E. Moravcsik (London, 1968), 297 ff.). In Owen's case, this is not to question his valid admission of constituent 'sub-ends' within the 'end' of the atonement (see *DD* 162), but to reject his thesis of a single, exclusive end.
16. e.g. 'the Son of man came to save that which was lost' (Matt. 18: 11); 'Christ Jesus came into the world to save sinners' (1 Tim. 1: 15); he came to 'give his life a ransom for many' (Matt. 20: 28). See *DD* 157.
17. *Dis. A.* 135.
18. *Comm. Rom.* 5: 18.
19. *Works*, ii. 8.
20. *Works*, xii. 113.
21. *Works*, ii. 343; also xii. 112.
22. *The Reformed Pastor* (London, 1974), 120.
23. *Institutes of Theology* (Edinburgh, 1849), ii. 404.
24. See John Locke (1632–1704), *An Essay Concerning Human Understanding*, ed. A. D. Woosley (London, 1964), IV. xvii. 4 (pp. 416 ff.), for a critique of Aristotelian logic; see George Berkeley (1685–1753), *The Principles of Human Knowledge* ed. G. J. Warnock (London,

1962), I. xi (p. 70), for a rejection of Aristotle's theory of matter. In his *Enquiry Concerning Human Understanding* I. 4 in *Enquiries*, ed. L. A. Selby-Bigge (2nd edn., Oxford, 1902), p. 7, David Hume (1711–76) writes, 'The fame ... of Aristotle is utterly decayed'.
25. *Journal*, vii. 340.
26. *Works*, xiii. 455.
27. Ibid. In his remarks on Locke's *Essay*, Wesley agrees with his empiricism, but he considers that 'The operations of the mind are more accurately divided by Aristotle than by Mr Locke' (ibid. 429).
28. *Works*, vi. 251 ff.
29. A. Skevington Wood, *The Burning Heart: John Wesley, Evangelist* (London, 1967), 237.
30. *PCC* 217.
31. *Letters*, vi. 298. Wesley may be regarded as typically 'latitudinarian' at this point. Tillotson warned against departing from the 'clear and plain' sense of the Bible (*TW* i. 436–7).
32. '... the hymns were the great weapons of this warfare. Forcible, earnest and ingenious, they admitted of no easy reply'. They were 'a treasure of great price' to those who wished to follow the Bible, rather than discuss the issues by 'metaphysical reasoning' (*The Poetical Works of John and Charles Wesley*, ed. G. Osborne (London, 1869), vol. iii. pp. xvi; xx).
33. H. Bett, *The Hymns of Methodism* (London, 1945), 26 ff.
34. *MHB* (1933), 75: 2. Bernard, Lord Manning, writes: 'Notice the stab at debased Calvinism in every line' (*The Hymns of Wesley and Watts* (London, 1942), 18).
35. E. Routley has written that 'you will search the hymns of Doddridge in vain for any clue to the minutiae of his theology' ('The hymns of Philip Doddridge', in *Philip Doddridge (1702–1751): His Contribution to English Religion*, ed. G. F. Nuttall (London, 1951), 68). Although Routley describes the 'tone quality' of Doddridge's hymns as 'Calvinistic', one cannot fail to see the perspicuous Arminianism of the Wesleys' hymns.
36. *MHB* (1933), 75: 3.
37. *Works*, v. 97.
38. *PCC* 221. See the Wesleyan theologian Richard Watson's view of the link between common grace and free will, in his *Theological Institutes* (1850), ii. 267; 364; 436.
39. *DD* 253.
40. *Works*, vii. 364.
41. *MHB* (1933), 75: 4.
42. *DD* 261.
43. *CT* I. ii. 38.
44. Ibid. 51.
45. Ibid. 53.

46. Ibid.
47. Ibid.
48. *DD* 159; 202; 287; 288; 383.
49. 'The fruits of Christ's mediation have been distinguished by some into those that are more general and those which are more peculiar, which, in some sense, may be tolerable; . . . there are . . . common gifts of light and knowledge, which Christ hath purchased for many for whom he did not make his soul a ransom' (*DD* 189; 362).
50. *Dis. A.* 134.
51. *Works*, xi. 640 (emphasis mine).
52. *Works*, iii. 236 (emphasis mine).
53. *Ibid.* 414.
54. The Westminster Confession is careful to distinguish between 'special grace' and the 'common operations of the Spirit' (ch. X. ii; iv). The Savoy Declaration (1658) and the Baptist Confession of Faith (1689) follow the same wording. The expression 'common operations of the Spirit' also appears in question 68 of the Larger Catechism. It seems there was some reluctance to speak of 'common grace', but during the debate on the Catechism 'common favours' was the wording used in the first draft (A. F. Mitchell and J. Struthers (eds.), *Minutes of the Sessions of the Westminster Assembly of Divines* (London, 1874), pp. lix, 369. There is clear ambiguity here. The acknowledgement of 'special grace' implies a variant of grace which is not special, i.e. common, and both the Confession (ch. VII. iii) and the Larger Catechism (q. 68) speak of 'Christ' and 'grace' respectively being offered to all. The Assembly probably felt uneasy over the concept of 'common grace' in view of its statement on the atonement (ch. VIII). To have used it might have been seen as a concession to the Amyraldians, whose view was seemingly rejected (Baxter's evidence notwithstanding). As it is, the Westminster standards cannot be said to proscribe the idea of common grace.
55. W. Cunningham was wrong to deny that Calvin taught a doctrine of common grace (*The Reformers and the Theology of the Reformation* (London, 1862; fac. London, 1967), 398). Calvin clearly accepted the common/special grace distinction, as a corollary to his doctrine of the atonement. 'Paul makes grace *common* to all men, not because it in fact extends to all, but because it is offered to all' (*Comm.* Rom. 5: 18); 'Therefore it was a wonderful thing when he poured out his grace upon all men in *common* . . . beyond the expectation of all men, salvation was offered to all nations' (*Sermons on the Epistle to the Ephesians*, trans. A. Golding, rev. L. Rawlinson and S. M. Houghton (Edinburgh, 1973), 57). Calvin describes faith as 'a *special* grace of God' (ibid. 146). Elsewhere he says that 'unless we are by *special* grace called to be sharers of the fruit of the death and passion of the Son of God, it will be useless to us' (*Sermons on the Saving Work of Christ*, trans. L. Nixon

(Grand Rapids, Mich., 1980), 100). Lastly, there is 'the *special* grace which the elect alone receive through regeneration' (*Inst.* II. ii. 6).
56. Calvinists of the Dutch school take this view. See A. Kuyper, *De gemeene gratie* (Leiden, 1902); H. Bavinck, 'Calvin and common grace', in Calvin and the Reformation (New York, 1909); H. Kuiper, *Calvin on Common Grace* (Goes, Holland, 1928). L. Berkhof states incorrectly that C.'s doctrine of common grace has no direct relationship with salvation (*Systematic Theology* (London, 1963), 434).
57. Ibid. 436.
58. *CT* II. 145.
59. *Works*, iii. 236.
60. Ibid. 236–7.
61. *EC* 160.
62. Ibid.
63. This point is cautiously granted by R. B. Kuiper, *For Whom Did Christ Die?* (Grand Rapids, Mich., 1982), 81–4.
64. Although the prefixes ('high' from Old English; 'hyper-' from the Greek) are both used to signify some form of 'exaggeration', their different uses facilitate an important distinction. 'High Calvinism' refers to a belief in limited atonement accompanied by the preaching of universal offers of grace; 'hypercalvinism' denotes a more pronounced stress on limited atonement to the exclusion of the 'free offer'. See G. F. Nuttall, 'Northamptonshire and the *Modern Question*', *JTS*, n.s. 16 (1965), at p. 101.
65. For Gill see *DNB*; M. R. Watts, *The Dissenters* (Oxford, 1978), 456 ff. See also Daniel, 'John Gill and Hypercalvinism', Ph.D. thesis (Edinburgh, 1983); R. E. Seymour, 'John Gill, Baptist theologian (1697–1771)', Ph.D. thesis (Edinburgh, 1954); O. C. Robison, 'The legacy of John Gill, *BQ* 24 (1971), 111–25; A. P. F. Sell, *The Great Debate* (Worthing, 1982), 76 ff.; K. Dix, 'Particular Baptists and Strict Baptists: an historical survey', *BSB* 13 (1976), 2–4.
66. J. Gill *A Collection of Sermons and Tracts* (London, 1773), ii. 123.
67. Baxter's soteriological dualism, i.e. his frequent use of the common–special and general–particular distinctions, raises the question of the influence of the bifurcated logic of the Ramists. Although Ramism had ousted Aristotelian logic at the Saumur Academy, Amyraut never seems to quote Ramus in his writings; the same seems to be true of Baxter. For Pierre de la Ramée (d. 1572) see Armstrong, *Calvinism*, pp. 37 ff.; 125 ff.; W. J. Ong, *Ramus, Method and the Decay of Dialogue* (Cambridge, Mass., 1958), *passim*; K. L. Sprunger, 'Ames, Ramus, and the method of Puritan theology', *Harvard Theological Review*, 50. 2 (1966), 133 ff.; Kendall, *Calvin*, p. 141. It is not denied that Aristotle was still quoted at the Saumur Academy in 'matters of common sense' (Armstrong, p. 46).

7
Doctrinal Dilemmas

It would seem that Owen and Wesley occupied their theological positions in the interests of strict logical consistency. As if to admit that Baxter's *via media* was a highly precarious tightrope exercise, they were not prepared to tolerate paradox in the way he did. They both tended to suppress or 'modify' textual data which seemed inconsistent with their respective theses. This is not to pretend that Baxter's synthesis was free from difficulty; but we must acknowledge his belief that the gospel should be accepted as it is revealed. He refused to allow the deductive process to eliminate paradox from the 'given' character of the scriptural data. There is definite evidence that neither Owen nor Wesley could sustain their more extreme viewpoints without avoiding serious doctrinal dilemmas. Furthermore, there is evidence that such dilemmas forced them to grant the kind of concessions Baxter repeatedly argued for. This emerges particularly in Owen's treatment of the sin of unbelief and Wesley's discussion of grace.

Under the influence of Aristotle's teleology and the commercial theory of the atonement, Owen proposes a 'dilemma to our universalists' in a powerful piece of reasoning. After stating that there was a qualitative[1] and quantitative[2] 'sameness' in the sufferings of Christ and the eternal punishment threatening those for whom he died, Owen affirms, 'God imposed his wrath due unto, and Christ underwent the pains of hell for, either all the sins of all men, or all the sins of some men, or some of the sins of all men'.[3] This is Owen's famous 'triple choice' proposition, which, in his view, conclusively settles the controversy in favour of a limited atonement. The last choice is quickly ruled out: if the atonement fails to deal with all sins, then the sinner has something to answer for. The first choice invites Owen's question, 'Why, then, are not all freed from the punishment of all their sins?'[4] He therefore concludes that the second choice alone fits the case; the atonement is exclusively related to 'all the sins of some men'.

Owen anticipates the universalist objection that men are only lost through an unbelieving rejection of the atonement. He asks:

But this unbelief, is it a sin or not: If not, why should they be punished for it? If it be, then Christ underwent the punishment due to it, or not. If so, then why must that hinder them more than their other sins for which he died from partaking of the fruit of his death?. If he did not, then did he not die for all their sins.[5]

For all its apparent cogency, this compelling argument raises some important problems. It is clear that unbelievers are guilty of rejecting nothing if Christ was not given for them; unbelief surely involves the rejection of a definite provision of grace. It also makes nonsense of the means of grace, depriving general exhortations to believe of all significance.[6]

A further objection arises from an unexpected quarter. In Owen's view the sufferings of Christ not only deal with the guilt of the believer's pre-conversion unbelief, they are causally related to the *removal* of unbelief. But Owen's pastoral experience taught him that even true believers—or those who have grounds to regard themselves as elect—continue to be plagued with unbelief.[7] Should this be the case if Christ had died to purchase faith for them, or are they perhaps deceived? Owen certainly denies that lapses of unbelief in the elect are not sinful if Christ has paid the penalty for them. Neither would he question the fact that doubting believers fail to participate fully in the subjective blessings Christ's death has purchased for them. In other words, his argument applies as much to supposed believers as it does to unbelievers, with interesting consequences. For if partial unbelief in a Christian hinders him from enjoying the fullness of those blessings Christ has died to purchase for him, this is no different in principle from saying that total unbelief in a non-Christian hinders him from 'partaking of the fruit' Christ's death makes available for him too.

Basic to Owen's argument is his theory of the nature of the atonement, which will be discussed in the next chapter. Suffice it to say that making the sufferings of Christ commensurate with the sins of the elect in a quantitative, commercialistic sense explains and reinforces his teleology of the atonement. This was the consideration which led him to modify the sufficiency–efficiency distinction. His apparent acceptance of it is really little more than lip-service; his deliberate redefinition of it means that the atonement is only

Doctrinal Dilemmas

sufficient for those for whom it is efficient.[8] In other words, if the atonement is strictly limited, then the 'credit facilities' of the gospel are only available to the elect.

This prevented Owen from seeing that there was an alternative way of dealing with his 'triple choice' challenge. For earlier generations of Calvinists the solution was a simple one. Viewing the sufficiency of the atonement in terms of a universal provision of grace, they would embrace the first choice (all the sins of all men) with respect to the atonement's sufficiency, and the second (all the sins of some men) with respect to its efficiency. As an earlier chapter has demonstrated, the sixteenth-century Reformers taught—both in their writings and in their confessions of the faith—that the atonement was relevant and applicable to all, though it was applied only to the elect. This much is clear: Calvin and his companions believed that the sufferings of Christ were related to the sins of the whole world;[9] men are lost, not for lack of atonement, but for not believing.[10] Unlike Owen, the Reformers had little difficulty in establishing the basis of human guilt. While guilt is undoubtedly defined in terms of transgressing the law, a very significant component of it arises from ungrateful neglect of the gospel remedy.[11] But on Owen's account, if the atonement relates only to the sins of the elect, then it is doubtful justice to condemn anyone for rejecting what was never applicable to them.

Owen's acceptance of common grace is surely in conflict with his view of the atonement's sufficiency, for it implies a broader view than his narrower theory will allow. As a corollary, his acceptance of the 'free offer' of the gospel is embarrassed by his strict commercialist position. He does indeed assert that the gospel is to be preached 'to every creature' because 'the way of salvation which it declares is wide enough for all to walk in'.[12] But how can this be if the atonement is really only sufficient for the elect? Calvin and his colleagues had no difficulty in speaking like this, but Owen cannot consistently do so. Not surprisingly, Gill and his fellow hypercalvinists employed the very kind of commercialism espoused by Owen, but did so to deny the validity of universal offers of grace.[13]

It is hardly surprising that Owen's conception of the 'free offer' is very different from those of Calvin and the Amyraldians. He denies that knowledge of a universal atonement is necessary for someone to come to Christ; in his view the gospel offer merely declares the duty of sinners to believe.[14] Thus the preaching of the gospel is a command to make bricks without straw. While there is definite New Testament evidence for urging the duty of sinners to repent and believe (Acts 17: 30; Romans 1: 5; 16: 26; 2 Thessalonians 1: 8; 1 John 3: 23), this is only half the story. Once the guilty sinner is informed of his duty to repent, the knowledge that Christ has died for him provides encouragement to believe. But Owen's view precludes this.

Since Owen does assert the reality of common grace, he cannot consistently invalidate the true sense of the free offer, with its suggestion of 'conditional credit'. Yet Owen was opposed to Arminianism *and* to Amyraldianism, otherwise known as hypothetical universalism or the 'conditional system'. W. H. Gould writes that Owen 'dwells with peculiar keenness and reiteration of statement upon a refutation of the conditional system'.[15] Now Owen does not object to the language of conditions as such; he rejects the idea that grace is offered on certain conditions. In his Aristotelian view, both the end (salvation) and the means (faith) for the attainment of the end are obtained for the elect alone. A necessary connection therefore exists between end and means;[16] in which case a conditional salvation for all must surely imply the eventual salvation of all. Grace to perform the conditions of salvation has been procured only for those for whom salvation itself was intended. Therefore Christ did not die for all, since they do not in fact perform the conditions.[17]

It is certain that Wesley did not grasp the implications of Owen's type of argument. However, it did receive his attention when he was asked to comment on a tract published in Bristol in 1758. Like Owen before him, the author argued that 'the gospel is a revelation of grace and mercy, not a proposal of convenant of terms and conditions . . .'[18] Using the simple analogy of a man stretching out his hand to receive a gift of money, Wesley still considered it consistent to say, 'We are justified freely by grace, and yet upon certain terms or conditions'.[19] But his analogy is entirely inappropriate; the ability to stretch out the hand is not dependent on the offered gift. Owen's argument is that the ability to receive salvation, as well as salvation itself, are both procured by Christ; the ability to receive Christ is part of the total donation of grace. In short (as Owen would say to Wesley), all but the elect are impotent or paralysed, and therefore unable to 'stretch out their hands' to grasp salvation. Christ has only purchased faith for the elect.[20]

To be fair to Wesley, Owen's argument makes salvation sound more like an imposition than a gift freely given. If there is a direct, causal connection between the atonement and the gift of faith, then the process of salvation seems as rigidly deterministic as any event in the physical world. Predictably, Wesley rejects Owen's thesis; otherwise, a man is no more 'than a tree or a stone'.[21] How then, Wesley would surely ask, can one avoid the idea that God fulfils 'his glorious promises' as if 'he had forced you to believe? And this he could not do, without destroying the nature which he had given you: for he made you free agents . . .'[22]

Owen would say that Wesley caricatures the Calvinist conception of grace. But arguing a necessary connection between the atonement and faith argues the very overtones of irresistibility Owen was also at pains to avoid. Indeed, contrary to their traditional image, neither the divines of Dort[23] nor Owen himself[24] were happy with the phrase 'irresistible grace'; they preferred 'efficacious grace'. The difference may be more terminological than real, but it does signify Owen's concern to meet Wesley's type of criticism. It was in fact the hypercalvinism of John Gill[25] that helped to bring Calvinistic phraseology into line with the initials of the popular mnemonic TULIP.

It was Richard Baxter who gave a more considered reply to Owen's view. After noting that the statement 'Christ died to purchase the act of faith for us' is 'no scripture-phrase so far as I know', he puts the issue in a more satisfactory light:

It must be considered that Christ did not die to purchase faith as immediately, and on the same account, as to satisfy for sin, and purchase us impunity or redemption. The proper direct reason of his sufferings, was to demonstrate the justice of God against sin . . . and thereby to procure pardon. We may well conceive Christ promising to the Father, as it were, (I will suffer for sinners, that they may not suffer). But you will hardly describe his undertaking thus, (I will die, if thou wilt give men faith) or (I will give thee so much of my blood for so much faith.).[26]

However, Baxter does not deny that the gift of faith is rooted in the atonement; it is so indirectly and through the instrumentality of the means of grace. In other words, it is through preaching and the blessing of the Holy Spirit that 'Christ causeth sinners to believe: so that faith is a fruit of the death of Christ in a remoter secondary sense'.[27]

This issue is closely related to the common–special grace

distinction. For as both Baxter and Owen allow, the 'free offer' of Christ is the subject matter of the means of grace, implying that the general display of grace is broader than its actual reception by the elect. However, it has been noted that Owen's doctrine of common grace sits uneasily with his major thesis in the *Death of Death*, and that to be consistent he must either discard his view of common grace or embrace a view of the atonement hardly distinguishable from Baxter's. This dilemma also has important implications for Owen's rejection of the 'conditional system'.

In the light of Owen's 'common grace' teaching, it may be asked, how incapable is the unbeliever of fulfilling the conditions of the gospel? Unlike John Gill and his hypercalvinist associates of the eighteenth-century, Owen did not discard the 'free offer', although he is arguably inconsistent and somewhat ill at ease with the idea.[28] Now Gill rejected the 'free offer' along with common grace because they jointly imply an ability to respond to the gospel which only comes from special or irresistible grace. This makes Owen's view of common grace all the more interesting. He argues very clearly that when 'common' influences of the Holy Spirit do not bring someone to faith, it is because 'they do not sincerely improve what they have received'. Full conversion is prevented 'not merely for want of strength to proceed, but, by a free act of their wills, they refuse the grace which is further tendered unto them in the gospel'.[29]

Under the influences of the means of grace, it is obvious that all possess some capability to 'proceed' towards fulfilling the conditions of the gospel. The issue is not one of ability, but of wilful non-compliance.[30] Owen declares that 'the common work of the Holy Ghost' causes 'a great alteration as to light, knowledge, abilities . . .' in many to whom the gospel is preached.[31] Even 'common illumination and conviction of sin have . . . a tendency unto sincere conversion'.[32] Therefore, if he admits common grace into his scheme, he cannot consistently reject the 'conditional system'. In short, if anyone 'sincerely improves what they have received', salvation will result. Then, without calling into question the influence of sovereign, efficacious grace, Owen can answer Wesley's charge that to punish the unbeliever without granting him some grace is unjust. The conclusion is clear: Owens' recognition of the 'free offer', his belief in common grace, and his concessions concerning the abilities of unbelievers all challenge the narrower thesis of the *Death of Death* in favour of Baxter's position.

Needless to say, Owen's strict particularism reflects a departure from the earlier Calvinist conception of the covenant of grace. Davenant's view that the universal gospel offer implies a covenant with all mankind is rejected by Owen. The covenant 'was not made universally with all, but particularly only with some'.[33] It is not, therefore, a conditional contract between God and man, since it consists of benefits 'absolutely promised' to the elect alone. But the key biblical texts[34] expounded by Owen reveal a declaration of intent on God's part, rather than a description of the terms of the covenant itself. In this respect, even Baxter admits, 'Predestination is well proved' from the texts in question.[35] However, Owen is adamant: 'for who dares affirm that God entered into a covenant of grace with the seed of the serpent?[36] To which Baxter replies: 'If you mean foreseen final enemies and unbelievers, Christ did not die for them as such, but as in their antecedent, recoverable, pardonable sin and misery.'[37]

The facts are clear: Owen's position is beset by incoherence. Common grace and its related themes challenge his narrower thesis. Indeed, he obviously sees common grace as a link in the *ordo salutis*; it has more than a soteriological aspect. Thus, from Berkhof's perspective,[38] even Owen seems to be forced to concede something to Arminianism.

If Owen is seen to make concessions only to Baxter's *via media*, the same may be said of Wesley. Like Owen, Wesley is also confronted by serious dilemmas, especially in his doctrine of grace. As we have seen, the logic of Wesley's case implies that ultimately the salvation of humankind is in human hands. He refuses to allow that God possesses the kind of absolute sovereignty attributed to him by the Calvinists; indeed, God's attributes are so 'unseparably joined' that his 'mercy' is not consistent with 'the right of reprobating any man'.[39] Wesley vehemently opposes the kind of theological determinism which condemns unbelievers for rejecting that grace which Calvinists suppose 'God had absolutely determined never to give them'.[40] This is why he rejects Owen's idea of a limited procurement of grace. Although Wesley never entertains the possibility of universal salvation, he dare not contemplate any injustice in the punishment of the unbeliever. God 'will punish no man for doing anything which he could not possibly avoid; neither for omitting anything which he could not possibly do'.[41] Therefore, the justice of God demands that grace be universal in provision.

Wesley's criticism touches on the most vulnerable point in the Calvinist case. Even though Owen admits the 'inexcusableness' of those who reject 'the word of reconciliation',[42] he fails to demonstrate the just basis for their guilt. However, something of an answer can be made to Wesley if Owen's teaching on common grace is consulted. But, in Wesley's view, grace which does not actually save without the addition of *special* grace hardly merits the name, if its success is only guaranteed by divine election. As such, he can only despise the Calvinist conception of common grace:

> Thou hast compell'd the lost to die,
>   Hast reprobated from Thy face;
>   Hast others saved, but them pass'd by,
>   Or mock'd with only damning grace.[43]

His solution is that a universal atonement has provided universal grace which is 'sovereign' and 'saving' as well as 'sufficient'.[44] But if he opposes a concept of 'efficacious universal grace' to Calvinist common grace, he must expect the embarrassing question, 'Why, then, are not all saved?' How can his species of grace be called sovereign if the unbeliever can nullify its influence? Merely clothing his idea of grace in Calvinistic language only adds to his difficulties. However, the dilemma he faces is no more problematic than the one confronting Owen. In other words, if Christ has not procured a general grace, how can unbelievers be justly punished (on Owen's thesis); and if Christ has procured efficacious grace for all, then why are not all saved (on Wesley's thesis)?

It is interesting to discover that Wesley, like Owen, felt obliged to admit a distinction in his theology of grace. Writing to John Mason in 1776, he hints at this very distinction: 'One of Mr Fletcher's *Checks*[45] considers at large the Calvinistic supposition 'that a natural man is as dead as a stone'; and shows the utter falseness and absurdity of it; seeing no man living is without some *preventing grace*, and every degree of grace is a degree of life.[46]

Wesley's notion of preventing grace correlates with his view of free will. While natural free will is a fiction in the case of fallen man, yet 'there is a measure of free will supernaturally restored to every man'.[47] The unbeliever as such does possess an ability to respond to the call of the gospel. The following statements by Wesley bear a fascinating resemblance to the common–special grace distinction used by Baxter and Owen:

Doctrinal Dilemmas

Salvation begins with what is usually termed (and very properly) *preventing grace*; including the first wish to please God, the first dawn of light concerning his will, and the first slight transient conviction of having sinned against him. All these imply some tendency toward life; some degree of salvation; . . . Afterwards we experience the proper Christian salvation; whereby 'through grace', we 'are saved by faith'; consisting of those two grand branches, justification and sanctification.[48]

This version of the *ordo salutis* is hardly consistent with Wesley's earlier portrayal of common grace as 'damning grace'. He obviously refuses to pretend that preventing grace is sufficient for salvation, but, like Baxter's and Owen's common grace, it has 'some tendency toward life'. Furthermore, a dualistic scheme of grace is reflected in Wesley's sermon on predestination: 'God . . . calls both outwardly and inwardly,—*outwardly* by the word of his grace, and *inwardly* by his Spirit. This inward application of his word to the heart seems to be what some term 'effectual calling'.[49] Thus Wesley seems to step outside the strictly Arminian doctrine of grace. In other words, if even Owen's Calvinism has something of an Arminian flavour, Wesley's Arminianism is tinged with Calvinism. J. I. Packer is right to remark that 'Wesley's teaching included so much Reformation truth about the nature of faith, the witness of the Spirit, and effectual calling. Wesley's Arminianism, we might say, contained a good deal of its own antidote.'[50]

Notwithstanding Wesley's standard Arminian response to Calvinism, no one can doubt the Calvinistic elements in his thought. Not forgetting his lifelong exposure to Puritan works,[51] the influence of Baxter's writings and the not entirely negative response to Whitefield in the 1740s probably left some favourable impressions. However impatient he was with high Calvinism, he still retained the essential evangelical emphasis of Reformation Calvinism. At the 1745 Methodist Conference it was admitted that the truth of the gospel lies 'very near' to Calvinism:

Wherein may we come to the very edge of Calvinism?
(1) In ascribing all good to the free grace of God.
(2) In denying all natural free will, and all power antecedent to grace, and
(3) In excluding all merit from man; even for what he has or does by the grace of God.[52]

Even after the publication of Wesley's main counterblast against Calvinism in *Predestination Calmly Considered* (1752), he continued to adopt a quasi-Calvinist, dualistic view of grace. This helped him to solve his dilemma. If all did not partake of 'saving grace', none were without 'preventing grace'. This was a theology which was at once evangelistic (all may be saved) and yet realistic (all would not be saved).

Although Wesley (unlike Baxter) refused to see any possible consistency between unconditional election and conditional reprobation,[53] it is surely arguable that had he not been confronted by the high Calvinism of Whitefield he might not have affirmed his Arminian distinctives so decisively. The doctrine of limited atonement probably turned the scales. Thereafter Wesley refused to tolerate ideas which in his view paralysed the work of evangelism, and opposition from Gill, Toplady, and others merely reinforced his Arminian convictions. However, there is sufficient evidence to suggest that Wesley continued to live on 'the very edge of Calvinism'.

It would seem that neither Owen nor Wesley could solve their theological dilemmas without resorting to a dualistic conception of grace. Thus Richard Baxter's *via media* is vindicated.[54] His scheme embraces many of the emphases of Owen and Wesley to the exclusion of others. In his view the Bible's message is an inscrutable, paradoxical blend of particularism and universalism; accordingly, Owen and Wesley were wrong to stress one aspect of the paradox at the expense of the other. From Baxter's perspective the theologies of the main contestants are—at their biblical best—different sides of the same coin. Thus, if Baxter's balanced position makes him the true heir of Calvin, there is a sense in which Owen and Wesley may be regarded as 'semi-Calvinists', albeit from differing (though complementary) points of view.

It cannot have escaped our theologians' notice that the New Testament writers never actually discuss grace in a dualistic manner. But the reason for this is obvious. Donald Guthrie reminds us that in the New Testament, there is 'no formal discussion of the problem of reconciling God's sovereignty with man's free will'.[55] Once such a discussion is forced upon theologians, it seems that a dualistic hermeneutic is necessary for a coherent theology of grace. Since the use of an extra-biblical term like 'trinity' has not been regarded as inimical to a coherent biblical exposition of that subject, the use of the adjectives 'common' and 'special' to describe grace may be justified, subject to usage within the thought patterns of the biblical writers. It is surely this realization which prompts Berkhof to conclude that 'There are no two kinds of grace in God, but only one', yet this 'one grace manifests itself . . . in different operations and gifts'.[56]

In the next chapter we will consider how the Calvinist–Arminian controversy raised questions about the nature of the atonement, and how two emerging theories contributed to conflicting theologies of grace.

NOTES

1. 'The punishment due to our sin . . . was upon him; which . . . was the pains of hell, in their nature and being, in their weight and pressure' (*DD* 173).
2. 'Christ . . . suffered for all the sins of all the elect in the world' (ibid.).
3. Ibid.
4. Ibid. 174.
5. Ibid.
6. For the indiscriminate provision of grace see John 6: 27 ff., esp. v. 32: 'my Father *giveth you* the true bread from heaven'. Many who heard these words rejected Christ (v. 66). See also Acts 3: 12 ff., esp. v. 26: 'God, having raised up his Son Jesus, sent him to bless *you*, in turning away *every one of you* from his iniquities.' All were thus embraced in the divine intention. See also the parable of the wedding feast (Matt. 22: 1 ff.) and the exposition of it in J. Bellamy, *True Religion Delineated* (Edinburgh, 1788), 308 ff.
7. 'I cannot think that they ever pray aright who never pray for the pardon of unbelief, for the removal of it, and for the increase of faith. If unbelief be the greatest of sins, and if faith be the greatest of the gifts of God, we are not Christians if these things are not one principal part of the matter of our prayers' (*Works*, iv. 277).
8. Owen is incorrectly assessed by A. A. Hodge, *The Atonement* (New York, 1907; fac. Grand Rapids, Mich., 1974), 367; Owen says, 'it is denied that the blood of Christ was a sufficient price and ransom for all and everyone' (*DD* 296). Christ's sacrifice would have been a sufficient ransom 'if it had pleased the Lord to employ it to that purpose' (ibid. 295). Baxter writes, 'they [the Schoolmen] cannot without absurdity be interpreted to mean, that his death is sufficient for all if it had been a price for them; and not a sufficient price for them; For that were to contradict themselves' (*UR* 59).
9. Calvin says, 'He alone bore the punishment of many, because the guilt

of the whole world was laid upon Him' (*Sermons on Isaiah's Prophecy*, trans. T. H. L. Parker (London, 1956), 136).
See also *Comm.* Isa. 53: 12.

10. Calvin says, '*To bear the sins* means to free those who have sinned from their guilt by his satisfaction. He says many meaning all, as in Romans 5: 15. It is of course certain that not all enjoy the fruit of Christ's death, but this happens because their unbelief hinders them' (*Comm.* Heb. 9: 27–8).
11. Calvin says, 'Our Lord Jesus suffered for all and there is neither great nor small who is not inexcusable today, for we can obtain salvation in Him. Unbelievers who turn away from Him and who deprive themselves of Him by their malice are today doubly culpable, for how will they excuse their ingratitude in not receiving the blessing in which they could share by faith' (*Sermons on Isaiah's Prophecy*, p. 141).
12. *DD* 297.
13. Gill denies that 'Christ has paid the debts of all men' (J. Gill, *A Body of Divinity* (London, 1838; fac. Grand Rapids, Mich., 1970), 464; Accordingly, 'by the covenant of grace ... provision is made of sufficient means of salvation ... but then this provision is made only for those who are interested in it, and they are only the elect of God' (*The Cause of God and Truth* (London, 1816), ii. 51). Consequently, 'that there are universal offers of grace and salvation made unto all men, I utterly deny' (*A Collection of Sermons and Tracts* (London, 1773), iii. 269–70). While Gill denies that there are 'offers of grace', he affirms the 'preaching of the gospel' to all. No one is guilty of rejecting what does not exist, but they will be punished for wilfully neglecting the gospel. But what they are guilty of neglecting if nothing is being offered is not made clear. For an attempted defence of Gill see T. J. Nettles, *By His Grace and For His Glory* (Grand Rapids, Mich., 1986), 89 ff. See also P. Toon, *The Emergence of Hyper-Calvinism in English Nonconformity, 1689–1765* (London, 1967), 70 ff.; C. Daniel, 'John Gill and Hypercalvinism', Ph.D. thesis (Edinburgh, 1983), *Passim*. Andrew Fuller opposed Gill's hypercalvinism and, in a letter to Jonathan Edwards' pupil Samuel Hopkins (1721–1803) dated 17 Mar. 1798, he lamented the continuing influence of Owen. (see Fuller's letter in the Angus Library, Regent's Park College, Oxford).
14. *DD* 300; 410.
15. Prefatory note to *DD* p. 140.
16. *DD* 202.
17. Ibid. 234.
18. Cited by Wesley, *Works*, x. 297.
19. Ibid. 297–8.
20. *DD* 202.
21. *Works*, vi. 299.

22. Ibid. 293.
23. Article 11 of the Third Canon speaks of 'the efficacy of the same regenerating Spirit'.
24. 'We do not affirm grace to be irresistible, as though it came upon the will with such an overflowing violence as to beat it down before it, and subdue it by compulsion.... But if that term must be used, it denoteth, in our sense, only such an unconquerable efficacy of grace' (*Dis. A.* 134).
25. 'No man is or can be truly converted to God, but by his powerful, efficacious and irresistible grace' (*Sermons and Tracts*, ii. 123). The caution evident in Owen is clearly cast aside.
26. *CT* II. 69.
27. Ibid.
28. 'The external offer is such as from which every man may conclude his own duty;... Their objection, then, is vain, who affirm that God hath given Christ for all to whom he offers Christ in the preaching of the gospel' (*DD* 300). Owen differs significantly from Calvin here, but also from Gill, for he understands that the 'offer of Christ' is the very content of the preached gospel.
29. *Works*, iii. 236.
30. Ibid. 236–7.
31. *Works*, xi. 640–1.
32. *Works*, iii. 236.
33. *DD* 236.
34. Jer. 31: 31–2; Heb. 8: 9–11.
35. *CT* I. iii. 56.
36. *DD* 238.
37. *CT* II. 72.
38. L. Berkhof, *Systematic Theology* (London, 1963), 437.
39. *PCC* 209–10.
40. Ibid. 213.
41. *Works*, x. 349.
42. *DD* 314.
43. *Poetical Works*, iii. 5 (verse omitted in *MHB* (1933), 75).
44. Ibid. 5; *MHB* (1933), 75: 3.
45. John Fletcher, 'Checks to Antinomianism' (1771–5), *The Works of John Fletcher* (London, 1830; fac. Salem, Ohio, 1974), ii. 1 ff.; also B. Semmel, *The Methodist Revolution* (London, 1974), 48 ff.
46. *Letters*, vi. 239.
47. *PCC* 221.
48. *Works*, vi. 482. Wesley uses the phrase 'preventing grace' just as Owen writes of 'common grace'; however, Owen also teaches that 'preventing grace' is the inward aspect of 'saving' or 'efficacious grace' (*Dis. A.* 135).

49. *Works*, vi. 213.
50. 'Arminianisms', in *The Manifold Grace of God* (PRSC, London, 1968), at p. 32.
51. R. C. Monk, *John Wesley: His Puritan Heritage* (1966), *Passim*; J. A. Newton, *Methodism and the Puritans* (London, 1964), *passim*.
52. *Works*, viii. 274; see A. Coppedge, 'John Wesley and the doctrine of predestination', Ph.D. thesis (Cambridge, 1976), 314.
53. Baxter says, 'God predestinateth men to faith, and perseverance, and to glory... not... *upon the foresight of faith* and perseverance: But that he predestinateth or decreeth men to damnation, *only on the foresight of final impenitence and infidelity*, but not to impenitence or infidelity itself' (*CT* I. i. 68; emphases mine).
54. Richard Watson's criticism of Baxter's dualistic view of grace ('No man is actually saved without something more than this "sufficient grace" provides'; *Theological Institutes* (London, 1850), i. 421) must also be levelled against his master Wesley. Even Wesley did not argue that 'common preventing grace' actually saves without 'saving grace' proper. Contrary to what Watson says, Baxter argues that 'no man is denied power to believe savingly, but for not using as he could his antecedent commoner grace' (*CT* II. 131). Such non-use is alone evidence of non-election to salvation. Watson argues that the unconverted have 'a sufficient degree' of grace to enable them to 'embrace the Gospel', plus a power to either 'use or spurn this heavenly gift and gracious assistance' (*Theological Institutes*, ii. 377). Baxter would rightly ask; 'Do you mean that man's will is more powerful than God's? (*CT* II. 145). In the final analysis Baxter leans towards Owen rather than Wesley.
55. *New Testament Theology* (Leicester, 1981), 640. In his *Treatise Concerning Grace and Free Will* (c. 1128) Bernard of Clairvaux gives his famous solution to this question: 'Take away free will, and there remaineth nothing to be saved; take away grace and there is no means whereby it can be saved' (cited in Anne Freemantle, *The Age of Belief* (New York, 1962), 102).
56. *Systematic Theology*, p. 435.

8
The Meaning of the Cross

During the seventeenth-century, divergent theories about the nature of the atonement came to underlie debates about its extent. In their response to the Arminians, the Calvinists insisted that a right understanding of the character of the atonement necessarily favoured their interpretation of the textual data. Thus, for Calvinist theologians, a theology of the atonement is, by definition, a theology of limited or definite atonement.[1] This was an axiomatic consideration in Owen's exposition of the subject. In his view, once the meanings of key concepts like redemption, reconciliation, satisfaction, and propitiation were grasped, then the idea of a universal atonement was self-contradictory if all were not saved.[2]

The gap between sixteenth- and seventeenth-century Calvinists over the extent of the atonement is no less conspicuous where its nature is concerned. If Calvin generally avoided speculative precision in favour of a soteriological dualism (i.e. grace was provided for all but not received by all), Owen was of a very different mind. His a priori, Aristotelian teleology prejudices his whole approach to the question. Paradoxically, Wesley's very aversion to theorizing about the atonement ensured that his view of the subject approximated in great measure to the original Reformation position.

Appealing to the parallel between Old Testament theocratic Israel and the New Testament church, Owen insists that 'universal redemption' is self-contradictory if any 'die in captivity'. The redeemed nation, 'delivered from bondage, preserved, taken nigh unto God, brought unto Canaan, was typical of God's spiritual church, of elect believers'[3] Israel was therefore a microcosm of the elect. However, the simple fact that not all those who were liberated actually reached the promised land demands a dualistic view of the nation's temporal deliverance, if deliverance from Egypt and settlement in Canaan were all of a piece. As a result of unbelief and disobedience, a significant proportion of the nation perished in the wilderness. On Owen's model this would imply that some of the elect might perish. But since, throughout Israel's long history, great stress is placed on the 'remnant' (Isa. 10: 20–1; Rom. 9: 27), the most that Owen can argue is that the nation was a type of the visible church, the latter consisting of 'nominal professors' and 'true believers'. Contrary to his view, one may argue that in certain respects theocratic Israel was a typical microcosm of the post-theocratic visible church and of the world. In other words, as there was a spiritual elect remnant within the church–state of Israel (Rom. 9: 6; 11: 5), so the elect are now to be found in visible churches gathered from all nations. On this model the spiritual privileges promised to national Israel became the privileges of 'all nations' (John 1: 29; Matt. 28: 19). Thus the 'sufficient for all, efficient for some' dualism once applying to Israel is now internationalized according to the New Testament.[4]

Owen's treatment of the New Testament concept of reconciliation is predictably restrictive. He insists that there is a strict correlation between God's work of reconciliation and the actual reconciliation of the elect.[5] It is this consideration which leads him to particularize Paul's use of κόσμος in 2 Corinthians 5: 19 (God was in Christ reconciling the world unto himself) to mean the 'elect'. However, the lack of strict equivalence between καταλλαγή and 'reconciliation' is important. There is more 'one-sidedness' in the Greek[6] permitting a distinction between 'reconcilation offered' and 'reconciliation received'.[7] There is not the strict correlation that Owen imagines, from which to make theological capital. In other words, it is quite admissible to say that God is reconcilable to all, even if all are not actually reconciled.[8]

When Owen comes to discuss the concept of 'satisfaction', he is well aware that, unlike redemption and reconciliation, 'satisfaction is not found in the Latin or English Bible applied to the death of Christ'.[9] However, he rightly insists that there are 'other words in the original languages' which are equivalent in meaning. Consequently, he employs all the 'commercialist' implications of Anselm's theory of the atonement,[10] expounding it in his rigidly particularist manner. Thus sin and guilt are given strictly quantitative connotations.[11] Observing commercial metaphors in the Bible, Owen argues that man is the debtor, sin is the debt, the obligation to pay is demanded by the law, God is the creditor, and the ransom is paid to the offended party on behalf of the offender by

Christ. This is the conceptual framework by which Owen establishes his doctrine of limited atonement: 'the debt thus paid was not for this or that sin, but for all the sins of all those for whom and in whose name this payment was made.'[12] He asks, with rigorous logic, 'If the full debt of all be paid to the utmost extent of the obligation, how comes it to pass that so many are shut up in prison to eternity, never freed from their debts?'[13] In other words, if Christ has died for all, and any perish, then God is demanding double payment for sin.[14] Therefore Christ did not die for all, but for the elect alone; his sufferings were commensurate with 'the whole punishment due to . . . all the sins of all those that he suffered and offered himself for'.[15]

Many orthodox Calvinist theologians have objected to the commercial theory of the atonement, including William Cunningham,[16] Charles Hodge,[17] and Robert L. Dabney.[18] Others have drastically modified their Calvinism because of their objections, such as Joseph Bellamy,[19] Andrew Fuller,[20] A. H. Strong,[21] Ralph Wardlaw,[22] Albert Barnes,[23] and Thomas Chalmers.[24] The general criticism of the theory is that it overworks the analogy between sins and debts; it fails to realize that 'analogy is not identity'.[25] After all, strictly speaking sin is crime, not debt; it is guilt, not actual failure in financial obligation. In short, the theory fails to distinguish between commercial and ethical categories. Excessive application of commercial concepts to the atonement treats sin in quantitative rather than qualitative terms.

Notwithstanding the justice of these criticisms, it is to Owen's credit that he saw the commercial theory as the *raison d'être* of the doctrine of limited atonement. Unlike others, he realized that the entire particularist edifice stands or falls by it. Indeed, as was noted in the previous chapter, it clearly explains why Owen modified the sufficiency–efficiency distinction. In reality, since the atonement provides only a limited satisfaction for the sins of the elect, it is only sufficient for those for whom it is efficient; thus the 'credit facilities' of the gospel are only available for the elect. As we have seen, this consideration poses difficulties for Owen's doctrines of common grace and the free offer of the gospel.

Had Richard Baxter been aware of the uneasy alliance between the doctrines of common grace and a limited satisfaction in Owen's writings, he might have exposed Owen's embryonic hypercalvinism more readily. Instead, much of the controversy revolved around the so-called 'governmental theory' of the atonement advocated by the Dutch jurist–divine Hugo De Groot, or Grotius (1583–1645).[26] This introduced an entirely new element into the discussion, which partly clarified and partly clouded the issues. In several respects Baxter followed Grotius in rejecting Owen's theory of a limited satisfaction.

Owen's concern over the theory of Grotius is easily understood. Intended as an orthodox response to Socinian denials of the atonement, the *Defensio fidei Catholicae de satisfactione Christi* (1617) actually threatened the very commercialism on which Owen's doctrine of limited atonement rested. Grotius argued that God demanded satisfaction not as a 'creditor', but as *rector*, or governor, of the universe. Since sin was an assault on the moral order, the death of Christ was necessary to show God's serious displeasure at sin; 'God was unwilling to pass over so many sins, and so great sins, without a distinguished example.'[27] He was not so much concerned with retributive as with public justice; sin was to be deterred and the good of the 'community' promoted. All was done in the interests of good government. Although the guilt of sinners occasioned his sufferings, Christ did not undergo the exact punishment due to anyone's sins. His satisfaction amounted to an equivalent substituted penalty, acceptable to God as rector in lieu of the punishment threatened to sinners. The lawgiver being satisfied, the law's threatenings might be relaxed where penitent offenders were concerned. The pardon of sin was therefore a matter of grace rather than a strict 'commercial' transaction. Since the atonement implied no quantitative limitation, it was available to all.

The inadequacies of the Grotian theory are well known. By introducing secular, utilitarian ideas of punishment into the Judaeo-Christian tradition, Grotius gave up, in the words of Ritschl, 'the idea of the penal satisfaction of past sins' for the 'penal example for the prevention of future sins'.[28] Owen was not slow to accuse Grotius, rightly, of replacing the doctrine of propitiation by the notion of governmental expediency;[29] 'the meaning of the word ἱλασμός, or 'propitiation' which Christ is said to be, is that whereby the law is covered, God appeased and reconciled, sin expiated, and the sinner pardoned . . .'[30]

Consistent with his commercialism, Owen insisted that God's justice was only satisfied by Christ's payment of the same *quantitative* penalty or debt owed by the elect to God on account of their sins—the *solutio ejusdem*.³¹ Baxter (following Grotius at the only point where he could do so with any real justification) argued that, in virtue of the differences (in detail and duration) between Christ's sufferings and the actual sufferings of the lost, Christ only paid a *qualitative* equivalent—the *solutio tantidem*.³² Since the penalty of the law threatens eternal punishment to impenitent offenders, Christ clearly did not suffer the identical punishment, for his resurrection terminated his banishment.³³ God therefore relaxed the law with regard both to the persons who should suffer (which Owen obviously agreed with)³⁴ and to the penalty suffered. Clearly, there was not the 'sameness' Owen pleads for.

Although a strict particularist like William Cunningham denied the importance of this issue,³⁵ Owen saw clearly that his doctrine of limited atonement hung upon the 'sameness' between Christ's sufferings and those deserved by the elect. However, he could only argue his case with the aid of Aristotle's metaphysics. His very language betrays him: 'When I say the same, I mean *essentially* the same in weight and pressure, though not in all the *accidents* of duration and the like; for it was impossible that he should be detained by death.'³⁶ He therefore resorts to Aristotle's dubious essence–accidents theory³⁷ to prove his point. In Baxter's view even this statement 'yieldeth the cause',³⁸ but after learning of Baxter's criticism Owen granted that 'There is a *sameness* in Christ's sufferings with that in the obligation in respect of *essence*, and *equivalency* in respect of *attendencies*.'³⁹

But Owen's use of this philosophical distinction simply obscures the fact that there is a real difference between Christ's temporary sufferings and the eternal sufferings deserved by the elect. He cannot establish his concept of 'sameness' without philosophical double-talk. If he is prepared to grant an equivalence in either respect, he is forced to concede that there is only a similarity, and not a sameness at all. Clearly, Aristotle's metaphysical formula⁴⁰ only serves to permit unreal and meaningless distinctions. Had Baxter been as nimble as David Hume⁴¹ at this point, he would have exploded Owen's case; however, Aristotle had a few more years to reign in scholastic circles. In view of later criticism of 'the philosopher' it is possible to see how Owen's questionable commercialism falls to the ground, and with it the classical doctrine of limited atonement. In other words, he cannot demonstrate that the sufferings of Christ were commensurate with the deserved sufferings of the elect without the doubtful support of Aristotle. He fails, therefore, to prove that the atonement is necessarily limited by its nature. Indeed, his thesis requires that the sinner be eternally saved at the 'expense' of the Saviour's eternal loss.

The *idem–tantundem* distinction automatically answers Owen's objection that if any suffer eternally for whom Christ died, then 'double payment' is being demanded. But assuming the commercialist analogy, there is no duplication of payment. Those who reject the gospel do not suffer again what Christ has suffered for them. He 'paid' the *tantundem*, or equivalent penalty; they will 'pay' the *idem*, or exact price.

Without denying that there are serious inadequacies in the governmental theory, the *tantundem* view of satisfaction is a valid and valuable insight. It is not handicapped by questions of intrinsic quantitative limitation. From this standpoint Christ may be seen as a substitute for all in general, though for the elect in particular. His satisfaction is applicable to all, if applied only to some. The question of numerical extent only arises in the application of the atonement, a point the Old Testament illustrates perfectly. Whereas the provision of atonement in Israel was coextensive with the nation, though enjoyed only by the faithful, the provision of Calvary extends to all the world, though many reject it. Furthermore, the commercial theory cannot really do justice to the gospel as a revelation of grace. Although Owen correctly argues that the giving of Christ to the elect was a gracious act of God,[42] he implies that salvation is simply the payment of what God owes them.[43]

J. I. Packer is right to point out the dangers of Richard Baxter's dependence on Grotius.[44] Even then, the Puritan's worst crime is to overdo political analogies to the point of using every aspect of secular government to illustrate sacred themes. That said, in fairness to Baxter, while there are govenmental and monarchical categories in the Bible (Pss. 67: 4; 96: 10; Isa. 9: 6–7), he does not stress the notion of governmental expediency as much as the Dutchman, especially in his later works.[45] Neither does he view the atonement as a mere deterrence of sin when he denies that Christ was a substitute for sinners in the commercial sense:

> Yet did he in the person of a mediator . . . suffer the penalty, *nostro loco*, in our stead . . . to satisfy God's wisdom, truth and justice, and to procure pardon and life for sinners . . . . The perfection of Christ's satisfaction consisteth not in its being instead of all the sufferings due to all for whom he

died, but . . . in its full sufficiency to those ends for which it was designed by the Father and Son . . .[46]

Christ therefore suffered the *tantundem*, not the *idem*. Baxter does not deny that Christ was 'cursed' instead of sinners in a penal, substitutionary sense; he only denies that his sufferings were identical in every respect with the 'curse of the law' (Galatians 3: 13).[47]

Packer criticizes Baxter for arguing that God relaxed the law rather than satisfying it;[48] but Baxter was surely correct to state that both Christ and his sufferings were inseparably substituted for the law's strict demands. Had the law not been relaxed with regard to the offender, none would be saved; had it not been relaxed with regard to the penalty, Christ himself would have suffered 'the everlasting torments of hell'.[49] Baxter's argument is irrefutable when he observes that the law did not permit the punishment of a substitute in the place of an offender: 'For the law made it due to the sinner himself. And another's suffering for him fulfilleth not the law (which never said, Either thou or another for thee shalt die). But [Christ's death] satisfied the Law-giver as he is above his own law, and could dispense with it, his justice being satisfied and saved.'[50] In other words, coupled with the infinite dignity of the suffering Saviour, his sufferings were accepted as a satisfactory equivalent for all that is deserved by mankind.

In his concern to oppose Owen's commercialistic particularism, it is unfortunate that Baxter allowed his insights to be clouded by excessive use of political metaphor. In this respect both men were in error. As has been noted, analogy is not identity; there is a difference between God's rule and secular kingship, and between sins and debts. In other words, the atonement is not correctly viewed in exclusively commercial or political terms, for it is neither a commercial transaction nor a political expedient. Rather, it is an ethical satisfaction. That said, Baxter did not discard the commercial analogies of the Bible entirely, any more than he denied retributive justive; he simply warned against pursuing metaphors too far.[51] Nor did Owen entirely reject governmental concepts,[52] for even he admitted that the law was relaxed rather than satisfied by Christ's substitution. Whereas it is common to associate the erosion of Calvinism with the adoption of governmentalism, it is important to note that John Gill insisted on governmental as well as commercial ideas in his theology of the atonement.[53]

It is interesting as well as refreshing to discover that John Wesley's deliberate policy was to avoid the metaphysical complexities of seventeenth-century debate. As has been shown, Wesley's method shares something of the anti-speculative mood of the Latitudinarians. However, he is markedly more simplistic than Tillotson, whose sermon on the atonement shows obvious signs of the influence of Grotius.[54] In his sermons and tracts, Wesley is generally content to quote verbatim sequences of biblical texts with virtually no exegetical gloss. The theories of Anselm and Grotius are conspicuously absent from his writings. In his debates with Calvinists or Socinians, Wesley believed he had a prima facie case in the bare word of God. But if his homiletic method is 'atheoretical', he does not contravene R. W. Dale's maxim[55] by shunning theoretical discussion altogether. Indeed, C. W. Williams affirms that the 'central point of the penal substitutionary theory was of great importance to Wesley'.[56] But Williams seems to imagine that Wesley's understanding did not assume a juridical context. Although Wesley certainly avoids a speculative use of governmental and commercial ideas, he does not hesitate to affirm a necessary link between the justice of God and the atonement: 'The attribute of justice was to be preserved inviolate; and inviolate it is preserved, if there was a real infliction of punishment on our Saviour.'[57]

There have been other attempts to drive a wedge between Wesley's theology and his Reformation heritage, almost to the point of assuming that John and Charles Wesley embraced something like the moral-influence theory of Abelard.[58] It is obvious that the emotional appeal of Methodism was more pronounced than earlier expressions of Protestantism, but the familiar theological emphases are just as evident. As far as John Wesley is concerned, Romans 3:25 and Galatians 3:13 demand that the atonement be seen in retributive and juridical terms. He writes that the atonement was a propitiatory sacrifice 'To appease an offended God. But if . . . God was never offended, there was no need of this propitiation.'[59] The 'curse of the law' was 'the curse of God', and, in his sufferings, Christ was 'made a curse for us'.[60] Charles Welsey's poetry is fully in accord with his brother's exegesis:

> The types and figures are fulfilled,
>   Exacted is the legal pain;
> The precious promises are sealed;
>   The spotless lamb of God is slain.[61]

In his controversy with the mystic William Law—who rejected the notion of 'vindictive justice in God'[62]—John Wesley explicitly affirms that the atonement involved 'the substitution of the Messiah in the place of his people, thereby atoning for their sins'.[63] Again, Charles is as explicit as his brother:

> For what you have done
> His blood must atone:
> The Father hath punished for you his dear Son.
>   The Lord, in the day
>   Of his anger, did lay
> Your sins on the lamb, and he bore them away.[64]

None can doubt the objective 'substitutionism'[65] of the Wesleys, even though they also stressed the subjective, experiential nature of Christianity. However, the Wesleys never confused the subjective impact of the death of Christ with the objective ground of the atonement. Indeed, the very satisfaction of divine justice, viewed in penal, retributive terms, was a necessary condition of the display of divine love to mankind. Therefore, the intensely emotional dimension of the atonement is not the ground of the sinner's forgiveness but its consequence:

> Then let us sit beneath His cross,
>   And gladly catch the healing stream,
> All things for Him account but loss,
>   And give up all our hearts to Him;
> Of nothing think or speak beside,
>   My Lord, my Love is crucified.[66]

John Wesley's lines are no less expressive than his brother's:

> Let the earth no more my heart divide,
> With Christ may I be crucified,
>   To Thee with my whole soul aspire;
> Dead to the world and all its toys,
> Its idle pomp and fading joys,
>   Be Thou alone my one desire.[67]

Since Calvinists and Arminians generally appealed to the commercial and governmental theories respectively, it is interesting to note Wesley's almost total disregard for Grotius.[68] In this respect his approach is in marked contrast to that of the Wesleyan theologian Richard Watson (1781–1833), whose discussion of the doctrine of satisfaction in his *Theological Institutes* (1850)[69] reveals considerable dependence on the Dutchman. The plain fact is that

Wesley's theology owes more to Reformation Anglicanism than to any other source. As we have seen, he frequently weaves together Scripture texts, quotations from the Prayer Book, and extracts from the homilies when he wishes to make a statement on the atonement.[70] Unlike Baxter and later Amyraldians, who fell back on the governmental view when opposing the high Calvinists, Wesley was content to quote the Prayer Book in affirming that Christ made 'a full sacrifice, oblation, and satisfaction for the sins of the whole world'.[71]

When Wesley used the key terms 'redemption' and 'satisfaction' to assert that 'the death of Christ is available for all the world',[72] he was actually aligning himself with Reformation Calvinism. Like Wesley, Calvin paid little or no attention to Anselm.[73] His theory of penal substitution assumes a universal satisfaction, notwithstanding its limited application.[74] Just as Wesley declares that God, through his servants, 'invites us, intreats us and, with the most tender importunity, solicits us, not to reject' the blessings of the gospel,[75] so Calvin concludes—with as little inhibition—that 'as He once suffered, so now every day He offers the fruit of His suffering to us through the Gospel which He has given to the world as a sure and certain record of His completed work of reconciliation.'[76]

The conclusion is thus inescapable that of all our theologians, with regard to their various understandings of the nature and extent of the atonement, John Wesley is closest to Calvin. Once considerations of election are introduced, the picture alters in favour of Baxter; but in his non-scholastic treatment of the atonement itself, Wesley is the Calvinist. In this respect Calvin would not recognize Owen's commercialistic particularism as his offspring, neither would he share the Puritan's attitude concerning 'millions of infants and others in barbarous nations': 'Were all these, are they that remain, all and everyone, bound to believe that Christ died for them, all and everyone in particular? Those that think so are, doubtless, bound to go tell all of them so . . .'[77]

It is a fact of the greatest significance that it was Baxter, rather than Owen, who supported so enthusiastically the work of John Eliot amongst the Indians of Massachusetts,[78] more than a century before William Carey and Andrew Fuller opened the era of modern missions proper.[79] Although Baxter's contribution to the 'downgrade' from Calvinism to rationalistic Arminianism and Unitarianism is seldom questioned,[80] it is at least as true that Owen's strict particularism contributed to the opposite 'downgrade'[81] from Calvinism to hypercalvinism. He thus helped to generate the fatalistic prejudices which Carey and Fuller had to overcome.[82]

Whatever are the relative merits of the Anselmic, Grotian, and Abelardian theories of the atonement, they all contain some element of truth. When pressed to their logical conclusions, distortion is the result. At their best, they may to some extent be harmonized, as Stott observes.[83] But under no circumstances can a theory which minimizes the concept of penal substitution claim fidelity to the Christian revelation.[84]

In the final analysis, the debate over the extent on the atonement is not to be settled with reference even to the position of John Calvin. The great Reformer's views can never be the final court of appeal for Protestants. In the next chapter, the scriptural evidence will be examined with a view to reaching an authoritative verdict.

NOTES

1. G. D. Long, *Definite Atonement* (Nutley, NJ, 1977), 3.
2. *DD* 258 ff. Hence the Dort expression 'efficacious redemption' is mere tautology; see J. Murray, *Redemption Accomplished and Applied* (London, 1961), 64.
3. *DD* 258.
4. Calvin says, 'And when he says *the sin of the world* he extends this kindness indiscriminately to the whole human race, that the Jews might not think the Redeemer has been sent to them alone. . . . Now it is for us to embrace the blessing offered to all, that each may make up his mind that there is nothing to hinder him from finding reconciliation in Christ if only, led by faith, he comes to him' (*Comm.* John 1: 29).
5. *DD* 262–3.
6. L. Morris, *The Apostolic Preaching of the Cross* (London, 1960), 200.
7. 'The work of reconciliation, in the sense of the New Testament, is a work which is finished, and which we must conceive to be finished, before the gospel is preached' (J. Denney, *The Death of Christ* (London, 1951), 85).
8. 'What Christ has done is in fact sufficient, to open a door for God through him to become reconcilable to the whole world' (J. Bellamy, *True Religion Delineated* (Edinburgh, 1788), 308).
9. *DD* 265.

10. Although Owen does not actually appeal to Anselm's treatise 'Cur Deus homo etc.' in the *Death of Death*, he had obviously studied it; see *Works*, i. 23.
11. 'Satisfaction is . . . a full compensation of the creditor from the debtor . . . If I owe a man a hundred pounds, I am his debtor, by virtue of the bond wherein I am bound, until some such thing be done as recompenseth him, and moveth him to cancel the bond; which is called satisfaction' (*DD* 265).
12. Ibi. 272–3.
13. Ibid. 273.
14. This argument was expressed poetically by A. M. Toplady (1740–78):

> And will the righteous judge of men
> Condemn me for that debt of sin,
>   Which, Lord, was charged on Thee?
>
> Payment God cannot twice demand,
> First at my bleeding Surety's hand,
>   And then again at mine.
>
> *Diary and Selection of Hymns* (London, 1969), 193.

The comfort derived from this argument applies only to those assured of their election.
15. *DD* 267.
16. W. Cunningham, *Historical Theology* (London, 1862; fac. London, 1960), ii. 331.
17. C. Hodge, *Systematic Theology* (New York, 1873; fac. London, 1960), ii. 554 ff.
18. R. L. Dabney, *Systematic Theology* (St Louis, 1878; fac. Edinburgh, 1985), 528.
19. Bellamy, *True Religion Delineated*, p. 306.
20. 'The gospel worthy of all acceptation', *The Complete Works of Andrew Fuller*, (London, 1831), i. 134.
21. A. H. Strong, *Systematic Theology* (New York, 1890), 409.
22. R. Wardlaw, *Systematic Theology* (London, 1856), ii. 368 ff.
23. A. Barnes, *The Atonement* (New York, 1860), 230.
24. T. Chalmers, *Institutes of Theology* (Edinburgh, 1849), ii. 403. For recent criticism of Owen's commercialism see J. N. Macleod, 'John Owen and the "Death of Death" ', in *Out of Bondage* (London, 1984), at p. 76.
25. The analogies between comparable ideas are never exact in every respect. Since parallels are limited, metaphors should not be pressed too far. Christ said, 'I am the door' (John 10: 7); but he is not made of wood.
26. For Grotius see *The Encyclopedia of Religion and Ethics*, ed. J. Hastings

(Edinburgh, 1913), vi. 440–3; A. P. F. Sell, *The Great Debate* (Worthing, 1982), 32.
27. *Defense of Catholic Faith concerning the Satisfaction of Christ against Faustus Socinus*, trans. F. H. Foster (London, 1889), 106.
28. Cited in R. W. Dale, *The Atonement* (London, 1875), 358.
29. *DD* 271 ff.
30. For Owen's doctrine of propitiation see *DD* 266; 269; 331 ff. Since Dale wrote in 1875 that the purpose of the atonement was to 'turn away the wrath of God' (*The Atonement*, p. 226), 20th-cent. scholarship has witnessed a rejection of the orthodox view of satisfaction and propitiation. See H. Rashdall, *The Idea of Atonement in Christian Theology* (London, 1919), 207; C. H. Dodd, *The Epistle of Paul to the Romans* (London, 1932), 21. More recent studies have agreed with Owen's view, e.g. E. Brunner, *The Mediator* (London, 1932), 519–20; Denney, *Death of Christ*, p. 188; K. Barth, *Church Dogmatics* trans. G. W. Bromiley (Edinburgh, 1957), v. 1, pp. 559–64; Morris, *Apostolic Preaching*, p. 155; id., *The Cross in the New Testament* (London, 1965), 349; Murray, *Redemption*, p. 30; R. S. Wallace, *The Atoning Death of Christ* (London, 1981), 113; J. R. W. Stott, *The Cross of Christ* (London, 1986), 168 ff. Unlike Owen, Brunner (p. 506), Barth (iv. 664 ff.), Denney (p. 151), Morris (*Apostolic Preaching*, pp. 200 ff.), and Stott (p. 199) all assume a universal dimension in the atonement.
31. *DD* 267 ff.
32. *Aphorismes of Justification* (London, 1649), Appendix, pp. 137 ff.
33. Baxter does not deny a qualitative similarity between Christ's actual sufferings and the deserved sufferings of sinners, but denies that there was a comprehensive, penal 'sameness'. 'Nor could Christ's sufferings be equal in degree, intensively and extensively, to all that was deserved by the world: . . . seeing our deserved suffering lay in things of such a nature, as to be left in sin itself, destitute of God's image, and love and communion, under his hatred, tormented in conscience; besides the everlasting torments of hell . . . Yet did Christ suffer more in soul than in body, being at the present deprived of that kind of sense of God's love, . . . and having on his soul the deep sense of God's displeasure with sinners and of his hatred of sin, though no sense of God's hatred to himself. . . . and so he bore the sorrow of our transgressions, and was so far forsaken of God for that time, and not further' (*CT* I. ii. 40).
34. *DD* 269–70.
35. *Historical Theology*, ii. 306–7. Cunningham fails to appreciate Owen's point that without the *idem* view, it is impossible to prove from the nature of the atonement that it is limited to the elect. The solution advanced by Cunningham is virtually indistinguishable from the view Owen is anxious to refute.

36. DD 269–70.
37. Bertrand Russell described this as a 'muddle-headed notion, incapable of precision' (*The History of Western Philosphy* (London 1961), 177).
38. *Aphorismes*, Appendix, p. 138.
39. *Works*, x. 448.
40. 'The essence of a thing is that which it is said to be *per se*'; '"Accident" also denotes that which belongs to a thing *per se*, though no part of its essence' (*Metaphysics*, trans. J. Warrington (London, 1956), 173; 46).
41. See Hume, *A Treatise of Human Nature*, I. vi. (London, 1911), i. 24. The metaphysical point which Hume highlights is that a thing is what its accidents are. Once the accidents or properties are logically separated from the essence or substance, nothing can be meaningfully said about the essence. In short, 'essence' denotes nothing at all. Therefore, if two things differ in their accidents, they are really different whatever else might be said of them. In other words, if the details and duration of Christ's sufferings are only *equivalent* to the threatened punishment of sinners, they are not the same, although they are undoubtedly similar. Owen's misconception may be illustrated by another: the theory of transubstantiation. After the prayer of consecration the sacramental bread is believed to be *essentially* different, though *accidentally* the same as before. But a real miracle would have occurred had the accidents of the bread (taste, texture, colour, etc.) become the accidents of Christ's actualy body. Applying this to Owen's analysis, an accidental difference between Christ's sufferings and the punishment threatening sinners means that they are really different, and not the same.
42. DD 268–9.
43. Fuller argues that the commercial theory is 'inconsistent with the free forgiveness of sin, and sinners being directed to apply for mercy as *supplicants,* rather than as *claimants*' (*Works*, p. 134). R. Wardlaw writes: 'the payment of debt, by strictly and literally cancelling all claim, leaves no room for the exercise of grace' (*Systematic Theology* (London, 1856), ii. 369).
44. 'The doctrine of justification in development and decline among the Puritans', in *By Schisms Rent Asunder* (PRSC, London, 1969), at p. 26.
45. Although Baxter did admit to a deterrent element in the atonement in the *Universal Redemption of Mankind* (written in the 1640s but published posthumously in 1694), the idea seems to have been omitted in such mature works as *Catholick Theologie* (1675) and *An End of Doctrinal Controversies* (1691). Even in the early work (at p. 10) the deterrent aspect is secondary to the retributive. He actually criticized Grotius for viewing satisfaction in exclusively governmental terms (*CT* I. ii. 69). He also lamented the Roman Catholic sympathies of Grotius (G. F. Nuttall, 'Richard Baxter and the Grotian religion', in

Reform and Reformation: England and the Continent, c. 1500–c 1750, ed. D. Baker (London, 1979), 245–50.
46. CT I. ii. 39.
47. See CT I. ii. 68 and 37 for Baxter's quotation of Gal. 3: 13; see also *The Scripture Gospel Defended* (1690), 47–8.
48. 'The doctrine of justification', p. 27; id., 'The redemption and restoration of man in the thought of Richard Baxter', D.Phil. thesis (Oxford, 1954), 303 ff.
49. CT I. ii. 40.
50. Ibid. 40.
51. Ibid. 67.
52. *DD* 270.
53. *A Body of Divinity* (Grand Rapids, Mich., 1970), 478.
54. 'Concerning the sacrifice and satisfaction of Christ' (1693), *TW* iii. 554 ff.
55. 'It is very possible for our theory of the atonement to be crude and incoherent, but it is hardly possible to have no theory at all' (*The Atonement*, p. 76).
56. *John Wesley's Theology Today* (New York, 1960), 84.
57. *Notes*, Rom. 3: 26.
58. F. Frost, 'Biblical imagery and religious experience in the hymns of the Wesleys', *WHS* 42. 6 (1980), at pp. 158 ff.
59. *Notes*, Rom. 3: 25.
60. *Notes*, Gal. 3: 13.
61. *A Collection of Hymns for the ... People Called Methodists* (London, 1877), 706: 4. The hymn appears in *MHB* (1904), 165, minus this verse, and was deleted altogether in *MHB* (1933).
62. Wesley, *Works*, ix. 464.
63. Ibid. 471.
64. *Collection of Hymns* (1877), 707: 2. This verse appears in *MHB* (1904), 161, but in line 3 'punished' is altered to 'stricken'. The verse is deleted from *MHB* (1933), 188, and the whole hymn from *Hymns and Psalms* (London, 1983).
65. Frost, 'Biblical imagery', p. 161.
66. *MHB* (1933), 186: 4; *Hymns and Psalms* (1983), 175: 3.
67. *MHB* (1933), 553: 3. Although this hymn is credited to Charles Wesley, H. Bett is persuaded that John wrote it (*The Hymns of Methodism* (London, 1945), 25).
68. There is just a hint of the governmental theory in *Notes*, Rom. 3: 26. John Wesley's father recommended Grotius to him: 'You ask me which is the best commentary on the Bible? I answer, the Bible itself .... But Grotius is the best, for the most part, especially on the Old Testament' (cited in A. Skevington Wood, *The Burning Heart: John Wesley, Evangelist* (London, 1967), 36). Wesley was actually reading

Grotius' *Annotationes in Vetus et Novum Testamentum* (1642) on the day of his examination for holy orders (ibid. 36). He quotes from them in a letter to Conyers Middleton in 1749 (*Letters*, ii. 316 n. 1). However, he seems to have preferred Bengel's *Gnomon Novi Testamenti* (1742) when preparing his own *Notes* (1755). Bengel, like Grotius, was an Arminian.

69. Watson did, however, criticize Grotius for leaning too much towards governmental expediency (*Theological Institutes* (London, 1850), ii. 139).
70. *Works*, v. 50; 56.
71. *Works*, vi. 219.
72. *Works*, v. 56; he also quotes from the *Homilies*, 310.
73. R. A. Peterson, *Calvin's Doctrine of the Atonement* (Phillipsburg, 1983), NJ, 85; 91.
74. Calvin says: 'For God, who is perfect righteousness, cannot love the iniquity which he sees in all. All of us, therefore, have that within which deserves the hatred of God . . . . Our acquittal is in this—that the guilt which made us liable to punishment was transferred to the head of the Son of God [Isa. 53: 12] . . . For, were not Christ a victim, we could have no sure conviction of his being . . . *our substitute-ransom and propitiation*' (*Inst.* II. xvi. 3; 5; 6). Elsewhere he says, '*To bear the sins* means to free those who have sinned from their guilt by his satisfaction. He says many meaning all, as in Romans 5: 15. It is of course certain that not all enjoy the fruit of Christ's death, but this happens because their unbelief hinders them' (*Comm.* Heb. 9: 27–8).
75. *Notes*, 2 Cor. 5: 20.
76. *Comm.* 2 Cor. 5: 19.
77. DD 405–6. In order to prove that Owen still stressed the free invitations of the gospel, Packer quotes a moving evangelistic appeal from Owen's *Glory of Christ* (1684) (Introductory Essay to *DD*, p. 18). Whatever was true of 'late' Owen, his language is very different from that of the *Death of Death* (1647).
78. Baxter, *Autobiography*, pp. xxvii; 96; 117. Although Owen also rejoiced 'that through the unwearied labours of some holy and worthy persons, sundry churches of Indians are lately called and gathered in America' (*Works*, xv. 72), his interest hardly compares with the fervent concern of Baxter. (See O.'s letter to John Eliot in *Correspondence*, pp. 153–5.) W. H. Goold fairly defends O. from the charge of 'indifference' to missions on grounds of circumstances (*Works*, xv. 72 n). But what was indeed generally true of 'British Christians' of O.'s day was certainly not true of Baxter, whose *Call to the Unconverted* was translated by Eliot after he had translated the Bible for the Indians (see *Autobiography* p. 96; N. B. Cryer, 'Biography of John Eliot', in *Five Pioneer Missionaries* (London, 1965), 171 ff.).

The Meaning of the Cross

79. This is not to forget the labours of John Wesley and David Brainerd in the 18th-cent.; for Carey's awareness of this see G. Smith, *The Life of William Carey* (London, 1909), 24–5.
80. Packer, Introduction to R. Baxter, *The Reformed Pastor*, ed. W. Brown (London, 1829; fac. Edinburgh, 1974), 10; P. Toon, *God's Statesman: The Life and Works of John Owen* (Exeter, 1971), 40; H. R. Jones, 'The death of Presbyterianism', in *By Schisms Rent Asunder*, 35 ff.
81. Robert Traill's famous remark can apply as much to those who go towards hypercalvinism from Arminianism as to those who drift in the opposite direction: 'usually such men that are for middle ways in points of doctrine, have a greater kindness for that extreme they go half-way to, than that which they go half-way from' (*Works* (London, 1810), i. 253).
82. Smith, *Life of Carey*, p. 23.
83. *Cross of Christ*, p. 230.
84. If some aspects of the Anselmic view are questionable, the same must be said about the reactionary theories of John McLeod Campbell and Gustaf Aulen. While it must be admitted that the former affirmed many of Calvin's insights, yet his views on the nature of the atonement place him closer to Abelard than to Calvin. (See M. C. Bell, *Calvin and Scottish Theology* (Edinburgh, 1985), 181 ff.; G. M. Tuttle, *So Rich a Soil: John McLeod Campbell on Christian Atonement* (Edinburgh, 1986), 65 ff.) While Aulen's emphasis on the victory of the cross is both true and valuable, his thesis has more to do with a consequence of the atonement than with its nature. The victory and satisfaction motifs are perfectly consistent. Indeed, the latter is the guarantee of the former according to Calvin, whose views Aulen failed to consider. If Anselm's theory tends to rationalize and moralize at the expense of the 'spontaneous love of God'—a charge which may be levelled against its high Calvinist derivative—the case is quite otherwise where Calvin, the English Reformers, and the Wesleys are concerned. (See G. Aulen, *Christus victor* (London, 1970), p. ix; Peterson, *Calvin's Doctrine*, pp. 46; 49).

9
The Verdict of Scripture

John Owen and John Wesley shared a common commitment to the Protestant rule of faith. Indeed, the *sola scriptura* principle was axiomatic for the four main theologians reviewed in this book. However, it is evident that the Calvinist–Arminian controversy placed great strain on Luther's doctrine of the perspicuity of Scripture. Although the early Reformed confessions reveal extensive agreement in both doctrinal content and simplicity of expression, the emergence of orthodox scholasticism precipitated the Arminian reaction. It now became necessary to safeguard the faith against misrepresentation. Ambiguities were carefully avoided, and cautious qualifications were introduced to eliminate all possibility of error. Thus the Canons of Dort and the Westminster Confession of Faith were seen to compensate for the deficiencies of the earlier confessions, which were now judged inadequate to deal with the heterodox developments of the day.[1]

Thus emerged the 'protestant magisterium'. The ordinary church member needed the scholastic theologian to expound and defend the faith; it was no longer possible for 'laymen' to satisfy their doubts by a mere appeal to the plain text of Scripture. Even the Authorized Version of 1611 seemed to require the Westminster Confession to safeguard its true meaning. In keeping with this mentality, John Owen despised those who appealed to the 'bare word' of Scripture, and whose only hermeneutic was 'away with the gloss and interpretation; give us leave to believe what the word expressly saith'.[2] His impatience was understandable, for, as Wesley himself was to point out, there were no texts in which it is said in 'express terms' that Christ did not die for all.[3]

Although Wesley was no enemy of sanctified scholarship, he was—his own academic training notwithstanding—in sympathy with much that Owen deplored. He still believed in the perspicuity of Scripture. As in his published sermons, preached and written '*ad populum*—to the bulk of mankind',[4] so in his *Explanatory Notes upon the New Testament* (1755), he wrote 'chiefly for plain, unlettered men, who understand only their mother tongue, and yet reverence and love the Word of God . . .'.[5] As far as Wesley was concerned, the doctrine of universal atonement was no recondite truth requiring 'philosophical speculations' and 'intricate reasonings'[6] to make it perspicuous; this view Owen had fiercely contested in the *Death of Death*. Accordingly, Wesley's *Notes* make an interesting comparison with Owen's textual comments as they appear in his treatise. Although Baxter's theological works abound in the kind of 'intricate reasonings' Wesley lamented, he too could edify the 'unlettered' man in his *Paraphrase on the New Testament* (1685). In view of the fact that Owen's theology is supposed to have the same pedigree as Calvin's, the Reformer's exegetical comments also possess considerable interest. Therefore, with the major philosophical and theological issues behind us, we may turn our attention to the 'bare word' of Scripture. By comparing the textual comments of our expositors, I shall attempt to evaluate their respective claims truly to represent the teaching of the Bible. Following the usual classification,[7] the relevant texts will be grouped into those implying a restricted view of the atonement, and those which suggest an unrestricted view.

THE EVIDENCE FOR A RESTRICTED OR LIMITED ATONEMENT

1. In Matthew 20: 28 and 26: 28 Christ declares that his life was to be given as a ransom, and his blood shed, for many. Although Owen admits that 'many' cannot legitimately be taken as 'some', yet, since those whom Christ is said to save are 'given to him by his Father' (John 17: 2–11) and called his 'sheep' (John 10: 15), 'many' cannot mean all.[8] For Wesley the texts pose no problems at all; the many are 'As many as spring from Adam'.[9] Baxter uses the sufficiency–efficiency distinction to say that whereas 'many' are ransomed efficaciously, yet Christ died as a ransom 'to purchase and seal the universal covenant of grace, which giveth free pardon and life to all true believing accepters'.[10] Calvin's remarks are surprisingly different from Owen's and more substantial than Wesley's: ' "Many" is used, not for a definite number, but for a large number, in that He sets Himself over against all others. And this is its

meaning also in Romans 5: 15 where Paul is not talking of a part of mankind but of the whole human race.'[11] Only by correlating the texts with others can Owen give them a restricted sense, a move Calvin has no sympathy with. In fact, his remarks seem more supportive of Wesley's universalism than even Baxter's comments do.

2. Owen cites the parable of the good shepherd (John 10) in support of a limited atonement: 'the good shepherd giveth his life for the sheep . . . I lay down my life for the sheep' (vv. 11, 15). Owen's words are emphatic; this passage 'is sufficient to evert the general ransom . . . all men are not the sheep of Christ . . . the sheep and the goats shall be separated . . . the sheep here mentioned are all his elect . . .'[12] Wesley's thoughts on these key statements are conspicuously non-existent. However, he seizes the opportunity to import his universalism into the parable, paraphrasing Christ's words 'I lay it down of myself' (v. 18) in Prayer Book expressions: by Christ's death a 'satisfaction is made for the sins of the whole world'.[13] This is a very questionable exegesis. Calvin, like Owen, has no doubts that the sheep are 'all God's elect',[14] but the very atmosphere of Calvin's exposition has little in common with Owen's extreme particularism. He says 'godly teachers' have the 'consolation' of knowing that Christ 'has His sheep whom He knows', yet 'They must do their utmost to bring the whole world into Christ's fold.'[15] Baxter, reflecting Calvin's soteriological dualism, resorts to the general–special distinction when he admits that the sheep are the 'chosen flock' and that Christ 'with a *special* love' lays down his life 'for their redemption and salvation'.[16]

If Wesley's exposition is deficient, Owen cannot demonstrate his exegesis of the parable without the questionable tactic of relating it to another, the parable of the sheep and the goats (Matt. 25: 31 ff.). There is, however, an alternative view of the parable which eliminates the question of the atonement's extent altogether. Notwithstanding the indirect reference to election in John 10: 26, Christ may be seen to highlight the quality of his love, compared with the 'pastoral care' of the elders of the synagogue. They had 'ejected' the man whose sight Christ had restored (John 9: 35–6). Unlike these 'self-appointed shepherds of Israel', the good shepherd would never 'eject' his own; on the contrary, he is willing to die for them. Therefore, instead of taking John 10: 11 and 15 as proof-texts for limited atonement, they may be seen as statements about the degree of Christ's commitment. In short, he would totally care for the sheep ('I will lay down my life for the sheep').

3. This alternative exegesis applies to Ephesians 5: 25: 'Husbands, love your wives, even as Christ loved the church, and gave himself for it.' Observing the conjugal analogy, Owen insists that Christ cannot have 'a love to others so as to die for them';[17] therefore the text demonstrates limited atonement.[18] For Wesley the text simply provides 'the true model of conjugal affection',[19] a point Calvin endorses: 'Let husbands imitate Christ in this respect, that he did not hesitate to die for the church'.[20] Aware of the way particularists appealed to Paul's statement, Baxter is careful to imply that Christ still has a general love for all: 'Husbands, imitate Christ, in loving your wives, as Christ did his church, for which (in a special sense) he gave himself by death'.[21] Although Baxter safeguards a point which Wesley seems unconcerned to stress, the text is best seen as a statement about the quality of a husband's love and commitment, especially since Paul had dealt with the question of promiscuity much earlier in the chapter (vv. 3–5). In other words, verse 25 means, 'Husbands, *so* love your wives, as Christ *so* loved the church . . .'.

4. Owen also cites Acts 20: 28 as a clear statement against a 'general mediation'. It was 'the church' which Christ 'redeemed with his own blood'.[22] This text presented no difficulties for Wesley; he would not quarrel with the view that Christ has died for 'the believing, loving, holy children of God',[23] but he rejects the negative inference made by Owen. As has been noted, Wesley knew the strength of his case; there are 'no scriptures' which declare in 'equally express terms' that Christ 'did *not* die for all'.[24] Indeed, Owen's thesis depends upon explicit, negatively qualified texts, and he virtually adds such a qualification in the course of his exegesis. Predictably, Baxter expounds Acts 20: 28 by saying, 'Christ's blood hath purchased the church in a fuller sense than he is said to die for all.'[25] Calvin would undoubtedly agree with this, but he goes much further. Indeed, his remarkable statement cannot possibly be understood without a universal atonement. He argues that pastoral negligence would make the Ephesian elders 'accountable for lost souls' and 'guilty of sacrilege, because they have profaned the sacred blood of the Son of God, and have made useless the redemption acquired by Him'.[26] Surprisingly, Calvin supports not Owen's, but Wesley's general thesis.

5. Owen cites Christ's intercession for his people in John 17 as proof of limited atonement. His basic argument is that the atonement and intercession of Christ are coextensive; for those for whom he died, he also interceded.[27] Althouh none can doubt that John 17: 9 is explicitly restrictive ('I pray not for the world, but for them which thou hast given me'), Wesley insists like Baxter that at this point in the prayer the disciples alone are intended, and that others are embraced later in the prayer (vv. 20–3). It is still arguable that the entire prayer embraces the elect in every generation, although Wesley is anxious to suppress the idea.[28] While Calvin concurs with Owen at this point, he also draws attention to Christ's prayer on the cross, 'Father forgive them, for they know not what they do' (Luke 23: 34), as evidence for an indiscriminate intercession for all. As was noted earlier,[29] Calvin also saw a correlation between the atonement and Christ's intercession, but in a very different manner from Owen. Whereas Owen's particularism forbids a 'general, successless intercession',[30] Calvin's dualism allows him to follow Christ's example by praying 'that this and that and every man may be saved and so embrace the whole human race', even though the efficacy of such prayer is 'still limited to God's elect'.[31]

Owen is distinctly ambivalent about the prayer on the cross, even to the point of contradicting himself.[32] After denying that it was a redemptive prayer, confined to the 'handful of the Jews by whom' Christ was 'crucified', he affirms that it was 'effectual and successful' in their conversion after the day of Pentecost (Acts 2: 14 ff.; 4: 4).[33] Even if the prayer on the cross does not support the idea of a broader intercession than the prayer of John 17, the evidence surely exposes a significant gap between Calvin and Owen. In this respect Calvin seems closer to Wesley, who declares that the prayer on the cross 'procured forgiveness for all that were penitent'.[34] Understandably, where Owen is excessively particular and Wesley excessively general, Baxter is concerned to balance complementary truths. In John 17 Christ prays for his elect 'out of a *special* love to them',[35] and like Calvin,[36] Baxter relates the prayer on the cross to 'reprobates'.[37]

6. Owen also claims support for his thesis from those texts where believers only are the subjects of the statements in question, e.g. Titus 2: 14, 'He gave himself for us, that he might redeem us.'[38] Such texts pose no problems for Wesley; after all, they are simply

The Verdict of Scripture

stating the obvious, that believers alone partake of the benefits of an atonement otherwise available for all. However, Romans 8: 32, 'He that spared not his own Son, but delivered him up for us all', is a special case, since it appears in the important predestinarian passage of Romans 8: 28 ff. If the Arminian view is correct, then, says Owen, 'God . . . had as great an act of love . . . to them that perish as to those that are saved'.[39] In short, distinguishing, electing love is quite meaningless.

Wesley is well aware of the implications of Romans 8: 32. He can only employ it as a proof-text for universal atonement by modifying the predestinarian assumptions of the passage, and this is precisely what he does.[40] To strengthen his argument, Wesley actually alters the AV translation of verse 29, 'For whom he did foreknow, he also did predestinate to be conformed to the image of his Son', replacing this with the doubtful alternative 'For whom he foreknew, he also predestinated conformable to the image of his Son.'[41] Wesley probably follows Philip Doddridge's *Family Expositor* (1738–46) at this point.[42] Whatever reasons led Doddridge to translate σύμμορφος as 'conformable' rather than 'conformed', Wesley clearly sees the theological potential of the English word. Since, in true Arminian fashion, he denies personal, unconditional election,[43] 'conformable' suits his purpose admirably. It introduces a hypothetical element into the divine purpose. Since all are conformable to Christ's image, they will be conformed, *if* they comply with the terms of the gospel. In other words, Wesley simply up-ends the text, turning a statement about God's election into a statement about human potential.[44]

Whatever weaknesses attend Wesley's exegesis, Owen's case is not thereby proven. After all, Paul does not say in verse 32 that Christ died 'for us *alone*'; only if that were the case could Owen demonstrate his thesis conclusively. It seems natural, however, to equate 'all' in verse 32 with 'predestined' in verse 29. Calvin expounds the passage accordingly,[45] but without taking the kind of inferential leap Owen does. Elsewhere, Calvin mingles Romans 8: 32 with John 3: 16, as if to imply that the 'all' of the former has a universal as well as particular connotation.[46] Accordingly, Baxter allows for any ambiguity in Paul's 'all'; Christ was 'given to all by a conditional covenant, of faith and acceptance, and actually to pardon and save all true believers, that accept him'.[47] Whatever Calvin and Baxter say about predestination,[48] their exegesis of

Romans 8: 32 is clearly more offensive to Owen than to Wesley. It thus seems that the more 'restrictive' textual data does not support Owen's thesis. If Wesley's treatment of Romans 8: 29 is a glaring example of textual tampering, Owen seems no less guilty of reading more into the other texts than is warranted.

THE EVIDENCE FOR A GENERAL OR UNRESTRICTED ATONEMENT

1. Although there are numerous texts which relate the atonement to 'all', 'all men', and 'everyman',[49] Owen firmly denies that they provide the Arminians with a prima facie case.[50] He admits that there are several instances of a non-redemptive kind where 'all' means 'all in general', but 'in the business of redemption', 'all' must mean, in a distributive sense, 'all of some sorts'.[51] Some of the examples cited by Owen are to a degree obvious (e.g. John 12: 32; Rev. 5: 9), and Wesley does not contest the point.[52] However, Owen believes that Romans 5: 18, 'the free gift came upon all men', is an example of the distributive 'all'.[53] His particularism demands that the 'all' be restricted to those who are actually saved. Wesley simply sees the text as stating that the 'purchase' of salvation is available for all men.[54] Likewise, Baxter comments that the 'free gift' is 'offered promiscuously to all, on condition of believing',[55] a view even more strongly expressed by Calvin: 'Although Christ suffered for the sins of the world, and is offered by the goodness of God without distinction to all men, yet not all receive him.'[56]

2. Owen seems to be on surer ground when he cites 1 Timothy 2: 5–6, 'the man Christ Jesus, who gave himself a ransom for all'. Since Paul is urging prayer 'for all men; for kings, and for all that are in authority', Owen insists that 'all' must mean 'some of all sorts'.[57] In other words, although Christ has only died for the elect, God has his elect within every rank of society. Owen is possibly correct here, although Paul's words are marginally ambiguous. Certainly Wesley exploits any ambiguity to the full when he declares that 'It is strange that any ... should doubt the universality' of God's grace, for Christ's ransom 'was more than equivalent to all mankind'.[58]

In Owen's view, Wesley's kind of exegesis is forbidden on account of verses 3–4, 'God our Saviour; who will have all men to be saved'. Distinguishing between God's will intending and his will commanding,[59] Owen says the text reflects God's sovereign, efficacious purpose, and this cannot be thwarted by man. Therefore, the 'all' must mean 'all the elect' saved from all ranks of society. If Owen's conception of the will of God is correct, then his exegesis is sound; 'all' cannot mean 'all in general' unless all are saved.

For once Owen has a degree of support from Calvin. The reformer writes that 'The universal term "all" must always be referred to *classes* of men but never to *individuals*'.[60] While this is not Calvin's invariable exegesis,[61] he insists that it applies in this instance.[62] There is, however, an important difference between Owen and Calvin which leads to an unnecessary anomaly in Calvin's own exegesis. Unlike Owen, Calvin believes that 1 Timothy 2:4 speaks not of God's secret, efficacious purpose, but of his revealed, conditional will.[63] If Owen's view of the divine will is correct in this instance, then he and Calvin are right to expound 'all' in the distributive sense. However, if, as Calvin argues, Paul is not speaking of God's secret purpose, the necessity for excluding a 'promiscuous' sense of 'all' does not arise. In other words, since Paul makes no reference to divine election in 1 Timothy 2:1–6, then Christ's 'universal' ransom may be understood as a provision of grace for all indiscriminately (including all ranks of society), albeit for the elect efficaciously. It is this consideration which enables Baxter to avoid a strained exegesis of the passage. He reflects Calvin's usual language when he comments, 'It is not only all sorts of men that Christ would have to be saved; but he willeth the salvation of all men in general, so far as to make a sacrifice sufficient for all, if all will believe . . . therefore he is so far willing of their salvation.'[64]

3. Another disputed text is 2 Peter 3:9, 'The Lord . . . is long suffering to us-ward, not willing that any should perish, but that all should come to repentance.' Predictably, Owen claims that the 'us' are the elect.[65] After all, how can God possibly allow any to perish if all are intended? Of course, Owen's conception of the will and decrees of God forbids an alternative view. As if Owen's position can only be sustained at the expense of severe violence to the text, Wesley's comments are brief: God is 'not willing that any soul which he hath made should perish'.[66] As if to confirm that Arminianism and high Calvinism are both at variance with Reformation theology, 2 Peter 3:9 occasioned one of Calvin's most

remarkable expositions (indeed, it was cited by Amyraut in his *Defense de la doctrine de Calvin* (1644)).[67] Calvin's words serve to challenge both Owen and Wesley, and deserve to be quoted in full:

> This is his wondrous love towards the human race, that he desires all men to be saved, and is prepared to bring even the perishing to safety. We must notice the order, that God is prepared to receive all men unto repentance, so that none may perish. It could be asked, if God does not want any to perish, why do so many in fact perish? My reply is that no mention is here made of the secret decree of God by which the wicked are doomed to their own ruin, but only of his loving kindness as it is made known to us in the Gospel. There God stretches out his hand to all alike, but he only grasps those (in such a way as to lead to himself) whom he has chosen before the foundation of the world.[68]

Calvin's firm adherence to the paradox of God's secret and revealed wills is especially evident in this quotation. The failure by Owen and Wesley to accept the totality of Calvin's balanced, biblical view—each one negating that half of the paradox which conflicts with his basic thesis—prevents them both from expounding 2 Peter 3:9 as Calvin does. The opposing extremes are alike rationalistic, and, as Amyraut observed, it was Calvin's doctrine of Scripture—to accept humbly the 'given' nature of revelation—that ensured 'he had no qualms about enterpreting the words of St Peter in this manner'.[69] Calvin's soteriological dualism underlies Baxter's own comment that 'God hath provided a sufficient sacrifice for their sin in Christ; . . . he giveth to all the world undeserved mercy, and obligeth them to repent in hope of more'.[70]

4. Owen is no less at ease with regard to Hebrews 2:9, 'But we see Jesus, crowned with glory and honour, for the suffering of death, . . . that by the grace of God he might taste death for every man.' Although he cites other texts to prove that 'every man' demands 'some restriction', his argument is not persuasive.[71] The assumed identity between the 'every man' of verse 9 and the 'many sons' and 'brethren' of verses 10 and 11 does not necessarily prove that one can substitute 'the elect' for 'every man'. It is just as valid to say that the author is descending from the general to the particular, as if a universally applicable salvation is effectually applied to believers alone.[72] Accordingly, Wesley interprets 'every man' as all 'that ever [were] or will be born into the world'.[73] Baxter writes that Christ 'suffered in the common nature of man, and the sins of all men had a causal hand in it'.[74] This was clearly Calvin's own view,[75]

although he considers the meaning of verse 9 too obvious to require more than that 'every man' means 'us'. Commenting on verse 5, where the prophecy of Psalm 8 is quoted, Calvin writes; 'David is here recounting the blessings which God bestows on the human race .... He is ... speaking ... of all mankind.'[76] Again, Calvin endorses Wesley's exegesis rather than Owen's.

5. Owen's treatment of 2 Corinthians 5: 14-15 illustrates how his scholastic method demands a priori that 'all' means 'the elect'. Paul's clear statement is up-ended in the process. Owen thus explains the words 'we thus judge, that if one died for all, then were all dead' to mean that 'so many [were] dead as Christ died for; not that Christ died for so many as were dead'.[77] Whereas Wesley understands the 'all' to be 'in a state of spiritual death', in the sense of Ephesians 2: 1, Owen links the statement with Romans 6: 1-11, where Paul teaches that baptism identifies the believer with Christ. Owen argues that since only believers 'die to sin' (Rom. 6: 11), then the 'all' for whom he died must be believers, or the elect. However, both Wesley and Owen are arguably incorrect in their exegesis of 'all were dead'. Scholars have pointed out that the AV wrongly construes the aorist ἀπέθανον as an imperfect. It should be rendered 'therefore all died', as in RV, RSV, NIV, and NKJV; in which case the Corinthians statement suggests the occurrence of two simultaneous deaths. The 'all' died as and when the 'one' died. This does not apply in the Romans passage, where the 'death of believers' (to a life of sin) takes place at their conversion. In other words, the Corinthians statement is simply affirming Christ's identification with the human race in his death,[78] this being the basis of the proclamation of salvation to the whole world (vv. 19-21).

Wesley's comments on 2 Corinthians 5: 15 are therefore in order: '*And that he died for all*' That all might be saved ...'[79] Neither Baxter nor Calvin labour the point. The entire drift of their remarks favours Wesley rather than Owen.

6. With regard to 1 Timothy 4: 10, 'we trust in the living God, who is the Saviour of all men, specially those that believe', Owen denies that Paul is discussing the atonement. He can include Calvin also when he takes the view, 'agreed upon by all sound interpreters', that Paul is dealing with the 'protecting providence of God, general towards all, special and peculiar towards his church'.[80] In other words, God is the σωτήρ of all in a providential rather than a redemptive sense. However, nothing in the context demands such

an exclusive exegesis. Neither Wesley nor Baxter deny that the providential element is present, but they give it a wider interpretation. Wesley says that God's soteriological activity includes his willingness 'to save [men] eternally' and believers are 'in a more eminent manner . . . saved everlastingly'.[81] Baxter agees that Paul means that 'God . . . giveth the mercies of this life and that to come . . . eternal good' as well as 'temporal good'.[82] It is interesting to note that although the eminent Reformed commentator William Hendriksen[83] rejects the exclusively redemptive exegesis of the Lutheran scholar R. C. H. Lenski, his own interpretation of 1 Timothy 4: 10 differs little from Baxter's. In other words, the text may be legitimately expounded in the light of Calvin's sufficiency-efficiency dualism, with reference to both providence and redemption.

7. The group of texts specifying the 'world' as the arena of redemptive activity is best represented by John 3: 16, 'For God so loved the world, that he gave his only begotten Son, that whosoever believeth in him should not perish, but have everlasting life'. In a carefully structured scheme, Owen seeks to prove that κόσμος, even in the writings of the Apostle John, has a variety of senses.[84] Much of what Owen says is rather obvious, e.g. that κόσμος sometimes means 'the physical fabric of heaven and earth' (as in John 1: 9), or 'the world of men' (7: 4), or 'the world corrupted' (1 John 2: 15–17). However, the sixth subdivision of his second category immediately appears questionable. He cites John 3: 16 as an example of the world of God's people, and 7: 7 as specifying the world of the wicked.[85] Thus the 'world' of 3: 16 is 'the elect of God only'.[86] He is forced to adopt this view because his extreme particularism confines the love of God to the elect.

High Calvinist semantics apart, it is doubtful if usage could ever justify Owen's somewhat artificial view. The twentieth century is familar with the scientific world, the world of the arts, and the world of sport. It is perfectly valid to speak of the Islamic world and the Third World. But there is no evidence in the New Testament for any usage remotely equivalent to 'the elect κόσμος', and Owen's view finds no support in any of the standard reference works.[87] Furthermore, unlike all the other instances of 'world', there are no contextual considerations which demand it. It has to be said that Owen's view is dictated solely by an a priori theological stance.

Although Owen attempts to rebut the charge, John 3: 16 is

The Verdict of Scripture

clearly reduced to incoherent nonsense if ἐκλεκτός is substituted for κόσμος. The 'whosoever believeth' then allows the possibility that some of the elect might perish.[88] It soon becomes obvious that Owen has drastically redefined the entire text in a highly rationalistic manner. In his view, it is stating something about the unconditional purposes of God, rather than the conditional promises of the gospel.[89] He also says that the divine love, ἀγάπη, is not a 'natural affection and propensity in God to the good of the creature', but 'an act of his will'.[90] By effectively replacing ἀγάπη with θέλημα Owen is yet again following Aristotle rather than the Bible.[91]

It has been noted that since Owen's day many supposedly orthodox Calvinists have retreated from his extreme particularism.[92] It is no less remarkable to discover Calvin's significantly different exposition of John 3: 16. From the evidence adduced thus far, Calvin's exegesis is almost predictable; even so, he clearly affirms that Christ 'was offered as our Saviour . . . because the heavenly Father does not wish the human race that he loves to perish'. On the subject of the 'whosoever', as well as the 'world', the gap between Calvin and Owen could hardly be greater. While Calvin admits that ultimately 'God opens the eyes only of the elect', yet without inhibition he says:

And he has used the general term, both to invite indiscriminately all to share in life and to cut off every excuse from unbelievers. Such is also the significance of the term 'world' which he had used before . . . . He nevertheless shows He is favourable to the whole world when he calls all without exception to the faith of Christ . . .[93]

It is almost unnecessary to quote Wesley's views on John 3: 16. However, while Calvin's exposition contains little that Wesley would disapprove of, he is unable to forget the high Calvinism of Owen, Whitefield, and others. His terse remarks, though embarrassing to Owen, are thoroughly consistent with much that Calvin taught: '*God so loved the world*—That is, all men under heaven; even those that despise His love, and will for that cause finally perish. Otherwise, not to believe, would be no sin to them. For what should they believe? Ought they to believe that Christ was given for them? Then He was given for them.'[94]

Baxter's paraphrase of John 3: 16 is perfectly straightforward and uncontroversial. However, his remarks on 3: 19 shed valuable light on the way he and the Amyraldians[95] viewed the position of unbelievers: 'For the true cause of men's condemnation is (not that they have no Saviour or ransom, being left as devils to remediless despair, but) that a Saviour as light is come into the world, and men loved darkness rather than light, and so reject him and his truth and grace . . .'[96]

In other words, the universalism of Baxter and the Amyraldians is a hypothetical one; all may be saved, if they believe. This dualistic view is rooted in the 'double aspect' decree of God. Hence God's gracious covenant dealings with mankind embrace the *foedus hypotheticum* and the *foedus absolutum*: the provision of grace is purposed for all conditionally, but for the elect absolutely. It is therefore giving only half the story to describe Amyraldians as 'hypothetic universalists', a description more applicable to the Arminians. As for Amyraut, he confidently appeals to Calvin for his teaching,[97] and there certainly is evidence in Calvin's writings to substantiate his claim.[98]

Whenever the Amyraldian position is discussed by unsympathetic theologians, criticism is usually directed at the implied temporal sequence in the decrees, with its suggestion of afterthought in the fact that the decree of election (which guarantees the success of the gospel) is subsequent to the decree to redeem.[99] In opposing the 'orthodox' alternative (which logically dictates a limited atonement if the decrees are reversed), Amyraut was only replacing one misconception with another, and Baxter actually distances himself from Amyraut at this point: 'all God's decrees are eternal without any order of time'.[100] This point is endorsed by R. L. Dabney: 'The whole all-comprehending thought is one coëtaneous intuition; the whole decree one act of will.'[101] If, therefore, John 3: 16 is expressing the gracious promises of the triune God, and if the basic Amyraldian idea still retains an important logical insight about the *foedus gratiae*, a question arises concerning the divine intention of the atonement. As we have seen, Baxter acknowledges a twofold intention: while Christ did not absolutely intend the salvation of all, yet he did intend that his death should provide a conditional salvation for all.[102] Baxter was thoroughly persuaded that the dualistic account alone made sense of all the textual data, and that high Calvinists and Arminians, from their opposing perspectives, paint only half the picture. They both rend the *foedus gratiae* asunder. In this light, Wesley is no more in error than Owen,[103] but in their extreme forms both theologies destroy the gospel.

8. 1 John 2: 2, unlike John 3: 16, contains an explicit reference to

the atonement: 'And he is the propitiation for our sins: and not for ours only, but also for [the sins of] the whole world.' Owen insists that the verse is not a statement about general redemption, but about the provision of grace for believers throughout the world. In short, ὅλος ὁ κόσμος is no more than the ἐκκλησία καθολική: the church universal, or the elect of God everywhere.[104] Owen carefully observes that the Apostle is seeking to 'give consolation' to believers by linking Christ's death with his present intercession for them (v. 1).[105] But in calling believers 'all nations', he effectively particularizes a general expression to suit his theological purposes. That said, he has the partial support of Calvin, who maintains that 'John's purpose was only to make the blessing' of Christ's propitiation 'common to the whole church'.[106] However, since Calvin was opposing the idea of an absolute universalism, even embracing the possible salvation of 'Satan himself', he needlessly went beyond his usual solution. In fact, he admits the truth of the sufficiency–efficiency distinction, while denying that it fits the passage. But Calvin's view of a universal satisfaction, as well as a twofold intercession, distances him from Owen's basic approach to 1 John 2: 2.

In the light of Calvin's 'usual solution', Wesley's understanding is perfectly valid. By Christ's propitiation 'the wrath of God is appeased'. Likewise, the atonement is applicable to all mankind: 'Just as wide as sin extends, the propitiation extends also'.[107] As one might expect, Baxter is careful to cover every aspect of the discussion when he asserts that Christ's death 'is a propitiation *sufficient* for the sins of the whole world', and that none 'shall be damned for want of a sufficient sacrifice, but only for want of accepting his grace'.[108]

9. Consistently with his general approach, Owen restricts Paul's use of κόσμος to the elect in 2 Corinthians 5: 19, 'God was in Christ reconciling the world unto himself, not imputing their trespasses unto them.' Owen observes that since believers alone are reconciled to God, and they alone are regarded as righteous in Christ (v. 21); therefore it is believers or the elect who are comprehended under the term 'world'. He further insists that since God's reconciling work is absolute rather than conditional, then Paul cannot be understood to mean the 'world generically'. It is therefore 'a blessed, justified world'.[109]

Apart from the forced nature of Owen's exegesis, there is a

glaring inconsistency. If God's reconciling work is absolute, then why does the Apostle plead with the Corinthians?[110] What more needs to be accomplished by exhortation if Owen is correct? Indeed, it is significant that Owen says nothing at all about Paul's impassioned appeal. As one would predict, Wesley finds no need to contest the meaning of 'world'; it is simply that 'which was before at enmity with God'.[111]

The close similarity between Wesley and Calvin's conceptions of reconciliation has been noted in an earlier chapter. It is necessary to observe here that Calvin offers no violence to κόσμος in the interests of election. For Calvin as well as Wesley, 2 Corinthians 5: 19 presented no difficulties at all. This is not quite the case with Baxter. He was well aware of Owen's type of exegesis: 'Verse 19 is mistaken by many, as if by [the world] were meant only [the elect] because reconciliation and not imputing trespasses are mentioned.'[112] However, Baxter is not blind to the fact that, in a very real sense, reconciliation is not 'consummated' until it is possessed by the believer: 'Yet no man is actually (but only conditionally) possessed of pardon and reconciliation, till that condition be performed: Yet God was forgiving them on his part, and was not imputing sin and unworthiness of redemption to them, when he gave them a Saviour.'[113] Indeed, common usage confirms this understanding. 'It's yours for the taking' implies a conditional possession prior to the act of receiving. Owen is inevitably embarrassed by the objection that if nothing substantial is really on offer to all, then ungrateful unbelief is quite meaningless.

TEXTUAL EVIDENCE IMPLYING THE LOSS OF THOSE FOR WHOM CHRIST DIED

If plain language is to be taken in its natural grammatical sense, then the final group of verses constitutes the greatest objection to Owen's hypothesis and the clearest vindication of Wesley's. The fact that Owen's language borders upon abuse suggests a distinct sense of unease; he says that the wits of the Arminians and their successors are 'wonderfully luxuriant' and 'full of rhetorical strains while they argue the fruitlessness of the blood of Christ in respect of the most for whom it was shed'.[114] In short, he flatly denies that 'Christ . . . did lay down his life for reprobates and them that perish.'[115]

The Verdict of Scripture

1. The language of the two Pauline statements is certainly challenging. Paul warns 'strong believers' not to abuse their Christian liberty by insensitively eating meat, formerly used in pagan ceremonies, in the presence, or with the knowledge, of 'weak believers', otherwise they might be tempted to return to pagan ways: 'If thy brother be grieved with thy meat, now walkest thou not charitably. Destroy not him with thy meat, for whom Christ died' (Rom. 14: 15); 'And through thy knowledge shall the weak brother perish, for whom Christ died?' (1 Cor. 8: 11.) The conclusion seems quite inescapable that, as a result of certain irresponsible behaviour on the part of a Christian, a fellow believer could suffer irretrievable harm, notwithstanding the fact that Christ has died for him. Owen rejects this conclusion outright: 'Though one could not perish in respect of the event, the other might sinfully give occasion of perishing in respect of a procuring cause';[116] in which case the danger of which Paul speaks is not a real one.

Owen does not deny that some might perish who, in the 'judgement of charity', are regarded as 'brothers' when they are not. On the other hand, if a brother is an elect believer, the actions of others cannot place his salvation in jeopardy. If he does perish, then he was not one of the elect. But by raising the question of the supposed election of the 'weaker brother', Owen effectively shifts the burden of responsibility from the 'strong' believer to the will of God in a fatalistic manner. Such an exegesis totally negates the thrust of Paul's warning. The validity of any believer's profession can never constitute a rule of thumb. Paul argues that such knowledge is ultimately God's alone (2 Tim. 2: 19). It is even arguable that the strong brother might not be a true believer, if he fails to act in a charitable manner (Jas. 2: 24; 1 John 3: 10). The Apostle can only mean that the weak brother must be viewed as a true believer; otherwise his fears are quite unjustified and his exhortation is without weight.

To add to the confusion, Owen rejects the very basis of the Apostle's concern: 'That by *perishing* here is understood eternal destruction and damnation I cannot apprehend.'[117] Owen is at his most vulnerable here, for all his critical acumen seems to escape him. He was surely aware that Paul uses the same verb ἀπόλλυμι, 'to destroy utterly' as in John 3: 16; there can be no doubt that the Apostle intends to convey the danger of eternal destruction. While it makes sense to infer that all who perish are non-elect, the irresponsibility of others is not to be viewed as a fiction, any more than the actions of those who effected the otherwise divinely appointed death of Christ (Acts 2: 23). In other words, Paul makes his exhortation in the context of the supreme paradox of divine predestination and human responsibility; but he never allows the former to be stressed at the expense of the latter (see 1 Cor. 9: 27; Phil. 2: 12–13; Col. 1: 23).

For Wesley there is no difficulty in reconciling the disputed texts with his view of the atonement: 'So we see, he for whom Christ died may be destroyed';[118] 'We see, Christ died even for them that perish.'[119] However, in making election conditional Wesley has completely eliminated any threat to his exegesis. In short, the problem is how to acknowledge the full force of the Apostle's exhortation without explaining election away. In this respect, Baxter sees Paul's words in the context of the *foedus hypotheticum*: 'Christ . . . hath a right of propriety unto all, having purchased for them a conditional gift of salvation'; 'thou wilt now rob Christ of his right, and them of their salvation, by the abuse of thy pretended knowledge'.[120] In Baxter's view Paul is neither questioning the ultimate efficacy of the atonement in the case of the elect, nor the validity of the weak brother's profession. These are separate questions, and quite foreign to the Apostle's purpose; indeed, he seems to be more concerned with the sincerity of the 'strong' brother.

Interestingly, Baxter claims the support of Calvin's comment on 1 Corinthians 8: 11 in his *Catholick Theologie*.[121] Calvin could not be more strikingly different from Owen at this point: 'If the soul of every weak person costs the price of the blood of Christ, anyone, who, for the sake of a little bit of meat, is responsible for the rapid return to death of a brother redeemed by Christ, shows just how little the blood of Christ means to him.'[122] What for Owen seems to be a theoretical impossibility is for Calvin a matter of the greatest pastoral and practical concern.[123] Again Calvin and Wesley are in perfect agreement over the meaning of Paul's unequivocal statement.

2. The final text to be considered is 2 Peter 2: 1, 'But there were false prophets also among the people, even as there shall be false teachers among you, who privily shall bring in damnable heresies, even denying the Lord that bought them, and bring upon themselves swift destruction.' Owen is not over-anxious about the

implications of this text fo three reasons. (*a*) He says it is not certain that 'Lord' refers to the 'Lord Christ', since the Greek is δεσπότης rather than κύριος. (*b*) It is uncertain whether the 'buying' spoken of in the text is referring to eternal redemption or some temporal deliverance. (*c*) It is not certain whether the Apostle is actually describing the true spiritual status of the persons concerned or simply relating their own opinion of themselves. Owen therefore concludes that they only possess 'common gifts of light and knowledge, which Christ hath purchased for many for whom he did not make his soul a ransom'.[124]

Although it is true that δεσπότης generally refers to God the Father (as in Luke 2: 29; Acts 4: 24; Rev. 6: 10), this is not always the case. In 2 Timothy 2: 21 the word is translated 'master', and in view of the reference to Christ in verse 19 it could be argued that it refers to him.[125] Since δεσπότης means one possessing absolute authority, it would not be inappropriate to use the word of Christ. Thus there are no conclusive reasons for denying that 'Lord' means 'the Lord Christ' in 2 Peter 2: 1.[126] This consideration is inextricably bound up with the next, namely the meaning of 'bought'. Owen denies that the 'purchase' referred to in the text has any redemptive connotations. He points out that the word translated 'bought' is αγηοράζω rather than λυτρόω, which 'signifieth primarily the buying of things'.[127] He says that wherever αγησράζω is used redemptively, the price of redemption is correspondingly spoken of, as in 1 Corinthians 6: 20 and Revelation 5: 9. In his view 2 Peter 2: 1 only signifies a non-redemptive acquisition.

There is, however, an important point to be made about the use of αγηοράζω which links it with δεσπότης. In 1 Corinthians 6: 20 and 7: 23 Paul is highlighting not so much the freedom of the redeemed as their obligations to the redeemer. Freedom from sin's guilt and power is not freedom to do as they wish;[128] they are now Christ's property. Although ἀηοράζω does not, strictly speaking, mean 'acquired by ransom', it clearly presupposes redemption, when used of believers. In Galatians 3: 13 the stronger form εγξαηοράζω is used with respect to the death of Christ. Therefore, αγηοράζω is used in 2 Peter 2: 1 to emphasize the obligations of the redeemed teachers faithfully to proclaim the truth. Peter is thus stressing Christ's sovereign right of ownership and the consequent obligations of those who had professed him. Teaching 'damnable heresies' was inconsistent with such obligations. For Owen to suggest that Peter merely alludes to the teachers' own opinion of themselves is simply to read something into the text. Even assuming his exegesis is valid, surely the 'common gifts of light and knowledge' which Christ had purchased for them are in the realm of 'common grace', and thus related to the atonement.

In the view of this discussion, Wesley's exegesis is, for all its brevity, perfectly adequate. 'The Lord that bought them' means 'With his own blood. Yet these very men perish everlastingly. Therefore Christ bought even them that perish.'[129] Baxter's soteriological dualism enables him to reject Owen's dubious exegesis with ease: 'Christ is called *The Lord that bought them*, not because they falsely professed that he bought them, as some say, but because he purchased and made them a deed of gift of Christ, pardon and life, to be theirs on condition of believing acceptance. And because they should not perish for want of a sufficient sacrifice for sin.'[130] Again, Baxter claimed the support of Calvin's comments on 2 Peter 2: 1:

Christ redeemed us to have us as a people separated from all the iniquities of the world, devoted to holiness and purity. Those who throw over the traces and plunge themselves into every kind of licence are not unjustly said to deny Christ, by whom they are redeemed .... He goes on to say that swift destruction comes upon them so that others do not involve themselves with them.[131]

Although Owen is right to say that universal atonement is not proved by 2 Peter 2: 1,[132] Calvin's comment shows that it demonstrates the underlying principle with respect to some, namely that the provision of the atonement was wider than its effectual application. Even nominal believers who become false teachers possess Christ to a degree, denying what they once accepted. Thus Calvin clearly taught a redemptive dualism. Whereas Owen's Aristotelian assumptions forbade the idea that redemption was not always efficacious, the reformer distinguished between 'redemption supplied' and 'redemption applied'. Calvin did not baulk at the idea of 'apparent wastage', as Owen did. When Calvin lamented those who 'went astray', he was prepared to say, 'We ought to have a zeal to have the Church of God enlarged, and increase rather than diminish; we ought to have a care also of our brethren, and so to be sorry to see them perish: for it is no small matter to have the souls perish which were bought by the blood of Christ.'[133]

Baxter used unusually strong language in dealing with the 'wastage' objection:

> When the Scripture most clearly telleth us *de facto*, that Christ died for all, even for them that perish, and that he bought them that denied him, be afraid of blaspheming God, by telling him, "If Christ died for any that perish, he died in vain" . . . Must Christ do all that our muddy brains will dictate to him, or else be reproached as an imperfect Saviour? O take heed![134]

He therefore appealed to the ambiguity of 'redemption'; it sometimes means 'the price or ransom paid' and 'often for the very liberation of the captive sinner'. To prove this was no novel task; he appealed to Augustine, Prosper of Aquitaine (d. *c*. 455), and Fulgentius of Ruspe (d. 533).[135]

Personalities and authorities apart, it seems fair to conclude that Owen cannot justify his particularist thesis exegetically. Without minimizing Wesley's deficiencies with regard to the ultimate success of the gospel, his exegesis of the disputed texts has more affinity with Reformation Calvinism than Owen's does. Only by imposing a preconceived theological strait-jacket on the textual data, and flying in the face of the criterion of perspicuity, can Owen's case appear credible. Without pretending that Baxter's overall presentation is flawless, his fundamental view of the atonement—a *via media* between Owen's particularism and Wesley's universalism—must surely commend itself as a valid biblical alternative. Notwithstanding minor exegetical variations, Baxter's position may now be seen as a basic reaffirmation of Calvin's soteriology. In short, Calvin's 'Calvinism' qualifies as the very 'ameliorated Calvinism' for which Alan Sell pleads. It is the conciliatory solution to a problem which has been shelved rather than solved.[136]

NOTES

1. The Thirty-nine Articles of the Church of England were open to an Arminian interpretation at certain points. Thus a major task of the Westminster Assembly was to 'vindicate' and 'clear' the 'doctrine of

the said Church from false aspersions and interpretations' (*The Westminster Confession of Faith* (Glasgow, 1973), 11).
2. *DD* 303.
3. *PCC* 217.
4. *Works*, v. 1.
5. Preface to the *Notes* (many editions).
6. *Works*, v. 1.
7. R. Watson, *Theological Institutes* (London, 1850), ii. 281 ff.; R. Wardlaw, *Systematic Theology* (London, 1856), ii. 459 ff.; C. Hodge, *Systematic Theology* (New York, 1873; fac. London, 1960), ii. 558 ff.; A. H. Strong, *Systematic Theology* (New York, 1890), 421 ff.; L. Berkhof, *Systematic Theology* (London, 1963), 392 ff.; L. Chafer, *Systematic Theology* (Dallas, 1976), iii. 201 ff.; R. L. Dabney, *Systematic Theology* (St Louis, 1878; fac. Edinburgh, 1985), 521 ff.
8. *DD* 214.
9. *Notes*, Matt. 26: 28.
10. *Paraphrase*, Matt. 26: 28.
11. *Comm.* Matt. 20: 28; see also *Comm.* Mark 14: 24; Isa. 53: 12.
12. *DD* 292.
13. *Notes*, John 10: 18.
14. *Comm.* John 10: 8.
15. *Comm.* John 10: 27.
16. *Paraphrase*, John 10: 15.
17. *DD* 294.
18. Dabney denies this (*Systematic Theology*, p. 521).
19. *Notes*, Eph. 5: 25.
20. *Comm.* Eph. 5: 25.
21. *Paraphrase*, Eph. 5: 25.
22. *DD* 189.
23. *Notes*, Acts 20: 28.
24. *PCC* 217.
25. *Paraphrase*, Acts 20: 28.
26. *Comm.* Acts 20: 28.
27. *DD* 293.
28. Commenting on John 17: 12, 'and none of them is lost, but the son of perdition', Wesley says, 'So one [Judas Iscariot] even of them whom God had given him is lost. So far was even that decree from being unchangeable' (*Notes*).
29. See above ch. 1 n. 97.
30. *DD* 195.
31. *Comm.* John 17: 9.
32. Owen says, 'Christ in those words doth not so much as pray for those men *that they might believe*' (*DD* 195); on the very next page he writes,

'It seems to me that this supplication was effectual and successful, that the Son was heard in this request also, *faith* and forgiveness being granted to them for whom he prayed' (emphases mine).
33. *DD* 196.
34. *Notes*, Luke 23: 34.
35. *Paraphrase*, John 17: 9.
36. *Sermons on Isaiah's Prophecy*, trans. T. H. L. Parker (London, 1956), 143.
37. *CT* II. 68.
38. *DD* 210.
39. Ibid. 293.
40. Wesley rejects the idea that in speaking of the 'called' in Rom. 8: 28–30 as foreknown, justified and glorified, Paul is discussing a fixed number of individuals. The apostle is only describing the 'method' by which God works, when anyone believes the gospel; the 'individuals' are a hypothetical number. (*Notes*, Rom. 8: 30; Wesley's sermon 'On predestination', *Works*, vi. 212 ff.)
41. *Notes*, Rom. 8: 29 (text).
42. There can be no doubt that Doddridge is writing in a Calvinistic manner when he paraphrases Rom. 8: 29 thus: 'For whom he foreknew, as the objects of his peculiarly favourable regards, ... he *did also predestinate* [*to*] stand in a peculiar relation to the great Redeemer, and [he] *made* in due time *conformable to the image of* that glorious and blessed person' (*Works*, viii. 465). Wesley expresses his debt to Doddridge in the preface to his *Notes*, even quoting an extract from Doddridge's own preface to his *Family Expositor*.
43. Wesley asks: 'Who are predestined? None but those whom God foreknew as believers' (*Works*, vi. 215).
44. W. Sanday and A. C. Headlam reject Origen's view which makes 'the foreknowledge a foreknowledge of character and fitness', but are even less inclined to a Calvinistic interpretation (*The Epistle to the Romans* (Edinburgh, 1898), 217). See also W. Bauer, W. F. Arndt, and F. W. Gingrich, *Greek–English Lexicon of the New Testament* (Chicago, 1964), 786, s. v. σύμμορφος.
45. *Comm*. Rom. 8: 32.
46. *Sermons on the Epistle to the Ephesians*, trans. A. Golding, rev. L. Rawlinson and S. M. Houghton (Edinburgh, 1973), 488; *Sermons on the Epistles to Timothy and Titus*, trans. L. T. (*sic*) (London, 1579; fac. Edinburgh, 1983), 5.
47. *Paraphrase*, Rom. 8: 32.
48. Notwithstanding his doctrine of reprobation, Calvin affirms that the proximate cause of condemnation is 'man's own fault' (*Institutes*, III. xxiii. 6); thus he denies a mechanistic necessitarianism. Baxter affirms

a 'chain of causes' from personal election to glorification, but he denies a positive decree of reprobation (*Paraphrase*, Annotations on Rom. 8).
49. Rom. 5: 18–19; 1 Cor. 15: 22; 2 Cor. 5: 14–15; 1 Tim. 2: 1–6; 4: 10; Titus 2: 11–12; Heb. 2: 9; 2 Pet. 3: 9.
50. *DD* 302–3.
51. Ibid. 309.
52. *Notes*, John 12: 32; Rev. 5: 9.
53. *DD* 309.
54. *Notes*, Rom. 5: 16.
55. *Paraphrase*, Rom. 5: 18.
56. *Comm.* Rom. 5: 18.
57. *DD* 344.
58. *Notes*, 1 Tim. 2: 1–6.
59. *DD* 344.
60. *Comm.* 1 Tim. 2: 5.
61. *Comm.* John 1: 29; Gal. 5: 12.
62. *Sermons on Timothy and Titus*, p. 149.
63. Ibid. 152; 1182.
64. *Paraphrase*, 1 Tim. 2: 4.
65. *DD* 348–9.
66. *Notes*, 2 Pet. 3: 9.
67. B. G. Amstrong, *Calvinism and the Amyraut Heresy: Protestant Scholasticism and Humanism in Seventeenth-century France* (Madison, Wisc., 1969), 166.
68. *Comm.* 2 Pet. 3: 9.
69. Armstrong, *Calvinism*, p. 166.
70. *Paraphrase*, 2 Pet. 3: 9.
71. See Col. 1: 28; 1 Cor. 12: 7. If the latter obviously limits 'every man' to the Corinthian believers, the former is not so clearly restricted (see Calvin, *Comm.* Col 1: 28).
72. J. Bellamy, *True Religion Delineated* (Edinburgh, 1788), 309 f.
73. *Notes*, Heb. 2: 9.
74. *Paraphrase*, Heb. 2: 9.
75. *Comm.* Isa. 53: 12.
76. *Comm.* Heb. 2: 5.
77. *DD* 350.
78. R. W. Dale states: 'According to St Paul, therefore, the death of Christ ... was a representative death. He so 'died for all' that the race died in Him. His death was the true crisis in the history of every man' (*The Atonement* (London, 1875), 322–3). J. Denney writes that the clause 'so then all died' puts 'as plainly as it can be put the idea that his death was equivalent to the death of all. In other words, it was the death of all men which was died by Him' (*The Death of Christ* (London, 1951), 84).

The Verdict of Scripture

79. *Notes* 2 Cor. 5: 15.
80. *DD* 190; see Calvin, *Comm.* 1 Tim. 4: 10.
81. *Notes*, 1 Tim. 4: 10.
82. *Paraphrase*, 1 Tim. 4: 10.
83. *Commentary on I and II Timothy and Titus* (London, 1959), 153 ff.
84. *DD* 303–5.
85. Ibid. 305.
86. Ibid. 321.
87. See the following works s.vv. 'world/κόσμος': J. H. Thayer, *Greek-English Lexicon of the New Testament* (Edinburgh, 1893); G. Abbot-Smith, *Manual Greek Lexicon of the New Testament* (Edinburgh, 1937); Bauer *et al.*, *Lexicon;* G. Kittel, *Theological Dictionary of the New Testament* (Grand Rapids, Mich., 1965).
88. *DD* 326. For Dabney's agreement with this criticism see his *Systematic Theology*, p. 525.
89. *DD* 326.
90. Ibid. 321.
91. J. B. Torrance, 'The incarnation and limited atonement', *EQ* 55. 2 (1983), at pp. 84 ff.
92. See above ch. 1 nn. 54, 62–6. W. Hendriksen criticizes the standard lexicons, but does not equate 'world' with 'the elect' (*A Commentary on the Gospel of John* (London, 1959), 79).
93. *Comm.* John 3: 16.
94. *Notes*, John 3: 16.
95. Armstrong, *Calvin*, pp. 177 ff.
96. *Paraphrase*, John 3: 19.
97. Armstrong, *Calvin*, pp. 186 ff.
98. *Comm.* Ezek. 18: 23; 2 Pet. 3: 9; *Concerning the Eternal Predestination of God*, trans. J. K. S. Reid (London, 1961), 105–6; *Sermons on Timothy and Titus*, pp. 152 ff.; *Institutes*, III. xxiv. 15.
99. B. B. Warfield, *The Plan of Salvation* (London, 1966), 94; D. Macleod, 'Misunderstandings of Calvinism II', *BOT* 53 (1968), at p. 19.
100. *CT* I. i. 58.
101. 'God's indiscriminate proposals of mercy', in *Discussions: Evangelical and Theological* (London, 1967), i. 296.
102. A. A. Hodge agrees (*Evangelical Theology* (London, 1890), 219).
103. William Ames' oft-quoted remark that 'Arminianism is not strictly heresy but a dangerous error tending toward heresy' (*De conscientia* (1632), IV, q. 4) may justly be applied to high Calvinism. Owen's 'error' may as easily lead to fatalism as Wesley's to humanism.
104. *DD* 336.
105. Ibid. 332 ff.
106. *Comm.* 1 John 2: 2.
107. *Notes*, 1 John 2: 2.

108. *Paraphrase*, 1 John 2: 2.
109. *DD* 339.
110. Although Paul's importunate language (v. 20) is directed to 'wayward believers', the basis of his appeal applies equally to evangelism. Calvin expounds the verse in terms of the believer's need for daily forgiveness, as well as for the time of conversion (*Comm.* 2 Cor. 5: 20).
111. *Notes*, 2 Cor. 5: 18.
112. *Paraphrase*, 2 Cor. 5: 19, Annotation II.
113. Ibid.
114. *DD* 359.
115. Ibid. 360.
116. Ibid.
117. Ibid. 361.
118. *Notes*, Rom. 14: 15.
119. *Notes*, 1 Cor. 8: 11.
120. *Paraphrase*, 1 Cor. 8: 11. Although Charles Hodge formally rejected the Amyraldian position, his exegesis of this text is virtually identical to Baxter's overall position *A Commentary on the First Epistle to the Corinthians* (London, 1958), 149; *Systematic Theology*, ii. 558.
121. *CT* II. 51.
122. *Comm.* 1 Cor. 8: 11.
123. For another equally strong statement by Calvin see *Sermons on Ephesians*, p. 521.
124. *DD* 362.
125. Hendriksen, *Commentary on I and II Timothy and Titus*, p. 271.
126. 'The Christology of 2 Peter, which Käsemann calls degenerate, is certainly a very exalted one. It is in relation to Him alone that God is called Father (1: 17). He is the δεσπότης of His followers (2: 1) whose ἐντολὴ they must obey (2: 21)' (E. M. B. Green, *2 Peter Reconsidered* (London, 1961), 16; see also D. Guthrie, *New Testament Theology* (Leicester, 1981), 480).
127. *DD* 363.
128. L. Morris, *The Apostolic Preaching of the Cross* (London, 1960), 54.
129. *Notes*, 2 Pet. 2: 1.
130. *Paraphrase*, 2 Pet. 2: 1, n. 2.
131. *Comm.* 2 Pet. 2: 1.
132. *DD* 364.
133. *Sermons on Timothy and Titus*, p. 817.
134. *CT* II. 66–7.
135. Ibid. 57–8. For Prosper and Fulgentius see S. Cheetham, *A History of the Christian Church during the First Six Centuries* (London, 1894), 324–5. For extracts from Prosper see Daniel, 'John Gill and hypercalvinism', Ph.D. Thesis (Edinburgh, 1983), 501–2.
136. A. P. F. Sell, *The Great Debate*, (Worthing, 1982), 95–8.

PART III
The Theology Faith and Justification

10
The Reformation Heritage

Even a casual acquaintance with the writings of John Owen and John Wesley shows that both men were equally committed to the principles of the Protestant Reformation. Like Martin Luther, they adhered to the centrality of justification by faith alone. Such a doctrine was indeed *articulus stantis vel cadentis ecclesiae*, the doctrine of a standing or a falling church. J. I. Packer's observation applies to Owen and Wesley, that 'justification by faith has been the central theme of the preaching in every movement of revival and religious awakening in Protestantism from the Reformation to the present day'.[1] But if Owen and Wesley were good Protestants in general, they both regarded themselves as champions of Reformed Anglicanism in particular. In his treatise *The Doctrine of Justification by Faith* (1677) Owen was careful to say, 'in what I have to offer on this subject, I shall not in the least depart from the ancient doctrine of the Church of England'.[2] Likewise, John Wesley was anxious to defend his churchmanship by publishing *The Doctrine of Salvation, Faith, and Good Works, Extracted from the Homilies of the Church of England* (1738).[3]

It soon becomes clear however, that Owen and Wesley interpret Anglican doctrine differently. Whereas Owen declares, 'the Church of England is in her doctrine express as unto the imputation of the righteousness of Christ, both active and passive, as it is usually distinguished',[4] Wesley emphatically denies the view of James Hervey and others that 'imputed righteousness' is spoken of in the Prayer Book, Articles, and Homilies.[5] This important difference serves to indicate that the Calvinist–Arminian controversy involved the doctrines of the atonement and justification, just as surely as the two subjects are themselves intimately bound together.

Much of the debate revolved around the issue of the imputed righteousness of Christ. Seventeenth-century orthodoxy believed that justification was more than the pardon of sin: Christ's passive and active obedience were imputed to the believer in his justification. Arminians and others believed that such teaching was inimical to the interests of practical piety, but their solution to an incipient antinomianism was itself regarded as inherently legalistic. Thus the doctrine of a standing church became a source of discord for a divided Protestantism. The issue of imputation coloured the discussion of every aspect of the doctrine of justification for two centuries, while theologians like Owen and Wesley wrestled to demonstrate that their view of the gospel was the authentic biblical teaching of the Protestant Reformation. As a background to the debates of a later period, it is useful to outline the views of the reformers, both English and continental, with special reference to the conflicting claims of Owen and Wesley.

Article XI of the Church of England makes reference to the Homily of Justification. Composed by Cranmer, the homily clearly states that the guilty man's 'righteousness or justification' before God consists in 'the forgiveness of his sins and trespasses'.[6] After denying that even a 'lively faith' has any intrinsic meritorious value, we are told that faith's role is to direct the sinner to Christ 'for to have only by him remission of sins, or justification'.[7] Furthermore, such forgiveness of sin is 'our perfect and full justification'.[8] Cranmer obviously equates 'justification' with 'pardon'. Accordingly, in his sermon 'Justification by faith' (1746), Wesley declared that 'the plain scriptural notion of justification is pardon, the forgiveness of sins'.[9] On the other hand, Owen considered it a mistake to say that 'remission of sin and justification are the same, or that justification consisteth only in the remission of sin'.[10] As I shall demonstrate more fully, Owen's remark reflects the high orthodoxy of a later generation, for even William Tyndale spoke of faith 'that justifieth, or receiveth forgiveness of sins'.[11] Likewise, Hugh Latimer argues that 'our sins must be remedied by pardon, or remission: other righteousness we have not, but the forgiving of our unrighteousness'.[12] John Hooper also assumes an equivalence when he writes of 'justification or remission of sin'.[13] Writing at a slightly later period, John Jewel concludes that no one is 'justified by his own deserts in God's sight', for only through Christ do we obtain 'forgiveness of our sins'.[14]

From the examples given, it would appear that Owen has entirely misread the Anglican Reformers, so that in his view they must be mistaken. The same must be said of the continental Reformers, for the evidence is equally persuasive; they were, of course, protesting against the Roman view of justification by inherent as well as

The Reformation Heritage

imputed righteousness. Thus Luther equates 'Christian righteousness' with 'the forgiveness of sins', that *'passive* righteousness which is the righteousness of grace, mercy and forgiveness of sins'.[15] Article IV of the Augsburg Confession (1530) assumes an equivalence between justification and pardon.[16] John Calvin's statements are thoroughly explicit on this matter: 'Justification by faith is reconciliation with God and . . . this consists solely in the remission of sins';[17] 'God justifies by pardoning';[18] 'this justification may be termed in one word the remission of sins';[19] 'Thus the Apostle connects forgiveness of sins with justification in such a way as to show that they are altogether the same.'[20] His view was also expressed in Article XVIII of the *Confessio fidei Gallicana* (1559).[21] We need not cite further examples; sufficient evidence has been adduced to challenge Owen's perception of the Reformers, and also to vindicate Wesley's claim to 'think on justification . . . just as Mr Calvin does'.[22]

It is obvious that Calvin's position has been something of an embarrassment to later Reformed theologians who, like Owen, wish to argue that justification is more than pardon.[23] Although Calvin did speak of 'the imputation of the righteousness of Christ',[24] he plainly regarded 'justification', 'imputation', and 'remission of sins' as synonymous terms.[25] Furthermore, it is precisely because justification is no more than forgiveness that Calvin never suggested the imputation of Christ's active obedience: 'Our righteousness has been procured by the obedience of Christ which he displayed in His death';[26] 'Christ has attained righteousness for sinners by His death'.[27] It was Theodore Beza who insisted that justification was more than pardon. Mere forgiveness was deemed insufficient; the believer needed a more 'positive' righteousness before God. Hence Christ's passive obedience in death, and his active obedience to the law, form the basis of that righteousness imputed to the believer.[28] While Calvin clearly grounds Christ's saving work in the whole of his obedience, he suggests that his 'active' obedience merely demonstrated his qualification to be the guiltless sin-bearer. His own obedience was thus immediately relevant to himself, and to the believer's justification only indirectly.[29]

Even William Cunningham grants that the Bezan view did not seem to occur to Calvin.[30] But from the perspective of Beza and Owen, Calvin's account of justification must be judged inadequate. Likewise the *Confessio*, which declares in Article XVII that by

'Christ's perfect sacrifice ... we are *fully* justified.'[31] We may therefore assume that Calvin considered the later idea neither necessary nor true, for once remission of sin is seen as the very substance of that gracious righteousness which is imputed to the believer, there is no need to propose a supplementary imputation. When Wesley registered his protest against the Beza–Owen 'double imputation' theory, on the grounds that the believer's personal, inherent righteousness is made redundant,[32] his objection did not apply to Calvin's view of imputation.

Furthermore, high orthodox unease over the scriptural expression 'faith is counted for righteousness' (Gen. 15: 6; Rom. 4: 3, 5; Gal. 3: 6) is not something Calvin shared. When Wesley insisted on its proper though non-meritorious use, Calvin was his ally: 'Now since men have not righteousness laid up in them, they obtain it by imputation, in that God accepts their faith in lieu of righteousness.'[33] Likewise, Luther does not hesitate to say that 'the righteousness of faith ... God through Christ, without works, imputeth unto us'.[34] Article IV of the Augsburg Confession concludes with the words 'This faith God imputes to us as righteousness.'[35] Among English Reformers, William Tyndale says that salvation is 'imputed ... unto faith only[36] and that 'Righteousness is even such faith'.[37] While the Reformers denied that Christ's righteousness was imputed through any intrinsic virtue in faith, they were not afraid of following scriptural phraseology. Therefore, when Owen said it was a mistake to affirm that 'faith itself ... is imputed unto us for righteousness'.[38] he placed himself at odds not only with the explicit language of scripture but also with the Reformers. While they were aware of the danger he was concerned to avoid, they did not adopt his dubious 'double imputation' theory in the process.

Another important question concerns the completeness of justification. It is generally assumed in the Reformed tradition that in the *ordo salutis*, justification is an event and sanctification a process. Luther's exposition of Romans 5: 1[39] seems to conform to this scheme, and Owen certainly believed that justification was an unrepeatable event.[40] Without denying the believer's need for repeated, daily forgiveness, Owen spurned the idea of multiple justifications, an obvious corollary to equating forgiveness with justification.[41] However, Wesley came to consider it dangerous to speak of being in a 'justified state'.[42]

There is some doubt as to whether Luther did adopt the

Reformed *ordo salutis*. McGrath has pointed out that Luther is closer to Augustine and the Council of Trent than is generally realized.[43] Indeed, Luther seems to regard justification as part of a lifelong, all-embracing process when he says: 'For God has not yet justified us, that is, He has not made us perfectly righteous or declared our righteousness perfect, but He has made a beginning in order that He might make us perfect.'[44] He was therefore somewhat ambivalent about the 'completeness' of justification, and the Anglican Reformers seem to reflect this too. Backsliders who 'fall into great sins' are encouraged by the homilies to seek for 'pardon and remission of the same', and thus to 'be received *again* into the favour of our heavenly Father'.[45] If justification means 'being received into God's favour through the remission of sins', then the idea of repeated justification seems perfectly valid. Luther's exposition of David's restoration further confirms this understanding.[46]

It is remarkable to find Calvin explictly teaching the 'continuous' nature of justification. In refuting the views of the 'sounder Schoolmen' that justification commences with the forgiveness of sins but is completed by good works, he argues that at every stage of his life the believer's justification is always that of forgiveness; 'Therefore we must have this blessedness not once only.'[47] He bases his argument on Psalm 32, where David describes his experience 'after a lengthy period of training in the service of God'. Thus, says Calvin, there is such a thing as the 'commencement of justification', also 'the unending continuance of free righteousness throughout our whole life'.[48] Calvin, therefore, opposes Trent not by insisting that justification is a one-off, 'lightning flash' event, but by arguing that it is always 'forgiveness'. Like the Anglican homily, he teaches that 'by a daily forgiveness God receives us into His favour'[49] and 'this alone keeps us in God's family'.[50] Justification, according to him, is a 'present continuous' reality rather than a complete, instantaneous event.[51]

Clearly, then, the high Calvinists of Owen's generation departed significantly from the Reformers. If anything, the Reformers' position raises questions about assurance if the high orthodox theologians root their doctrine of assurance in the completeness of justification. But on Calvin's terms, the unrepeatable event for the Christian in his union with Christ and adoption into God's family. Assurance of salvation is derived from the evidences of such union: 'if we are in communion with Christ, we have proof sufficiently clear and strong that we are written in the Book of Life'.[52] In other words, Calvin's teaching of 'continuous justification' only raises problems for the 'slothful' who rest on some past experience of justification rather than on present communion with Christ. Wesley's warning about complacency, therefore, is not necessary where Calvin is concerned. Even though divine election is the ultimate basis of salvation, Calvin does not forget the 'ethical' aspect of assurance: 'One argument whereby we may prove that we are truly elected by God and not called in vain is that our profession of faith should find its response in a good conscience and an upright life.'[53]

This brings us to consider the relationship between justification and the believer's obedience. Although Owen was just as concerned as Wesley to stress the necessity of holiness in the Christian life, he had difficulty in convincing his critics.[54] His theory of imputation invited the question, 'If Christ's active obedience is imputed to the believer, where is the necessity for the believer's own obedience?' For Wesley no such problem existed; justification does not exclude the necessity of holiness. Although such obedience is not meritorious, it is still necessary for final salvation. Thus Christ's righteousness *imputed* does not exclude Christ's holiness *imparted*. What, then, was the verdict of the Reformers on this issue?

Thomas Cranmer affirms that a 'lively Christian faith' is necessarily accompanied by repentance and 'a steadfast determination with ourselves, through [God's] grace, to obey and serve Him in keeping His commandments'.[55] The Homily on Good Works declares that 'the moral commandments of God be the very true works of faith, which lead to the blessed life to come'.[56] The conclusion is inescapable that whereas Christ's death is the sole meritorious cause of justification, obedience is also a necessary condition of salvation. William Tyndale could not be clearer: 'For God promiseth them only forgiveness of sins, which turn to keep his laws.'[57] John Hooper is remarkably insistent on the absolute necessity of obedience. He asks how antinomianism can be consistent with 'the doctrine of Christ, which only teacheth ... all verity and virtuous life'.[58] Although Owen would not question this statement, one wonders whether his theory of imputation would permit him to conclude, with Hooper; 'I believe that good works are necessary for salvation.'[59]

There can be no doubt that when Wesley rejected Luther's

Galatians in 1741 as a 'dangerous treatise', he was quite unaware of Luther's strong polemic against antinomianism.[60] Although Luther insisted that a sinner cannot make any meritorious contribution towards his salvation, he also held that a believer must be active in holiness: 'Now he believeth not truly, if works of charity follow not his faith .... Christ ... shutteth out all slothful and idle persons which say: If faith justify without works, then let us work nothing .... faith, which, after it hath justified, is not idle, but occupied and exercised in working through love.'[61] Although, generally speaking, Luther stresses the necessity of good works simply because God has commanded them (see Articles VI and XX of the Augsburg Confession), he seems here to ratify Hooper's strong and unequivocal statement.

Calvin's teaching is no less clear; the imputation of Christ's righteousness does not exclude the necessity of obedience. Indeed, he affirms, 'We dream not of a faith which is devoid of good works, nor of a justification which can exist without them.'[62] He also suggests that justification is no less dependent on the believer's obedience than it is on Christ's righteousness: 'we cannot be justified freely by faith alone, if we do not at the same time live in holiness'.[63] This is no isolated utterance. Calvin insists on the necessary relationship between imputed and imparted righteousness. He describes the conditional passage, 'But if we walk in the light, ... the blood of Christ cleanseth us from all sin' (1 John 1: 7), as 'remarkable': 'From it we learn ... that the expiation of Christ, effected by his death, belongs properly to us when we cultivate righteousness .... For Christ is Redeemer only to those who are turned from iniquity and begin a new life.'[64]

Calvin's belief in the sole meritorious work of Christ and the certain efficacy of regeneration does not deter him from writing as he does. Although he is careful to distinguish justification from sanctification, he does not adopt the view that the one is an unrepeatable event, the other a process. They are distinct yet inseparable correlates: 'Christ cannot be divided into parts, so the two things, justification and sanctification, which we perceive to be united together in him, are inseparable.'[65] In short, the process of salvation is a continuum of 'justifying–sanctifying' instants, in which the believer's deficiencies are constantly remedied by remission of sin and the renewing work of the Holy Spirit.[66] What is clear is that Calvin's exegesis no more fits the later high orthodox scheme than it does the Roman Catholic fusion of justification and sanctification. It is instructive to compare Calvin and Owen on the *ordo salutis*

		union		
(Calvin)	election→	with→ Christ	⎰ justification→ ⎱ ⎱ sanctification→ ⎰	→glorification
(Owen)	election→	union with→ Christ	justification→ sanctification→	glorification

FIG. 1. Calvin and Owen in the *ordo salutis*

The final question concerns the status of the *sola fide* principle. As we have seen, Owen argued tenaciously for it whereas Wesley became somewhat ambivalent. Although McGrath is correct to say[67] that *sola fide* and *sola gratia* may be reduced to their common denominator 'justification through Christ alone' (*solo Christo*), it must be said that 'faith alone' is a phrase nowhere used in the New Testament (except Jas. 2: 24, where it is rejected). Calvin partially concedes this, although he defends its use.[68] At best the slogan was unnecessarily provocative, and generally the Reformers explained their use of it with great care. It seems that Luther was in difficulties when he rejected the 'wicked gloss of the schoolmen' that 'faith then justifieth, when charity and good works are joined withal'.[69] On the other hand, Cranmer argues that saving faith 'hath charity always joined unto it'.[70] Similarly, Calvin asserts that 'faith cannot possibly be disjoined from pious affection'.[71] Therefore if faith is never alone, Cranmer and Calvin must view *sola fide* differently, and this is what they do. Cranmer writes that *sola fide* is 'spoken for to take away clearly all *merit* of our works';[72] similarly, in Calvin's mind, 'faith alone' simply means 'mercy alone'.[73] In other words, *sola fide* was not a statement about the psychological constituents of a believer's experience, but a statement about the merits of Christ; it is a synecdochal expression meaning 'faith in the merits of Christ only'. Luther himself denied that faith was alone 'after it hath justified',[74] but his anxiety to defend the *sola gratia* principle made him view *sola fide* psychologically rather than synecdochally. This was quite unnecessary; if 'faith alone' promoted a cavalier attitude to good works, it was best used to emphasize the exclusive place of Christ's merits in the sinner's justification. Approving of the best of the medieval theologians, Cranmer says that they never viewed *sola fide* to mean 'to be justified without our good works';[75] hence it

The Reformation Heritage

means that 'we are justified by faith in Christ only'.[76] Tyndale affirms that 'faith only' means 'trust only in Christ's deserving'.[77] In the context of merit, Calvin describes faith as an 'empty vessel'.[78] Since faith is 'turning to Christ only'.[79] Zacharias Ursinus wrote, 'We are justified by faith only, that is, by the merits of Christ alone.'[80] Lastly, John Jewel declared that to 'be justified before God by only faith' means 'only by the merits and cross of Christ'.[81]

The *sola fide* slogan, properly understood, is simply a way of stressing the objective, meritorious basis of justification. In this respect, faith—viewed as the divinely energized human response—does not itself justify, a truth Cranmer[82] and Calvin[83] sought to clarify. To say otherwise is to revert to the Roman Catholic view that justification is by 'an infusion of grace', with faith as the fruit of regeneration. What J. H. Thornwell says of obedience applies as much to faith in this respect: 'To be justified by graces is not to be justified by grace.'[84] Once the synecdochal view of *sola fide* is strictly adhered to, it at once makes unnecessary the debate as to whether faith, love, or any other spiritual graces justify; the answer is that none of them do. If it is said that works can never justify because of their imperfection, the same has to be said of faith. The theological conundrum 'How does faith alone justify when faith itself is never alone?' becomes a non-starter. The issue then is not whether faith is ever isolated or unaccompanied in justification—which it is not—but what is the sole object of trust. Although love, hope, and obedience are the necessary concomitants of faith, Christ and his merits are the sole focus of attention in faith's nonetheless unique role.

In his discussions about faith Calvin was greatly concerned to rescue justifying faith from Roman Catholic misrepresentations. He argued clearly that 'faith is more a matter of the heart than the head, of the affection than the intellect. For this reason, it is termed "the obedience of faith"'.[85] Even for him faith was never devoid of moral content: 'We, indeed, acknowledge with Paul, that the only faith which justifies is that which works by love (Galatians 5: 6)'.[86] In his comment on that key verse (a text often used by Roman theologians to refute *sola fide*) he denies that saving faith is 'naked': 'Faith ... is always joined with good works.'[87] In a statement penned a few weeks before his death (1564), Calvin insisted, 'The proposition, that faith without works justifies by itself, is false, because faith without works is void.'[88]

Therefore, viewing the issue from a psychological rather than a meritorious perspective, Calvin and the Anglican Reformers rejected justification *sola fide* precisely because faith is never alone. Even when faith is directed to the merits of Christ, it does not function in isolation. In several respects, the later Caroline divines restored the Reformers' teaching in the process of reacting to the high orthodoxy of the early seventeenth-century.[89] If some of their 'antisolifidian' expressions were excessive, many of their insights were anticipated by the reformers. George Bull (1634–1710) was thought to be overturning the doctrine of the Reformation in his *Harmonia apostolica* (1669) by insisting that 'faith comprehends all the obedience required by the gospel'.[90] But such a view is strongly implied in Cranmer's Homily on Faith,[91] and it has an explicit precedent in Miles Coverdale, who affirmed that 'The righteousness of faith comprehendeth the fear of God, love of thy neighbour, patience and all virtue.'[92] Indeed, all the Reformers were anxious to maintain that 'faith is pregnant with good works',[93] although the ambiguity of *sola fide* tended to obscure this. The chief thrust of Reformation theology in the controvesy with Rome was not that man must do nothing, but that he can do nothing of meritorious value in the sight of God.[94] Calvin is not in the least intimidated by the 'rewards' promised to faithfulness in the Bible; they are granted by God's 'free kindness'. They could never derive from some supposed merit, since even perfect obedience is nothing more than our duty. Since we all fail, the 'heathenish' idea of merit should not arise.[95]

Sola fide should therefore mean no more than 'faith in Christ's merits alone'. This is arguably the Apostle's meaning in Romans 3: 28; 'faith' is opposed, not to love and obedience *per se*, but to the idea that they possess any meritorious worth. After quoting with approval a statement by Philip Melanchthon to this effect, Bull concludes: 'And in this sense the gospel obedience expressed in the word faith, excludes that obedience, and all those works which are repugnant to the free promise of and reliance on Christ the Mediator.'[96] Since therefore justification is by Christ (Gal. 2: 17), the object of faith, 'faith' (which always implies an object) is very probably Paul's shorthand for 'faith in his blood' (Rom. 3: 25; 5: 9), Christ's death being the sole meritorious basis of justification. The issue then centres on the theology of merit, not the psychology of faith; it was at this point that the theologies of Rome and the

Reformation parted company. In this respect even George Bull did not betray the Reformation.[97]

It seems that Wesley's understanding of the Anglican and continental Reformers is more accurate than Owen's. Whereas Owen seems quite oblivious to Calvin's theology of justification, Wesley derived his knowledge of Calvin via the Arminian Puritan John Goodwin's treatise *Imputatio fidei* (1642). Both Goodwin[98] and Arminius[99] claimed to concur with many of Calvin's sentiments. This would suggest that the Arminians rather than the scholastic Calvinists were the true heirs of Calvin, a thought which surely demands a redrawing of the theological map. Indeed, what applies to the atonement also applies in some measure to the doctrine of justification. Once the Beza–Owen–Cunningham–Packer school assume that the views of Calvin and the other sixteenth-century reformers coincide with their own, they are committed to regarding Arminius, Goodwin, Bull, and Wesley with suspicion. The views of the Reformers are therefore something of an embarrassment to the 'orthodox', which obliges them either to ignore these views or to 'up-rate' them according to seventeenth-century criteria.

As surely as the medieval and Tridentine theologians mistakenly affirmed a doctrine of merit to check antinomianism, so the high orthodox Reformed theologians needlessly embraced a double-righteousness theory of imputation in order to check legalism. In fact, all aspects considered, both positions were at variance with the true genius of the Reformation. Having outlined the Reformation doctrine of justification, it is now possible to provide an accurate interpretation and evaluation of the views of John Owen and John Wesley. The discussion to date has largely been confined to historical theology; where the truth lies remains an open question. Criteria of biblical exegesis must now be introduced in an attempt to determine whose interpretation seems most in accord with the teaching of the New Testament.

NOTES

1. Introductory Essay in J. Buchanan, *The Doctrine of Justification* (London, 1961), at p. 2.
2. *JF* 164.
3. *Works*, xiv. 209.

4. *JF* 164.
5. *PJ* 305–6. For Wesley and Hervey see B. Semmel, *The Methodist Revolution* (London, 1974), 48 ff.
6. *Homilies*, p. 13; see S. Motyer, 'Righteousness by faith in the New Testament', in *Here We Stand*, ed. J. I. Packer (London, 1986), at p. 34. The Reformers were well aware that 'justification' meant 'righteousness'.
7. *Homilies*, p. 18.
8. Ibid. 13. Cranmer seems to confirm Owen's view of the reformers: 'Christ is now the righteousness of all them that truly do believe in him. He for them paid their ransom by his death. He for them fulfilled the Law in His life' (ibid. 15). However, he does not teach that Christ's 'active obedience' is imputed to the believer, as a later orthodoxy did. It is simply part of the 'cause meritorious' of justification (ibid. 18), a point which is not in dispute. Cranmer obviously treats 'righteousness', 'justification', and 'forgiveness' as synonymous terms.
9. *Works*, v. 32.
10. *JF* 271.
11. W. Tyndale, *Doctrinal Treatises* (Cambridge, 1848), 525.
12. *Sermons by Hugh Latimer* (Cambridge, 1844), 528. Latimer seems to contradict the simplicity of this statement when he says elsewhere, 'Christ giveth unto us his holiness, righteousness, justice, fulfilling of the law' (ibid. 330). But this statement may be taken to mean that Christ's total obedience became the meritorious basis for justification or pardon, rather than that justification is more than pardon.
13. *Early Writings of John Hooper, DD*, (Cambridge, 1848), 264. See also *Later Writings of Bishop Hooper* (Cambridge, 1852), 58–9.
14. *The Works of John Jewel* (Cambridge, 1848), iii. 66.
15. *A Commentary on St Paul's Epistle to the Galatians*, ed. P. S. Watson (London, 1953), 16; 21–3.
16. H. B. Smith and P. Schaff, *The Creeds of the Evangelical Protestant Churches* (London, 1877), 40. (Hereinafter cited as '*Creeds*.')
17. *Inst.* III. xi. 21.
18. Ibid. 11.
19. Ibid. 21.
20. Ibid. 22.
21. *Creeds*, p. 369; also A. C. Clifford, 'John Calvin and the Confessio fidei Gallicana', *EQ* 58. 3 (1986), at p. 204.
22. *Journal*, v. 116.
23. See W. Cunningham, *The Reformers and the Theology of the Reformation* (London, 1862; fac. London, 1967), 403 ff.; L. Berkhof, *Systematic Theology* (London, 1963), 514.
24. C. Hodge and J. I. Packer create the impression that Calvin held the later view by quoting *Institutes*, III. xi. 2: 'justification consists in the

forgiveness of sins and the imputation of the righteousness of Christ'. But this is to fly in the face of overwhelming evidence to the contrary, as John Goodwin made clear. He cites David Pareus of Heidelberg, who disputed Cardinal Bellarmine's similar misinterpretation of Calvin's words: 'his meaning was not, that there should be a double (formal) cause of justification (for so he would fight against himself, and against the Scriptures) but his intent was, by two Scripture-terms equipollent, the one to the other, to express one and the same formal cause, or to join these two expressions together exegetically . . . so that one might help to explain the other' (J. Goodwin, *Imputatio fidei, or a Treatise of Justification* (London, 1642), 121-4). Cunningham is similarly mistaken in his view of Calvin's comment on 1 Cor. 1: 30: 'He atoned for our sins by his death, and his obedience is imputed to us for righteousness.' But for Calvin Christ's obedience is his death; since justification is pardon, nothing more than the imputation of Christ's passive obedience is necessary to effect this. (For Hodge see his *Systematic Theology* (New York, 1873; fac. London, 1960), iii. 133-4; for Packer, see 'The doctrine of justification in development and decline among the Puritans', in *By Schisms Rent Asunder* (PRSC, London, 1969), at p. 21 n. 11; id., 'Justification in Protestant theology', in *Here We Stand*, at pp. 90-1; for Cunningham see his *Reformers*, p. 403.)

25. *Inst.* III. xi. 4; *Comm.* Gal. 3: 6; Luke 1: 77.
26. *Comm.* Rom. 4: 25.
27. *Comm.* Rom. 5: 9.
28. T. Beza, *Tractationes theologiae* (Geneva, 1570-82), iii. 248; 256.
29. *Inst.* II. xvi. 5.
30. *The Reformers*, p. 404.
31. *Creeds*, p. 369.
32. *Works*, v. 227.
33. *Comm.* Gal. 3: 6.
34. *Commentary on Galatians*, p. 22.
35. *Creeds*, p. 40.
36. *Doctrinal Treatises*, p. 15.
37. Ibid. 494.
38. *JF* 271.
39. 'Lectures on Romans', *Works*, xxv. 285 ff.
40. *JF* 144.
41. Ibid. 138.
42. *Works*, viii. 325. Wesley thought this would encourage complacency: 'And think not to say, "I was justified once; my sins were once forgiven me . . ."' (*Works*, v. 88).
43. A. E. McGrath, *Iustitia Dei* (Cambridge, 1986), ii. 18.
44. *Works*, xxv. 245.

45. *Homilies*, p. 372; also p. 367.
46. *Commentary on Galatians*, p. 515.
47. *Inst.* III. xiv. 11.
48. *Comm.* Rom. 3: 21; 4: 6.
49. *Comm.* 2 Cor. 5: 20.
50. *Comm.* 1 John 1: 7.
51. 'That peace of conscience, which is disturbed on the score of works, is not a one-day phenomenon, but ought to continue through our whole life. It follows from this that until our death we are justified only as we look to Christ alone in whom God has adopted us, and now regards us as accepted' (*Comm.* Rom. 3: 21; see also *Comm.* Luke 1: 77).
52. *Inst.* III. xxiv. 5.
53. *Comm.* 2 Pet. 1: 10.
54. *Works*, ii. 314 ff. Motyer says 'it has always been hard for Protestant theology to show the *theological* necessity for sanctification' ('Righteousness by faith', p. 55).
55. *Homilies*, p. 24.
56. Ibid. 34.
57. *Doctrinal Treatises*, p. 525.
58. *Early Writings*, p. 53.
59. *Later Writings*, p. 59.
60. 'What Christ has merited for us is not only *gratia*, "grace", but also *donum*, the "gift" of the Holy Ghost, so that we might not only have forgiveness of sin, but also cease from sinning. Whoever, then, does not cease from sinning, but continues in his former wicked life, must have another Christ from the antinomians' (editor's Preface, *Commentary on Galatians*, p. 14 n. 2).
61. Ibid. 466.
62. *Inst.* III. xvi. 1.
63. *Comm.* 1 Cor. 1: 30.
64. *Comm.* 1 John 1: 7.
65. *Inst.* III. xi. 6.
66. Paul's speaking here of the righteousness of works is not at all inconsistent with the free righteousness of faith .... God begins righteousness in us through the regeneration of the Spirit, so what is lacking is supplied through the remission of sins, yet so that all righteousness depends on faith' (*Comm.* Phil. 1: 11).
67. *Iustitia Dei*, ii. 38–9.
68. *Inst.* III. xi. 19. Luther incorrectly added 'allein' to Rom. 3: 28 in his German New Testament (1522).
69. *Commentary on Galatians*, p. 141.
70. *Homilies*, p. 24.
71. *Inst.* III. ii. 8.
72. *Homilies*, 14 (emphasis mine).

73. *Comm.* Rom. 3: 21; Hab. 2: 4.
74. *Commentary on Galatians*, p. 466.
75. *Homilies*, 16.
76. Ibid. 17.
77. *Doctrinal Treatises*, p. 509.
78. *Inst.* III. xi. 7.
79. Ibid. xvi. 1.
80. *The Commentary of Dr Zacharias Ursinus on the Heidelberg Catechism*, trans. G. W. Williard (Columbus, Ohio, 1852; fac. Phillipsburg, NJ, 1985), 332.
81. *Works*, iii. 243.
82. *Homilies*, p. 17.
83. *Inst.* III. xi. 7.
84. *Collected Writings* (Richmond, Virg., 1875; fac. Edinburgh, 1974), iii. 353.
85. *Inst.* III. ii. 8. This statement surely challenges R. T. Kendall's idea that for Calvin, faith is seated exclusively in the mind (*Calvin and English Calvinism to 1649* (Oxford, 1979), 19; 28).
86. *Inst.* III. xi. 20.
87. *Comm.* Gal. 5: 6.
88. *Comm.* Ezek. 18: 14–17.
89. A. E. McGrath, 'The emergence of the Anglican tradition on justification 1600–1700', *CM* 98; 1. (1984), at p. 33.
90. *Harmonia Apostolica* (Oxford, 1842), 64.
91. 'For the very sure and lively Christian faith is, not only to believe all things of God which are contained in Scripture; but also an earnest trust and confidence in God . . . that he will be merciful to us for his only Son's sake . . . whensoever we, repenting truly, do return to him with our whole heart, steadfastly determining with ourselves, through his grace, to obey and serve him in keeping his commandments . . . Such is the true faith that the Scriptures doth so much commend' (*Homilies*, p. 24).
92. *The Remains of Bishop Coverdale* (Cambridge, 1846), 93.
93. A. E. McGrath, *Justification by Faith* (Basingstoke, 1988), 31.
94. Calvin clearly stresses the passivity of faith where meriting justification is concerned, without denying its active character psychologically: 'For in regard to justification, faith is merely passive' (*Inst.* III. xiii. 5); 'We, indeed, acknowledge with Paul, that the only faith which justifies is that which works by love (Gal. 5: 6)' (ibid. xi. 20).
95. *Comm.* Luke 17: 7–10; *Inst.* III. xv. 2–4. Calvin's answer to the Tridentine doctrine of merit (whether condign or congruous) may be summarized as follows: (1) God is never under any obligation to man for anything performed by him. (2) Man is always in God's debt; even the believer's good works and faithfulness (the fruit of regeneration)

are imperfect and in need of pardon. (3) God accepts our persons and our works only on account of the merits of Christ. (4) The only sense in which God becomes our debtor is with regard to his gracious promises, not because of anything we might offer to him. (Calvin, 'Antidote to the Council of Trent', *Tracts and Treatises* (Edinburgh, 1851), iii. 108 ff.) Although he would take issue with the ARCIC II statement 'Salvation and the church' (1987) over the ambiguous retention of 'merit' and its related 'penitential disciplines and other devotional practices' (paras. 22–4), the document clearly makes a number of concessions he would approve of, as was actually the case with the decrees of Trent (see 'Antidote', pp. 108–9). Contrary to McGrath's criticisms of the 1987 statement, it was no part of Calvin's polemic against Rome to insist that justification was a complete and perfect event followed by sanctification. Consequently, for Calvin the believer's assurance is not based on such an event; rather it is derived from (*a*) union with Christ by faith on the basis of his finished work, and (*b*) an on-going continuum of redemptive experience. Thus he really occupies a middle position *vis-à-vis* Rome and a later (equally questionable) Reformed orthodoxy; but neither McGrath nor Chadwick seem aware of Calvin's actual position or its importance. As I have noted, there is evidence that Luther shared Calvin's conception. Although McGrath is aware of Luther's semi-Augustinian position in *Iustitia Dei* ('semi'-since neither Luther nor Calvin adopts the Augustinian 'justification–sanctification' synthesis), he uses him to justify a very different position against the conclusions of 'Salvation and the Church.' (A. E. McGrath, *ARCIC II and Justification: An Evangelical Anglican Assessment of 'Salvation and the Church'* (Oxford, 1987), 40–2; H. Chadwick, 'Justification by faith: a perspective', *One in Christ*, 20. 3 (1984), at pp. 192 ff.) See also T. H. L. Parker, *Commentaries on the Epistle to the Romans 1532–1542* (Edinburgh, 1986), 197–200.

96. *Harmonia apostolica*, p. 71.
97. Bull did in fact confirm and clarify several 'neglected' emphases of Cranmer, Calvin, and the other reformers, in opposition to both Tridentine and high Calvinist views. Although his exegesis of Jas. 2: 24 obviously differs from Calvin's, it is actually consistent with Calvin's overall position. For Calvin, no less than for Bull, only a living, obedient faith justifies, a view which makes sense of Jas. 2: 24. The heart of the matter is the question of merit; here Bull could not be more at one with Calvin (or even Luther in his more cautious moments): 'But because the promise of eternal life given in the Gospel is founded in the meritorious satisfaction of Jesus Christ, and confirmed by His most precious blood, therefore the obedience of faith continually refers to Christ, as the only propitiation: and His most perfect obedience in life and death is the only circumstance, which

makes our imperfect and spiritless obedience acceptable to God unto salvation, and to carry off the reward of eternal life' (ibid. 70-1).

98. After quoting Calvin's views extensively, Goodwin comments: 'He that in the presence of all these witnesses speaking so distinctly and fully from the author's own pen, will yet say, that Calvin held not remission of sins to be our entire and complete justification; had need be able to prove to the world, that Calvin's head and hand were at odds, when these things were written; or that his pen was suborned and bribed by some adversary to conspire against his meaning, and to betray his judgement in the point' (*Imputatio fidei*, pp. 121-2).

99. When the 'orthodox' Calvinists accused Arminius of heterodoxy over justification, he replied, 'Whatever interpretation may be put upon these expressions, none of our divines blames Calvin, or considers him to be heterodox on this point; yet my opinion is not so widely different from his as to prevent me from employing the signature of my own hand in subscribing to those things which he has delivered on this subject, in the Third Book of his *Institutes*; this I am prepared to do at any time, and to give them my full approval' (*Works*, i. 636).

11
Christ's Righteousness and Ours

When Owen published his treatise *The Doctrine of Justification by Faith* in 1677, Puritan theology and piety had been officially proscribed for several years. Sustained attacks had also been made on Calvinistic orthodoxy from outside and inside the Reformed churches, the primary cause of concern being the growth of antinomianism. Against this background, Baxter had published his *Aphorismes of Justification* in 1649, the first of many treatises on the subject. Bull's *Harmonia apostolica* (1669) was an attempt to reconcile the seemingly conflicting teachings of the apostles Paul and James on the subject of justification, thus dealing with the antinomian problem at its source. Protestants consequently joined with Roman Catholic and Socinian theologians in rejecting the principle of *sola fide*, as commonly understood. The main focus of their objections was the doctrine of the imputed righteousness of Christ.

Owen's treatise was itself a response to the growing disenchantment with the orthodox doctrine of justification. In 1674 William Sherlock wrote against Owen's earlier treatise *On Communion with God* (1657), in which Owen had argued that Christ's passive and active obedience were imputed to the believer. Sherlock objected that Owen's theory made personal obedience and holiness quite redundant. Owen replied with his *Vindication* (1674), asserting a position he was to defend three years later in his main treatise on the subject.

In *Justification by Faith* Owen is concerned both to vindicate the gospel and to answer those who 'cried out against' his theory of imputation as being 'inconsistent with a necessity of personal holiness and obedience'.[1] The Socinians argued that it was irrational to assert both the imputation of Christ's active obedience and the necessity of personal holiness, and the Roman theologians rejected the idea of imputed righteousness as unscriptural. In Owen's view 'imputed righteousness' was in the same category as the doctrines of the trinity and the incarnation; it was above reason but not contrary to it.[2] As for the Roman Catholic objection, Owen was amazed at its audacity, especially when much Roman theology was based on 'terms, distinctions and expressions' which were coined in 'Aristotle's mint, or that of the schools deriving from him'.[3] It is quite remarkable that he should advance this criticism, since he too had resorted to Aristotelianism.

Owen's views on the nature of justification and imputation have already been touched on. The indications are that a significant gap exists between his own views and those of the reformers. How, then, does he demonstrate that justification is more than pardon, and that Christ's active obedience is as necessary for justification as his passive obedience? His reply is that Christ 'fulfilled the whole law for us; he did not only undergo the penalty of it due unto our sins, but he also yielded that perfect obedience which it did require'.[4] 'He was born to us, and given to us; lived for us, and died for us;—that "by the obedience of one many might be made righteous".'[5] He therefore denies that Christ's personal obedience was merely relevant to himself. He 'was not a private but a public person'.[6]

Owen also argues that pardon is not by itself sufficient for justification. It is therefore insufficient to be merely not unrighteous, or innocent. The believer's justification must relate to the precept as well as the penalty of the law. Although Christ's death delivers the sinner from the curse of the law, Owen concludes, 'we are not thence esteemed just or righteous, which we cannot be without respect unto the fulfilling of the law, or the obedience by it required'.[7]

Owen seeks to demonstrate his thesis exegetically by citing Galatians 4: 4, 'But when the fulness of the time was come, God sent forth his Son, made of a woman, made under the law, to redeem them that are under the law, that we might receive the adoption of sons.' Owen argues that Christ had sufficient 'habitual grace' to qualify himself as the sin-bearing mediator by virtue of his incarnation; thus his active obedience had direct bearing on the believer's justification. Recognizing that Paul's statement covers the ceremonial as well as the moral law, but that the latter is 'of eternal obligation', Owen still insists that by his passive and active obedience Christ has delivered the believer from both the penalty and the precept of the law: 'And if the Lord Christ hath redeemed us only from the curse of it by undergoing it, leaving us in ourselves to answer its obligation unto obedience, we are not freed nor delivered ....'.[8] He also appeals to Romans 5: 19, Philippians 2: 8, and Hebrews 5: 8, insisting that the references to Christ's obedience must include his passive and active obedience.[9]

This exegesis is questionable on several counts. To argue that Christ's imputed active obedience is a truth 'above reason' is unnecessary and beside the point; it is to plead for an idea for which there is no real evidence, unlike the doctrines of the trinity and the virgin birth. Undoubtedly Christ's active obedience had a 'public' significance; but the 'habitual grace' of the 'second Adam' had to be publicly evidenced in order to prove his 'high priestly' qualifications (Heb. 7: 26–7). To assume that his active obedience had the same vicarious significance as his death cannot but encourage an antinomian mentality. Indeed, no real parallel exists between them; the statement 'Christ died a penal death in our stead' makes 'gospel sense', but 'Christ lived a holy life in our stead' is antinomian nonsense.[10] The antinomians proper, whose outlook Owen rightly deplored,[11] argued on his very principles.[12] As for the other texts, the subject of discourse is in every case the death of Christ. If Owen is correct, then Paul's expression 'justified by his blood' (Rom. 5: 9) states only half the truth.

John Wesley was entirely aware of the weaknesses of this type of argument. He accepted without question that Christ's active obedience demonstrated his fitness to make a perfect atonement for sin, but saw no necessity to give the statements 'Christ lived for me' and 'Christ died for me' the same kind of status. 'Therefore, though I believe he hath lived and died for me, yet I would speak very tenderly and sparingly of the former, (and never separately from the latter) even as sparingly as do the Scriptures.'[13] Thus he was reluctant to employ the expression 'imputed righteousness'; it was unscriptural, unnecessary, ambiguous, and dangerous, 'For if the very personal obedience of Christ (as those expressions directly lead me to think) be mine the moment I believe, can anything be added thereto? Does my obeying God add any value to the perfect obedience of Christ? On this scheme, then, are not the holy and unholy on the very same footing?'[14] In Wesley's view the expression should only refer to Christ's passive obedience or death; 'His "becoming obedient unto death", that is, dying for man, is certainly the chief part, if not the whole, which is meant by that expression.'[15]

Wesley backs up his exegesis with two powerful arguments.

Firstly, he says that by his death alone Christ has fully satisfied the law. The law 'required only the alternative, obey *or* die. It required no man to obey *and* die too. If any man had perfectly obeyed, he would not have died'.[16] Secondly, he argues that if Christ's perfect obedience is imputed to the believer, then the believer has no more need of pardon than Christ had; 'If his obedience be ours, we still perfectly obey in him.'[17] In other words, Christ's passive obedience alone is sufficient to guarantee the believer's justification. In reply to Owen's argument that 'It is one thing to be acquitted before the throne of a king ... another to be made his son by adoption',[18] Wesley says this might apply to a 'rebel against an earthly king', but not to a 'rebel against God'. Pardon necessarily implies acceptance. The two 'cannot be divided ... In the very same moment that God forgives, we are the sons of God. Therefore, this is an idle dispute'.[19] For this reason Wesley affirms, with Luther, Calvin, and the Anglican Reformers, that 'The plain scriptural notion of justification is pardon, the forgiveness of sins.'[20]

Wesley is certain that his view accords with Scripture. He agrees with Owen that in Galatians 4: 4 Christ was 'Both under the precept, and under the curse' of the law.[21] However, redemption from the law only applies to the 'curse of it'. Elsewhere he links the text with Galatians 3: 13, 'Christ hath redeemed us from the curse of the law, being made a curse for us.' This text, he says, 'speaks not a word of redeeming us from the law, any more than from love or heaven'.[22] 'But from what did he redeem them? Not "from the law", but "from guilt, and sin, and hell". In other words, He redeemed them from the "condemnation of this law", not from "obedience to it". In this respect they are still "not without law to God, but under the law to Christ" (1 Corinthians 9: 21)'.[23] Wesley's quotation of Corinthians surely clinches the argument. In short, the gospel 'repeals', not the precept, but the penalty of the law.

Wesley's claim to adhere to Calvin's exposition of the subject has already been noted. Indeed, in Calvin's detailed exegesis, his views on justification, Christ's obedience, and the law fully confirm Wesley's claim.[24] As we have seen, his knowledge of the Reformer's views was probably derived from John Goodwin, who quotes Calvin extensively in his *Imputatio fidei* (1642), abridged and republished by Wesley in 1765. Although Arminius himself refused to commit himself on the passive–active obedience debate,[25] he explicitly endorsed Calvin's *Institutes* on the subject of justification.[26] All this confirms that it was the Arminian tradition that tended to perpetuate the true Calvinistic and Reformation position. Indeed, the differences between Calvin and the Westminster Confession are even more pronounced in the Savoy Declaration.[27] According to Baxter, these far-reaching doctrinal changes were master-minded by Owen himself.[28]

It should be noted that Calvin's teaching on Christ's obedience was expounded more explicitly by the German Reformed theologian Johannes Fischer (Piscator) (1546–1625),[29] professor at Herborn in Nassau. Whether or not Wesley was influenced directly by his views, Owen actually pays attention to Piscator's arguments, albeit unsatisfactorily.[30] Indeed, it was Piscator who exposed the inherent contradiction in the Bezan view of imputation, although his trenchant analysis failed to prevent Reformed orthodoxy from embracing it.[31]

Piscator made explicit Calvin's suggestion that Christ's active obedience demonstrated his fitness to be the innocent sin-bearer; his own obedience was relevant to himself, and only to the believer's justification indirectly. Furthermore, if man's obedience to the law was still necessary, then Christ's active obedience could have no substitutionary significance. Since the law only demanded 'do or die', Christ did not produce a double righteousness for the sinner on the basis of 'do and die'; otherwise, says Piscator, God would be demanding 'the same debt twice paid'.[32] It was Christ's duty to obey the law for himself; however, by his voluntary death he completely satisfied the demands of justice for others. Had his life merited righteousness for others by satisfying the precept of the law, there would have been no need for his death. Therefore, since the Scriptures always attribute salvation to the death of Christ, the believer's righteousness before God derives from Christ's passive obedience. Thus believers are delivered not from the precept of the law, but from its penalty. Lastly, as Calvin himself taught, Piscator held that 'justification', 'remission of sins', and 'imputation of righteousness' are synonymous expressions.

Like Calvin and Piscator, Wesley affirms the believer's perpetual legal obligations in his sanctification. Although Owen maintains this too, his theory of imputation creates a serious anomaly. Where is the necessity for the believer's obedience, if the statements 'Christ kept the law for me' and 'Christ died for me' have the same status? Although Wesley, like Calvin,[33] was happy to extend the basis of justification to the whole of Christ's obedience, as its meritorious ground (i.e. a guilty mediator could never mediate), Christ's obedience is seen as the model for the believer's sanctification according to 1 John 2: 6, 'He that saith he abideth in him ought himself to walk, even as he walked.' In short, Christ's active obedience is for imitation rather than imputation.[34] Despite his denials, Owen cannot press the necessity of that 'holiness without which no man shall see the Lord' (Heb. 12: 14). For Wesley, his questionable perfectionism apart, Christ's passive and active obedience are seen as the foundation for imputed and imparted righteousness, both of which are necessary for salvation.[35]

This brings us to the 'middle men', Richard Baxter and John Tillotson. Like Wesley in the eighteenth-century, both were accused of Roman and Socinian tendencies in their critiques of high orthodoxy; but they were no less critical of Roman and Socinian divines than of their high orthodox brethren. Of course, if Owen's type of orthodoxy is regarded as normative, it is difficult to view some of their emphases with favour. But if the theological controversies of the seventeenth and eighteenth centuries are seen from a sixteenth-century perspective, a very different evaluation is demanded, not only of Owen and Wesley, but also of Baxter and Tillotson. Both men made a significant contribution to Wesley's theology, so that their views assume an added importance.

From the moment Baxter's *Aphorismes* were published, his assault on antinomianism raised many an orthodox eyebrow. Ever since the seventeenth century his views have been regarded as something of an embarrassment to Protestant theologians, a fact reflected in J. I. Packer's ambivalent assessment of his contribution: 'Baxter was a great and saintly man; as a pastor, evangelist, and devotional writer, no praise for him can be too high; but as a theologian he was, though brilliant, something of a disaster.'[36] This is a predictable response by one who endorses the criteria of Owen's orthodoxy. But if such criteria are valid beyond question, Packer is obliged to pass a similar judgement on some of the teachings of the Protestant Reformers themselves. This is not to suggest that Baxter's theology is flawless, but to question Packer's critical perspective and the accuracy of some of his observations.[37]

Although Baxter denies that 'Christ's righteousness imputed' is a 'Scripture phrase', he is prepared to include even the active obedience of Christ as part of the 'meritorious cause' of the believer's righteousness.[38] What he rejects is the incoherence of the Beza–Owen theory of imputation. If this is correct, says Baxter, 'we could need no pardon, for he that is reputed to be innocent, by fulfilling all the law, is reputed never to have sinned.... Therefore, such an imputation of Christ's righteousness to us would make his satisfaction null or vain'.[39] If Baxter's obvious agreement with Piscator is interesting, a certain parallel with Calvin is equally so. Baxter's view of faith as the formal though not meritorious cause of justification, and of its role in the imputation of righteousness, is virtually identical to Calvin's in his discussion of the subject.[40] This is not to defend every aspect of the scholastic 'four-fold cause of justification'[41] but to suggest that Calvin is equally vulnerable to criticisms commonly levelled at Baxter.[42]

Baxter's neonomian or new law conception of the gospel is a highly ingenious amalgam of gospel theology and seventeenth-century politial theory. Packer is correct to question the propriety of Baxter's 'political method', although one may doubt that he has grasped the significance of all the details of Baxter's system. To describe God the Father as 'Rector' and Christ as 'the Father's administrator' in God's kingdom is certainly 'quaint', but, stripped of all dubious metaphor, Baxter's emphases are not as 'theologically vicious' as Packer makes out. Baxter's greatest methodological mistake is an excessive use of political analogy, though, to be fair, there are monarchical analogies in the Bible, and much of Baxter's exposition does full justice to the Reformation understanding of Christ's threefold office of prophet, priest, and king.

Packer gives the impression that Baxter has simply 'legalized' the gospel at the expense of the law, but this is to misrepresent Baxter's thesis entirely. In Baxter's view the great bulk of the biblical revelation falls within the era of the Covenant, or Law of Grace, which, coming into force after the fall of man, superseded the Law of Innocency. The 'first edition' of the 'new law' was made with all mankind in Adam and Noah. Even the Mosaic covenant falls within the era of the law of grace, for God 'hath proclaimed his name ... even in the terrors of Mount Sinai, to be a God gracious, merciful, long suffering, pardoning, etc.'[43]

The 'last edition' of the law of grace is contained in the New Testament, being the full revelation of God's covenant in Christ, the prophet, priest, and king of his people. In his critique of antinomianism Baxter is anxious to demonstrate that Christ is king as well as saviour. The covenant of grace being one in all ages, Baxter is concerned to stress that just as Old Testament saints were never graceless, so New Testament believers are never lawless; the covenant has always involved the believer in duties and obligations as well as privileges and blessings. In other words, the law of grace has never been 'strong' on grace and 'weak' on law, as Packer seems to suggest. Even the 'last edition' still includes 'Moses' Decalogue' as well as the remedial provision of grace and particular Christian duties.[44] In short, the whole economy is one of balance.

Baxter teaches that the law of grace was occasioned by the advent of sin. Had God dealt with fallen man by the law of innocency alone, salvation would have been impossible. When Packer accuses Baxter of saying that the new law waives the penal requirement of the original law, he fails to grasp the significance of the pre-lapsarian law. It did not allow the concept of satisfaction by the sufferings of a substitute, as Baxter is careful to point out: 'He that is judged by the Law of Innocency, must be justified by personal, perfect, perpetual obedience (not by another's) or be condemned.'[45] Had God strictly executed the old law (which made no gracious provision), then only God's justice and holiness would have been satisfied. However, the 'legislative amendment' which led to the new law did not introduce an element of grace at the expense of God's justice and holiness. The change of which Baxter speaks was one of addition, not subtraction. In other words, there was no dilution of God's righteousness at all, since the new still embraced the main features of the old. In short, if the old law is X, then the new law is $(X+Y)$. 'The Scripture assureth us', says Baxter, 'that it is the law of grace, and *not only* that of innocency, which all the world is governed by.'[46]

In Baxter's view the law of grace gives a fuller revelation of the nature of God than the law of innocency could have provided. 'The nature of God is infinitely good . . . and so that he first seeketh the glory of his mercy; and exerciseth justice in man's destruction, but as his second work.'[47] However, Baxter does not stress the benevolence of God at the expense of his holiness. Even though he does include a utilitarian dimension in his discussion, this is never at the expense of God's justice. While God is able to pardon all penitent offenders on account of Christ's penal sufferings, the wrath of God is not jettisoned in Baxter's scheme. For those who reject the gospel, under the law of grace, 'The sentence is peremptory, excluding all hope of dispensation and pardon, to the final rejectors of its grace, forever.'[48]

Baxter's neonomian scheme was his way of saying that the imputation of Christ's righteousness has not abrogated the precept of the law. Believers, therefore, are not lawless. However, valuable as many of Baxter's insights are, there is evidence that he carried his protest against antinomianism too far; notwithstanding the sincerity of his reactionary emphases, he was unable to avoid the idea of a twofold justification. Contrary to Packer's verdict, his error was not to deny the imputed active obedience of Christ, but to apply the term 'justification' to both pardon and obedience. As we shall see later, this was his way of reconciling the apostles Paul and James; but while recognizing the importance of obedience in the life of the believer, Baxter prejudiced his entire case by employing 'justification' in this double sense.[49] Whereas Calvin teaches a necessary correlation between justification and sanctification, Baxter describes both these *correlata* in terms of two types of justification. In other words, sanctification is viewed as a secondary justification.

Much as antinomianism was distasteful to Baxter, his ambiguous use of terminology was both confusing and provocative. Whatever misgivings he had about Owen's theology, he could have secured all his emphases had he adopted Calvin's view.[50] Indeed, once the ambiguities are eliminated, the parallels are remarkable. One major difference is little more than terminological. Although Baxter asserts that 'To dream of meriting from God . . . is blasphemy and madness' and that 'To say that we can merit pardon, or justification, or salvation merely by observing Moses' Law, was the Jews' pernicious error',[51] he tolerated something very close to congruous merit.[52] It is remarkable that Baxter, notorious as he was for drawing intangible distinctions, failed to distinguish between merit and reward as Calvin did. While his thinking here was an incidental aberration, he would have done better to follow Calvin in spurning the word 'merit' as 'heathenish'.[53]

Tillotson shared Baxter's concern about antinomianism. In his sermons on justification he probably popularized the views of Bull's *Harmonia apostolica*, as was usual among latitudinarian divines. However, he was particularly lucid in presenting his position. For instance, he warns against the idea of 'being admitted to heaven "by proxy"'. The notion of imputing Christ's active obedience is absurd, he argues, because 'the holiest man that ever was upon earth, can no more assign and make over his righteousness, or repentance, or any part of either, to another who wants it, than a man can bequeath his wisdom, or learning to his heir, or his friend'.[54] Of course, judged from Owens' high orthodox perspective, such an account sails dangerously close to Roman and Socinian views. But, unlike Baxter, Tillotson has no time for the doctrine of merit. He repudiates the 'doctrine of the Church of Rome' in no uncertain terms. They teach 'as if they could drive a strict bargain with God for eternal life and happiness; and have treated Him in so insolent a manner, by their doctrine of the merit of their devotions and good works'.[55] While the Council of Trent rejected the terms *congruo* and *condigno* in relation to merit,[56] its ambiguous declarations encouraged the kind of popular understanding Tillotson was opposing.

Tillotson is therefore concerned to steer an unambiguous middle course between the Roman doctrine of merit and antinomianism. 'Indeed, our blessed Saviour hath merited for us all the reward of eternal life, upon the conditions of faith and repentance and obedience: But the infinite merit of his obedience and sufferings will be of no benefit and advantage to us, if we ourselves be not really and inherently righteous.'[57] Any hint of a similarity of emphasis here between Tillotson and Calvin[58] is reinforced by the archbishop's view of justification. While acknowledging that 'justification' has other uses in the New Testament, Tillotson still affirms that 'when it is applied to a sinner, it signifies nothing else but the pardon of his sin'.[59] He seems to be well aware that, *vis-à-vis* Rome, 'to justify' is not 'to *make* righteous' (as implied by the Latin verb *justificare*), but rather 'to *declare* righteous' (the meaning of the Greek verb δικαιόω). But equally, he rejects the Beza–Owen view of imputation. In expounding Acts 13: 38–9 and Paul's citation of Psalm 32 in Romans 4: 6–8, his exegesis is identical to Calvin's:

The man unto whom God imputeth righteousness, is the man whom God justifies .... From hence I reason, if according to the Apostle those propositions be equivalent, *Blessed is the man whose iniquities are forgiven,* and *Blessed is the man whom God justifies,* then according to the Apostle, justification and forgiveness of sins are all one: but those propositions are equivalent, if the Apostle cites the text out of the Psalms pertinently.[60]

Unlike those scholars who still insist that justification is more than forgiveness[61], Tillotson expounds 'justification' precisely as the sixteenth-century Reformers did, and as John Wesley was to do in the next century. What is more, he adheres strictly to his definition; it always means that the sinner is 'right with God' through the forgiveness of sins. His account is therefore more satisfactory than Baxter's.

Having affirmed that the work of Christ is the sole meritorious basis of justification, Tillotson, like Calvin, argues that a necessary connection exists between justification and sanctification, even when they are carefully distinguished; 'The great condition of our justification and acceptance with God, is the real renovation of our hearts and lives.'[62] It is interesting to detect here the same continuum view as was taught by Calvin. Subjective renewal is the necessary concomitant or perpetual correlate of justification, 'whether by justification be meant our first justification upon our faith and repentance, or our continuance in this state, or our final justification by our solemn acquittal and absolution at the Great Day'.[63]

Calvin's and Tillotson's 'semi-Augustinianism' is clearly at variance with both the medieval and high orthodox views of justification. It at once avoids the fallacies the other views are prone to. On the one hand, it shuns the Augustinian theory that justification is by 'an infusion of grace', which confuses justification with sanctification; on the other, it denies that an 'imputation of righteousness' ever takes place without 'an infusion of sanctifying grace'. Scholars have pointed out that the linguistic discrepancies between the Latin and Greek verbs have contributed to mutual misunderstanding between Rome and the Reformed churches. If *justificare* permits a confusion of justification and sanctification at the expense of the gratuitousness of salvation, so the reactionary use of δικαιόω lends weight to the idea that the pardoned and accepted sinner may remain unsanctified. Allowing for an element of caricature, this is certainly how the opposing sides have perceived the other's position.

If the Latin-based English verb is an unsatisfactory translation of the Greek, and if no other English equivalent in the 'right' word-group (e.g. 'rightify') exists,[64] perhaps *rectificare* will provide a solution to the embattled alternatives. Its Latin origin notwithstanding, 'rectify' is an established form without any supicious theological overtones. 'Rectification' would cover the necessarily connected aspects of salvation without confusing them; the sinner's standing with God is 'put right' by imputed righteousness or pardon, and his state before God is 'put right' by imparted righteousness or sanctification. Such a 'doctrine of rectification' encapsulates Calvin's (and Luther's?) distinctive semi-Augustinianism, effectively blending what remains biblically valid in the opposing Augustinian and anti-Augustinian viewpoints.

It may be argued that Baxter and Tillotson were seeking to articulate this 'semi-Augustinian' *via media*. As for Baxter, his scheme of justification involved a conceptual ambiguity rather than a fundamental error. Where he was confusing (if not confused), Tillotson lucidly clarified the issues. He advocates—albeit more coherently and without the embarrassment of Wesley's perfectionism—the very view propagated by the mature Wesley in the eighteenth-century. The latter's residual difficulties largely arose from Baxter's influence. However, judged from a sixteenth-century perspective, much that was taught by Baxter, Tillotson, and Wesley may be rehabilitated and regarded as a legitimate expression of Reformation theology. If their views are not entirely satisfactory, the same must be said of Owen, whose high Calvinist orthodoxy cannot be traced to the biblical theology of Calvin and his fellow Reformers.

NOTES

1. *JF* 53.
2. Ibid. 47.
3. Ibid. 55-6.
4. Ibid. 253.
5. Ibid. 258.
6. Ibid. 260.
7. Ibid. 266.
8. Ibid. 272.
9. Ibid. 274.
10. A. C. Clifford, 'The gospel and justification', *EQ* 57. 3 (1985), at p. 266; also E. F. Kevan, *The Grace of Law* (London, 1964), *passim*.
11. Owen argues that the 'necessity of holiness' is 'proved from the commands of God in the law and the gospel' (*Works*, iii. 604; see also *The Savoy Declaration of Faith and Order*, ed. A. G. Matthews (London, 1959), ch. XIX. vi. for Owen's view).
12. They argued that the believer's deliverance from the law was total and perpetual. Therefore, to return to the law after justification as a continuing rule of duty in sanctification amounted to a return to

legalism. Tobias Crisp affirmed that 'Free grace is the teacher of good works' (P. Toon, *The Emergence of Hyper-Calvinism in English Nonconformity, 1689–1765* (London, 1967), 54). See also J. Murray, *Principles of Conduct* (London, 1957), 181–201.
13. *PJ* 318.
14. *Works*, x. 303.
15. *PJ* 318.
16. Ibid. 312.
17. Ibid. 313.
18. *JF* 267.
19. *PJ* 311.
20. *Works*, v. 52. See also *Appeal II*, p. 45.
21. *Notes*, Gal. 4: 4.
22. *DA I*, p. 261.
23. *DA II*, p. 270.
24. Calvin writes: 'Moreover, we are not so exempted from the law by Christ's benefit that we no longer owe any obedience to the teaching of the law and may do what we please. For it is the perpetual rule of a good and holy life' (*Comm.* Gal. 4: 4; see also *Comm.* Rom. 6: 15; Gal. 3: 25).
25. *Works*, i. 632.
26. Ibid. 636.
27. Ch. XI of the Westminster Confession speaks of the imputation of 'the obedience and satisfaction of Christ', which is changed in the Savoy Declaration to 'Christ's active obedience unto the whole law, and passive obedience in his death for their whole and sole righteousness'.
28. The double-imputation doctrine 'was Dr O[wen].'s doing' (*Catholick Communion Defended* (1684), II. 8; see also *EC* 266).
29. For Piscator see P. Schaff, *The New Schaff–Herzog Encyclopedia of Religious Knowledge* (New York, 1957), ix. 73.
30. *JF* 334 ff.
31. Although L. Berkhof (*Systematic Theology* (London, 1963), 524–5) and J. Buchanan (*The Doctrine of Justification* (Edinburgh, 1867; fac. London, 1961), 189) view Piscator's position with suspicion, John Knox's successor Andrew Melville considered 'that the opinion was one which might be fairly tolerated among those who were agreed in other respects on the doctrine of justification by faith' (A. F. Mitchell and J. Struthers (eds.), *Minutes of the Sessions of the Westminster Assembly of Divines* (London, 1874), p. xxiv).
32. See translated extracts of Piscator's views in J. Arminius, *The Works of James Arminius, DD*, trans. J. Nichols (London, 1825), i. 634. Piscator's major treatise on the subject is *Apologia disputationis de causa meritoria justificationis hominis coram deo* (Herborn, 1618).
33. Calvin thinks that Paul 'extends the ground of pardon which exempts from the curse of the law to the whole life of Christ' (*Inst.* II. xvi. 5).

Thus are we 'clothed' with Christ's 'innocence' (ibid. III. xiv. 12). However, Calvin never hints that Christ's active obedience is imputed to us, since justification is merely pardon.
34. Wesley, *Notes*, 1 John 2: 5–6; Calvin, *Comm.* 1 John 2: 6.
35. *Works*, v. 227; vii. 300.
36. 'The doctrine of justification in development and decline', among the Puritans', in *By Schisms Rent Asunder* (PRSC, London, 1969), at p. 27. (This paper provides a partial summary of Packer's D.Phil. thesis.)
37. A number of Packer's detailed criticisms of Baxter are highly misleading. (1) 'Baxter's scheme ... fails to come to terms with the representative headship of Christ, the second Adam, as this is set forth in Romans 5: 12 ff.' ('The Doctrine of justification', p. 27). But Baxter affirms 'That as we are told that Adam was the natural root or parent of mankind; so also that Christ was the Federal root of all the saved' (*CT* I. ii. 77–8; see also *Paraphrase*, Rom. 5: 12 ff.). (2) Packer (p. 27) accuses Baxter of directing the distressed sinner to his faith rather than to 'the cross of Christ'. But Baxter clearly says, 'Christ's sacrifice for sin, and his perfect holiness, are so far satisfactory and meritorious for all men, as that they render Christ a meet object for that faith in him which is commanded men' (*CT* I. ii. 51). (3) He also implies (ibid.) that by adopting his 'political method' Baxter 'externalises sin' as if it were 'crime', underestimating its personal and 'demonic corporate influence'. But Baxter is fully aware of the nature and influence of sin:

> All ministers, tutors, parents, Christians; yea, persons find how woefully hard it proveth to cure one sin; to cure the ignorant, the unbelieving, the hard-hearted, the proud, the lustful, the covetous, the passionate; much more the malignant enemies of God and holiness. What need of the sanctification of the Spirit, or the medicinal grace of Christ, if the very depraved will can do all in a moment of itself, and depose its enmity? (*CT* II. 84.)

(4) Packer (p. 27) criticizes Baxter for seeing Christ as 'the Head of God's government rather than of His people'. But Baxter could not be clearer: 'And Christ is first filled with his Spirit personally himself, that he may be a fit Head of vital influence to all his members, who by the previous operations of his Spirit are drawn and united to him' (*CT* II. 178). (5) He suggests (ibid.) that Baxter viewed the death of Christ as 'one presupposition of our sins being remitted rather than the procuring cause of it'. But Baxter distinctly affirms that 'Christ's righteousness, merit and satisfaction may be said to be imputed to us, ... God reputeth or judgeth us righteous ... which indeed is done for Christ's meritorious righteousness procuring it' (*CT* I. ii. 64). (6) Baxter is charged with viewing the remission of sins 'as public pardon rather than personal forgiveness', making Christ 'remote' and 'more

like a judge than a Saviour'. Here Packer seems to fly in the face of 2 Cor. 5: 10, 'we must all appear before the judgement seat of Christ'. Even so, Baxter declares that 'all our past sins are pardoned at our first faith or conversion', while justification is completed at the day of judgement 'which ... is done by Christ as Judge, and so is an act of his kingly office' (*CT* I. ii. 85). As for Christ seeming 'remote', even in a somewhat technical treatise like *Catholick Theologie* B. can write of Christ's mediatorial work as 'the way to the Father, to bring man home to his creator', and says that the Holy Spirit's work is to apply what is 'given by Christ' by 'giving us the love of God, and other graces' and 'by giving us the comfort of all' (*CT* I. ii. 88–90).

It is also strange that Packer can lament Baxter's theological activity yet praise his pastoral accomplishments. After all, many of the ideas he objects to in the theological treatises can be found in the very devotional and practical writings he praises so highly. Baxter's theological and pastoral activities were all of a piece. It is true that the 'political' terminology is much less prominent in his more popular works, but there is no solid basis for Packer's dichotomy.

Lastly, it is not altogether just to accuse Baxter of having 'a streak of legalism' in his theological system. Merely stressing that Christ's kingdom involves the believer in duties and obligations is bound to appear legalistic from an antinomian perspective. What Baxter does is recognize that Christ is both Saviour and Lord, and that saving faith has passive and active features. That said, he carefully distinguishes between means and motive. One does not observe the requirements of Christ the king in a mercenary manner; 'Other service is undertaken for the love of the wages, but this is undertaken for the love of the Master and work, and is wages itself to them that go through with it' ('Directions to a sound conversion', in *Practical Works* (1981 edn.), 584).

38. *CT* I. ii. 63–4.
39. Ibid. 59.
40. Baxter says of faith that 'the formal reason of its office as to our justification is its being the performed condition of the Covenant', and that 'our faith now is instead of our innocency .... Paul saith, that faith is imputed to us for righteousness. To deny this sense, is to use violence with the text' (*CT* I. ii. 82; 86). Likewise Calvin: 'what can the formal or instrumental cause be but faith?' (*Inst.* III. xiv. 17); 'For it is not said that faith was imputed to him as a part of his righteousness but simply as righteousness. Hence his faith was truly in place of righteousness for him.' (*Comm.* Gal. 3: 6.)
41. *Inst.* III. xiv. 17; T. Lane, 'The quest for the historical Calvin', *EQ* 55. 2 (1983), at p. 98.
42. C. F. Allison, *The Rise of Moralism* (London, 1966), 162.

43. *CT* I. ii. 50.
44. Ibid. 43–4.
45. *EC* 154; see also *CT* I. ii. 40.
46. *CT* I. ii. 49 (emphasis mine).
47. Ibid. 50.
48. Ibid. 49.
49. 'So far as we are sinners, a pardon is our righteousness: but so far as we are holy, it is not so ...'. Writing of 'sincere obedience', Baxter adds, 'This is the justification by works (as many are willing to call it, to make it odious) which I assert and defend, and which I judge so necessary to be believed' (*Rich. Baxter's Confession of His Faith* (London, 1655), Preface, pp. ix, x (unnumbered); see also *CT* I. ii. 69 ff.).
50. Baxter almost did adopt Calvin's definition of justification: 'I think it had been well for the church, if we had used less in our disputes the term justification.... If we had treated more fully about remission of sin alone, and under that term ... I think the church would reap much benefit by it. Doubtless we might much easier convince a papist ... when so many of ours do take remission and justification for the same thing' *Confession*, p. vii (unnumbered).
51. *CT* I. ii. 80.
52. 'To deny *subordinate comparative merit* ... and presupposing Christ's total merits ... is to subvert all religion and true morality, and to deny the scope of all the Scriptures, and the *express assertion* of an Evangelical *worthiness*, which is all that this *merit* signifieth' (ibid. 80).
53. *Comm.* Luke 17: 7–10. For the history of the concept of merit see A. E. McGrath, *Iustitia Dei* (Cambridge, 1986), i. 22 ff.
54. 'The parable of the ten virgins', *TW* iii. 370.
55. Ibid. 366.
56. McGrath, *Iustitia Dei*, ii. 68 ff.
57. *TW* iii. 370.
58. Calvin, *Inst.* III. xvi. 1; *Comm.* 1 Cor. 1: 30; 1 John 1: 7.
59. 'Of the Christian faith which sanctifies, justifies and saves', *TW* ii. 479.
60. *TW* ii. 479–80.
61. J. R. W. Stott, *The Cross of Christ* (London, 1986), 182; Berkhof, *Systematic Theology*, p. 515.
62. 'Of the nature of regeneration, and its necessity, in order to justification and salvation', *TW* i. 390.
63. Ibid.
64. S. Motyer, 'Righteousness by faith in the New Testament', in *Here We Stand*, ed. J. I. Packer (1986), at p. 34; also P. Toon, *Justification and Sanctification* (London, 1983), 20 ff.

12
The Obedience of Faith

The true character of a saving response to the gospel was no less a problem of definition to our theologians than the objective, meritorious ground of justification. The nature of faith, the relationship between faith and good works, and the place of obedience in the *ordo salutis* were issues which occasioned the greatest perplexity. Challenged by Tridentine Romanism and Socinian rationalism, Reformed theologians were anxious to demonstrate that a biblical theology of grace excludes legalism and antinomianism alike. The problem was compounded by the fact that the Bible itself appeared ambiguous. Thus, those who embraced the *sola scriptura* principle were obliged to provide a coherent exegesis which was at once perspicuous and persuasive.

Doctrinal and practical considerations led the seventeenth-century high orthodox Puritans to modify the Reformers' conception of faith and assurance. Agreeing with the Westminster Confession that 'infallible assurance doth not so belong to the essence of faith',[1] John Owen argued that it was a mistake to 'place the essence of faith in the highest acting of it'.[2] In other words, it was possible for a Christian to possess a genuine faith while plagued with doubts and robbed of spiritual comfort. John Wesley eventually embraced the same judgement. In his sermon 'Justification by faith' (1746) he was happy to endorse the reformers' view of faith as 'a sure trust and confidence in the mercies of God'.[3] The first Methodist Conference of 1744 had agreed that 'no man can be justified and not know it'.[4] However, after correspondence with 'John Smith' (in fact Dr Thomas Secker (1693–1768), later archbishop of Canterbury),[5] Wesley modified his thinking. Writing to his brother Charles in 1747, he denied that 'justifying faith is a sense of pardon'; indeed, it was 'contrary to reason' and 'flatly absurd'. Never afraid to be independent when truth demanded it, Wesley admitted that the Church of England did teach what he now denied, but he insisted that Scripture taught otherwise, and that 'All men may err.'[6]

Recent scholarly discussion[7] suggests that while Calvin did include assurance in his definition of faith, he did not deny that true faith might have conflict with doubt.[8] This seeming contradiction is not really resolved by the idea that Calvin's definition was more prescriptive than descriptive.[9] Calvin clearly implies two levels of assurance, a truth made explicit by Baxter. Distinguishing between objective and subjective certainty, Baxter agrees with Calvin's definition: 'There is assurance in this faith', an 'assurance that God's promises and all his words are true'; indeed, it is impossible for faith to be exercised without such assurance. This objective certainty may still coexist with subjective uncertainty: 'For sometimes a man may doubt, merely as doubting . . . the sincerity of his own faith, and not at all doubting whether the promises be sure.' Even then, 'when it is doubting whether the promises be sure, which makes a man doubt whether he shall be saved, this doubting is the debility of faith'.[10] Baxter's distinction thus eliminates the confusion surrounding this issue.

On the subject of justification, Owen was a champion of justification *sola fide*. In his view justifying faith is a passive reception of Christ, and 'no other grace is capable of that office which is assigned unto faith in our justification'.[11] Although 'the assent of the mind . . . is the root of faith',[12] it is, psychologically speaking, more than merely notional; it also consists in 'the heart's approbation' of the way of salvation,[13] the will performing a consenting role in the receiving of Christ.[14] Thus defined, faith alone justifies, 'as we are justified by it, . . . no other grace, duty or work, can be associated with it'.[15] Anticipating Roman and Socinian objections, Owen denies that faith is a barren, lifeless disposition. *Sola fide* respects faith's 'influence unto our justification, not its nature and existence. And we absolutely deny that we can be justified by that faith which can be alone . . . which is not itself . . . a spiritually vital principle of obedience and good works'.[16] To dispel any lingering suspicions of antinomianism, he declares that true faith 'virtually and radically contains in it universal obedience, as the effect is in the cause, the fruit in the root'.[17] He even concedes that 'justifying faith includeth in its nature the entire principle of evangelical repentance';[18] in short, faith is more than 'assenting trust'. However, anxious to avoid making any concessions to the medieval view of faith as *fides caritate formata*, 'faith formed by love' (as in Gal. 5: 6), he up-ends the idea by saying that faith 'gives life and efficacy unto all other graces, and form unto all evangelical obedience'.[19]

Earlier discussion of the *sola fide* principle is relevant at this point. Whereas the Reformers' view of it avoided the suggestion that faith itself possesses any innate justifying virtue,[20] Owen's emphasis on faith creates a very different impression, even though he denies justification *propter fidem*, 'on account of faith'.[21] To insist that faith alone has the 'capability' of justifying *vis-à-vis* other graces is to miss the Reformers' point and to focus attention on faith rather than its object. Committed to a psychological view of *sola fide*,[22] Owen's emphasis on the exclusive role of faith involves him in a delicate and unnecessary balancing act. To exclude the intrusion of works, he argues that justifying faith is passive; then to offset any antinomian tendency he half surrenders faith's passivity by insisting that it contains the root of obedience.

While Owen admits that faith cannot exist apart from other graces, he needlessly insists that it functions apart from them. The syndecdochal view of *sola fide* avoids this double-talk completely. While faith has a unique role in 'receiving' or 'laying hold' of Christ, it is never unaccompanied; justifying faith is necessarily associated with love and obedience (Gal. 5: 6; 1 Cor. 13: 2; Rom. 1: 5) because regeneration is not piecemeal. Rather than say that 'faith gives life and efficacy unto all other graces', it is held that regeneration is the common efficacious cause of them all. The real issue is not the relationship between the constituents of the believing response in justification, but the object of trust. In this respect the believer is not justified by faith alone; faith is associated with, not isolated from, other graces. Yet the justified believer trusts neither his obedience, nor his love, nor his faith, but the Christ who alone justifies (Rom. 5: 9; Gal. 2: 17), a fact which the popular view of *sola fide* tends to obscure. However Owen qualifies his position, the history of *sola fide* has revealed a cavalier attitude to good works which a rejection of the ambiguous and unscriptural slogan would help to cure.

Without doubting that 'trust' in the merits of Christ is the heart of faith, there were those who argued in exegetical grounds that Paul's conception of πίστις in Romans and Galatians is a more comprehensive thing than Owen seems to allow. John Wesley reflected on this, and his view of faith was constantly under review during his life. Following his earlier 'Lutheran' phase, he stated at the 1744 Methodist Conference that 'love and obedience' were 'the inseparable properties of faith'.[23] With reference to the key text, Galatians 5: 6, he affirms, 'But I say, you have not true faith, unless your faith "worketh by love" '.[24] True faith is by its very nature a loving and obedient grace. Wesley is not defecting from the correct understanding of *sola fide*; he is merely expounding the Pauline conception of saving faith. In other words, it is more than mere assent and trust; there is also an active element. Faith as trust is therefore *prima* rather than *sola*.

As we have noted, Wesley's acquaintance with Baxter's *Aphorismes* led him to adopt the theory of a twofold justification.[25] Predictably, he was much maligned for this, but his modified conception of faith never assigned a meritorious place to good works. That said, he was ever anxious to clarify the subjective requirements of the gospel. Indeed, as late as 1789 he was still exercised by the question: 'Our Lord expressly commands us [to] labour, ἐργάζεσθε, literally, "work", . . . for . . . everlasting life.'[26] This was the conclusion of many years' careful reflection and almost ceaseless controversy. Man's salvation depended as much on his 'faithfulness to God' as on the merits of Christ. To say otherwise was to promote antinomianism:

We have received it as a maxim, that 'a man is to do nothing in order to justification'. Nothing can be more false. Whoever desires to find favour with God, should 'cease from evil, and learn to do well'. So God teaches by the prophet Isaiah. Whoever repents, should 'do works meet for repentance'. And if this is not in order to find favour, what does he do them for? . . . Who of us is now accepted of God? He that now believes in Christ with a loving, obedient heart . . . . Is not this salvation by works? Not by the merit of works, but by works as a condition.[27]

Wesley's doctrine of faith is clear. Faith is not a simple but a complex response; it comprehends obedience as well as assent and trust, all of which are necessary for a correct definition of saving faith.

Baxter's appeal for Wesley is easily explained. Keeble makes the key observation that for Baxter justifying faith is a 'practical or working faith'.[28] 'As accepting of Christ for Lord . . . is as essential a part of justifying faith as the accepting Him for our Saviour, so consequently sincere obedience . . . hath as much to do in justifying us before God as affiance.'[29] Baxter's discussion of faith suggests another link with Calvin. Indeed, he develops the Reformer's brilliant exposition of Christ's threefold office of prophet, priest, and king[30] as it relates to the believer's true response to the gospel. For Baxter, justifying faith is more than 'self-renouncing trust'.[31] Without denying that 'trusting Christ as a Saviour' involves 'the renouncing and letting go all other trust',[32] he argues that 'the very nature of faith is to take Christ as Christ, as he is offered in the Gospel: as our teacher to guide us in the way of holiness, and as our king to rule us, as well as a sacrifice for our sins'.[33]

The threefold office formula became a basic feature of orthodox Puritan Christology, featuring prominently in Chapter VIII of the Westminster Confession. Baxter was thus expounding his position within an accepted framework; however, he works out the full implications of the formula in a way Calvin certainly hints at.[34] Faith has a comprehensive, tripartite character, each of the three constituents relating to the corresponding office of Christ: the assent of the mind, the trust of the heart, and the obedience of the will constitute justifying faith's response to Christ. 'Whenever justification and life is promised to faith, all these three are the essential parts of it.'[35] Therefore 'The object of justifying, saving faith, is one only undivided Christ',[36] and 'There is no justification by a partial faith.'[37] Thus, to deny any one element of faith would negate a corresponding office in Christ.

Owen's definition of faith may be evaluated in this context. While he admits that faith contains the 'root' of obedience—a concession suspiciously close to Baxter's thesis—he denies that obedience itself is a constituent of faith. To establish his case he must deny that Christ's kingly office is relevant to justifying faith. This is precisely what he does. 'Justifying faith . . . respecteth Christ in his priestly office alone.'[38] The antinomian implications of this admission are obvious, and R. L. Dabney took strong exception to Owen's view in the nineteenth-century.[39] Current controversy has focused attention on this subject, with J. I. Packer responding in a decidedly Baxterian manner.[40]

Owen therefore faces a dilemma. Although Baxter argues that actual acts of obedience are to be distinguished from faith, his entire case rests on the very thing Owen grants, that 'subjection to Christ

... is taking him for our Lord and Saviour to be obeyed, which is all future obedience in the root'.[41] If, therefore, Owen wishes to deny that Christ's kingly office is relevant to justifying faith, where is the necessity for faith to include the root of obedience? If he insists on his view of faith, he must adopt Baxter's position; only then can he avoid the charge that the believer is justified 'by a part of faith'.[42] Although Baxter committed a terminological blunder in calling obedience a secondary justification rather than the necessary subjective correlate of justification, as Calvin understood it, Owen's thesis can hardly be regarded as a satisfactory deterrent to antinomianism.

This entire debate depends ultimately upon biblical exegesis, as Owen was aware. He was even prepared to reconsider his position if the evidence demanded it.[43] The evidence was close at hand, according to John Tillotson, who lucidly handled texts Owen seems to have ignored. After citing Romans 1: 5 and 10: 16, he compares 1 Timothy 4: 10 with Hebrews 5: 9, and Galatians 5: 6 with 1 Corinthians 7: 19, to prove that true faith involves '*obedience* of the heart and life to the precepts and commands of the Gospel, as well as an *assent* of the understanding to the truth of the Gospel-Revelation and *relying* upon the merits of Christ'. He reinforces his point from such texts as Hebrews 3: 12 and 4: 11, John 3: 36, and 1 Peter 2: 7, 'where unbelief and disobedience are equivalently used'.[44]

Although this kind of exegesis is currently receiving some support,[45] Owen saw it as a surrender of the doctrine of justification by faith.[46] After his early prejudice against Tillotson, Wesley came to share the archbishop's views. As for Tillotson, he was adamant: 'So ... we cannot be said to be justified by faith alone, unless that faith include in it obedience.'[47] In his view such an understanding would 'silence and put an end to those infinite controversies about faith and justification, which have so much troubled the Christian world, to the great prejudice of practical religion and holiness of life'.[48]

Tillotson evidently sees his tripartite view of faith—assent, reliance, and obedience—in the context of the triple office formula. A Christian acknowledges Christ as:

the great guide and teacher sent from God .... This is to believe his *prophetical office*. He believes ... that we ought to rely upon him only for salvation, to own him for our Saviour .... This is to believe his *priestly office*. And lastly, he believes that the precepts of the Gospel ... ought to have the authority of laws upon us, and that we are bound to be obedient to them; and this is to believe the *kingly office* of Christ.[49]

Although Tillotson shares many of Baxter's emphases, he neither regards obedience as a secondary justification nor tolerates the idea of merit; the very imperfection of the believer's assent, trust, and obedience disqualify him from ever meriting salvation. While he insists that the subjective *causa sine qua non* of salvation is 'Faith in Christ, and a sincere and universal obedience to the precepts of his Holy Gospel',[50] yet, for 'the sake of the perfect righteousness and obedience, and the meritorious sufferings of our blessed Saviour', God is pleased 'to forgive the defects and imperfections of our obedience'.[51] Tillotson had a clear Reformation understanding of *sola fide*; it was a statement about the exclusive merits of Christ:

> But there is a wide difference between the doctrine of the Papists about justification and this doctrine. They say that obedience and good works are not only a condition of our justification, but a meritorious cause of it; which I abhor as much as anyone. It is the doctrine of merit that the Protestants cheifly oppose in the matter of justification.[52]

The early Methodist disapproval of Tillotson must therefore be put down to ignorance and antinomianism. However, if the late primate was considered an enemy to justification by faith alone, even Owen could lapse into Tillotsonian language, including those 'conditional' overtones he preferred to avoid: 'Salvation is confined to believers; and those who look for salvation by Christ, must secure it unto themselves by faith and obedience. It is Christ alone who is the cause of our salvation; but he will save none but those that obey him.'[53]

This last quotation suggests that Owen was ambivalent about the necessity of good works. In response to Sherlock's challenge, he could only say that they were necessary because God had commanded them. This still begs the question, 'Why has God commanded them?' Owen's incipiently antinomian view of imputation and faith is an obvious embarrassment to him. He is reluctant to deny that good works have no bearing on salvation at all: 'We are neither justified nor saved without them, though we are not justified by them, nor saved for them.'[54] In what different senses does he both affirm and deny the necessity of the believer's holiness? Elsewhere he provides an answer which suddenly closes the gap between himself and Baxter, Tillotson, and Wesley. In his comment on Hebrews 12: 14, 'holiness, without which no man shall see the Lord', Owen concedes: 'Now this future sight of the Lord doth depend peremptorily on our present holiness. It doth not do so as the meritorious cause of it; for be we ever so holy, yet in respect of God we are "unprofitable servants", and "eternal life is the gift of God by Jesus Christ".'[55] Owen seems here to be going beyond the Thirty-nine Articles[56] and the Westminster Confession,[57] which teach that the believer's active obedience is merely evidence of a 'true and lively faith'. Faced by the antinomian challenge, Owen's position becomes almost indistinguishable from that of our other theologians. That said, his timely stress on holiness is self-contradictory, for it places a strain on his theory of imputation. Doubtless Tillotson had Owen in mind when he acknowledged those 'worthy and excellent divines, who ... have always pressed the necessity of holiness and obedience' but whose principles logically led to antinomianism.[58] In the eighteenth century John Gill repudiated the necessity of good works with a vehemence Owen never used.[59] This was the background to Wesley's crusade against antinomianism. In 1774 he summed up his position in terms which neither Baxter, Tillotson, nor Owen could object to:

None of us talk of being accepted for our works: that is the Calvinist slander. But we all maintain, we are not saved without works; that works are a condition (though not a meritorious cause) of final salvation. It is by faith in the righteousness and blood of Christ that we are enabled to do all good works; and it is for the sake of these that all who fear God and work righteousness are accepted of him.[60]

The ultimate incoherence of Owen's position emerges in his discussion of the doctrine of a twofold justification. He objects to both Tridentine and Protestant formulations of it, since 'Justification through the free grace of God, by faith in the blood of Christ, is evacuated by it. Sanctification is turned into justification, and corrupted by making the fruits of it meritorious.'[61] Since a second justification casts doubt on the adequacy of the first, the two justifications are mutually destructive; We must therefore 'part with the one or the other, for consistent they are not'.[62] Owen is surely correct to say that the concept of a twofold justification is foreign to the apostle Paul and the New Testament writers in general. But while he laments the introduction of 'arbitrary distinctions, without Scripture ground for them',[63] it is remarkable that he could infringe his own rule without apparent concern. This is a matter requiring careful demonstration, for once again Aristotle's influence is evident, with serious implications for Owen's overall thesis.

Owen's basic view is that since the 'meritorious procuring cause' of justification (Christ's death) was 'complete', the believer's justification was 'complete' at the moment of trust.[64] That said, he obviously finds difficulty in bridging the time-gap between the believer's instantaneous justification and the day of judgement. Packer's view that 'Justification is decisive for eternity, being in effect the judgement of the last day brought forward',[65] is too simple a view for Owen. While he had no time for the hypercalvinist dogma of eternal justification,[66] neither did he reduce the day of judgement to a virtual non-event. However, his solution is a definition obviously foreign to Paul, couched in Aristotelian terms, and suspiciously similar to the one he is refuting:

Justification by faith in the blood of Christ may be considered either as to the nature and essence of it, or as unto its manifestation and declaration. The manifestation of it is two-fold: First, initial, in this life. Second, solemn and complete, at the day of judgement . . .'.[67]

But he cannot have it both ways. If the earlier criticism of Aristotle's essence–accidents distinction—here lurking in Owen's definition—is valid, then Owen must either settle for Packer's simplistic view or adopt a straightforward theory of twofold justification. If, according to this criticism, a thing is what its accidents (or 'manifestations') are, then he is really committed to the latter option. This is in fact the position he eventually adopts.

For all Owen's concern with 'the true state of the question', insisting on 'one justification only', he distinguishes between the justification of a sinner, *qua* sinner, and the justification of a believer, *qua* believer. The matter of this latter justification is not Christ's righteousness imputed, but the believer's 'evangelical righteousness', and Owen's ambivalence about it is clear. On the one hand, it is 'pleadable' evidence against the accusations of Satan, men, and conscience in this life; they are 'judges' of the believer's 'godly sincerity'. On the other, it is even regarded by God as evidence of the believer's standing in Christ. Had Owen left matters there, his account could be consistent with a theory of justification which makes the day of judgement a foregone conclusion, a mere 'declaratory' formality. It is therefore remarkable to find Owen admitting, in language more akin to Baxter's doctrine of final justification,

> That upon it [evangelical righteousness] we shall be declared righteous at the last day, and without is none shall so be. And if any shall think meet from hence to conclude unto an evangelical justification, or call God's acceptance of our righteousness by that name, I shall by no means contend with them. And wherever this enquiry is made,—not how a sinner, guilty of death, and obnoxious unto the curse, shall be pardoned, acquitted, and justified, which is by the righteousness of Christ alone imputed unto him— but how a man that professeth evangelical faith, or faith in Christ, shall be tried, judged, and whereon, as such, he shall be justified, we grant that it is, and must be, by his own personal, sincere obedience.[68]

This is an astonishing concession, and hardly consistent with his high doctrine of imputation. For all his protestations to the contrary, Owen's view is barely distinguishable from Baxter's theory, which he was so anxious to refute. It is significant that when Wesley and John Fletcher of Madeley were criticized for holding the twofold justification theory, Fletcher cited Owen's statement as a precedent for the view.[69]

Despite dubious assistance from Aristotle, Owen is in complete disarray. If, as he grants, the believer's evangelical righteousness does not acquit him 'from any real charge in the sight of God',[70] what purpose does this justification serve? If a genuine 'trial' is envisaged, what if a believer should not be acquitted? How would this affect his 'first' and 'complete' justification? Furthermore, if Owen is so anxious to avoid unscriptural and 'arbitrary distinctions', how can he justify his own? Indeed, if he saw himself as a champion of the Pauline doctrine of justification, what statement of the apostle's is he defending? In one paragraph, it seems that he has suddenly swung from ultra-orthodoxy to sub-orthodoxy, unless Fletcher has misread him completely.

Is Owen also guilty of a conceptual blunder? Certainly he cannot avoid aligning himself with Baxter. Viewing an individual with a double status is a meaningless manœuvre, for in the final analysis, the 'one' individual requires the double righteousness of which Owen speaks. He even grants that 'evangelical obedience' is the same thing as sanctification, and this, according to his comment on Hebrews 12: 14, is necessary for salvation. If this sanctification is a basis of a secondary justification, what cause need there be for alarm concerning the twofold theory? Baxter seems to speak for Owen in his comment on Hebrews 12: 14: '*That without holiness none shall see God*; And if any be accused as unholy (and on that account no member of Christ or a child of God, or heir of heaven) his holiness must be the matter of his justification.'[71] Should Owen suggest that inherent righteousness is merely evidential, then, concludes Baxter, he must 'allow it some place in justification: for evidence hath its place in judgement'.[72]

Owen, therefore, cannot rescue his position from the charge of incoherence. From the moment he granted that justifying faith included the root of obedience, and that holiness was necessary for salvation, his case for the imputation of Christ's active righteousness began to lack cogency. Conversely, when he reverts to his theory of imputation, his arguments for holiness lack weight. The antinomian potential of this position is obvious. He even grants that because believers are in a justified state, the avoidance of sin 'is not so required of them as that if in anything they fail of their duty, they should immediately lose the privilege of their justification'.[73] He also insists that to admit an alternative view of justification undermines the believer's assurance,[74] an objection to which his own version of the twofold theory is not immune. John Wesley was surely right to question Owen's thesis. An instantaneous justification is not a valid ticket for all future sins: 'Does not talking, without proper caution, of a justified or a sanctified state, tend to mislead men; almost naturally leading them to trust in what was done in one moment? Whereas we are every moment pleasing or displeasing to God, according to the whole of our present inward tempers and outward behaviour.'[75] This 1789 statement indicates the extent to which Wesley had shaken off his earlier aversion for Tillotson, whose lucid view of assurance sounds an identical note:

If we daily mortify our lusts, and grow in goodness, and take care to add to our faith and knowledge, temperance and patience and charity and all other Christian graces and virtues, we certainly take the best course in the world to make our calling and election sure (2 Peter 1: 10). And without this it is impossible that we should have any comfortable and well-grounded assurance of our good condition.[76]

Tillotson seems to make the most coherent sense of the labyrinth of issues discussed in this chapter. Unlike Baxter, Wesley, and Owen, he stresses obedience to Christ in his kingly office without making obedience itself a secondary justification. Obedience is necessary for justification and salvation insofar as saving faith includes the element of obedience in its nature. Careful to distinguish between meritorious obedience and obedience as such, he is able to stress the conditional nature of justification (albeit fulfilled by regenerating grace and union wich Christ) without detracting from the exclusive, meritorious mediation of Christ.

It is remarkable that of all the theologians in this study, Owen the high Calvinist least reflects Calvin's overall position. The same is fascinatingly true of the recognized guardian of eighteenth-century Calvinistic orthodoxy, Jonathan Edwards.[77] It is hard to resist the bizarre thought that, from the perspective of Calvin and Piscator, both Owen and Edwards invest the believer with a triple justifying righteousness, that is, the pardon of sin *plus* Christ's active obedience imputed *plus* the believer's own evangelical obedience. On the other hand, the close similarities between Tillotson's view of justification and Calvin's rather special view are both interesting and important. Wesley's claim to follow Calvin has considerable support. However, in following Baxter's lead Wesley mistakenly came to view the believer's obedience as a secondary justification, rather than the necessary subjective correlate of justification as Calvin saw it. That said, the error of Baxter and Wesley was more terminological than real.

Whatever was true of a later orthodoxy, Calvin did not subscribe to the 'lightning flash', once-for-all idea of justification. This was no part of his polemic against Rome. His uncluttered continuum view is exegetically valid and thoroughly coherent. From an exegetical point of view, Paul's use of the aorist in Romans 5: 1, 'Being justified by faith', merely proves that whenever any sins are confessed, either at conversion or subsequently, the believer is—there and then—pardoned or justified. The term 'justification' simply expresses the forgiveness of sins in legal terminology or metaphor.[78] If 'justification' is used in an absolute sense in Romans and Galatians, then Paul's other writings, not to speak of the epistles of Peter and John, are seriously deficient, assuming that the doctrine of justification is fundamental. However, they do speak of the forgiveness of sins, which is the same thing. For all its simplicity, the Lord's Prayer contains the doctrine of justification as surely as the epistle to the Romans does.[79]

The continuum view of justification makes coherent sense from every angle. There is no necessity for a 'lightning flash' account in the truth that Christ's death is the once-for-all meritorious cause of justification. To say that the sinner's justification is complete because the gracious basis of acquittal is complete is to confuse a single cause with a multiplicity of effects. Sin is not forgiven until it is committed and repented of. Justification is never in advance, though one may say that a provision is made for the pardon of future sin. Furthermore, the believer's life is a continuum or a sequence of justifying instants. At any instant, 'I have been justified' and 'I am being justified' are perfectly compatible statements. The just man is living by faith on a day-to-day basis. Thus the continuum view avoids the unbiblical idea of a twofold justification. At no stage in the believer's life, from conversion to the day of judgement, is his justifying righteousness other than the forgiveness of sin. Good works themselves require a pardon for their deficiencies. Even if they were perfect, neither faith and repentance nor obedience are meritorious since they are divinely commanded duties (Luke 17: 10; Acts 17: 30; 1 John 3: 23). It might be objected that by equating justification with forgiveness one is admitting a theory of multiple justifications.[80] However, the idea only appears odd until one remembers that Paul's 'legal' exposition in Romans assumes 'current charges against the accused' (as implied in Rom. 3: 25). In a sense the believer 'goes to court daily', assured that the just judge is seated on a throne of grace.

I have employed Calvin's theological contribution as a point of reference throughout this book to advertise the belief that his exegesis provides an accurate, balanced, biblical exposition of the issues in question. On the subject of justification, unlike the high orthodox Calvinism of the Beza–Owen school, Calvin's teaching meets all the objections of Tridentine Romanism without being unduly provocative. He can even be seen as a conciliator. If his position were adopted, Rome could discard her doctrine of merit without surrendering the necessity of good works, and the ultra-Reformed could reduce their doctrine of imputation without sacrificing the doctrine of gratuitous justification. In short, Calvin's authentic teaching is a rebuke to inadequate and exaggerated theologies alike.

Of the four main theologians in this study, Tillotson is nearest to Calvin. His lucid exposition of the issues amounted to a conciliatory critique of Reformed high orthodoxy on the one hand, and Roman and Socinian heterodoxy on the other. Faced by the 'errors of Popery' and 'the luscious doctrines of the antinomians',[81] he pursued the true *via media* of the Protestant Reformation. It only remains to consider the apparent conflict between the apostles Paul and James in their teachings on justification, an exegetical embarrassment which has never ceased to cast its shadow over the doctrine of gratuitous justification. It will be shown that, consistently with Calvin's overall position,[82] Tillotson actually clarifies and rectifies the one questionable element in the Reformer's otherwise cogent theology of justification.

NOTES

1. Ch. XVIII. iii.
2. *JF* 86.
3. *Works*, v. 56.
4. *Works*, viii. 265.
5. *Letters*, ii. 43 ff.
6. Ibid. 108.
7. R. T. Kendall, *Calvin and English Calvinism to 1649* (Oxford, 1979), 18.
8. P. Helm, *Calvin and the Calvinists* (Edinburgh, 1982), 24.
9. Ibid. 26.
10. *CT* I. ii. 88.
11. *JF* 105.
12. Ibid. 100.
13. Ibid. 96.
14. Ibid. 101.
15. Ibid. 291.
16. Ibid. 73.
17. Ibid.
18. Ibid. 213.
19. Ibid. 104.
20. See *Homilies*, p. 17; *Inst.* III. xi. 7.
21. *JF* 109.
22. This view holds that 'faith alone' = 'faith to the exclusion of all other graces'. The syndecdochal view is: 'faith alone' = 'faith in Christ's merits alone'.
23. *Works*, viii. 266.
24. *DA II*, p. 269; also *Appeal II*, p. 65.
25. *Works*, v. 52–3; *Appeal II*, pp. 54, 67; *Works*, x. 369–74.
26. *Works*, viii. 324.

27. Ibid.
28. N. H. Keeble, *Richard Baxter: Puritan Man of Letters* (Oxford, 1982), 141.
29. *Aphorismes*, pp. 69, 72.
30. J. I. Packer, 'Calvin the theologian', in *John Calvin*, ed. G. Duffield (Abingdon, 1966), at p. 168.
31. J. I. Packer, 'The doctrine of justification in development and decline among the Puritans', in *By Schisms Rent Asunder* (PRSC, London, 1969), at p. 27; id., 'Justification in Protestant Theology', in Packer (ed.), *Here We Stand* (London, 1986), at p. 97.
32. *CT* I. ii. 45.
33. 'Treatise on conversion', *Practical Works* (1981 ed.), at p. 421.
34. Calvin writes that 'the name of Christ refers to those three offices' (*Inst.* II. xv. 2), and that 'faith embraces Christ as he is offered by the Father' (III. ii. 8). Therefore, 'He unites the offices of King and Pastor towards believers, who voluntarily submit to him' (II. xv. 5). In criticizing Baxter's view of faith, Packer fails to see the full implications of the very theory he praises Calvin for expounding.
35. *CT* I. ii. 45.
36. 'Directions to sound conversion', *Practical Works* (1981 edn.), at p. 592.
37. *CT* I. ii. 86.
38. *JF* 117.
39. 'A phase of religious selfishness', *Discussions: Evangelical and Theological* (Richmond, Virg., 1890; fac. London, 1967), i. 694–8. C. Hodge also distances himself from Owen's position, without seeing the full implications of his dissent (*Systematic Theology* (New York, 1873; fac. London, 1960), iii. 99; 43). See also J. Edwards, *The Works of Jonathan Edwards*, ed. E. Hickman (2 vols., London, 1834; fac. Edinburgh, 1974), ii. 590; T. Chalmers, *Institutes of Theology* (Edinburgh, 1849), ii. 152; 160; 178.
40. Foreword to J. F. MacArthur, *The Gospel According to Jesus* (Grand Rapids, Mich., 1988), at p. ix.
41. *The Scripture Gospel Defended* (1690), 46. Baxter is adamant that subjection to Christ as king entails the believer in legal duties: 'But as to them that insist on it, that the Gospel and New Covenant are no Laws, and that we have none from Christ but the Decalogue and Old Testament; were I to write against them to purpose, I would plentifully prove them subverters of Christianity itself, and give full evidence against them, to any that believe the Holy Scriptures. And contrarily I would prove, that there are no Divine Laws but what are truly the Laws of our Redeemer, now in the world, . . . and that he that feareth not breaking the Laws of Christ, shall hear at last; *Those mine enemies that*

would not that I should reign over them, bring them hither and slay them before me, Luke 19: 27.' (*CT*, I. ii. 43–4.)
42. *JF* 122.
43. Ibid. 105.
44. 'Of the Christian faith, which sanctifies, justifies and saves', *TW* ii. 475. G. Bull refers to Rom. 6: 16–17 (*Harmonia apostolica* (Oxford, 1842), 62 ff.
45. MacArthur, *Gospel According to Jesus*, pp. 172 ff.; McGrath, *Justification by Faith*, (Basingstoke, 1988), 30–1.
46. *JF* 103.
47. *TW* ii. 476.
48. Ibid.
49. 'The necessity of repentance and faith', *TW* ii. 3.
50. 'Christ the author, and obedience the condition of salvation', *TW* i. 500.
51. 'The possibility and necessity of gospel obedience, and its consistence with free grace', *TW* i. 510.
52. 'Of justifying faith', *TW* ii. 485.
53. 'An exposition of the Epistle to the Hebrews' (1674), *Works*, xxi. 540.
54. 'A vindication . . . of communion with God' (1674), *Works*, ii. 321.
55. *Works*, xxiv. 287.
56. Esp. Article XII.
57. Esp. Ch. XVI. ii.
58. 'Of justifying faith', *TW* ii. 485.
59. 'I cannot say that good works are necessary to salvation, that is to obtain it, which is the only sense in which they can be said with any propriety to be necessary to it . . . which I charge as a Popish and Socinian tenet, and I hope I shall ever oppose, as long as I have a tongue to speak, or a pen to write with, and am capable of using either' ('The necessity of good works unto salvation considered' (1738), *A Collection of Sermons and Tracts* (1773), ii. 185).
60. *Letters*, vi. 76–7.
61. *JF* 138.
62. Ibid. 143.
63. Ibid. 142.
64. Ibid. 144.
65. *Here We Stand*, p. 91; see also McGrath, *Justification by Faith*, p. 27.
66. 'For . . . evangelical justification, whereby a sinner is completely justified, that it should precede believing, I have not only not asserted, but positively denied, and disproved by many arguments' (*Works*, x. 449).
67. *JF* 139.
68. Ibid. 159–60.

69. R. C. Monk, *John Wesley: His Puritan Heritage* (London, 1966), 128–9.
70. *JF* 159.
71. *EC* 250.
72. Ibid. 251.
73. *JF* 149.
74. Ibid. 145.
75. *Works*, viii. 325.
76. 'The distinguishing character of a good and bad man', *TW* iii. 170.
77. According to H. Simonson, *Jonathan Edwards: Theologian of the Heart* (Grand Rapids, Mich., 1974), 41–4, Edwards held a conventional *sola fide* position. But this is far from being the case. Although he seems to share Owen's major emphases, he paradoxically makes concessions in the direction of Baxter and Tillotson. He clearly adopts a synecdochal view of *sola fide*, declaring that 'faith is not the only condition of salvation or justification; for there are many things that accompany and flow from faith, with which justification shall be, and without which it will not be, and therefore are found to be put in Scripture in conditional propositions with justification and salvation, in multitudes of places; such are love to God, and love to our brethren, forgiving men their trespasses, and many other good qualifications and acts'. Therefore, *sola fide* is to be understood in terms of 'the relation faith has to the ... mediator, in and by whom we are justified .... And thus it is that faith justifies, or gives an interest in Christ's satisfaction and merits' ('Justification by faith alone', *Works*, i. 623; 624; 626). Like Baxter and Tillotson, Edwards even grants that 'acts of evangelical obedience are indeed concerned in our justification itself, and are not excluded from that condition that justification depends upon, without the least prejudice to that justification by faith' (ibid. 643). He is most at variance with Owen over the nature of faith. He acknowledges that no one word 'clearly and adequately expresses the whole act of acceptance, or closing of the soul or heart with Christ'; therefore, like Baxter and Tillotson, he says faith is more than mere assenting trust. 'Love either is what faith arises from, or is included in faith .... Good works are in some sort implied in the very nature of faith ...' ('Concerning faith', *Works*, ii. 582; 579; 583). Edwards even contradicts Thomas Goodwin, who shared Owen's aversion for the medieval view of justifying faith as *fides caritate formata* (ibid. 588). He quotes with approval the twofold justification theory of Thomas Manton, which perfectly reflects Baxter's much maligned view (ibid. 591). His own view of Jas. 2: 24 could not be more in accord with Baxter's: 'For if we take works as acts or expressions of faith, they are not excluded; so a man is not justified by faith only, but also by works' (ibid., i. 652). Edwards like Owen, is self-contradictory. Unlike Owen, his doctrine of faith provides him

with the kind of solution adopted by Tillotson; i.e. if, as Edwards grants, faith does include good works in its nature, one can say that justification is by faith alone—in the synecdochal sense—without implying that 'faith' is a lifeless, barren disposition in an antinomian sense.

78. See Calvin, *Comm.* 1 Cor. 6: 11. One may argue that Romans and Galatians contain the gospel of forgiveness clothed in legal language, whereas Hebrews expresses the same gospel in ceremonial language. Had the first two letters never been written, the Reformation might have witnessed the rediscovery of the doctrine of sanctification by faith alone. While it is conventional to distinguish between justification and sanctification as separate aspects of salvation, and to make the former prior to the latter, the terms might be seen as representing two sets of equivalent metaphorical ideas. 1 Cor. 6: 11 even hints that the order should be reversed. According to the alternative view, this might explain why Paul does not include 'sanctification' in the *ordo salutis* of Rom. 8: 30; otherwise—if the hypothesis holds—he would be repeating himself. What is usually understood by 'sanctification' is possibly seen by the apostle as the subjective correlate of 'justification', in the manner assumed by Calvin. In 1 Cor. 1: 30, where the juxtaposition of δικαιοσύνη and ἁγιασμός seems to indicate the conventional order, this need not be Paul's intention any more than in 6: 11; he is just as likely to be expressing the fullness of salvation under different metaphors. See J. A. T. Robinson, *Wrestling with Romans* (London, 1979), 49–50.
79. Calvin himself discusses the petition for forgiveness in exactly the same way as justification, but without actually using the term 'justification' (*Inst.* III. xx. 45).
80. *JF* 138.
81. 'Of the necessity of good works', *TW* ii. 359.
82. 'We dream not of a faith which is devoid of good works, nor of a justification which can exist without them' (*Inst.* III. vxi. i); 'We, indeed, acknowledge with Paul, that the only faith which justifies is that which works by love (Gal. 5: 6)' (III. xi. 20); 'Faith . . . is always joined with good works' (*Comm.* Gal. 5: 6). For Calvin's views *vis-à-vis* the medieval debates over faith, see A. Vos, *Aquinas, Calvin, and Contemporary Protestant Thought* (Grand Rapids, Mich., 1985), 28 ff. Accordingly, Tillotson argues that 'tho' we be justified at first by faith without works preceding, yet faith without good works following it will not finally justify and save us' (*TW* ii. 364). The fundamental issue is not the necessity but the supposed merit of good works; thus Calvin writes that 'justification is free . . . no *merit* of works can at all be associated with it' (*Comm.* Rom. 3: 28). Likewise, Tillotson argues: 'What a senseless piece of arrogance is it to say, that a creature can merit

anything at God's hand? Whatever we give God is of his own, and when we have done all we can, we have done no more than our duty .... Besides that, all our obedience is imperfect, and is so far from meriting, that it stands in need of pardon; and can a man demerit, and merit by the same action? Can he who deserves to be punished for an action, because he did it no better, deserve to be rewarded for the same action, because he did it so well? And to say that Christ hath merited that our imperfect obedience should merit, either signifies only this, that Christ hath merited that our imperfect obedience should be accepted by God, notwithstanding its imperfection; (and this is true, but nothing to the purpose of merit;) or else it signifies, that Christ hath merited that *that* which is no wise meritorious, should be so; that is, that the nature of things should be alter'd; which is not only false, but senseless.' ('The condition of the gospel covenant, and the merit of Christ, consistent', *TW* ii. 491).

13
Paul and James

The seeming discrepancy between the apostles Paul and James (Rom. 3: 28; Jas. 2: 24) has been a perpetual source of embarrassment since the time of the Reformation. To complicate matters, this 'apostolic antinomy' has always had implications for the doctrine of Scripture as well as the theology of justification. For Protestants *sola scriptura* must be seen to harmonize with *sola fide*, but as Henry Chadwick points out, 'there is on the face of it a sharp tension between *sola fide* and recognition of the supreme authority of canonical scripture'.[1] Likewise, P. H. Davids writes, 'Because of this possible conflict, James 2: 24 must be viewed as a *crux interpretum*, not only for James but for New Testament theology in general.'[2]

John Owen confesses that the issue is highly problematic. His doctrine of Scripture demands that the words of Paul and James 'are certainly capable of a just reconciliation', yet he honestly admits 'that we cannot any of us attain thereunto' because of 'the darkness of our minds, the weakness of our understandings, and, with too many, from the power of prejudices'.[3] He was well aware that, for many, the only solution to the 'seeming repugnance between the apostles Paul and James' was the doctrine of a twofold justification.[4] In his view this involves the surrender of the Reformation and a return to medieval error.

Before the Reformation any seeming clash between Paul and James was but dimly perceived. In the patristic tradition, Augustine simply viewed Romans 3: 28 as excluding works prior to justification.[5] He frequently appeals to Galatians 5: 6 (*fides caritate formata*) as a comment on James 2: 14ff., to demonstrate that good works produced by grace and true faith are rewarded with eternal life.[6] It is impossible to ignore Augustine's use of merit in this context, which for all its sophistical ambiguity 'appears to have been quite innocent of the overtones of "works-righteousness" which would later be associated with it'.[7] Thomas Aquinas largely follows

Augustine here,[8] and he too appealed to Galatians 5: 6 to argue that 'the act of faith is meritorious only if faith works through love'.[9] Consequently, 'Man merits growth in grace by any meritorious act ... he merits the consummation of grace, which is eternal life'.[10] In short, faith and good works have a combined role in the process of justification and the obtaining of salvation.

This was also the view of John Wycliffe, who nevertheless retained the later concept of congruous merit while firmly rejecting condign merit.[11] For all his anticipation of Luther, he seems quite unaware of any inconsistency between Paul and James. Accordingly, for him James 2: 24 simply teaches that 'belief by itself is not sufficient to men's salvation, without good works'.[12] The Augustinian Paul–James synthesis is thus very evident in Wycliffe: 'To believe in God, as St Augustine saith, is, in belief to cleave to God through love, and to seek busily to fulfil his will.'[13] Such statements as these led Philip Melanchthon to say that Wycliffe was 'ignorant of the righteousness of faith'. However, Vaughan insists that Wycliffe's absolute dependence on Christ's atonement was no less conspicuous than Luther's, but that he saw 'the word salvation ... as comprehending the articles of justification and sanctification'.[14]

The Reformation witnessed a radical redefinition of justification. The concept of process was replaced by that of forensic declaration, a revolution which produced the inherent righteousness–imputed righteousness antithesis. Thus, the Paul–James antinomy emerged as a problem with Luther's affirmation of *sola fide*. He rejected Augustine's conception of justifying faith in favour of something more passive, although he denies that faith is passive after justification. Faced by James 2: 24, Luther relieved his theological and exegetical difficulties at a stroke by denigrating James as 'the epistle of straw'.[15] Although Calvin differed from Augustine on the nature of justification, his view of faith is virtually identical.[16] He is less critical than Luther, especially where the epistle of James is concerned; however, he established a precedent in dealing with James 2: 24. To 'make James consistent with the other Scriptures and with himself, you must give the word *justify*, as used by him, a different meaning from what it has with Paul'.[17] In short, James writes of the 'manifestation not of the imputation of righteousness';[18] the believer's righteousness is thus demonstrated before men.

The Anglican Reformers, for the most part, approached the

problem as Calvin did. Cranmer understood James 2: 14–26 to be saying simply that 'Thy deeds and works must be an open testimonial of thy faith';[19] good works are thus merely evidential. Elsewhere, Cranmer is somewhat ambivalent. While admitting that the two apostles use 'justify' in different senses, he considers that James speaks of the 'continuation, and increase of that justification which St Paul spake of before'.[20] This rather contradictory concession implies that James was, to a degree, thinking of justification just as Paul did. If Cranmer seems to hesitate over the evidential view, Hooker clearly thought the idea too simple; he even resorts to terminological latitude, suggesting that when James wrote 'justification' he really meant 'sanctification'.[21] As well as virtually rewriting Scripture, Hooker significantly departs from Calvin and Cranmer by allowing the doctrine of a twofold justification: 'To be justified so far as remission of sins, it sufficeth if we believe what another hath wrought for us: but whosoever will see God face to face, let him show his faith by his works, demonstrate a first justification by a second as Abraham did: for in this verse Abraham was justified (that is to say, his life was sanctified) by works.'[22]

The evidence suggests that James 2: 24 was indeed a problem, and the solutions are far from unanimous. Cranmer seems hesitant, while Calvin and Hooker lean effectively in Luther's direction, not by denigrating the epistle but in suggesting (albeit differently) that the 'inspired' penman meant something other than what he wrote.

The English Puritans tended to follow Calvin's exposition of James 2: 24, with minor variations. Presbyterians such as John Flavel (1628–91),[23] Thomas Manton (1620–77),[24] Matthew Poole (d. c.1685),[25] and Walter Marshall (1620–80)[26] relate the text to the believer's vindication from the charge of hypocrisy as well as a positive 'manifestation' of his justification before God. The Independent Thomas Goodwin (1600–79)[27] took the same position, as did the Baptist John Bunyan (1628–88). In a treatise concerned to oppose the increasing 'torrent of iniquity' in restoration England, Bunyan asks, 'Is there, therefore, no need at all of good works, because a man is justified before God without them? Or can that be called a justifying faith, that has not for its fruit good works, Job 22: 3; James 2: 20, 26? Verily good works are necessary, though God need them not.'[28]

Samuel Wright (1683–1746) assisted in the completion of the

famous *Exposition of the Old and New Testament* by the Presbyterian Matthew Henry (1662–1714). Reflecting Henry's Baxterian views, Wright's comment on James 2: 24 suggests discontent with the merely evidential view: 'Paul may be understood as speaking of that justification which is inchoate; James of that which is complete; it is by faith only that we are put into a justified state, but then good works come in for the completing of our justification at the last great day.'[29]

Thus Calvin's English disciples were no longer satisfied with their mentor's exposition. Indeed, had Calvin been correct, James really meant that men are publicly 'approved' δόκιμοι by works, a word which he did use in 1: 12 and might have used in 2: 24. Did he not realize that his readers would interpret ἐξ ἔργων δικαιοῦται ἄνθρωπος (2: 24) with reference to Paul's concept of δικαίωσις? In short, why did he employ a term perfectly understood in a Pauline context, if he intended to teach a different truth?

The *Considerationes* (1658) of William Forbes (1585–1634) possibly helped create the latitudinarian view of justification, as formulated by George Bull (1634–1710) in his *Harmonia apostolica* (1669).[30] While Tillotson was the most popular exponent of these views, his friend Gilbert Burnet (1643–1715) also argued that the solution to the Paul–James antinomy lay in the nature of faith. James is not intending 'to contradict the doctrine delivered by St Paul, but only to give a true notion of the faith that justifies.... So that the faith mentioned by St Paul is the complex of all Christianity; whereas that mentioned by St James is a bare believing, without a life suitable to it'.[31]

In the eighteenth-century dissenting opinion was as divided as ever. John Gill (1697–1771) seems content to expound James 2: 24 as the justification of a man's faith rather than of his person.[32] Revealing the influence of Baxter and Tillotson, Philip Doddridge (1702–51) thought that James was simply clarifying the nature of justifying faith: 'Faith in Christ is a very extensive principle, and includes in its nature and inseparable effects the whole of moral virtue.'[33] In America, Jonathan Edwards (1703–58) seems to have gone further than Doddridge, entertaining a theory of twofold justification little different from Baxter's.[34]

During the nineteenth-century, James Buchanan (1804–70), for all his high Calvinist orthodoxy, regarded it as a 'defective statement' to say that James 'speaks only of a justification before men', notwithstanding his distinction between actual and declarative justification.[35] The 'moderate' Calvinist Ralph Wardlaw (1779–1853) made a similar point; in his lucid lectures on James he advocates a doctrine of twofold justification.[36] He was clearly not satisfied by the merely evidential view held by Robert Haldane (1764–1842).[37]

Among the numerous twentieth-century scholars and commentators the same diversity of opinion exists. J. H. Ropes insists that James does not attach a different meaning to δικαίωσις from Paul. Thus 'Abraham's justification depended not merely on the initial act of faith, but also on his confirmatory manifestation of this faith under trial.'[38] Rudolph Bultmann considers that James' treatment of faith and works is simply a corrective to certain misunderstandings of Paul's theology.[39] Likewise, Karl Barth sees the solution to the Paul–James antinomy in the correct view of faith: 'Paul never even dreamed of the kind of πίστις envisaged and criticised in James 2: 14–26—the faith which has no ἔργον, which is inactive... There is no other faith than that "which worketh by love".'[40]

In much the same vein, Alan Richardson argues that James is not discussing the works excluded by Paul in Romans 3: 28: 'it may be said that Abraham was justified by works without contradicting Paul's assertion that no one is justified by works of the law in the sense of the meritorious observance of a legal code'.[41] J. Gresham Machen makes the same observation: 'The faith about which Paul has been speaking is not idle faith which James condemns, but a faith that works.'[42] Herman Ridderbos similarly argues that faith and works are only mutually exclusive where the question of merit is concerned; otherwise, 'That faith and works ... belong inseparably together is evident from the whole of Paul's preaching. Not only is faith at work through love (Galatians 5: 6), but the Apostle speaks in so many words of "the work of faith".'[43] Faith therefore has active as well as passive features, an idea also expounded by D. M. Lloyd-Jones: 'In faith there is always the element of trust, the element of committal, the element of obedience.' That said, Lloyd-Jones views the 'works' of James 2: 24 as mere 'proofs'.[44] Despite some misgivings, Berkhof takes the same position.[45]

On the other hand, P. H. Davids definitely teaches a twofold justification. Unlike other contemporary scholars, he denies the validity of expounding James 2: 24 with 'Pauline definitions in mind'; James should be allowed 'to speak out of his own background'.[46] Donald Guthrie disagrees: 'The kind of works that James is concerned about is the kind that results from genuine faith .... Paul would have been as opposed as James is to mere intellectual assent.'[47] Thus James is really correcting misunderstandings of Paul's conception of faith. While John Stott is not certain that Paul and James were using the verb 'justify' in different senses, he holds that 'both teach that an authentic faith works, Paul stressing the faith that issues in works, and James the works that issue from faith'.[48]

Three clear viewpoints emerge from this cursory, merely representative survey, for opinion is certainly divided on the place of good works in justification. The classification cannot be exact, and overlap cannot be excluded. The Augustinians proper teach a twofold justification (the first by an infusion of grace at baptism, the second by faith and works; the theory modified by some Protestants as 'first by faith and a second by works'); this group includes Wycliffe, Hooker, Wright, Edwards, Wardlaw, and Davids. The semi-Augustinians teach that good works are necessary for justification in the sense of a concomitant or feature of justifying faith; among these are Cranmer, Forbes, Bull, Burnet, Doddridge, Barth, Richardson, Ridderbos, and other modern scholars. The anti-Augustinians argue that good works are merely evidence of justification; they include Luther, Calvin, Flavel, Manton, Poole, Marshall, Goodwin, Bunyan, Gill, Haldane, Buchanan, Berkhof, and Lloyd-Jones. While these categories are defined in terms of the exegesis of James 2:24, there is evidence that Calvin's unique continuum view of justification actually places him in the middle ground, even if his view of the text makes him an anti-Augustinian. If these categories are valid, they would indicate that the anti-Augustinian position is something of an over-reaction to the medieval Augustinian view. Whereas the earlier view is clouded by the concept of merit, the later one appears ambivalent and suspicious about the necessity of good works.

With the terms of the discussion duly clarified, it should now be possible to assess correctly the view points of John Owen and John Wesley.

Owen provided the most thorough and detailed exposition of the Paul–James antinomy from a high orthodox, anti-Augustinian position. Since the root of the difficulty lies in the apparent ambiguity of the terms 'justified', 'faith', and 'works' in James 2: 24, he lays it down as a basic exegetical principle that the verse is to be interpreted in the light of Paul's more comprehensive treatment of justification. Paul must illuminate James, rather than (as Bull argued) the other way round.[49] Accordingly, Owen makes four crucial observations on the 'seeming repugnance' between the two apostles. (1) The apostles differ in purpose; Paul explains how sinners may be justified before God, whereas James is exposing the emptiness of a merely nominal profession of faith.[50] (2) In criticizing *sola fide* James is not rejecting Paul's conception of faith but a 'dead faith.'[51] (3) Whereas Paul discusses the believer's absolute justification before God, James speaks of the evidence or manifestation of it before men.[52] (4) The works that James says are necessary for justification are identical with those Paul rejects, which proves that they are speaking of justification in different senses.[53]

Although Owen is right to insist that Paul is the real exponent of justification *coram Deo*, it cannot be said that James is ignoring this, even though his emphasis is different. If Romans 3: 28 is dealing with man's justification before God, the question in James 2: 14, 'can [dead] faith save him?', proves beyond doubt that James is not discussing merely evidential considerations. While James is clearly refuting nominalism, he is also clarifying something Paul largely assumes. Indeed, with regard to the nature of saving faith, James is illuminating and amplifying in 2: 14–20 what Paul says in Romans 6: 16–17 and elsewhere. In other words, if James does not discuss the objective basis of justification (Christ's atoning work) as Paul does (Rom. 3: 25; 5: 1–11), he endorses Paul's not exactly inconspicuous teaching on the nature of a valid saving response to the gospel.

Owen's second main observation, that the two apostles 'speak not of the same faith', is only partially true, and his discussion at this point is questionable. He correctly refutes Bellarmine's contention that James is discussing justifying faith as such in verses 14–20, for true faith is more than the mere mental assent that demons might possess (v. 19). Owen then grants that Abraham's faith (vv. 21–3) is of a different order from that which James had earlier 'treated with such severity'.[54] This would imply that here James and Paul assume the same faith. That said, Owen denies that James attributes justification partly to faith and partly to works since, in his view, verse 24 places faith and works in antithesis.[55] In other words, James is describing an evidential justification by works, not an absolute justification by faith *and* works. But if Owen is right, why does James refer to Genesis 15: 6 (v. 23), quoted by Paul to prove that Abraham was justified by faith 'absolutely' before God (Rom. 4: 4; Gal. 3: 6)? Of course, if at this point, James's conception of faith is identical to Paul's, then there is an obvious and serious discrepancy; but even this assumes that Paul meant 'faith alone'—a phrase he never used—in the very sense denied by James. However, in his attempt to discredit the twofold justification theory, Owen is simply ignoring the facts; James 2: 24 obviously reflects the conjunction of the faith and works of verse. 21–2. Assuming that Paul and James are not really in conflict, there must be an alternative solution. But, for the moment, one may say that the faith–works conjunction seems to support Owen's own dubious quasi-Augustinian theory of twofold justification, but his overall view of James 2 forbids any assistance from this quarter.

In his third observation, Owen insists that Paul and James are not using 'justified' in the same sense.[56] Unlike Paul, James is simply concerned with the believer's public justification before men. Without doubting that this is included, it would have been sufficient for James to say that the believer is approved δόκιμος rather than justified δικαιοῦται before men. Had he done so, the history of theological controversy would have been very different. The fact that he is thinking of justification δικαίωσις makes Owen's position questionable, especially since James also assumes the wider context of salvation (v. 14). In short, Owen and the anti-Augustinians are virtually rewriting Scripture. To be fair, all three positions are committed to a degree of 'terminological adjustment'. The question then becomes, which position makes the most coherent sense of all the data with the least degree of adjustment? That said, it is difficult to imagine that James intended something so very different from Paul, especially when both apostles appeal to Abraham's justification in the sight of God (Gen. 15: 6).

Owen's fourth and final observation concerns James's use of 'works'. In his view, both apostles mean 'the works of the law'.[57] Therefore, since Paul excludes 'the works of the law' from justification in Romans 3: 28, James must be thinking of another justification if such works are necessary for it. This is plausible, but Abraham's 'works' could not be defined by a law which was not introduced until 430 years later (Gal. 3: 17). It is surely significant that James does not employ Paul's expression 'works of the law'. He is probably assuming Paul's own distinction between works, i.e. deeds performed without regeneration for meritorious ends, and good works, i.e. 'gospel obedience', consistent with the moral law but performed in the strength of regeneration (Eph. 2: 9–10). In other words, the relevant issue is the status of the persons concerned. Paul has in mind the merit-seeking Jew, James the professing believer. Ignoring for a moment Owen's paradoxical concession over the twofold theory, he admits that such an exegesis would 'easily solve this difficulty', if there was scriptural warrant for it. But he denies that Paul was sufficiently explicit on this.[58] However, without granting every aspect of the twofold theory, there were those who thought Paul's conception of faith involved a necessary connection between trust and obedience, without assuming that either had any meritorious significance. Indeed, the apostle's statement in Ephesians 2: 8–10 seems to demand the view that a believer is only saved by a 'good-works-producing' faith. In short, faith without works will not save. Interestingly, one of Owen's statements seems to express this perfectly: 'We are neither justified nor saved *without* them, though we are not justified ... for them.'[59] This would surely solve the difficulty; but Owen's 'official' passive doctrine of *sola fide* precludes this. His exposition of James 2: 14–15 thus confirms the suspicion that the anti-Augustinian view fails to do justice to the textual difficulties involved.

As early as the 1744 Methodist Conference Wesley and his companions were troubled by the Paul–James antinomy. The agreed solution was that the apostles speak of different justifications at separate periods in Abraham's life. Also, Paul is 'speaking of works that precede faith' and James 'of works that spring from faith'.[60] Wesley thus resorts to an Augustinian position, obviously implying that Paul's justification is incomplete and insufficient without a subsequent, secondary justification. In his *Explanatory Notes* (1755) the 1744 view is confirmed, but with some important elaborations. Wesley treats the variations between the apostles quite differently from Owen; James 'purposely' repeats Genesis 15: 6 to refute those who abused Paul's teaching, but basically, the two apostles are thinking of 'different kinds of men'. Wesley points out that James himself 'pleaded the cause of faith (Acts 15: 13–21)', and Paul also 'strenuously pleads for works, particularly in his later epistles'; in short, Paul and James both teach justification by faith and works. Wesley's obvious impatience with the evidential view is indicated by his view of faith. Interpreting James 2: 14 in the light of Galatians 5: 6, he concludes, 'Can that faith "which is without works" save him? No more than it can profit his neighbour.'[61]

In dealing with James 2: 21 Wesley plainly contradicts his 1740 view that 'justification ... is not the being made actually just and righteous. This is sanctification'.[62] He now declares that Abraham 'was justified in St James's sense [that is, made righteous], by works, consequent to his faith. So that St James' justification by works is the fruit of St Paul's justification by faith'.[63] Thus in fifteen years Wesley had swung from an anti-Augustinian to an Augustinian position. Like Hooker before him, he assumes that James is concerned with sanctification ἁγιασμός rather than justification δικαίωσις. Wesley has resorted to a highly unscholarly manœuvre. Like Owen, albeit differently, he effectively rewrites Scripture.

Predictably, Wesley interprets the 'works' of James and Paul in typically Augustinian fashion. Thus Abraham returned from the Genesis 22: 12 trial of his faith 'far higher in the favour of God'.[64] Apart from the dubious suggestion that there are degrees of divine favour, for one is either justified or not, Wesley does have the advantage over Owen in distinguishing between the pre-conversion 'works' and post-conversion 'good works'. However, influenced by Baxter's twofold theory of justification, he failed to exploit this coherently. His own solution to the Paul–James antinomy is almost as questionable as Owen's.

Adopting an Augustinian stance, Baxter distinguishes between a constitutive and a sentential justification. Defining the first in terms of pardon of sin, Baxter does admit that it 'is the sense that we are said to be justified by faith in, primarily in Scripture'.[65] However, he interprets the New Testament stress on 'doing' as the basis of a secondary justification. Notwithstanding his timely stress on good works, he fails to meet the objection that the twofold theory finds no place in Paul's theology of justification. If Baxter and others are right, Paul's account is seriously deficient. None the less, his doctrine of faith is itself the key to solving the apparent conflict between Paul and James. Baxter was right to expound James 2: 24 by saying that 'this practical faith ... justifieth the man himself',[66] but it was Tillotson who successfully worked out the implications of this simple insight.

Tillotson's solution is lucid and uncomplicated. He virtually avoids attaching different meanings to James's expressions to reconcile him with Paul. Neither does he resort to a twofold justification; like Calvin, he adopts a continuum view, with justification always defined as remission of sins. But unlike Calvin, Tillotson sees no need to assume that James is using 'justification' differently from Paul. Since James is not dealing with the meritorious basis of justification, his rejection of *sola fide* is not a negation of Paul, but only a rejection of false faith. In line with Calvin's overall semi-Augustinian emphasis ('We dream not of a faith which is devoid of good works, nor of a justification which can exist *without* them'),[67] Tillotson uses his tripartite conception of faith to make Calvin's anti-Augustinian exegesis of James 2: 24 quite unnecessary. Since πίστις consists of assent, trust, and obedience, Tillotson concludes:

But if Abraham were justified by works, viz. by offering up his son upon the altar, in obedience to God's command . . . how was the Scripture fulfilled, which saith, that faith was imputed to him for righteousness, that is, he was justified by faith; unless faith take in the works of obedience? From whence he concludes, that by works a man is justified, and not by faith only; not by naked assent to the truth, but by such a faith as includes obedience.[68]

When Tillotson disqualifies other exegeses, he does so in the simplest and most persuasive manner. He actually 'outdoes' the Puritan exegetes, renowned as they were for a meticulous attention to the text of Scripture. He has no time for the view that 'faith justifies the person, and works justify the faith'; this distinction 'only serves an opinion', and 'at this rate a man may maintain anything, though it be never so contrary to Scripture, and elude the clearest text in the Bible'.[69] After showing the inconsistency of the evidential view of James 2: 24 in the light of 2: 14 ('can [dead] faith save him?'), he shows that the final solution is as decisive as it is simple:

And this doth not contradict St Paul, who saith, Galatians 2: 16, *that a man is not justified by the works of the law: but by the faith of Jesus Christ*. For how does this, that we are justified not by the legal dispensation, but by the faith of the Gospel, which includes obedience and good works, contradict what St James says, that we are not justified by a bare assent to the truth of the Gospel, but by obedience to the commands of it? And I do not see that upon the contrary supposition, viz. that the faith of the Gospel doth not include obedience in it, it is possible to reconcile these two apostles.[70]

Allowing that James himself distinguishes between what he calls Abraham's faith (assent plus trust) and the faith of demons (mere assent), Tillotson's lucid insights permit the following paraphrase of James 2: 20–4: A faith without the commitment implied by obedience is not a living, saving faith. In Abraham's case, obedience was coupled with his assent and trust, thereby proving that his faith was complete and genuine. So, by an obedient faith a man is justified, and not by mere assent and trust. Needless to say, 'by' is not to be construed meritoriously; it simply denotes the appropriating factor in justification.

One might add that from the moment Abraham decided to depart for Canaan, his faith was, at its very inception, of the kind Tillotson describes. James is therefore merely clarifying what Paul assumed, that from the first moments of conversion true faith possesses all the right ingredients. In other words, true faith has active as well as passive features. Where Paul is primarily concerned with the objective character of divine grace, James is concerned with the subjective character of the human response. Their different emphases are perfectly complementary. That said, Paul largely assumes the very conception of faith for which James is pleading. James, therefore, is not thinking of a different conception of justification, but arguing for a view of faith that Paul generally takes for granted.

Tillotson's semi-Augustinian synthesis effectively solves the knotty problems of the Paul-James antinomy. It also helps to reconcile the apostles with their Lord. It is arguable from Christ's own teaching on justification in Luke 18: 11–14 and Matthew 12: 36–7 that the proceedings of the day of judgement will terminate the justification continuum. In the former case, where the publican 'went down to his house justified' rather than the Pharisee, the stress is placed on the objective, meritorious basis of justification (i.e. the publican appealed to God's mercy, v. 13). In the other passage Christ is pointing out the appropriating factor of justification: 'For by thy words thou shalt be justified' (v. 37) (i.e. by words which indicate a genuine faith wrought in the heart, (v. 35). However, these two aspects correlate at every stage of the believer's experience; they do not represent two justifications any more than the teachings of Paul and James do. Neither should a continuum view be confused with a theory of progressive justification. While santification is progressive, pardon or justification admits of no degrees; one is either justified or not. At any instant in the believer's experience, present confession of sin and faith in Christ is accompanied by present justification.

Tillotson's solution also reconciles the apostles' theological utterances in their epistles with their evangelistic and pastoral practice in the book of Acts, where repentance is made as much a condition of salvation as faith (Acts 17:30; 20: 21 26:18). Tillotson's view suggests that faith necessarily includes repentance, if a believer is justified by an obedient faith. Since faith involves assent, trust, and obedience, so repentance implies a change of mind, heart, and will. Put differently, faith and repentance are simply positive and negative sides of the same coin. They are necessarily connected, the one implied by the other. This is surely the reason why Paul's stress on justification by faith (where repentance is not specifically mentioned) is consistent with his stress on repentance elsewhere.[71]

Tillotson's (and Baxter's) discussion of faith in the context of Christ's threefold office also makes sense psychologically, since a correlation obtains between the believer's psychology and the faith he exercises in Christ. In other words, when a person receives Christ, the whole person (mind, heart, and will) embraces a whole Christ (prophet, priest, and king) with a whole faith (assent, trust, and obedience). Each constituent of faith has a corresponding office in Christ's person, which in turn is an expression of each aspect of the believer's psychology. When James attributes Abraham's justification to faith and works, 'faith' denotes assent and trust and 'works' denotes obedience. At this point in his argument, the faith James attributes to the patriarch is different both from the 'faith' demons may possess and the full-blown conception of Paul. One may say that, for the sake of argument, James deliberately separates faith from works to make his point, 'works' being the equivalent of Paul's 'obedience of faith'. This may be represented symbolically. If assent $=f_a$, trust $=f_t$, and works $=f_o$, then James 2: 24 is stating: 'by f_o a man is justified, and not by f_a and f_t only'. In other words, Paul (from evidence already supplied) assumes the very conception of faith (F) for which James is pleading, i.e. $F=f_a+f_t+f_o$'. In terms of the triple office formula, James 2: 24 may be paraphrased thus: 'By receiving Christ as king a man is justified, and not by receiving him as priest and prophet only.' James, therefore, is not arguing for a different conception of justification, but for a view of faith that Paul takes for granted.

Despite adverse criticism, Tillotson denied that he was reintroducing a 'works-righteousness' gospel. Whilst he stressed the necessity of an obedient faith for justification, he carefully distinguished between the meritorious and the non-meritorious conditions of salvation. This, he insisted, was the fundamental issue in the controversy with Rome. But in order to preserve the gospel of free grace, the high orthodox had insisted that Christ's righteousness (both passive and active) was the formal cause of justification, while a passive faith was its instrumental cause. In line with Calvin's anti-scholastic instincts,[72] Tillotson and the other latitudinarians rejected the 'formal–instrumental' distinction,[73] preferring the simpler—and arguably more scriptural–'meritorious–non-meritorious' alternative.[74] This endorses the concern lying behind the earlier distinction without encouraging an antinomian view of faith. Indeed, had the high orthodox theologians restricted their notion of the formal cause of justification to Christ's passive righteousness, the 'holy living' school[75] might not have opposed it. According to the latter, the anti-Augustinian thesis, that a passive view of faith alone avoids infringing Christ's all-sufficient merit, is not the only option.[76] Neither is it necessary, for the imperfectly fulfilled duties of gospel obedience are no more qualified to merit divine favour than a passive faith is. But Tillotson still insists that while trust in Christ alone appropriates God's grace, it never does so in isolation from other spiritual graces. Thus legalism and antinomianism are both avoided.

Tillotson's lucid solution of the Paul–James antinomy was greeted with widespread suspicion, for one simple reason: his Calvin-like insistence that there is no justification without good works was thought to threaten the merits of Christ. But the real cause of all the confusion lay elsewhere: the ambiguous *sola fide* slogan had created an unnecessary antipathy towards good works. This was to a degree understandable in the wake of the medieval doctrine of merit. Thus James's rejection of *sola fide* was seen as a threat to Paul, even though the latter never dreamed of the notion James was repudiating. If Luther seemed to miss the point, most of the other Reformers realized that a necessary connection existed between faith and good works. However, despite his own polemic against antinomianism, Luther's solifidian tendencies gained popular acceptance. Faced by solifidian antinomianism, Baxter and others over-reacted towards medieval theology. By distinguishing between the supposed merit of good works and good works *per se*, and by viewing *sola fide* as a statement about Christ's merits rather than about the supposed isolated function of justifying faith, Tillotson was able to provide a coherent *via media*. His insights effectively rectified the one exegetical anomaly in Calvin's otherwise cogent and unique theology of justification. More importantly, he rescues the gospel from both legalistic presumption and antinomian abuse:

So that no man hath reason to fear, that this doctrine of the necessity of obedience to our acceptance with God, and the obtaining of eternal life, should be any ways prejudicial to the law of faith and the law of grace. For so long as these three things are but asserted and secured,

1st, That faith is the root and principle of obedience and a holy life, and that without it, it is impossible to please God.

2nd, That we stand continually in need of the divine grace and assistance to enable us to perform that obedience which the gospel requires of us . . . . And

3rd, That the forgiveness of our sins, and the reward of eternal life, are founded in the free grace and mercy of God, conferring these blessings upon us, not for the merit of our obedience, but only for the merit and satisfaction of the obedience and sufferings of our blessed Saviour and Redeemer; I say, so long as we assert these three things, we give all that the gospel anywhere ascribes to faith, and the grace of God revealed in the gospel.[77]

This is a position neither Wesley, Baxter, nor Owen could disagree with.

NOTES

1. 'Justification by faith: a perspective', *One in Christ*, 20. 3 (1984), at p. 197.
2. *The Epistle of James* (London, 1982), 130.
3. *JF* 384.
4. Ibid. 138.
5. 'On the spirit and the letter', in Augustine, *Works*, ed. P. Schaff (New York, 1887; fac. Grand Rapids, Mich., 1956), v: *Anti-Pelagian Writings*, at p. 102.
6. 'On grace and free will', ibid. 451.
7. A. E. McGrath, *Iustitia Dei* (Cambridge, 1986), i. 109. Calvin (*Inst.* III. xv. 2.) asks pertinently, 'what need was there to introduce the word

Merit, when the value of works might have been fully expressed by another term, and without offence?' See also 'Salvation and the Church' (ARCIC II, 1987), 22 n. 5.
8. McGrath, *Iustitia Dei*, i. 114; 160.
9. *Summa Theologiae*, ed. C. Ernst (London, 1972), xxx. 213.
10. Ibid. 225.
11. McGrath, *Iustitia Dei*, i. 117; R. Doyle, 'The death of Christ and the doctrine of grace in John Wycliffe', *CM* 99. 4 (1985), 317–35.
12. *The Poor Caitif: The Writings of the Revd and Learned John Wickliffe, DD* (London, n.d. [1838]), 50.
13. Ibid. 53.
14. R. Vaughan, *The Life and Opinions of John de Wycliffe, DD* (London, 1831), ii. 324–6.
15. While some Lutheran scholars suggest that Luther changed his attitude towards the Epistle, Woolf says that in the 1546 edition of his German New Testament he 'adopts in some respect a milder tone than in the few words in the last paragraph of his general introduction to the New Testament, or at least a form of words that leaves less room for scoffing or parody. But his critical attitude is as firm as ever' (*Reformation Writings of Martin Luther*, trans. B. L. Woolf (1956), ii. 306).
16. *Inst.* III. xi. 15; xi. 20; *Comm.* Gal. 5: 6.
17. *Inst.* III. xvii. 12.
18. *Comm.* Jas. 2: 21.
19. *Homilies*, p. 30.
20. 'Notes on justification', *Miscellaneous Writings of Thomas Cranmer* (Cambridge, 1846), 208.
21. 'A learned discourse of justification', *The Works of That Learned and Judicious Divine Mr Richard Hooker*, ed. J. Keble (Oxford, 1836), iii. 2, pp. 630–1.
22. Ibid., II. 704.
23. 'Exposition of the Shorter Catechism', *The Works of John Flavel* (London, 1820; fac. London, 1968), vi. 196–7; see also *DNB*.
24. *An Exposition of the Epistle of James* (Edinburgh, 1870; fac. London, 1962), 260 (this work was first published in 1658). It seems that Manton moved away from the strictly evidential view, to judge by his posthumous sermons; see J. Edwards's quotation of Manton's twofold theory in *The Works of Jonathan Edwards*, ed. E. Hickman (London, 1834; fac. Edinburgh, 1974), ii. 591. For Manton see *DNB*.
25. *A Commentary on the Holy Bible* (London, 1963), iii. 888; see also *DNB*.
26. *The Gospel Mystery of Sanctification* (Edinburgh, 1896), 146; esp. 'The doctrine of justification opened and applied', ibid. 442. See also *DNB*.

27. Sermon XXIII, *The Works of Thomas Goodwin, DD* (Edinburgh, 1861), ii. 245; see also *DNB*.
28. 'A holy life the beauty of Christianity' (1684), *The Works of John Bunyan*, ed. G. Offor (London, 1855), ii. 507.
29. M. Henry, *An Exposition of the Old and New Testament* (London, 1886), ix. 619; see also *DNB*.
30. A. E. McGrath, 'The emergence of the Anglican tradition on justification 1600–1700', *CM* 98. 1 (1984), 28–43.
31. G. Burnet, *An Exposition of the Thirty-nine Articles of the Church of England*, ed. J. R. Page (London, 1841), 163.
32. *A Collection of Sermons and Tracts* (London, 1773), i. 207; see also *DNB*.
33. 'The family expositor', *The Works of the Revd P. Doddridge, DD* (ed. E. Williams and E. Parsons), (Leeds, 1802–5), v. 218; see also *DNB*.
34. *Works* (1974), i. 652; see also *DAB*.
35. *The Doctrine of Justification* (Edinburgh, 1867; fac. London, 1961), 257; see also *DNB*.
36. *Lectures on the Epistle of James* (London, 1862), 179–85; see also *DNB*.
37. *Exposition of the Epistle to the Romans* (Edinburgh, 1874; fac. London, 1963), 155; see also *DNB*.
38. *The Epistle of James* (Edinburgh, 1916), 218–19.
39. *Theology of the New Testament* (London, 1955), ii. 131.
40. *Church Dogmatics*, trans. G. W. Bromiley (Edinburgh, 1957), iv. 2, p. 731.
41. *An Introduction to the Theology of the New Testament* (London, 1958), 240–1.
42. *The New Testament* (Edinburgh, 1975), 239.
43. *Paul: An Outline of His Theology*, trans, J. R. De Witt (Grand Rapids, Mich., 1977), 132.
44. *Romans: Atonement and Justification* (London, 1970), 123.
45. L. Berkhof, *Systematic Theology* (London, 1963), 521.
46. *The Epistle of James* (London, 1982), p. 132.
47. *New Testament Theology* (Leicester, 1981), 599.
48. *The Cross of Christ* (London, 1986), 192.
49. *Harmonia Apostolica* (Oxford, 1842), 56 ff.
50. *JF* 387; 9.
51. Ibid. 390.
52. Ibid. 392.
53. Ibid. 394.
54. Ibid. 391.
55. Ibid.
56. Ibid. 392.
57. Ibid. 394.

238 The Theology: Faith and Justification

58. Ibid. 379.
59. *Works*, ii. 321.
60. *Works*, viii. 266.
61. *Notes*, Jas. 2: 14.
62. *Works*, v. 51.
63. *Notes*, Jas. 2: 21.
64. *Notes*, Jas. 2: 22.
65. *EC* 245.
66. *Paraphrase*, Annotations on Jas. 2.
67. *Inst.* III. xvi. 1. See also *Comm.* Ezek 18: 14–17.
68. 'Of justifying faith', *TW* ii. 482.
69. Ibid. 483.
70. Ibid.
71. In Acts 20: 21 repentance and faith are coupled together, the former signifying a general response to the triune God, and the latter a particular response to the person of Christ.
72. While Calvin accepted a version of the scholastic fourfold cause of justification, he did not say that Christ's righteousness was the formal cause of justification, as a later high orthodoxy did. Of course, he only uses the fourfold cause to prove a point, namely that works have no meritorious causal significance, even when—as Tillotson does—he allows them to have an 'inferior causality' (*Inst.* III. xiv. 21). Calvin actually reduces the 'four causes' to three: the efficient, the material, and the formal or instrumental, the last two terms being treated as virtually synonymous. Christ' obedience is the material rather than the formal cause of justification, the latter being ascribed to faith (see *Inst.* III. xiv. 17). Elsewhere Calvin drops the term 'formal' altogether, while his fourth cause becomes God's 'justice and goodness' (*Comm.* Rom. 3: 22–4; *Inst.* III. xiv. 17). See T. H. L. Parker, *Commentaries on the Epistle to the Romans 1532–1542* (Edinburgh, 1986), 197.
73. Improving on Calvin's view, but consistently with his generally anti-scholastic exposition of faith, Tillotson rightly says that to speak of faith as the instrumental cause of justification is to invoke the invalid necessitarian analogy of physical causality (*TW* ii. 480). T. denies that the language of physical causality is appropriate to moral concepts like faith. In short, this way of speaking involves a category mistake. While divine grace may be said to cause faith, it does not do so in a mechanistic manner.
74. While the concept of merit is alien to the New Testament, Tillotson uses it to express the New Testament idea that justification is 'founded in the free grace and mercy of God' (*TW* i. 508). Tillotson's idea of 'meritorious cause' is equivalent to Calvin's 'material cause'.
75. McGrath, *Iustitia Dei*, ii. 105 ff.; P. Toon, *Justification and Sanctification* (London, 1983), 97 ff.

76. Both J. I. Packer ('The doctrine of justification in development and decline among the Puritans', in *By Schisms Rent Asunder* (PRSC, London, 1969), at p. 27) and R. T. Kendall (*Calvin and English Calvinism to 1649* (Oxford, 1979), 205–8) fail to distinguish between meritorious actions and actions *per se*. As P. Helm points out (*Calvin and the Calvinists*, (Edinburgh, 1982), 71 ff.), insisting on the conditionality of active faith is not to make it the meritorious ground of salvation. Whatever inhibitions Owen and others may have had about 'conditions' (*JF* 105 ff.), Calvin evidently did not share them (see *Concerning the Eternal Predestination of God* (trans. J. R. S. Reid (London, 1961), 105–6; *Sermons on the Epistles to Timothy and Titus*, trans. L. T. (*sic*), (London, 1579; fac. Edinburgh, 1983) 1181–2; *Inst.* I. xvii. 14).
77. 'The possibility and necessity of gospel obedience and its consistence with free grace', *TW* i. 508.

Conclusion

From the perspective of the twentieth-century, the heated debates of post-Reformation theology seem remote, obscure, and irrelevant. Generally speaking, our interests and preoccupations are very different from those of Owen's and Wesley's generations. Indeed, Dr Alan Sell points out that such issues as biblical criticism, the Oxford movement, and evolutionary theory had a marginalizing effect on the Calvinist–Arminian controversy throught the nineteenth-century.[1] Since then an increasingly secular mentality has tended to dominate much theology. Yet it would seem that the combined pursuits of a vague ecumenism, the 'new hermeneutic', humanistic liberalism, and even 'liberation theology'—not to speak of charismatic pietism—are no closer to solving contemporary problems. The modern approach largely ignores the basic biblical evaluation of law and grace, faith and action, and religion and life, which was of such paramount importance to Owen, Baxter, Tillotson, and Wesley. Our theologians were no less concerned with the human predicament than modern secular theologians, but they were aware that for a response to be truly Christian it must remain within the God-given constraints of the Scriptural revelation. Accordingly, Dr Sell says that a return to so basic an issue as the divine–human relationship 'would be a refreshing change from that neutralism and relativism into which so much recent theology has fallen'.[2]

Dr Sell is surely correct to say that the older debates were not solved but only shelved.[3] However, without ignoring the theological trends he justly laments, we may note that Reformed theology has witnessed a significant revival since about 1960. In its wake, the interest aroused by R. T. Kendall's revisionist contribution surprised many. The very mixed reception given to Dr Kendall's findings gives added significance to Dr Sell's plea for a renewed concern for 'doctrinal clarity, provided it could be fostered without acrimony'.[4]

Conclusion

In this book a number of Dr Kendall's conclusions have been endorsed. Certain detailed differences remain, but the general validity of his revisionist approach is not questioned. Taking the debate further, the theological emphases of John Owen and John Wesley have been evaluated with reference to the Baxter–Tillotson *via media* in the broader context of Reformation theology. The towering genius of John Calvin appears at almost every stage, his own contribution emerging as the very 'ameliorated Calvinism' pleaded for by Dr Sell.[5] In short, Calvin's own exposition of the issues possesses, at one and the same time, the hallmarks of biblicity, catholicity, and contemporary relevance.

In relation to theological developments after his death, Calvin's 'Calvinism' exhibits a positive basis for reconciliation. The evidence would suggest that Owen's high Calvinism and Wesley's Arminianism are very largely the result of theological imbalance. Unlike Calvin, neither Owen nor Wesley seemed able to acknowledge the presence of paradox in the Bible. In their radically different approaches to the issues in question, their methods were arguably rationalistic. High Calvinism may be styled the rationalism of the right, and Arminianism the rationalism of the left. While both men claimed support for their doctrinal peculiarities in the teaching of the Bible, their conclusions can only be upheld at the expense of significant textual evidence.

Owen's particularism and Wesley's universalism are alike one-sided accounts of the gospel. At their best, both men may be regarded as semi-Calvinists, albeit from opposing perspectives. They both stress different sides of the paradox that Calvin held in tension. An alternative is offered by Richard Baxter, who was concerned to expound the textual data in an integrated manner without suppressing either the general or the particular aspects of the gospel. Like Calvin, Baxter accepted the fact of paradox, urging the need to restrict theological activity to the confines of the evidence; thus he adopted a dualistic hermeneutic in his theology of grace. The atonement is to be seen in a two-sided manner: it is general in provision, though particular in application, both aspects being part of the divine intention. While Baxter was accused of compromise, his concern was not merely dictated by the demands of an ecumenical vision; his was a convinced theological evaluation of the issues. He was not, therefore, diluting truth but restoring what had become a 'super-concentrate' to its proper biblical 'strength'.

In this latter respect, Baxter has a clear precedent in Calvin. It is fascinating to conclude that, logically speaking, Calvin has to be disqualified by his high orthodox sons. Judged by seventeenth-century criteria, Calvin was no more of a 'Calvinist' than Baxter.

Calvin's precise position on the atonement raises obvious questions for the remaining 'four points' of Calvinism. Although he clearly taught the doctrine of total depravity, he admits a carefully defined concept of free will which an Arminian could hardly contest. Indeed, some of his utterances about man's response to the gospel seem thoroughly Wesleyan.[6] Calvin's chief contention is that a man's volitions are free from compulsion, but ultimately conditioned by his nature; man is thus a willing slave to sin. The grace of regeneration is necessary to enable a person to choose and act aright. Against Arminius and Wesley, Calvin clearly taught unconditional election; only by the most undisguised textual tampering can the Bible be said to teach otherwise. Yet Calvin makes plain that election is only known indirectly; Christ is the 'mirror' of election. Therefore, without faith in Christ and a godly life, no one can learn of their election. If election is ultimately unconditional, knowledge of it is conditional. God's sovereign, inscrutable will apart, there can be no doubt—to judge by his numerous utterances—that Calvin would have endorsed the lines of Charles Wesley:

> O for a trumpet voice,
> On all the world to call!
> To bid their hearts rejoice
> In Him who died for all;
> For all my Lord was crucified,
> For all, for all my Saviour died.[7]

It is doubtful whether Calvin would have aquiesced in the idea of 'irresistible grace'. His view of free will forbids a thoroughgoing mechanistic determinism. 'Efficacious grace', an expression even preferred by the divines of Dort and by John Owen, would better describe Calvin's view of the Holy Spirit's work of regeneration. But Calvin's common grace–special grace dualism allows the conclusion that while special grace is ultimately efficacious, common grace is resistible. Lastly, while Calvin was committed to the 'final perseverance of the saints', his teaching is only an encouragement to those who make progress in faith and obedience.

Conclusion

There is no room for complacency in Calvin's Calvinism. His views of union with Christ, and of the perpetual connection between justification and sanctification, forbids the very possibility of antinomianism. Indeed, Calvinism's traditional image has suffered from misrepresentation by its friends and caricature by its enemies, a treatment which is as unnecessary as it is fallacious.

If Baxter shared many of Calvin's emphases concerning the atonement, this is less true where justification is concerned. His fear of antinomianism produced an over-reaction to the generally misconceived idea of *sola fide*. Where Calvin insisted on a perpetual, necessary connection between justification and good works, Baxter argued for a twofold justification. The differences are largely terminological, but Baxter's timely emphasis on holiness was not helped by his highly confusing utterances. By contrast, Owen's theory of imputation was significantly different from the doctrine of Calvin and the other reformers. The doctrine of the imputed active obedience of Christ produced a labyrinth from which even Owen could not finally extricate himself. Even his stress on holiness constrained him to adopt a variant of the twofold theory of justification that differed little from Baxter's. In his discussion of the atonement and justification, his resort to Aristotle only confused the issue by creating self-contradictory conceptual illusions. The approach of archbishop Tillotson could not be more different. His own exposition of the issues confirms the conclusion that, at many points, the Arminian tradition perpetuated Calvin's theology of justification. This observation holds good in Wesley's case too, although his residual difficulties were largely inherited from Baxter.

Having assessed the evidence, the case for redrawing the theological map is inescapable. Indeed, the area in question is even greater than Dr Kendall seems to assume. Suffice it to say that Calvin's own explicit teaching has emerged as a tenable, scriptural, and doubtless surprising, point of reference throughout this book. This is not to imply a belief in Calvin's infallibility, but to acknowledge his unique competence as the Reformed theologian *par excellence*. Even his brilliant exposition of Christ's triple office of prophet, priest, and king and his late clarification of the *sola fide* principle[8] inspire a rejection of his exegesis of James 2: 24. This, in the hands of Tillotson, led to a clarification of the nature of saving faith, which in turn produced a more coherent solution to the Paul–James antinomy than Calvin and others could offer.

The primary aim of this book has been to evaluate a number of complex theological issues by the criterion of 'Scripture perspicuity'. With our terms carefully and biblically defined, readers must now judge whether the attempt to harmonize *sola gratia* and *sola fide* with *sola scriptura* has been successful.

NOTES

1. A. P. F. Sell, *The Great Debate* (Worthing, 1982), 94.
2. Ibid. 95.
3. Ibid.
4. Ibid.
5. Ibid. 98.
6. Calvin writes: 'Being messengers from God to men, their first duty is to offer the grace of God, but their second is to strive with all their might to ensure that it is not offered in vain' (*Comm.* 2 Cor. 6: 1).
7. *MHB* (1933), 114: 7; *Hymns and Psalms* (1983), 226: 7.
8. Calvin wrote in 1564, 'Thus it still remains true, that faith without works justifies, although this needs prudence and a sound interpretation; for this proposition, that faith without works justifies is true and yet false, according to the different senses which it bears. The proposition, that faith without works justifies by itself, is false, because faith without works is void . . . faith cannot justify when it is without works, because it is dead, and a mere fiction' (*Comm.* Ezek. 18: 14–17).

Bibliography

Place of publication is London unless stated otherwise. In some cases, modern facsimile reprints are given in preference to the original edition.

I. THE PRINCIPAL THEOLOGIANS

BAXTER, R., *Aphorismes of Justification* (1649).
—— *Rich. Baxter's Confession of His Faith* (1655).
—— *Certain disputations of Right to Sacraments* (1658).
—— *Richard Baxter's Catholick Theologie* (1675).
—— *Catholick Communion Defended* (1684).
—— *A Paraphrase on the New Testament* (1685).
—— *The Scripture Gospel Defended* (1690).
—— *An End of Doctrinal Controversies* (1691).
—— *Universal Redemption of Mankind*, ed. J. Read (1694).
—— *Reliquiae Baxterianae, or Mr Richard Baxter's Narrative of The Most Memorable Passages of his Life and Times*, ed. M. Sylvester (1696).
—— *The Reformed Pastor*, ed. W. Brown (1829; fac. Edinburgh, 1974).
—— *The Practical Works of the Revd Richard Baxter*, ed. W. Orme (23 vols.; 1830).
—— *The Autobiography of Richard Baxter*, ed. J. M. Lloyd-Thomas (1931).
—— *The Practical Works of Richard Baxter: Select Treatises* (Grand Rapids, Mich., 1981).
OWEN, J., *The Works of John Owen, DD*, i, ed. T. Russell, (1826).
—— *The Works of John Owen, DD*, ed. W. H. Goold (24 vols.; 1850–5).
—— *The Correspondence of John Owen (1616–1683): With an Account of His Life and Work*, ed. P. Toon (Cambridge, 1970).
TILLOTSON, J., *The Works of the Most Revd Dr John Tillotson* (folio edn.); vols. i–ii (posthumous), ed. R. Barker (1712); vol. iii. 6th edn. (1710).
—— *The Works of Dr John Tillotson*; i, ed. T. Birch (1752; repr. 1820).
WESLEY, J., *Explanatory Notes upon the New Testament* (1755).
—— *The Works of the Revd John Wesley, AM*, ed. T. Jackson, 4th edn. (14 vols.; 1840–2).
—— *The Poetical Works of John and Charles Wesley*, ed. G. Osborne 3 vols.; 1869).

—— *The Journal of the Revd John Wesley, AM*, ed. N. Curnock (8 vols.; 1909–16).
—— *The Letters of the Revd John Wesley, AM*, ed. J. Telford (8 vols.; 1931).

Note. Since only eight volumes of the new (originally OUP, now Abingdon) edition of Wesley's works have appeared to date, (vols. 1–4, 7, 11, and 25–6 of an intended thirty-four), all references will be made to the Jackson edition.

2. OTHER WORKS

ABBOT-SMITH, G., *Manual Greek Lexicon of the New Testament* (Edinburgh, 1937).
ALLISON, C. F., *The Rise of Moralism* (1966).
AMES, W., *De conscientia* (n.pl. 1632).
AQUINAS, T., *Summa theologiae*, xxx, ed. C. Ernst (1972).
ARISTOTLE, *The Ethics of Aristotle*, trans. J. A. K. Thompson (1953).
—— *Metaphysics*, trans. J. Warrington (1956).
ARMINIUS, J., *The Works of James Arminius, DD*, trans. J. Nichols (3 vols.; 1825).
ARMSTRONG, B. G., *Calvinism and the Amyraut Heresy: Protestant Scholasticism and Humanism in Seventeenth-century France* (Madison, Wisc., 1969).
ASTY, J., 'Memoirs of The Life of John Owen', in *A Complete Collection of the Sermons of John Owen* (1721).
AUGUSTINE, *Works*, ed. P. Schaff, v; *Anti-Pelagian Writings* (New York, 1887; fac. Grand Rapids, Mich., 1956).
AULEN, G., *Christus victor* (1970).
AYLING, S., *John Wesley* (1979).

BAINTON, R., *Here I Stand* (New York, 1950).
BAKER, F., *Charles Wesley as Revealed by His Letters* (1948).
BANGS, C., *Arminius: A Study in the Dutch Reformation* (Nashville, Tenn., 1971).
—— 'Arminius as a Reformed theologian', in *The Heritage of John Calvin*, ed. J. H. Bratt (Grand Rapids, Mich., 1973).
BARNES, A., *The Atonement* (New York, 1860).
BARTH, K., *Church Dogmatics*, iv. 2; v, trans. G. W. Bromiley (Edinburgh, 1957).
BAUER, W., Arndt, W. F., and GINGRICH, F. W., *Greek–English Lexicon of the New Testament* (Chicago, 1964).
BAVINCK, H., 'Calvin and common grace', in *Calvin and the Reformation*, (New York, 1909).

Bibliography

BEARDMORE, J., *Memorials of John Tillotson* (1752).
BELL, M. C., *Calvin and Scottish Theology* (Edinburgh, 1985).
BELLAMY, J., *True Religion Delineated* (Edinburgh, 1788).
BERKELEY, G., *The Principles of Human Knowledge* ed. G. J. Wanock (1962).
BERKHOF, L., *Systematic Theology* (1963).
—— *History of Christian Doctrines* (1969).
BETT, H., *The Hymns of Methodism* (1945).
BEZA, T., *Tractationes theologiae* (Geneva, 1570–82).
Biographia Britannica, v (1760); vi (1763).
BIRRELL, A., *Miscellanies* (1901).
BOLAM, C. G., GORING, J., SHORT, H. L., and THOMAS, R., *The English Presbyterians: From Elizabethan Puritanism to Modern Unitarianism* (1968).
BOSWELL, J., *Life of Johnson* (2 vols.; 1960).
BOYCE, J. P., *Abstract of Systematic Theology* (Philadelphia, 1887).
BRADFORD, J., *Sermons*, i. (Cambridge, 1848).
BREADY, J. W., *England: Before and After Wesley* (1939).
BROWN, J., *An Exposition of Hebrews* (Edinburgh, 1862; fac. 1961).
BRUNNER, E., *The Mediator* (1934).
BUCHANAN, J., *The Doctrine of Justification* (Edinburgh, 1867; fac. 1961).
BULL, G., *Harmonia apostolica* (Oxford, 1842).
BULLINGER, H., 'The Second Helvetic Confession (1566)', in *Reformed Confessions of the Sixteenth Century*, ed. A. Cochrane (1966).
BULTMANN, R., *Theology of the New Testament* (1955).
BUNYAN, J., *The Works of John Bunyan*, ed. G. Offor, ii (1855).
BURNET, G., *A Sermon Preached at the Funeral of ... John ... Lord Archbishop of Canterbury* (1695).
—— *An Exposition of the Thirty-nine Articles of the Church of England*, ed. J. R. Page (1841).

CALAMY, E., *Divine Mercy Exalted: Or Free Grace in Its Glory* (1703).
CALVIN, J., *Tracts and Treatises* (3 vols.; Edinburgh, 1851).
—— *Sermons on Isaiah's Prophecy*, trans. T. H. L. Parker (1956).
—— *Calvin's Commentaries*, ed. D. W. and T. F. Torrance (12 vols.; Edinburgh, 1959–72).
—— *Concerning The Eternal Predestination of God*, trans. J. K. S. Reid (1961).
—— *Institutes of the Christian Religion*, trans. H. Beveridge (2 vols.; 1962); also ed. J. T. McNeill, trans. F. L. Battles (2 vols.; 1960).
—— *Sermons on the Epistle to the Ephesians*, trans. A. Golding, rev. L. Rawlinson and S. M. Houghton (Edinburgh, 1973).
—— *Letters of John Calvin*, selected from the Bonnet Edition (Edinburgh, 1980).

—— *Sermons on the Saving Work of Christ*, trans. L. Nixon (Grand Rapids, Mich., 1980).

—— *Sermons on the Epistles to Timothy and Titus*, trans. L. T. (*sic*) (1579; fac. Edinburgh, 1983).

CANNON, W. R., *The Theology of John Wesley: With Special Reference to the Doctrine of Justification* (New York, 1946).

CARPENTER, E., *Cantuar: The Archbishops in their Office* (1971).

CARRICK, J., 'Jonathan Edwards and the Deists', *BOT* 299–300 (1988), 22–34.

CARRUTHERS, S. W. (ed.), *Digest of the Proceedings of the Synods of the Presbyterian Church of England 1876–1905* (1907).

CELL, G. C., *The Rediscovery of John Wesley* (New York, 1935).

CHADWICK, H., 'Justification by faith: a perspective', *One in Christ*, 20. 3 (1984), 191–225.

CHAFER, L., *Systematic Theology*, iii (Dallas, 1976).

CHALMERS, T., *Institutes of Theology*, ii (Edinburgh, 1849).

CHEETHAM, S., *A History of the Christian Church during the First Six Centuries* (1894).

CHILLINGWORTH, W., *The Religion of Protestants a Safe Way to Salvation* (1638).

CLIFFORD, A. C., 'Orthodoxy and the Enlightenment: Theology, philosophy, and religious experience in the thought of Philip Doddridge, DD (1702–51)', M. Litt. thesis (Newcastle upon Tyne, 1977).

—— 'Philip Doddridge and the Oxford Methodists', *WHS* 42. 3 (1979), 75–80.

—— 'The Christian mind of Philip Doddridge', *EQ* 56. 4 (1984), 227–42.

—— 'The gospel and justification', *EQ* 57. 3 (1985), 247–67.

—— 'John Calvin and the Confessio fidei Gallicana', *EQ* 58. 3 (1986), 195–206.

—— 'Faith, assurance and the gospel offer', *The Monthly Record of the Free Church of Scotland* (Sept. 1988), 204.

COLES, E., *A Practical Discourse on God's Sovereignty* (1673).

Collection of Hymns for the use of the People called Methodists (1877).

Confession of Faith of the Calvinistic Methodists or the Presbyterians of Wales (Caernarfon, 1900).

COOK, P. E. G., 'Hearts strangely warmed'. John and Charles Wesley, May 1738', in *Not by Might nor by Power* (Westminster Conference, 1988).

COPPEDGE, A., 'John Wesley and the Doctrine of Predestination', Ph.D. thesis (Cambridge, 1976).

COVERDALE, M., *The Remains of Bishop Coverdale* (Cambridge, 1846).

CRAGG, G. R., *From Puritanism to the Age of Reason* (Cambridge, 1966).

CRANMER, T., *The Works of Thomas Cranmer* (Cambridge, 1846).

—— *Miscellaneous Writings of Thomas Cranmer* (Cambridge, 1846).

Bibliography

CROW, E. P., 'John Wesley's conflict with antinomianism', Ph.D. thesis (Manchester, 1964).
CRYER, N. B., 'Biography of John Eliot', in *Five Pioneer Missionaries* (1965).
CUNNINGHAM, W., *Historical Theology*, ii (1862; fac. 1960).
—— *The Reformers and the Theology of the Reformation* (1862; fac. 1967).
Cyffes Ffydd: y corph o Fethodistiaid Calfinaidd, yn Nghymru (Gwrecsam, [Wrexham], 1861).
DABNEY, R. L., *Discussions: Evangelical and Theological*, i (Richmond, Virg., 1890; fac. 1967).
—— *The Westminster Confession and Creeds* (Dallas, 1983).
—— *Systematic Theology* (St Louis, 1878; Edinburgh, 1985).
DALE, R. W., *The Atonement* (1875).
DALLIMORE, A. A., *George Whitefield* (2 vols.; 1970–80).
DANIEL, C., 'John Gill and hypercalvinism', Ph.D. thesis (Edinburgh, 1983).
DAVENANT, J., 'A dissertation on the death of Christ' [*Dissertatio de morte Christi*], trans. J. Allport, in *A Commentary on the Epistle to the Colossians* (1832), ii.
DAVIDS, P. H., *The Epistle of James* (1982).
DAVIES, D. H. M., *Worship and Theology in England from Watts and Wesley to Maurice, 1690–1850* (Princeton, NJ, 1961).
—— *Worship and Theology in England from Andrewes to Baxter and Fox, 1603–1690* (Princeton, NJ, 1975).
DAVIES, A. P., *Isaac Watts* (1943).
DE YONG, P. Y. (ed.), *Crisis in the Reformed Churches: Essays in the Commencement of the Great Synod of Dort (1618–1619)* (Grand Rapids, Mich., 1968).
DEMAUS, R., *Hugh Latimer* (1903).
DENNEY, J., *The Death of Christ* (1951).
DESCHNER, J., *Wesley's Christology* (Dallas, 1960).
Dictionary of American Biography (1928–).
Dictionary of National Biography (1885–).
DIX, K., 'Particular Baptists and Strict Baptists: an historical survey', *BSB* 13 (1976), 1–19.
DODD, C. H., *The Epistle of Paul to the Romans* (1932).
DODDRIDGE, P., *The Works of the Revd P. Doddridge, DD*, ed. E. Williams and E. Parsons (10 vols.; Leeds, 1802–5).
—— *The Correspondence and Diary of Philip Doddridge, DD*, ed. J. D. Humphreys (5 vols.; 1829–31).
—— *Calendar of the Correspondence of Philip Doddridge, DD (1702–1751)*, ed. G. F. Nuttall (1979).
DOUTY, N. F., *The Death of Christ* (Swengel, Pa., 1972).

DOWNEY, J., *The Eighteenth Century Pulpit* (Oxford, 1969).
DOYLE, R., 'The death of Christ and the doctrine of grace in John Wycliffe', *CM* 99. 4 (1985), 317–35.
DRYSDALE, A. H., *History of the Presbyterians in England* (1889).
EDWARDS, D. L., with STOTT, J. R. W., *Essentials: A Liberal–Evangelical Dialogue* (1988).
EDWARDS, J., *The Works of Jonathan Edwards*, ed. E. Hickman (2 vols.; 1834; fac. Edinburgh, 1974).
EDWARDS, M. L., 'George Whitefield after two hundred years', *WHS* 37 (1970), 178–9.
EDWARDS, T., *The Paraselene Dismantled of Her Cloud, or Baxterianism Barefac'd* (1699).
ENGLISH, J. C., 'John Wesley and the Anglican moderates of the seventeenth century', *ATR* 51. 3 (1969), 203–20.
EVANS, E., *Daniel Rowland and the Great Evangelical Awakening in Wales* (Edinburgh, 1985).

FERGUSON, S. B., *John Owen on the Christian Life* (Edinburgh, 1987).
FISHER, E., *The Marrow of Modern Divinity* (1645).
FISHER, G. P., *The History of the Christian Church* (1904).
—— 'The writings of Richard Baxter', *Bibliotheca sacra*, 9 (1851), 135–69; 301–29.
FLAVEL, J., *The Works of John Flavel*, iii; vi (1820; fac. 1968).
FLETCHER, J., *The Works of John Fletcher*, ii (1830; fac. Salem, Ohio, 1974).
FORBES, W., *Considerationes modestae pacificae* (Oxford, 1850).
FREEMANTLE, A., *The Age of Belief* (New York, 1962).
FROST, F., 'Biblical imagery and religious experience in the hymns of the Wesleys', *WHS* 42. 6 (1980), 158–66.
FULLER, A., *The Complete Works of Andrew Fuller*, ed. A. G. Fuller (5 vols.; 1831).

GERRISH, B. A., *Grace and Reason: A Study in the Theology of Luther* (Oxford, 1962).
GILL, F. C., *Charles Wesley: The First Methodist* (1964).
GILL, J., *A Collection of Sermons and Tracts* (3 vols.; 1773).
—— *The Cause of God and Truth* (2 vols.; 1816).
—— *A Body of Divinity* (1838; fac. Grand Rapids, Mich., 1970).
GODFREY, W. R., 'Reformed thought on the extent of the atonement', *WTJ* 37 (1975), 133–71.
GOODWIN, J., *Imputatio fidei, or a Treatise of Justification* (1642).
—— *Redemption Redeemed* (1651).
GOODWIN, T., *The Works of Thomas Goodwin, DD*, ii (Edinburgh, 1861).
GORDON, A., 'Richard Baxter's Calvinism', *PHSE* 1 (1915), 35.
GREEN, E. M. B., *2 Peter Reconsidered* (1961).
GREEN, V. H. H., *John Wesley* (1964).

―― *Luther and the Reformation* (1964).
―― *The Young Mr Wesley* (1961).
GRIFFITH THOMAS, W. H., *The Principles of Theology* (4th edn., 1951).
GROTIUS, H., *A Defense of the Catholic Faith concerning the Satisfaction of Christ against Faustus Socinus*, trans. F. H. Foster (1889).
GUELZO, A. C., 'Jonathan Edwards and the New Divinity', in *Pressing Toward the Mark: Essays Commemorating Fifty Years of the Orthodox Presbyterian Church*, ed. C. G. Dennison and R. C. Gamble (Philadelphia, 1986).
GUTHRIE, D., *New Testament Theology* (Leicester, 1981).
HALDANE, R., *Exposition of the Epistle to the Romans* (Edinburgh, 1874; fac. 1963).
HALÉVY, E., *A History of the English People* (1924).
―― *The Birth of Methodism*, trans. B. Semmel (1971).
HALL, B., 'Calvin against the Calvinists', in *John Calvin*, ed. G. Duffield (Abingdon, 1966).
HALLER, W., *The Rise of Puritanism* (New York, 1957).
HARDIE, W. F. R., 'The final good in Aristotle's Ethics', in *Aristotle: A Collection of Critical Essays*, ed. J. M. E. Moravcsik (1968).
HARRISON, A. W., *Arminianism* (1937).
HASTINGS, J. (ed.), *The Encyclopedia of Religion and Ethics* (13 vols.; Edinburgh, 1908–26).
HELM, P., *Calvin and the Calvinists* (Edinburgh, 1982).
―― 'Calvin and Calvinism', *Evangel* (Winter, 1984), 7–10.
HENDRIKSEN, W., *A Commentary on the Gospel of John* (1959).
―― *Commentary on I and II Timothy and Titus* (1959).
HENRY, M., *An Exposition of the Old and New Testament*, ii; ix (1886).
HOBBES, T., *Leviathan* (1965).
HODGE, A. A., *The Atonement* (New York, 1907; fac., Grand Rapids, Mich., 1974).
―― *Evangelical Theology* (1890).
HODGE, C., *A Commentary on the First Epistle to the Corinthians* (1958).
―― *Systematic Theology*, ii (New York, 1873; fac. London, 1960).
HOEKSEMA, H., *The Triple Knowledge: An Exposition of the Heidelberg Catechism*, i (Grand Rapids, Mich., 1976).
HOOKER, R., *The Works of that Learned and Judicious Divine Mr Richard Hooker*, ed. J. Keble, iii (Oxford, 1836).
HOOPER, J., *Early Writings of John Hooper, DD* (Cambridge, 1848).
―― *Later Writings of Bishop Hooper* (Cambridge, 1852).
HOWELL, W. S., *Logic and Rhetoric in England 1500–1700* (Princeton, NJ, 1956).
HUME, D., *Enquiries concerning Human Understanding and concerning the Principles of Morals*, ed. L. A. Selby-Bigge (Oxford, 2nd edn. 1902).
―― *A Treatise of Human Nature* (2 vols.; 1911).

HUNT, J., *Religious Thought in England* (2 vols.; 1871).
HUTCHINSON, F., *The Life of the Most Reverend Father in God John Tillotson, Archbishop of Canterbury* (1717).
HUTTON, W. H., *A History of the English Church from the Accession of Charles I to the Death of Anne, 1625–1714* (1903).
Hymns and Psalms (1983).

JEWEL, J., *The Works of John Jewel*, iii (Cambridge, 1848).
JONES, H. R., 'The death of Presbyterianism', in *By Schisms Rent Asunder* (PRSC, 1969).
JONES, R. T., *Congregationalism in England, 1662–1962* (1962).

KEEBLE, N. H., *Richard Baxter: Puritan Man of Letters* (Oxford, 1982).
KENDALL, R. T., *Calvin and English Calvinism to 1649* (Oxford, 1979).
KERR, W. N., 'Baxter, Richard, and Baxterianism', *Encyclopedia of Christianity*, ed. E. H. Palmer, i (Wilmington, Del., 1964).
KEVAN, E. F., *The Grace of Law* (1964).
KIRKBY, A. H., 'Andrew Fuller—evangelical Calvinist', *BQ* 15 (1954), 195–202.
—— 'The Theology of Andrew Fuller and its relation to Calvinism', Ph.D. thesis (Edinburgh, 1956).
KITTEL, G., *Theological Dictionary of the New Testament* (Grand Rapids, Mich., 1965).
KUIPER, H., *Calvin on Common Grace* (Goes, Holland, 1928).
KUIPER, R. B., *For Whom Did Christ Die?* (Grand Rapids, Mich., 1982).
KUYPER, A., *De gemeene gratie* (Leiden, 1902).

LADELL, A. R., *Richard Baxter: Puritan and Mystic* (1925).
LANE, T., 'The quest for the historical Calvin', *EQ* 55. 2 (1983), 95–113.
LATIMER, H., *Sermons by Hugh Latimer* (2 vols.; Cambridge, 1844).
LAWSON, A., 'John Wesley and some Anglican evangelicals of the eighteenth century', Ph.D. Thesis (Sheffield, 1974).
LAWTON, G., *Within the Rock of Ages: The Life and Work of Augustus Montague Toplady* (Cambridge, 1983).
LEE, U., *John Wesley and Modern Religion* (New York, 1936).
LEIBNITZ, G. W., *Discourse on Metaphysics*, trans. P. G. Lucas and L. Grint (Manchester, 1953).
LEWIS, P. *The Genius of Puritanism* (Haywards Heath, 1979).
LINDSAY, T. M., 'Amyraldism', in *The Encyclopedia of Religion and Ethics*, ed. J. Hastings, i (Edinburgh, 1908).
LINDSTRÖM, H., *Wesley and Sanctification* (Stockholm 1946).
LLOYD-JONES, D. M., *Romans: Atonement and Justification* (1970).
LOCKE, J., *An Essay Concerning Human Understanding*, ed. A. P. Woosley (2 vols.; 1964).
LOCKE, L. G., 'Tillotson: a study in seventeenth century literature', *Anglistica*, 4 (Copenhagen, 1954).

Bibliography

LONG, G. D., *Definite Atonement* (Nutley, NJ, 1977).
LONGSTAFFE, W. H. D., (ed.), *Memoirs of Ambrose Barnes* (1867).
LUTHER, M., *A Commentary on St Paul's Epistle to the Galatians*, ed. P. S. Watson (1953).
—— *Reformation Writings of Martin Luther*, trans. B. L. Woolf, ii (1956).
—— *The Bondage of the Will*, trans. J. I. Packer and O. R. Johnson (1957).
—— *Works*, xxv; xxx (St Louis, Mo., 1963).
MACARTHUR, J. J., *The Gospel According to Jesus* (Grand Rapids, Mich., 1988).
MACAULAY, LORD, *History of England*, iii (1967).
MCGRATH, A. E., 'The emergence of the Anglican tradition of justification 1600–1700', *CM* 98. 1 (1984), 28–43.
—— *Iustitia Dei* (2 vols.; Cambridge, 1986).
—— *The Intellectual Origins of the European Reformation* (Oxford, 1987).
—— *ARCIC II and Justification: An Evangelical Anglican Assessment of 'Salvation and the Church'* (Latimer House, Oxford, 1987).
—— *Justification by Faith* (Basingstoke, 1988).
MACHEN, J. G., *The New Testament* (Edinburgh, 1975).
MACLEOD, D., 'Misunderstandings of Calvinism II', *BOT* 53 (1968), 15–26.
MACLEOD, J. N., 'John Owen and the "Death of Death"', in *Out of Bondage* (London, 1983).
MCPHEE, I., 'Conserver or transformer of Calvin's Theology? A study in the origins and development of Theodore Beza's thought, 1550–1570', Ph.D. thesis (Cambridge, 1979).
MANNING, BERNARD, LORD, *The Hymns of Wesley and Watts* (1942).
MANTON, T., *An Exposition of the Epistle of James* (Edinburgh, 1870; fac. 1962).
MARCHANT, J., *Dr John Clifford, CH: Life, Letters and Reminiscences* (1924).
MARTIN, H., *Puritanism and Richard Baxter* (1954).
MATTHEWS, A. G., *The Works of Richard Baxter* (1932).
—— (ed.), *Calamy Revised* (Oxford, 1934).
—— (ed.), *The Savoy Declaration of Faith and Order* (1959).
Methodist Hymn Book (1904).
Methodist Hymn Book (1933).
MITCHELL, A. F., and STRUTHERS, J. (ed.), *Minutes of the Sessions of the Westminster Assembly of Divines* (1874).
MITCHELL, W. F., *English Pulpit Oratory from Andrewes to Tillotson* (1932).
MOFFAT, J., *The Golden Book of John Owen* (1904).
—— *The Golden Book of Tillotson* (1926).
MONK, R. C., *John Wesley: His Puritan Heritage* (1966).
MOORMAN, J. R. H., *A History of the Church of England* (1953).

Morning Exercise at Cripplegate, or Several Cases of Conscience Practically Resolved by Sundry Ministers (1661).

MORRIS, L., *The Apostolic Preaching of the Cross* (1960).

—— *The Cross in the New Testament* (1965).

MOTYER, S., 'Righteousness by faith in the New Testament', in *Here We Stand*, ed. J. I., Packer (1986).

MOULE, H. C. G., *Charles Simeon* (1892).

MURRAY, I. H., *Jonathan Edwards: A New Biography* (Edinburgh, 1987).

MURRAY, J., *Principles of Conduct* (1957).

—— *Redemption Accomplished and Applied* (1961).

—— *Collected Writings of John Murray*, i (Edinburgh, 1976).

NETTLES, T. J., *By His Grace and For His Glory* (Grand Rapids, Mich., 1986).

NEWTON, J., *The Works, of the Revd John Newton*, iv (1808).

NEWTON, J. A., *Methodism and the Puritans* (1964).

NICHOLS, J., *Calvinism and Arminianism Compared* (1824).

NICOLE, R., 'Amyraldianism', in *Encyclopedia of Christianity*, ed. E. H. Palmer, i (Wilmington, Del., 1964), 184–93.

—— 'John Calvin's view of the extent of the atonement', *WTJ* 47 (1985), 197–225.

NUTTALL, G. F., *Richard Baxter and Philip Doddridge: A Study in a Tradition* (1951).

—— *Visible Saints: The Congregational Way 1640–1660* (Oxford, 1957).

—— *Richard Baxter* (1965).

—— 'Northamptonshire and the *Modern Question*', *JTS* NS 16 (1965), 101–23.

—— 'Cambridge Nonconformity, 1660–1710: from Holcroft to Hussey', *URC* 1. 9 (1977), 241–58.

—— 'Richard Baxter and the Grotian religion', in *Reform and Reformation: England and the Continent, c.1500–c.1750*, ed. D. Baker (1979).

—— (ed.), *Calender of the Correspondence of Philip Doddridge, DD (1702–1751)* (1979).

ONG, W. J., *Ramus, Method and the Decay of Dialogue* (Cambridge, Mass., 1958).

ORME, W., 'Memoirs of Dr Owen', in *The Works of John Owen, DD*, ed. T. Russell i (1826).

—— 'A life of the author', in *The Life and Writings of Richard Baxter*, i, ed. W. Orme (1830).

OUTLER, A. C., *John Wesley* (New York, 1964).

OVERTON, J. H., *John Wesley* (1891).

PACKER, J. I., 'The redemption and restoration of man in the thought of Richard Baxter', D.Phil. thesis (Oxford, 1954).

—— Introductory Essay in J. Owen, *The Death of Death* (1959).

—— Introductory Essay in J. Buchanan, *The Doctrine of Justification* (1961).
—— *Evangelism and the Sovereignty of God* (1961).
—— 'Calvin the theologian', in *John Calvin*, ed. G. Duffield (Abingdon, 1966).
—— 'Arminianisms', in *The Manifold Grace of God* (PRSC, 1968).
—— 'The doctrine of justification in development and decline among the Puritans', in *By Schisms Rent Asunder* (PRSC, 1969).
—— Introduction to R. Baxter, *The Reformed Pastor*, ed. W. Brown (1829; fac. Edinburgh, 1974).
—— ed., and 'Justification in Protestant theology', in *Here We Stand* (1986).
—— review of J. R. W. Stott, *The Cross of Christ*, in *Christianity Today* (4 Sept. 1987), 35–6.
PACKER, J. W., *The Transformation of Anglicanism 1643–1660* (Manchester, 1969).
PALMER, E. H., *The Encyclopedia of Christianity*, i (Wilmington, Del., 1964).
PARKER, T. H. L., *Commentaries on the Epistle to the Romans 1532–1542* (Edinburgh, 1986).
PASCAL, B., *Pensées*, trans. J. Warrington, ed. L. Lafuma (1960).
—— *The Provincial Letters*, trans. A. J. Krailsheimer (1967).
PETERSON, R. A., *Calvin's Doctrine of the Atonement* (Phillipsburg, NJ, 1983).
PIETTE, M., *John Wesley and the Evolution of Protestantism* (1937).
PISCATOR, J., *Apologia disputationis de causa meritoria justificationis hominis coram Deo* (Herborn, 1618).
PLUMB, J. H., *England in the Eighteenth Century* (1965).
POLLARD, A., *English Sermons* (1963).
POOLE, M., *A Commentary on the Holy Bible*, iii (1963).
POWICKE, F. J., *A Life of the Revd Richard Baxter 1615–1691* (1924).
—— *The Revd Richard Baxter: Under the Cross 1662–1691* (1927).
PRESTWICH, M. (ed.), *International Calvinism 1541–1715* (Oxford, 1985).
PROCTOR, F., and FRERE, W. H., *A New History of the Book of Common Prayer* (1929).

RASHDALL, H., *The Idea of Atonement in Christian Theology* (1919).
REED, R. C., *The Gospel as Taught by Calvin* (Grand Rapids, Mich., 1979).
RICHARDSON, A., *An Introduction to the Theology of the New Testament* (1958).
RIDDERBOS, H., *Paul: An Outline of His Theology*, trans. J. R. De Witt (Grand Rapids, Mich., 1977).
ROBERTS, J., *The Calvinistic Methodism of Wales* (Caernarfon, 1934).
ROBINSON, J. A. T., *Wrestling with Romans* (1979).
ROBISON, O. C., 'The legacy of John Gill', *BQ* 24 (1971), 111–25.

ROGERS, H., *The Life and Character of John Howe, MA* (n.d.).
ROLSTON, H., *John Calvin versus the Westminster Confession* (Richmond, Tenn., 1972).
ROPES, J. H., *The Epistle of James* (Edinburgh, 1916).
ROUTLEY, E., 'The hymns of Philip Doddridge', in *Philip Doddridge (1702–1751): His Contribution to English Religion*, ed. G. F. Nuttall (1951).
—— *English Religious Dissent* (1960).
RUSSELL, B., *The History of Western Philosophy* (1961).
RYLE, J. C., *Expository Thoughts on the Gospels; St John*, i (1865).
—— *Light from Old Times* (1902).
—— *Christian Leaders of the Last Century* (London, 1885; fac. Edinburgh, 1978).

SANDAY, W., and HEADLAM, A. C., *The Epistle to the Romans* i (Edinburgh, 1898).
SCHAFF, P., *The History of the Christian Church*, viii (Edinburgh, 1883).
—— *The New Schaff–Herzog Encyclopedia of Religious Knowledge*, ix (New York, 1957).
SCHMIDT, M., *John Wesley: A Theological Biography* (1973).
Second Anglican–Roman Catholic International Commission, 'Salvation and the Church' (ARCIC II; 1987).
SELL, A. P. F., *The Great Debate* (Worthing, 1982).
SELLECK, J. B., 'The Book of Common Prayer in the Theology of John Wesley', Ph.D. thesis (Drew, NJ, 1983).
SEMMEL, B., *The Methodist Revolution* (1974).
Sermons or Homilies, Appointed to be Read in Churches (1833; fac. Lewes, 1986).
SEYMOUR, R. E., 'John Gill, Baptist Theologian (1697–1771)', Ph.D. Thesis (Edinburgh, 1954).
SIMEON, C., *Horae homiletisae*, i; xviii (1832–3).
SHEDD, W. G. T., *Dogmatic Theology*, ii (New York, 1894).
SHEPHERD, N., 'The covenant context for Evangelism', in *The New Testament Student and Theology*, ed. J. H. Skilton (Phillipsburg, NJ,. 1976).
SIMON, J. S., *John Wesley the Master Builder* (1927).
SIMONSON, H., *Jonathan Edwards: Theologian of the Heart* (Grand Rapids, Mich., 1974).
SKEVINGTON WOOD, A., *The Burning Heart: John Wesley, Evangelist* (1967).
SMITH, G., *The Life of William Carey* (1909).
SMITH, H. B., and SCHAFF, P., *The Creeds of the Evangelical Protestant Churches* (1877).
SPRUNGER, K. L., 'Ames, Ramus, and the method of Puritan theology', *Harvard Theological Reviews*, 50. 2 (1966), 131–51.

SPURGEON, C. H., *The New Park Street Pulpit*, iv (1859).
—— *The Treasury of the Old Testament*, i (n.d.; post-1934).
—— *The Early Years* (1962).
—— 'John Wesley', *BOT* 68 (1969), 15–20; 69 (1969), 43–8; 70–1 (1969), 54–8.
STEPHEN, L., *English Thought in the Eighteenth Century* (2 vols.; 1876).
STOTT, J. R. W., *Basic Christianity* (1958).
—— *The Cross of Christ* (1986).
—— with Edwards, D. L., *Essentials: A Liberal–Evangelical Dialogue* (1988).
STRONG, A. H., *Systematic Theology* (New York, 1890).
SURMAN, C. E., *Richard Baxter* (1961).
SYKES, N., *Churh and State in England in the Eighteenth Century* (Cambridge, 1934).
—— *From Sheldon to Secker* (Cambridge, 1959).
TELFORD, J., *The Life of John Wesley* (1899).
TEMPERLEY, H. W. V., *The Cambridge Modern History*, vi, ed. A. W. Ward, G. W. Prothero, and S. Leathes (Cambridge, 1909).
THAYER, J. H., *Greek–English Lexicon of the New Testament* (Edinburgh, 1893).
THOMAS, G., 'Edward Williams and the rise of "modern Calvinism"', *BOT* 88 (1971), 43–8; 90 (1971), 29–35.
THOMAS, R., *Daniel Williams: 'Presbyterian Bishop'* (1964).
THOMPSON, A., 'Life of Dr Owen', in *The Works of John Owen, DD*, ed. W. H. Goold, i (1850).
THORNWELL, J. H., *Collected Writings*, iii (Richmond, Virg., 1875; fac. Edinburgh, 1974).
TOON, P., *The Emergence of Hypercalvinism in English Nonconformity, 1689–1765* (1967).
—— (ed.), *The Correspondence of John Owen (1616–1683): with an Account of his Life and Work* (Cambridge, 1970).
—— *God's Statesman: The Life and Work of John Owen* (Exeter, 1971).
—— *Justification and Sanctification* (1983).
TOPLADY, A. M., *The Works of Augustus M. Toplady, AB* (6 vols.; 1825).
—— *Diary and Selection of Hymns* (1969).
TORRANCE, J. B., 'The incarnation and limited atonement', *EQ* 55. 2 (1983), 83–94.
'The strength and weaknesses of Westminster theology', in *The Westminster Confession in the Church Today*, ed. A. I. Heron (Edinburgh, 1982).
TRAILL, R., *The Works of the late Revd Robert Traill, AM*, i (Edinburgh, 1810; fac. Edinburgh, 1975).
TUTTLE, G. M., *So Rich a Soil: John McLeod Campbell on Christian Atonement* (Edinburgh, 1986).
TUTTLE, R. G., *John Wesley: His Life and Theology* (1979).

TYERMAN, L., *The Life and Times of the Revd John Wesley* (3 vols.; 1875).
—— *The Life of the Revd George Whitefield* (2 vols.; 1876).
TYNDALE, W., *Doctrinal Treatises* (Cambridge, 1848).

URSINUS, Z., *The Commentary of Dr Zacharias Ursinus on the Heidelberg Catechism*, trans. G. W. Williard (Columbus, Ohio, 1852; fac. Phillipsburg, NJ, 1985).

VAUGHAN, R., *The Life and Opinions of John de Wycliffe, DD* (2 vols.; 1831).
VOS, A., *Aquinas, Calvin, and Contemporary Protestant Thought* (Grand Rapids, Mich., 1985).
VULLIAMY, C. E., *John Wesley* (1931).

WALLACE, R. S., *The Atoning Death of Christ* (1981).
WARDLAW, R., *Discourses on the Nature and Extent of the Atonement* (1854).
—— *Systematic Theology*, ii (1856).
—— *Lectures on the Epistle of James* (1862).
WARFIELD, B. B., *The Plan of Salvation* (1966).
WATKINS, O. C., *The Puritan Experience* (1972).
WATSON, R., *Theological Institutes* (2 vols.; 1850).
WATTS, I., *The Works of the Reverend and Learned Isaac Watts, DD*, vi, ed. D. Jennings and P. Doddridge (1753).
WATTS, M. R., *The Dissenters* (Oxford, 1978).
WESLEY, C., *The Journal of Charles Wesley*, ed. T. Jackson (2 vols.; 1849; fac. Kansas City, Mo., 1980).
—— *Charles Wesley's Earliest Evangelical Sermons*, ed. T. R. Albin and O. A. Beckerlegge (1987).
WESLEY, S., *Poem on the Death of His Grace John, Late Lord Archbishop of Canterbury* (1695).
Westminster Confesion of Faith (Glasgow, 1973).
WHITEFIELD, G., *The Works of the Revd George Whitefield*, ed. J. Gillies, ii (1771).
—— *George Whitefield's Journals*, ed. I. Murray (1960).
WILLIAMS, C. W., *John Wesley's Theology Today* (New York, 1960).
WILLIAMS, D., *Gospel-truth Stated* (1692).
WILLIAMS, E., 'Life of Owen', in J. Owen, *Exposition of the Epistle to the Hebrews* (1790).
WILLIAMS, J. B., *Memoirs of the Life, Character and Writings of the Revd Matthew Henry* (1828; fac. Edinburgh, 1974).
WOOD, A., *History of the University of Oxford*, ii, ed. J. Gutch (Oxford, 1791).
WRIGHT, T., *The Life of Augustus Toplady* (1911).
WYCLIFFE, J., *The Poor Caitif: The Writings of the Revd and Learned John Wycliffe, DD* (2 vols.; n.d. [1838]).

Index of Biblical Citations

OLD TESTAMENT		28: 19	126
Genesis		Mark	
15: 6	172, 228	14: 24	162
22: 12	230	16: 15–16	80
Deuteronomy		Luke	
29: 29	86	1: 77	181, 182
Job		2: 29	159
22: 3	223	13: 34	97
Psalms		17: 7–10	183, 201
32: 1–2	173, 195	17: 10	214
67: 4	130	18: 11–14	232
96: 10	130	19: 27	217
119: 136	48	23: 34	94, 146
Isaiah		John	
9: 6–7	130	1: 9	152
10: 20–1	126	1: 11	97
53:4	48	1: 29	72, 84, 98, 126, 164
53:5	98	3: 15	83
53: 12	122, 140, 162, 164	3: 16	x, 72, 73, 76, 82, 90,
Jeremiah			97, 147, 152–4, 157, 165
31: 31–2	123	3: 19	153
Lamentations		3: 36	207
2: 18	48	5: 40	100
Ezekiel		6: 27–32	121
18: 14–17	183, 238, 244	6: 32	97, 121
18: 23	165	6: 51	84
Habakkuk		7: 4	152
2: 4	183	7: 7	152
Zechariah		9: 35–6	144
12: 10	48	10: 7	136
NEW TESTAMENT		10: 8	162
Matthew		10: 11	144
7: 12	48	10: 15	143–4
12: 36–7	232	10: 18	144
18: 11	107	10: 26	144
20: 28	107, 143	10: 27	162
22: 1–14	121	11: 52	83
22: 39	48	12: 32	148
25:31–46	144	17: 1–26	146
26: 24	86	17: 2–11	143
26: 28	48, 143	17: 9	94, 146
27: 51	48	17: 12	162

Index of Biblical Citations

Acts			
2: 14–47	146	8: 11	157–8, 166
2: 23	158	9: 21	189
3: 12–26	121	9: 27	158
4: 4	146	12: 7	164
4: 24	159	13: 2	204
13: 38–9	195	15: 22	164
15: 13–21	229	2 Corinthians	
17: 30	114, 214, 233	5: 10	200
20: 21	233, 238	5: 14–15	72, 81, 151, 164
20: 28	145	5: 18	83, 166
26: 18	233	5: 19	97, 126, 140, 155–6
Romans		5: 20	140, 166, 182
1: 5	114, 204, 207	6: 1	244
3: 21	182, 183	Galatians	
3: 22–4	238	2: 16	231
3: 25	132, 178, 214, 227	2: 17	178, 204
3: 26	139	3: 6	172, 181, 200, 228
3: 28	178, 182, 219, 221–8	3: 13	131, 132, 139, 159, 189
4: 3–5	172	3: 17	229
4: 4	228	3: 25	198
4: 6	182	4: 4	187, 189, 198
4: 6–8	195	5: 12	85, 164
4: 25	181	5: 6	177, 183, 204, 205, 207,
5: 1–11	227		219, 221–2, 225, 230
5: 1	172, 213	Ephesians	
5: 9	178, 188	2: 1	151
5: 12–21	199	2: 8–10	229
5: 15	122, 140, 144	5: 25	145
5: 16	164	Philippians	
5: 18	85, 109, 148, 164	1: 11	182
5: 18–19	164	2: 7	48
5: 19	188	2: 8	188
6: 1–11	151	2: 12-13	158
6: 15	198	Colossians	
6: 16–17	217, 227	1: 14	85
8: 28–39	147	1: 23	158
8: 29	147–8, 163	1: 28	164
8: 30	163, 219	2 Thessalonians	
8: 32	147–8	1: 8	114
9: 6	126	1 Timothy	
9: 27	126	1: 15	107
10: 16	207	2: 1–6	148–9, 164
11: 5	126	2: 4	149
14: 15	84, 157	2: 5–6	148
16: 26	114	2: 5–7	85
1 Corinthians		4: 10	151–2, 164, 207
1: 30	181, 182, 201, 219	2 Timothy	
6: 11	219	2: 19	157, 159
6: 20	159	2: 21	159
7: 19	207	Titus	
7: 23	159	2: 11–12	164
		2: 14	146

Index of Biblical Citations

Hebrews		2 Peter	
2: 5	151	1: 10	182, 212
2: 9	72, 150, 164	1: 17	166
3: 12	207	2: 1	158–60, 166
4: 11	207	2: 1–3	84
5: 8	188	2: 21	166
5: 9	207	3: 9	100, 149–50, 164, 165
7: 26–7	188	1 John	
8: 9–11	123	1: 7	175, 201
9: 27–8	122, 140	2: 2	72, 84, 86, 93, 154–5
12: 14	191, 209, 211–12	2: 5–6	199
James		2: 6	191, 199
1: 12	224	3: 10	157
2: 14–26	221-32	3: 23	114, 214
2: 24	157, 176, 184, 221–33, 243	5: 3	41, 48
1 Peter		Revelation	
2: 7	207	1: 7	48
2: 21	42	5: 9	148, 159, 164
3: 15	43	6: 10	159

General Index

Abelard 132, 141
 See also atonement, moral influence theory of
Abbot-Smith, G. 165
Allison, C. F. 30, 200
Ames, W. 165
Amyraut, M. 11, 16, 26, 74, 76, 97, 110, 150, 154
Amyraldianism *passim*
annihilationism 47
Anselm 126, 132, 134, 141
 see also atonement; commercial theory of
antinomianism *passim*
 see also law of God; neonomianism
Aquinas, T. 74, 95, 106, 221
Aristotle, 95–8, 105–8, 110, 111, 129–30, 153, 187, 210–11, 243
Aristotelianism 8, 43, 82, 95–110, 111, 114, 125, 129, 160
 and transubstantiation 138
Arminius, J. 9, 69–71, 83–4, 179, 185, 189, 242
Arminianism *passim*
Armstrong, B. G. 16, 83–4, 106, 110, 164–5
Arndt, W. F. 163, 165
Arrowsmith, J. 26
assurance 4, 54–5, 173–4, 184, 202–3, 212
 see also faith; perseverance
Asty, J. 14
atonement *passim*
 commercial theory of 9–10, 112, 126–7, 130–1, 133–4
 ethical theory of 131
 governmental theory of 127–8, 130–2
 limited *passim*
 moral influence theory of 132
 penal substitutionary theory of 132–3, 135, 140
 universal *passim*
  see also faith; grace; Jesus Christ; propitiation; reconciliation; redemption; satisfaction
Augsburg Confession
 and faith 172
 and good works 175
 and justification 171
Augustine 77–8, 91, 105, 161, 173, 221–2
Augustinianism, semi-, anti- 196–7, 221–6
Aulen, G. 141
Ayling, S. 51, 62

Baillie, R. 26
Bainton, R. 105
Baker, F. 63
Baldwin, S. 61
Báñez, D. 77
Bangs, C. 84
Baptist Confession of Faith
 ultra-orthodoxy of 75
 and grace 109
Barksdale, C. 80
Barnes, Albert 77, 90, 127
Barnes, Ambrose 14
Barth, K. 93, 137, 225–6
Bauer, W. 163, 165
Bavinck, H. 110
Baxter, R. *passim*
Baxterianism *passim*
Beardmore, J. 44
Bell, M. C. 86, 88–9, 141
Bellamy, J. 77, 89–90, 121, 127, 135, 164
Bellarmine, R. 181, 227
Bengel, J. A. 140
Berkeley, G. 98, 107
Bett, H. 99, 139
Berkhof, L. 103, 110, 117, 162, 198, 225–6
Bernard of Clairvaux 124

General Index

Beza, T. 12, 69–71, 74–5, 78, 82, 84, 91, 95, 171, 179, 192, 214
Birch, T. 36, 44
Birrell, A. 63
Boswell, J. 19
Boyce, J. P. 77, 90
Bradford, J. 79
Brunner, E. 137
Buchanan, J. 16, 179, 198, 224, 226
Bull, G. 39, 44, 178–9, 184, 186, 194, 217, 224, 226, 227
Bullinger, H. 94
Bultmann, R. 225
Bunyan, J. 14, 75–6, 87, 223, 226
Burnet, G. 44, 46, 106, 224, 226

Calamy, E. (I) 4, 26, 75–6, 89
Calamy, E. (II) 76, 88
Calvin, J. *passim*
Calvinism, high-, hyper-, moderate- *passim*
Campbell, J. M. 141
Cannon, W. R. 62, 64
Canons of Dort
  and Arminianism 71
  Baxter on 27
  and Calvin's Calvinism 73
  and earlier confessions 142
  and efficacious grace 123
  and efficacious redemption 135
  and sufficiency of the atonement 27, 87
Carpenter, E. 33
Carrick, J. 46
Cell, G. 62, 65
Chadwick, H. 184, 221
Chafer, L. 162
Chalmers, T. 76, 88, 98, 127, 216
Charles, T. (Bala) 89
Cheetham, S. 166
Cheynell, F. 28
Chillingworth, W. 36
Clifford, A. C. 45, 63, 86, 88, 89, 180, 197
Clifford, J. 62
Coles, E. 64
conditional reprobation 120
  see also predestination
Confessio Fidei Gallicana
  and extent of the atonement 74
  and justification 171
  and justification by Christ's sacrifice alone 171–2

Cook, P. E. G. 63
Coppedge, A. 62, 124
Coverdale, M. 178
Cragg, G. R. 34, 43, 47
Cranmer, T. 79, 170, 174, 176, 177, 178, 180, 184, 223, 226
Crisp, T. 23, 198
Crow, E. P. 62
Cryer, N. B. 140
Cunningham, W. 10, 87, 90, 109, 127, 129, 137, 171, 179, 181
Cyffes Ffydd
  and extent of the atonement 89

Dabney, R. L. 77, 87, 90, 91, 127, 154, 162, 165, 206
Daille, J. 26
Dale, R. W. 62, 132, 137, 164
Dallimore, A. 52, 64
Daniel, C. 85, 93, 110, 122, 166
Davenant, J. 26, 27, 75, 78, 80, 81, 97, 117
Davids, P. H. 221, 225
Davis, A. P. 88
Davies, D. H. M. 33, 34, 41, 47
Decrees of the Council of Trent
  Calvin on 86, 183–4
  and extent of the atonement 73
Demaus, R. 106
Denney, J. 135, 137, 164
Deschner, J. 62, 65
Dix, K. 110
Dodd, C. H. 137
Doddridge, P. vii, 3, 15, 19, 29, 34, 45, 56, 76, 88, 108, 147, 163, 224, 226
Douty, N. 16
Dowden, E. 31
Downey, J. 34, 41, 44, 47
Doyle, R. 236
Drysdale, A. H. 61–2

Edwards, D. L. 47
Edwards, J. 46, 77, 89–90, 122, 213, 216, 218–19, 224, 226, 236
Edwards, M. L. 52
Edwards, T. 29
effectual calling 119
  see also grace
ejusdem-tantidem distinction 10, 129–30
  see also atonement; satisfaction

General Index

election *passim*
empiricism 43, 98
  see also Berkeley; Hume; Locke
English, J. C. 64
Episcopius, S. B. 84
Evans, E. 63

faith 169–244
  nature of 174, 177, 202–8, 224–35
  and *sola fide* principle 59, 65, 176–8, 203–5, 208, 221–2, 227, 229, 234–5, 243
  see also assurance; atonement; grace; justification
Farrar, F. W. 61
federal theology 13
Ferguson, S. B. 14, 15, 16, 84
Fisher, E. 88
Fisher, G. P. 24, 31, 107
Flavel, J. 106, 223, 226
Fletcher, J. 85, 118, 211
Forbes, W. 224, 226
forgiveness, *see* justification
Freemantle, A. 124
free offer 76, 82–3, 86, 89, 91, 113, 116, 148
free-will 99–100, 118–19, 124, 242
  see also human ability
Frere, W. H. 30, 46
Frost, F. 139
Fulgentius 161, 166
Fuller, A. 76, 88, 122, 127, 135, 138

Gardiner, S. R. 17
Gerrish, B. 105
Gill, F. C. 63
Gill, J. 62, 94, 104, 110, 113, 115–16, 120, 122, 123, 131, 209, 217, 224, 226
Gingrich, F. W. 163, 165
Gladstone, W. E. 61
Godfrey, W. R. 86
good works 174, 208–9, 225, 243
  see also inherent righteousness; obedience; sanctification
Goodwin, J. 65, 72, 85, 179, 181, 185, 189
Goodwin, T. 35, 36, 218, 223, 226, 237
Goold, W. H. 3, 9, 10, 13, 15, 16, 27, 114, 140
Gordon, A. 87

grace *passim*
  common and special 64, 102–5, 113–24, 160, 242
  covenant of 117, 143, 154, 192
  efficacious 70, 115, 118, 242
  irresistible 115, 242
  preventing and saving 118–20
  see also atonement; effectual calling; faith; merit
Green, E. M. B. 166
Green, V. H. H. 62, 105
Griffith Thomas, W. H. 81, 92
Grotius, H. 128–141
  see also atonement; governmental theory of
Guelzo, A. C. 90
Guthrie, D. 120, 166, 226

Haldane, R. 225, 226
Hall, B. 84
Hall, J. 26, 54
Haller, W. 46
Hardie, W. F. R. 107
Harrison, A. W. 84
Headlam, A. C. 163
Heidelberg Catechism
  and extent of the atonement 74–5
Helm, P. 85, 93, 215, 239
Helvetic Confession, second
  Calvin's Calvinism reflected in 94
Hendriksen, W. 152, 165
Henry, M. 19, 29, 34, 54, 224
Hervey, J. 169, 180
Heshusius, T. 87
Hill, R. 59, 78
Hobbes, T. 106
Hodge, A. A. 121, 165
Hodge, C. 77, 90, 91, 162, 166, 180–1, 216
Hoeksema, H. 86
holiness, *see* sanctification
Hooker, R. 79, 223, 226, 230
Hooper, J. 78, 79, 170, 174, 175
Hopkins, S. 122
Howe, J. 38
Howell, W. S. 106
human ability 116–20
  see also free-will
Hume, D. 35, 98, 108, 129, 138
Hunt, J. 44
Hutchinson, F. 44
Hutton, W. H. 30, 47

imputed righteousness 7, 12, 169–72, 186–97, 243
  see also justification
inherent righteousness 170, 195, 212
  see also good works; merit; obedience; sanctification

Jansen, C. 77
Jesus Christ
  active and passive obedience of; see imputed righteousness
  deity of 39, 42
  incarnation of 39, 42, 187–8
  intercession of 94, 146
  threefold office of 192, 205–8, 233, 243
  union with 173, 176, 213
  see also atonement; justification
Jewel, J. 79, 170, 177
Johnson, S. 19, 22, 34
Jones, H. R. 141
Jones, T. (Denbigh) 89
justification 5, 7, 21, 25, 44, 54–5, 59–60, 169–244
  ARCIC on 184
  completeness of 172, 210
  continuous nature of 173, 196, 213–14, 231–3
  definition of 170, 195, 201, 222–3
  eternal, idea of 210
  formal cause of 181, 192, 234
  meritorious cause of 180, 234
  Roman Catholic view of 177, 183–4, 195–6, 209
  twofold theory of 59, 194, 205, 207, 209–13, 221, 225, 230–1, 243
  see also faith; imputed righteousness; Jesus Christ; merit

Käsemann, E. 166
Keeble, N. H. 19, 23, 24, 29, 31
Kendall, R. T. vii, 11, 28, 84, 85, 86, 92, 94, 106, 110, 183, 215, 239, 240–1
Kerr, W. N. 17, 30, 31
Kevan, E. F. 197
Kirkby, A. H. 88
Kittel, G. 165
Kuiper, H. 110
Kuiper, R. B. 77, 91, 110
Kuyper, A. 110

Ladell, A. R. 28
Lane, T. 105, 200
Latimer, H. 78–9, 106, 170, 180
law of God 128–31, 187–90, 228–9
  see also antinomianism; neonomianism
Law, W. 133
Lawson, A. 62
Lawton, G. 62
Lee, U. 65
Leibniz, G. W. 106
Lenski, R. C. H. 152
Lewis, P. 85
Limborch, P. van 84
Lindsay, T. M. 16
Lindström, H. 62, 65
Lloyd-George, D. 61
Lloyd-Jones, D. M. 225, 226
Lloyd-Thomas, J. M. 28
Locke, J. 34, 98, 107–8
Locke, L. G. 34, 35, 44, 47
Lombard, P. 74
Long, G. D. 135
Luther, M. 59, 61, 69, 70, 83, 92, 95, 105, 106, 142, 169, 171, 172–3, 174–5, 176, 182, 184, 189, 197, 222–3, 226, 234, 236

MacArthur, J. F. 216, 217
Macaulay, Lord 34, 60
McGrath, A. E. 84, 91, 106, 173, 176, 183, 184, 201, 217, 236, 237, 238
Macleod, D. 165
Macleod, J. N. 136
McPhee, I. 84, 106
Machen, J. G. 225
Manning, B. L. 108
Manton, T. 218, 223, 226, 236
Marshall, W. 223, 226
Martin, H. 30, 31
Melanchthon, P. 178, 222
Melville, A. 198
merit 60, 176–9, 183, 191, 194–6, 204, 208, 214, 221–2, 229–35
  see also grace; inherent righteousness; Jesus Christ; justification; obedience
Miller, P. 13
Mitchell, W. F. 47
Moffat, J. 14, 34, 44, 47
Molina, L. de 77

Monk, R. C. 62, 65, 124
Montemayor, P. 77
Moorman, J. R. H. 33
Morley, Lord 17
Morris, L. 135, 137, 166
Motyer, S. 180, 182, 201
Moule, H. C. G. 63
Moulin, L. Du 26
Murray, I. 90
Murray, J. 77, 85, 91, 135, 137, 198

neonomianism 192–4
  see also antinomianism; law of God
Nettles, T. J. 87, 122
Newton, J. 80
Newton, J. A. 124
Nichol, W. 44
Nichols, J. 84
Nicole, R. 16, 85, 86
Nuttall, G. F. 4, 19, 29, 30, 45, 88, 108, 110, 138

obedience 174, 208–9, 225–35
  see also good works; inherent righteousness; Jesus Christ; merit; santification
Ong, W. J. 110
ordo salutis 103, 117, 119, 172–3, 176, 202
Orme, W. 9–10, 13, 14, 28, 30, 31, 46, 86
Outler, A. 62, 64
Overton, J. H. 62, 63
Owen, J. *passim*

Packer, J. I. vii, 8, 9, 11, 13, 17, 19, 30, 63, 71, 81, 85, 92, 119, 130, 139, 141, 169, 179, 180–1, 191–4, 199–200, 206, 210, 216, 239
Packer, J. W. 92
Parker, T. H. L. 184, 238
Pareus, D. 75–6, 181
Pascal, B. 77, 91
Pelagius 83
Pelagianism 9, 44
Perkins, W. 78, 91, 95
perseverance 84, 91, 124, 242
  see also assurance; free-will; predestination
Petersen, R. A. 85, 93, 140, 141
Piette, M. 65

Piscator, J. 190–2, 198, 213
Pollard, A. 47
Poole, M. 223, 226
Powicke, F. J. 23, 28, 30
predestination
  and Arminianism 69–70, 147
  Calvin and Beza on 70
  Caroline divines on 80
  and covenant of grace 117
  and efficacy of the atonement 101
  and federal theology 13
  and human responsibility 158
  Thirty-nine Articles on 58, 78, 92
  see also conditional reprobation
Preston, J. 26, 106
Prestwich, M. 94
Proctor, F. 30, 46
propitiation 128, 155
  see also atonement
Prosper 161, 166

Ramism 110
Ramus, P. 110
Rashdall, H. 137
reconciliation 126, 134, 155–6
  see also atonement
redemption 125–6, 134, 159–61
  see also atonement
Reed, R. C. 93
Richardson, A. 225, 226
Ridderbos, H. 225, 226
Ridley, N. 78
Ritschl, A. 128
Roberts, J. 63
Robinson, J. A. T. 219
Robison, O. C. 110
Rogers, H. 46
Rolston, H. 84
Ropes, J. H. 225
Routley, E. 4, 108
Russell, B. 138
Ryle, J. C. 28, 51, 55, 61, 81

sanctification 175–6, 194–6, 209, 223, 230–2
  see also good works; inherent righteousness; merit; obedience
Sanday, W. 163
satisfaction 126, 134
  and double payment 127, 130, 136
  see also atonement

General Index

Savoy Declaration of Faith and Order
  and Calvin's Calvinism 190
  and grace 109
  and imputation 12, 198
  and the law 197
  Owen and the 6, 190
  ultra orthodoxy of 75
  and Westminster Confession 12, 190
Schaff, P. 31
Schmidt, M. 62, 64
scholasticism, *see* Aristotelianism
Scougal, H. 54
Seaman, L. 26
Secker, T. 202
Sell, A. P. F. 16, 83, 88, 110, 137, 161, 240–1
Selleck, J. B. 62
Semmel, B. 61, 62, 64, 123, 180
Seymour, R. E. 110
Shedd, W. G. T. 77, 90–1
Sherlock, W. 12, 186, 208
Simeon, C. 56, 63, 81
Simonson, H. 218
Skevington Wood, A. 61, 64, 108, 139
Smith, G. 141
Socinus, F. 137
Socinianism *passim*
Sprunger, K. L. 110
Spurgeon, C. H. 19, 29, 51, 93–4
Stephen, Sir L. 34
Stott, J. R. W. 47, 81, 92, 135, 137, 201, 226
Strong, A. H. 77, 90, 127, 162
sufficiency-efficiency distinction 9–10, 27, 73–5, 79–81, 83, 86, 91, 112–13, 126, 143, 149, 150, 152, 155, 160
  see also atonement; satisfaction
Surman, C. E. 17
Sykes, N. 41, 47

Telford, J. 61, 62
Temperley, H. W. V. 61
Thayer, J. H. 165
Thirty-nine Articles
  and Arminianism 161
  and faith and obedience 209
  and justification 170
  and predestination 58, 80, 92
  and universal atonement 58–9, 78–9

Thomas, G. 88
Thomas, R. 45, 87
Thompson, A. 8–10, 13, 14, 16
Thornwell, J. H. 177
Tillotson, J. *passim*
Toon, P. 3, 11, 13, 14, 15, 16, 122, 198, 201
Toplady, A. M. 56, 62, 72, 78, 91, 120, 136
Torrance, J. B. 93, 165
Traill, R. 141
Trench, R. C. 19
Tudur Jones, R. 4, 34, 88
Tuttle, G. M. 141
Tuttle, R. G. 62, 63, 64, 65
Twisse, W. 26, 35, 89
Tyerman, L. 45, 49, 61, 62, 63, 64
Tyndale, W. 170, 172, 174, 177

Unitarianism 134–5
Ursinus, Z. 75, 76, 177
Ussher, J. 26

Vaughan, R. 222
Vermigli, P. Martyr 95
Vines, R. 26
Vos, A. 219
Vulliamy, C. E. 62, 63

Wallace, R. S. 137
Wardlaw, R. 76, 88, 127, 138, 162, 225, 226
Warfield, B. B. 165
Watkins, O. C. 28
Watson, R. 108, 124, 133, 140, 162
Watts, I. 76, 88
Watts, M. R. 110
Wesley, C. 53–7, 99, 133, 139, 242
Wesley, J. *passim*
Wesley, S. 53, 62
Wesley Bready, J. 61
Westminster Confession of Faith
  and Amyraldianism 26–7
  and assurance 202
  Baxter on 27
  and Calvin's Calvinism 190
  and Christ's threefold office 206
  and earlier confessions 75, 142
  Edwards, J. on 90
  and faith and obedience 209
  and grace 109
  and imputation 12, 198

Westminster Confession of Faith (*cont.*)
   and later Presbyterians 76–7, 88
   and Savoy Declaration 198
   ultra orthodoxy of 28, 71, 85
Whitefield, G. vii, 19, 29, 35, 44, 51–9, 61, 64, 72, 78, 80, 119–20, 153
Willet, A. 91
Williams, C. W. 62, 64, 132
Williams, D. 76, 87
Williams, E. 14, 76, 88
Williams, J. B. 29, 45
Williams, W. (Pantycelyn) 89
Wood, A. 3, 15
Woolf, B. L. 236
Wright, S. 223–4, 226
Wright, T. 62
Wycliffe, J. 222, 226

Zanchi, G. 95
Zwingli, U. 93, 94